Pitt Latin American Series

UNEQUAL GIANTS

Diplomatic Relations

Between the

United States

and Brazil,

1889–1930

Joseph Smith

University of Pittsburgh Press

Published by the University of Pittsburgh Press, Pittsburgh, Pa., 15260
Copyright © 1991, University of Pittsburgh Press
All rights reserved
Eurospan, London
Manufactured in the United States of America

Library of Congress Cataloging-in-Publication Data

Smith, Joseph, 1945–
    Unequal giants : diplomatic relations between the United States
and Brazil, 1889–1930 / Joseph Smith.
        p.   cm. – (Pitt Latin American series)
    Includes bibliographical references and index.
    ISBN 0-8229-3676-3
    1. United States–Foreign relations–Brazil.   2. Brazil–Foreign
relations–United States.   I. Title.   II. Series.
E183.8.B7S55   1991
327.73081–dc20   90-25379
                                                           CIP

A CIP catalogue record for this book is available from
the British Library.

CONTENTS

PREFACE

A voluminous list of titles awaits anyone who consults a scholarly bibliography on U.S.–Latin American relations. There are several general texts containing broad overviews of the subject. Also available are many studies devoted to the constant American preoccupation with developments in Mexico, Central America, and the Caribbean. Less well served is the history of U.S. relations with the individual nations of South America. My purpose in writing a case study of U.S.-Brazilian diplomatic relations is to help correct this neglect and to show that knowledge of the past is by no means irrelevant to an understanding of the present state of inter-American relations. I am indebted to the University of Pittsburgh Press for including my study in their Pitt Latin American series.

For the financial assistance which greatly facilitated my archival research in London, the United States, and Brazil, I wish to thank the British Academy, the United States Information Service, and the Committee of Deans of the University of Exeter. The task of research was considerably assisted by the staffs of the following libraries: in England, the Public Record Office, the Institute of Historical Research, and the Inter-Library Loans section of the University of Exeter Library; in the United States, the Library of Congress, the National Archives, the Hoover Presidential Library, and the library of the University of Texas at Austin; in Brazil, the Arquivo Histórico.

I wish to express my personal gratitude to John Lynch for helping me in the early stages of this project. I owe also a great deal to Bill Golant for his friendly counsel and indefatigable enthusiasm. My visits to Brazil could never have been so personally and professionally rewarding without the friendship and hospitality of Francisco Vinhosa. I also have fond memories of my old cat, Koo, who sat so often by my side as I typed out endless drafts of the manuscript. Most of all, I must thank Rachael for her enduring support.

vii

UNEQUAL GIANTS

CHAPTER 1

Sister Republics, 1889–1901

I T WAS NOT until the last quarter of the nineteenth century that Brazilian affairs intruded directly into the American political consciousness and affected what had long been an outwardly friendly but distant relationship between the two giants of the Western Hemisphere. The most dramatic event occurred in November 1889 when a military coup suddenly brought down the Brazilian empire. Americans were gratified to see monarchy replaced by republicanism. "Nothing so grand or so excellent has ever been achieved in the history of any nation," declared Senator John T. Morgan of Alabama.[1]

The new American awareness of Brazil also reflected economic motives already highlighted by the decision to hold a Pan-American conference at Washington in 1889.[2] "The countries of Central and South America," affirmed Congressman James McCreary of Kentucky, "need the products of our furnaces, of our factories, and of our farms."[3] The conference was viewed as part of a wider strategy designed to oust European competition and thereby secure American commercial ascendancy in Latin American markets. But ambitious projects such as an inter-American customs union proved impracticable. Instead, American diplomacy stressed the promotion of increased trade by means of the negotiation of separate reciprocal trade agreements.[4]

In fact, Brazil hoped to gain special commercial advantages by negotiating the first treaty, but these calculations were dashed as the United States proceeded to sign similar agreements with other governments. Aside from modest commercial dealings, the two peoples were still historically and culturally far apart. Their common location in the Western Hemisphere gave a misleading sense of geographical proximity as the direction of sailing winds facilitated travel between Brazil and Europe rather than to the United States. While increasing numbers of Europeans headed for São Paulo, only a few Americans traveled to Brazil.[5]

With so little contact and so few interests at stake Brazil was scarcely a significant or prestigious diplomatic posting.[6] Like appointments throughout the civil service, American officials were chosen for partisan political reasons

3

rather than previous diplomatic or consular experience. The emergence of a republic in Brazil was irrelevant to the process of nominating ministers from Robert Adams in 1889 to Thomas L. Thompson in 1893 and Edwin Conger in 1897, all of whose appointments coincided with new administrations assuming office in Washington.[7] Both Adams and Conger, however, possessed diplomatic qualifications. More controversial was the choice of Thompson, a journalist and Democratic party loyalist from California. Thompson's inadequacies were sharply exposed during the Naval Revolt and were a fitting reminder of the awkward nature of diplomatic relations between the United States and Brazil.

Despite the words of the new national motto, the proclamation of the Brazilian republic in 1889 ushered in not "order and progress" but a decade of political turbulence and financial crisis. The new political system was designed to differ radically from that of the empire in its emphasis on decentralization. Significant powers were reserved to the states, but the practicalities of ruling a country as large as Brazil and the example of almost a century of imperial direction from Rio ensured the continuance of a strong central government.[8]

The republic exhibited a democratic facade by providing for regular elections to federal and state office. But the extent of popular participation in politics was severely restricted by the granting of the vote only to literate males. Enmeshed within a web of kinship and clientist relationships, the mass of society was indifferent to political affairs. Consequently, the revolutionary theories of positivism and electoral reform soon foundered on the innate conservatism and elitism of the rural and urban oligarchy, whose influence and power increased rather than diminished under the Old Republic.[9] The newly emerging state political machines were inward-looking and entered national politics only to protect and promote their own local interests. The lure of federal patronage and appropriations motivated state delegations to compete for ministerial offices and positions on the congressional committees of finance, public works, or justice. Foreign affairs offered few spoils and possessed little political attraction.[10]

Although the foreign ministry was relocated to the splendid Itamaraty palace in 1897, its total staff and resources steadily dwindled during the 1890s.[11] Diplomacy seemed almost an irrelevance in a period of political violence, mounting financial chaos, and widespread anxiety over the survival of the republic itself. Moreover, the lack of political consensus at the beginning of the republic resulted in a decade of executive weakness. The prevailing atmosphere of internal political crisis and international indifference was demonstrated by the fact that there were no fewer than ten foreign ministers during the first nine years of the republic. Until the appointment of Olinto de Magalhães in 1898 all of these ministers came to office lacking diplomatic experience. Most were middle-ranking politicians with varied legal and military backgrounds.

It was not surprising that Brazilian diplomacy should focus greater attention on the United States during the last decade of the nineteenth century. By its issue of invitations to the Pan-American conference, the "northern colossus" had served notice of its intention to take an active role in hemispheric affairs. Moreover, the growing significance of the United States as a market for exports of Brazilian sugar, coffee, and rubber meant that the governments of the republic could not ignore the American desire to negotiate reciprocity treaties.

In Brazilian eyes, the United States was not only a power to be reckoned with, it was also a well-disposed nation and one from which the new Brazilian republic had much to learn. The 1889 coup may have been inspired by French positivism, but the debates over the framing of the new constitution revealed a close knowledge of American political theory and practice.[12] Moreover, a strain of common diplomatic idealism with its sister republic of the north was reflected in the adoption of the formal title of the "Republic of the United States of Brazil." This idealism led to Brazil's support for Pan-Americanism and resulted in a close identification with American policy.

In 1895 the American minister at Rio, Thomas Thompson, remarked that "the masses" had "the most friendly feeling for our country." A year later, he alluded, however, to the existence of "a large faction" that was hostile to close relations with the United States.[13] History had made Brazilians peculiarly sensitive toward alleged foreign interference or encroachment. There was traditional animosity against the British and especially the Portuguese, but feeling could also run high against other nationalities.[14] The United States and Brazil were sister republics at last, but their mutual friendship could not entirely be taken for granted.

RECOGNITION

The visit of Emperor Pedro II to the United States in 1876 symbolically lifted the barriers of geography and history that had kept Brazil and the United States apart for so long. The emperor was received at the White House by President Grant, but such state formalities were reduced to an absolute minimum. The main purpose of the visit was to attend the centennial exhibition at Philadelphia. Unaccustomed to Brazilian visitors and even more so to emperors, Americans were intrigued and impressed by the tall, fair-complexioned and blue-eyed Dom Pedro, who preferred to dress in a plain black suit. He could also speak and understand English and was plainly delighted and fascinated by the marvels displayed at the exhibition. Although bemused by his appearance,

Americans resolved the puzzle by calling him "the Yankee Emperor" and considering him to be like themselves. Monarch he might be, but Brazilians were surely fortunate to have such an enlightened and dignified ruler. The impression he left was both affectionate and lasting.[15]

Dom Pedro came to the United States primarily to indulge his personal passion for discovery and travel. Political motivation was lacking. His visit was a gesture of friendship and it was sincerely reciprocated. He did allude, however, to the desirability of closer commercial ties between the two countries. In fact, only a few years previously in 1872 the United States Congress had removed the duty on imports of coffee. The resulting boost to coffee exports attracted less notice than Dom Pedro's visit, but it was ultimately much more significant for United States–Brazilian relations. Up to the Civil War, Americans had bought their coffee in the form of unroasted green beans. After 1865 the market expanded considerably as a result of developments in roasting and packaging. In 1873 Arbuckles and Co. took advantage of the elimination of duty and introduced *Ariosa,* the first successful national brand of package coffee. Selling roasted coffee "in little paper bags like peanuts" initially aroused ridicule, but it soon formed the basis of one of the world's great commercial enterprises.[16]

Americans showed a distinct preference for the good quality and mild flavors of Brazilian coffee and provided Brazil with its largest export market. The image of Brazil became indelibly associated with coffee as its cultivation flourished in the fertile *terra roxa* of São Paulo. While shipments of coffee boomed from Santos to New York, the pattern of trade in the other direction was markedly different as there was no similar lucrative item that Brazil desired in return. Trade between the two countries was growing during the late nineteenth century, but Brazil was the main beneficiary. While its annual exports to the American market during the 1870s and 1880s ranged from $40 to $50 million, imports from the United States were less than $10 million a year.[17]

The imbalance in trade reflected several generations of American commercial indifference and inertia. After reading the official report of the 1884–1885 Trade Commission to Latin America, the American minister at Rio concluded that "one is led to infer that Brazil is the least important of all the countries in this Hemisphere south of the Equator."[18] The *Rio News* charged that American merchants were "in a great measure to blame" for the low level of exports.[19] They showed little interest in cultivating the Brazilian market and refused to set up the shipping and credit facilities enjoyed by their well-established European competitors.

Commerce was conducted in a triangular fashion. European ships carried their own goods to Brazil and then loaded Brazilian cargoes for their return trip home or, just as frequently, for carriage to the United States. A relatively small number of American sailing ships plied the same waters, but made only a small dent in what amounted to a virtual European monopoly. Profits were made by Americans from the import-export business with Brazil, but these were traditionally controlled by the merchants of Baltimore who sought to restrict competition from other East Coast ports. Although Baltimore continued to dominate the flour trade, more and more Brazilian business in other products was transferred to New York after the Civil War. From 1859 onward New York established itself as the largest importer of Brazilian coffee, and the foundation of the New York Coffee Exchange in 1882 confirmed that city's preeminence in the coffee business.[20]

Nevertheless, the merchants of Baltimore attempted to resist the trend of events. Their early primacy in the trade with Brazil was greatly assisted by the fact that the sailing time from Baltimore was 48 hours less than from New York. Dismayed by the introduction of steam power, they lobbied Congress to reject the pleas of entrepreneurs such as John Roach for financial subsidies to operate a line of steamships from New York to Brazil. Democrats saw an opportunity for partisan political advantage and seized upon the issue to berate their Republican opponents. "The American people," remarked one Democratic congressman in 1878, "have been cheated and deceived and millions have been taken out of the treasury under the false delusion of aid to American commerce."[21] Without subsidies, American shipping lines could not compete with their bigger and more efficient European rivals. Roach struggled on, but his lack of success was appropriately reflected in the nickname given to the United States and Brazil Steamship Company (USBMSC) of the "Unusually Slow and Badly Managed Steamship Company."[22]

The subject of trade with Brazil attracted, however, a new political interest in 1887. As part of his electoral strategy to win the White House in 1888, President Cleveland stressed the promotion of American overseas commerce. The significance attached to Brazil was made apparent when he discussed his plans in an interview with the Brazilian consul-general at New York, Salvador de Mendonça. After praising Brazil as the most important nation of South America, Cleveland suggested the formation of a customs union or *Zollverein* between the two countries.[23] In the case of Germany, the dismantling of commercial barriers had led to full economic and political union. The president's proposal was studiously vague and was not intended to be so far-reaching in its implications. Nevertheless, he wished it to be communicated to Rio.

Salvador's report was so unexpected that the Brazilian government initially treated it with some skepticism.[24] While Brazilian officials understood that the president was only making a suggestion, they assumed that what he wanted was nothing less than a formal commercial treaty between Brazil and the United States. If so, it was a matter that demanded considerable study and discussion because commercial negotiations were invariably highly sensitive. The Brazilian government was dependent upon customs duties for a large portion of its revenue. A move toward a *Zollverein* would require a substantial tariff reduction, which could only have an adverse effect upon government revenue. Opposition could also be expected from local merchants and foreign interests fearful of advantages being gained by their American competitors. Moreover, the desire to avoid diplomatic complications and the memory of economic subordination to Britain earlier in the century had created a traditional Brazilian aversion to the conclusion of entangling alliances and commercial treaties with noncontiguous countries.

Cleveland's initiative reflected, nonetheless, the new assertive mood of American diplomacy and prompted a thorough reappraisal of Brazilian policy. An arrangement with the rising power of the northern colossus was not without danger, but it was also attractive in itself and would offset Brazil's dependence on the great European powers.[25] Furthermore, the proposal coincided with widespread concern over the declining fortunes of the sugar industry and an awareness that tariff concessions might usefully be offered to promote sugar exports. After a study of the question by a special commission, the imperial government decided to welcome a commercial agreement with the United States, although this was expressed cautiously in terms of allowing American kerosene into Brazil as an exchange for American tariff concessions on Brazilian sugar. The tone of the reply was guarded but encouraging. "Altogether, it seems to me," noted the American consul-general at Rio in late 1888, "that we now have an opportunity such as seldom occurs for extending our trade."[26]

While Brazilian officials carefully pondered their course of action, Cleveland was defeated by Harrison in the 1888 presidential election. Although no direct reference to Brazil was made during the campaign, both candidates endorsed the desire for increased commercial contact between the United States and all the countries of Latin America. This was confirmed in their respective party political platforms and by the wide degree of congressional support given earlier for the holding of a Pan-American conference. The conference was scheduled to assemble at Washington in October 1889.

The Brazilian government saw the conference as a convenient opportunity to send a delegation to discuss a possible commercial treaty. Cleveland's electoral defeat meant, however, that the Brazilian delegates would have to deal with the newly elected Harrison administration in which James G. Blaine was secretary of state. The controversial Blaine had acquired a reputation throughout Latin America for diplomatic recklessness during the War of the Pacific, but he was regarded as an enthusiastic advocate of closer Pan-American relations. His views on Brazil were known to be friendly and he had written some years previously that "Brazil holds in the South much the same relationship to the other countries that the United States does in the North." The Brazilian chargé d'affaires at Washington reported the new secretary's cordial attitude and hinted that he was disposed to make commercial concessions.[27]

Diplomats in Rio, however, remained suspicious of American motives in holding the Pan-American conference. After all, it marked a dramatic reversal of decades of traditional American opposition to such meetings. Foreign Minister José Francisco Diana feared that Blaine's well-known desire to establish machinery for the arbitration of disputes was really intended to create an American protectorate over Latin America. Diana informed the British minister that the broad aims of the conference evoked lukewarm enthusiasm and that practical results were not expected. No doubt, such statements were deliberately designed for European ears, but the foreign minister was being truthful when he observed that Brazil had commercial relations with only a few Latin American nations so that there could be little advantage for his country in the idea of a general customs union. A Brazilian mission would attend, but its primary object was to negotiate a commercial treaty with the United States.[28]

The three-man delegation consisting of Lafayette Pereira, Amaral Valente, and Salvador de Mendonça left for Washington in July 1889. The conference convened briefly at the beginning of October and then adjourned whilst the delegates were taken on a six-week deluxe railroad tour of the United States. Just before the resumption of the conference the sensational news arrived from Rio that the Brazilian empire had fallen on November 15. Out of loyalty to the emperor, Lafayette Pereira withdrew from the conference. Amaral Valente and Salvador de Mendonça decided to remain as representatives of the new republican government. Their exact status became, however, a matter of temporary uncertainty when the conference declared that it lacked authority to recognize "the new order of things in Brazil."[29]

Recognition of the new Brazilian government was forthcoming from Uruguay on November 20 and Argentina on November 29. The other Latin American countries followed suit in December. The United States government adopted a more cautious and legalistic response. American officials were genuinely astounded by events. The American minister at Rio, Robert Adams, viewed the revolution as "the most remarkable ever recorded in history."[30] In his opinion, the imperial era was definitely over, and he wished to establish official relations immediately with the new government. But the dictates of diplomatic procedure and propriety persuaded his own government and those of the European powers to act with circumspection. While maintaining friendly relations with the new rulers of Brazil, the Harrison administration decided to withhold official recognition until such time as its minister at Rio reported sufficient evidence of popular support for the new regime.[31]

The delay was puzzling because American politicians and press opinion clearly welcomed the victory for republicanism.[32] More than 60 years earlier President Monroe had similarly hesitated to recognize the change of government in Brazil. Suspicion of monarchy had clouded the issue on that occasion.[33] Ironically, American action in 1889 was complicated by the existence of genuine sympathy and sadness for the much-admired Dom Pedro. With characteristic dignity and unselfishness, the emperor had yielded to the ultimatum presented by the leader of the coup, Marshal Manoel Deodoro da Fonseca, that he leave immediately for exile in France. "In departing," replied Dom Pedro to Deodoro, "I with all the persons of my family, shall always retain the most tender remembrances of Brazil in offering ardent prayer for its greatness and prosperity."[34]

Moreover, the conservative instincts of American politicians were alarmed at the overthrow of a symbol of authority and stability by military violence. The ambivalence was underlined in the Senate on December 20 when a resolution calling for recognition of the new republic was defeated. Democratic senators urged that Congress should welcome "this new sister into the family of republics." Further hesitation would only encourage "despotic" influences to plan a restoration of the monarchy. But Republican senators argued that caution was necessary. Senator Sherman regarded the coup as "one of the greatest events in our times," but he also regretted Dom Pedro's deposition. The majority of his Republican colleagues shared this feeling and voted that recognition be delayed to soften the blow to the old emperor. Disquiet was also expressed about the exact nature of the new regime. It was known that the coup had been engineered by army officers and that the provisional government had already interfered with the freedom of the press and telegraphic communications. Senator Teller observed: "We have had in the past some experience with republics in South America that were republics only in name, unworthy even of the name of republic, and that brought disgrace upon republican government the world over. We do not want to make that mistake. Whenever the people of Brazil say that there is a republican government in that country, then we are for Brazil."[35]

With the exception of the *New York World,* which consistently praised the new Brazilian government,[36] the New York press mirrored the wary attitude shown by the Senate. "What at present confronts us in Brazil," declared the *New York Sun,* "is a military dictatorship." The *Nation* commented that "it is not enough . . . to get rid of a monarch in order to set up a republic," while the *New York Times* argued that American recognition could not be accorded "until it has been shown by experience that the Brazilian Government is a responsible one, and can perform its part in any agreement that may be made with it."[37]

American apprehensions were confirmed by the continuing unsettled political conditions in Brazil and the declaration of a state of siege at the close of 1889. The provisional government headed by Marshal Deodoro da Fonseca was preoccupied with internal affairs, but it was also aware that international recognition would be a useful means of strengthening its domestic authority.

Moreover, a bold and positive approach to diplomacy was forthcoming from the distinguished journalist and one of the founders of the Republican party, Quintino Bocaiúva, who was appointed as the republic's first foreign minister. Quintino Bocaiúva seized the opportunity to implement his long-held philosophy that Brazil's diplomatic aim should be the promotion of hemispheric peace by the cultivation of friendly relations with all governments, especially those of Argentina and the United States.

While the provisional government discussed new directions of foreign policy, the actual conduct of Brazilian diplomacy fell into disarray. Lacking precise instructions, Amaral Valente and Salvador de Mendonça had remained at the Pan-American conference in Washington since November and had sensibly adopted a low profile. In January 1890, however, they attracted notice by their approval of the controversial stand taken by the Argentine delegates in favor of the compulsory arbitration of disputes. Chile was most alarmed by this unexpected development. Since its victory over Peru and Bolivia in the War of the Pacific, Chile had sought an understanding with Brazil to counter Argentine hostility toward its territorial gains. The Chilean delegates at the Pan-American conference claimed that they had been promised Brazilian support and now feared the emergence of an Argentine-Brazilian rapprochement detrimental to Chilean interests.[38] But Brazilian policy was motivated by confusion rather than calculation. Salvador revealed this when he reminded officials at Rio that he lacked specific guidance as to the attitude he should adopt on the question of arbitration.[39]

In fact, the diplomatic confusion prevailing in South America arose directly from Argentina's astute initiative in extending a speedy welcome to the new Brazilian republic. Past rivalries and animosities between the two peoples were seemingly cast aside at the beginning of December when a national holiday was proclaimed in Argentina to celebrate the change of government in Brazil. The provisional government was grateful for Argentina's diplomatic and moral support. Moreover, it genuinely wanted friendly relations with its powerful neighbor and demonstrated this by responding warmly to the timely Argentine proposal that the long-standing Misiones boundary dispute should be settled. To expedite agreement, negotiations were conducted by telegraph on January 5, 1890. Details were glossed over and within two hours the contested territory was divided almost equally between the two countries.

The fixing of the boundary between Brazil and Argentina represented a momentous historical achievement. Quintino Bocaiúva journeyed to Buenos Aires to affirm what appeared to be a new era of friendship. But the provisional government had not reckoned on the degree of Brazilian hostility to the proposed treaty. A century of bitter and, sometimes violent, rivalry to control the Plate region could not be easily set aside. No matter how persuasively argued, Pan-American idealism was insufficient compensation for the loss of national territory to Argentina. Street demonstrations occurred in Rio and were a prelude to congressional rejection of the settlement. Both governments confessed defeat and agreed to submit the boundary question to the arbitration of the president of the United States. Argentine opportunism, seeking to exploit Brazil's political difficulties, had been foiled. But Brazil's diplomatic prestige and credibility had also been seriously damaged. Further humiliation followed in March 1890 when, to Chile's satisfaction, Argentina formally denied the rumors of an anti-Chilean alliance between Buenos Aires and Rio.[40]

In the meantime, a more pleasing outcome had materialized in the United States. Friendship between the two sister republics was especially desired by Quintino Bocaiúva. The foreign minister admired the United States where he had lived during the Civil War and had even actively assisted the emigration of Confederate exiles to Brazil.[41] His pursuit of close diplomatic relations was ably supported by Salvador de Mendonça who had represented his country's interests in the United States since 1875, principally as consul-general at New York. Despite a long friendship with the emperor, Salvador was also an ardent republican and resolutely supported Deodoro da Fonseca's government. Although technically junior in rank to Amaral Valente, Salvador's singular knowledge of American affairs meant that he soon superseded his colleague.[42] Not only had Salvador resided in the United States for 15 years, he was also married to an American and was already an established and popular figure in Washington society. Moreover, his access to American political leaders was particularly impressive and belied Brazil's somewhat lowly international standing. Prominent among his friends and political contacts were Republican businessmen such as Charles Flint, Thomas Jefferson Coolidge, and Andrew Carnegie. Most notably, the Brazilian minister was able to cultivate a close working relationship with Secretary of State Blaine.[43]

Salvador's immediate objective was to persuade the United States government to recognize the republic.[44] The question, however, was complicated by Republican party politics. Although the "magnetic" Blaine had failed to win the presidency in 1884 and 1888, he had not quite entirely given up his presidential ambitions. Salvador believed that Blaine had a high regard for Brazil, but was hesitant to grant recognition for fear of annoying prominent Republicans such as Senator Sherman. Throughout January 1890 Salvador campaigned persistently, either by means of personal interviews or the use of his Republican friends as intermediaries, to convince the secretary of state that speedy recognition was vital if the republic was to survive. He argued that the present state of uncertainty only encouraged European thoughts of interference although, with somewhat inverted logic, he also declared that the European powers were awaiting American action and would not themselves recognize the republic until the United States had done so.[45]

One weekend toward the close of January, Blaine's hesitation was suddenly overcome and he approved American recognition. Thomas Jefferson Coolidge called at Salvador's home on January 29 to say that Blaine wished to speak with him without delay. In the secretary of state's office, Salvador was told the gratifying news about recognition. The whole episode was characteristic of Blaine in that it reflected his swings of behavior between vacillation and impulsiveness.[46] The personal and unilateral nature of the decision was also in keeping with the customs and practice of the nineteenth-century State Department. No embarrassment was shown over the apparent contradiction with the administration's earlier stated policy of allowing its minister in Brazil to judge the correct moment to recognize. In fact, the decision had been taken without the knowledge of Adams who, according to British reports, was "much hurt," especially as he had only very recently denied that such a step was being contemplated by his government. The decision was made so casually and unexpectedly that the *Rio News* doubted the accuracy of the report: "Had the United States taken so important a step as to officially recognize a republic . . . it is certain that the Legation here would have been at once advised to that effect and instructed to comply with the usual diplomatic formalities required by the circumstances. But no such message has been received, nor even the slightest intimation that such a policy was under consideration." Adams confided to his British colleague that he believed it was a mistake to recognize a regime that had deteriorated into a "military dictatorship." In the circumstances his position had become untenable and he judged that his only course was resignation.[47]

The shabby treatment of Adams underlined the unilateral nature of American decision making. However, the decision to recognize attracted little notice in the United States and Congress gave its approval in February. The drama of the November coup had quickly subsided and Brazilian affairs now possessed meager news value. A sufficient interval had elapsed as a mark of respect to Dom Pedro, and it was only a matter of judging the right moment for recognition. If the United States had acted ahead of the European governments, so much the better. An exchange of naval visits in June allowed the two sister republics a suitable opportunity for mutual celebration.

Some apprehension still lingered that a military dictatorship was being imposed upon Brazil. At the beginning of 1890 Salvador had considered, however, that press opinion was adopting a more favorable tone toward Deodoro's government. By the summer he was able to report a very encouraging reaction to the draft of the proposed new Brazilian constitution. Americans were flattered to find that it rejected the European parliamentary system and proposed a federal government openly modeled on that of the United States. The *New York Daily Tribune* called it "the best possible augury for the future of the country," while the *New York Times* predicted that "the future of the republic is regarded as most encouraging."[48] These articles, however, were merely minor items of political news. Americans were kindly disposed to the new sister republic, but no special diplomatic relationship was forthcoming. After the drama of the 1889 coup, Brazilian affairs simply became submerged within the general debate that was unfolding over the Latin American policy of the Harrison administration.

RECIPROCITY

Holding the Pan-American conference at Washington illustrated the rising hemispheric preeminence of the United States, but few tangible results emerged from the meeting. As Francisco Diana had predicted, the delegates were unwilling to reach agreement on arbitration procedures. Although there was an evident desire for closer commercial links, the idea of a *Zollverein* found little support. The American delegates, however, were able to persuade the committee on the customs union to recommend the negotiation of separate commercial treaties. In fact, this was in keeping with the original purpose of the Brazilian mission sent to the conference. The Harrison administration was keen to conclude a treaty with Brazil and preliminary discussions had actually commenced between Blaine and Mendonça independently of the Pan-American conference. But these talks were suspended when the issue became entangled with the Republican party's political priority of preparing a new congressional tariff bill. Only a few months earlier, Congress had frustrated attempts to recognize the Brazilian republic. It now similarly put at risk the Pan-American commercial ambitions of Harrison and Blaine.

The most contentious question concerned sugar. While Republican congressmen fully endorsed the drive for increased exports, they were also politically committed to making sugar imports duty-free. A reduction in the price of sugar was part of the strategy of the "free breakfast table" designed to win votes in the 1890 congressional elections. The Harrison administration argued, however, that "free sugar" would take away its most important bargaining lever in commercial negotiations with Latin American countries. Brazil was cited as a pertinent example of a country that was prepared to give important tariff concessions in return for free sugar. This was precisely what the American Congress was offering but without demanding anything in return.[49]

The proposed treaty with Brazil became in effect a vital element in the administration's attempt to persuade Congress to modify the tariff bill. All possible sources of support were called upon. Salvador even put aside diplomatic reserve and directly joined the campaign by publishing two letters in the *New York Post* in which he optimistically outlined Brazilian trade prospects and answered various objections that had been raised against reciprocity treaties.[50] Despite strenuous lobbying, Harrison and Blaine could not undo their party's commitment to free sugar. Nevertheless, a satisfactory compromise eventually emerged. In October 1890 an amendment was added to the tariff bill that allowed President Harrison the discretionary power to manipulate the "free list" in order to secure the negotiation of reciprocal commercial arrangements with foreign countries. Nothing was therefore to be given away after all. Latin American countries would enjoy the provisions of the free list only if they "reciprocated" by granting tariff concessions to their imports of American goods.[51]

Talks were immediately resumed between the United States and Brazil. For John W. Foster, the principal American negotiator, the treaty with Brazil was crucial to the success of the reciprocity policy. He later recalled that it "was to be the test case of success or failure and we awaited the result not without some misgivings."[52] Fortunately, Salvador de Mendonça proved to be most cooperative. By responding positively the Brazilian minister hoped to clinch an agreement that would give his country a virtual monopoly of the American sugar market and thus effect the "salvation of our states from Rio to Maranhão."[53] A treaty would also underline American support for the republic and demonstrate to the other South American countries that Brazil enjoyed a privileged relationship with the United States.

The delay caused by the congressional tariff debate had, however, resulted in a tougher American bargaining mood. The "free list" had been extended and included not only sugar but also coffee, hides, and molasses. Accordingly, Foster told Salvador that the United States expected extra tariff concessions from Brazil. Salvador replied by offering to remove duties on various American goods including wheat, flour, and certain manufactured items such as tools and machinery. Brazil would also reduce existing duties by 25 percent on a wide range of other American products.[54] Despite these apparent American gains, Foster argued that it was Salvador who had secured "a great triumph." In Foster's opinion, the significant concessions had been made by the United States and he added: "Nothing but the earnest desire of the rulers and people of the United States of America to extend to the new republic of Brazil hearty sympathy and encouragement, and to give as little embarrassment as possible to its much needed revenues, could have influenced the President and Secretary of State to agree to accept as satisfactory the reciprocity arrangement proposed."[55]

Salvador arrived in Rio with the draft agreement in November 1890. After some weeks of secret discussion with government officials, his views prevailed and he was able to return to the United States to give his government's formal adherence to the treaty on January 31, 1891. The new American minister at Rio, Edwin Conger, sent his congratulations to Blaine and predicted enthusiastically that the "successful reciprocity negotiations have opened the doors of Brazilian trade to wonderful opportunities for our people." But only a few weeks later, he was writing that public reaction was "by no means as cordial as we had a right to expect." In April he confirmed sadly that local opinion was still adverse to the treaty and that Congress would vote its repeal.[56] The *Rio News* summed up: "The Brazilian press, Congress, the foreign mercantile houses, and even the Brazilians themselves, are almost unanimous in condemning the recent commercial treaty with the United States."[57]

The reciprocity question coincided with a period of acute political controversy in Brazil. The 1889 coup had been carried out by army officers and their retention of political power incurred growing resentment. Particular criticism was directed at President Deodoro da Fonseca. The latter's personal prestige and decisive role in the events of 1889 had brought him the presidency, but his arbitrary style of leadership provoked increasing discontent and culminated in the wholesale resignation of cabinet ministers in January 1891. When Deodoro threatened to enforce the reciprocity agreement by executive decree, his political opponents accused him of high-handedness and insisted that the arrangement required congressional approval. A diplomatic issue was therefore swiftly transformed into a battle over the constitutional authority of the executive power.[58]

A succession of congressional debates demonstrated the unpopularity of both Deodoro and the reciprocity treaty. Critics argued that the proposed reductions in the Brazilian tariff would seriously reduce government revenues. It was also feared that the grant of concessions solely to the United States would provoke protests from European countries and consequently lead to foreign complications. National sensitivities were aroused and in one particularly stormy debate the warning that Brazilians must not become the slaves of the North Americans was greeted with much applause.[59]

Doubts were also voiced about the benefits supposedly to be enjoyed by sugar producers. It was pointed out that the American concession was too limited as it gave exemption from duty only to specific grades of sugar. In addition, reports were cited that the United States was seeking a similar commercial arrangement with Spain on behalf of Cuba and Puerto Rico. Should this materialize, it would effectively destroy Brazilian expectations of capturing a monopoly of the American sugar market and thereby defeat the main purpose of seeking a commercial agreement with the United States. In March 1891 the acting British minister at Rio reported with some satisfaction that it was "a foregone conclusion" that Congress would reject the treaty.[60]

Like the Misiones settlement with Argentina, the political cost of reciprocity was much greater than initially envisaged by the Deodoro government.[61] Salvador's concessions to Foster had been approved by the government in Rio, but the wisdom of that decision was thrown into question in May when it was learned that the United States had concluded an identical arrangement with Spain. Cuban sugar would now also have free entry into the United States. Conger relayed Brazilian annoyance to Washington, but only drew the comment of Second Assistant Secretary of State Alvey Adee that President Harrison would regard any move by Brazil against the treaty as "most unfortunate for the good relations of the two countries." Furthermore, Conger was instructed to stress the president's "deep interest" in this matter, although the minister was warned to avoid his actions' being construed as interference in Brazilian domestic affairs.[62] In June the Brazilian government decided to take the direct approach and instructed Salvador by telegraph to express officially its misgivings and state that Brazilian public opinion "requires good ground to sustain the agreement before the country." But a sympathetic response was not forthcoming. Foster answered that Harrison was "taken greatly by surprise by attitude of Brazilian government." The arrangement with Brazil did not preclude the negotiation of a similar agreement with Spain. Foster declared:

> President will be constrained to regard present attitude of Brazil as evasive, and that failure of executive to support it and of Congress of Brazil to ratify it will be interpreted as an unfriendly act to the United States, which has been so prompt to recognize the new Republic and extend to it most cordial sympathy and support. The consequences to the future relations of the two countries cannot fail to be most unfortunate and dangerous. He calls attention to fact that after ratification if found to work unfavorably, Brazil has perfect right to denounce it, but that good faith requires that it should first be fairly tested.[63]

A suspicion lingered in Rio that Salvador had been tricked into making the agreement by the promise of the "special favor" of free sugar,[64] but in the light of the rather unyielding though correct attitude of the Harrison administration, the Brazilian government could hardly do otherwise than stand by the arrangement. The consequences were extremely awkward because the treaty had been transformed from a commercial matter into a test of Deodoro's political strength. His government proceeded to mobilize all its resources of persuasion and patronage to win congressional ratification. Salvador was brought back from Washington to lead the campaign. While admitting that the treaty with Spain was unfortunate, Salvador stressed that this only made free access to the American market even more vital for Brazilian exports. In his opinion, any reduction of revenue caused by tariff concessions would soon be outweighed by the benefits of increased trade. He pointed out that most American goods were relatively expensive and even with the reduced tariff they would not seriously undercut the prices of Brazilian merchants or the well-established European businesses. To those still concerned that American goods might become too competitive, Salvador suggested that the government could simply raise the overall level of duties and thus restore the original tariff advantage to the Brazilian producer.[65]

The cogency of Salvador's arguments, combined with the government's use of political pressure and patronage, secured a close but favorable vote to ratify the treaty in September 1891.[66] Edwin Conger had special praise for Deodoro's leadership and described the Marshal as "a true friend of the policy of reciprocity."[67] But Conger's pleasure was short-lived. A military coup had been predicted for some time and eventually materialized in November 1891 when a naval squadron commanded by Admiral Custódio José de Melo threatened to bombard Rio. Fearful of unleashing civil bloodshed, Deodoro resigned.

Edwin Conger was alarmed by Deodoro's fall from power. Despite some initial apprehension, he was, however, relieved that the new regime headed by Vice President Floriano Peixoto made no move against the reciprocity treaty. But government support could no longer be taken for granted. On his departure for a period of leave in January 1892, Conger reported that Floriano was believed to be an opponent of the treaty. When he returned to Rio in August the American minister remarked that there was only "a little improvement in the feeling" in favor of reciprocity.[68] British dispatches suggested that the Brazilian government found the arrangement "very unpalatable" and that modification or even abrogation was likely. "The present Government in this country," commented the British minister at Rio, "does not wish to surrender itself to the 'Pan American' policy of the United States."[69]

In his defense of the arrangement Salvador de Mendonça had ingeniously noted that, if Brazilian goods were adversely affected by the preferential reductions given to American products, then the Brazilian tariff should be raised to restore the original price differential. Floriano responded to the growing protectionist mood of Congress by adopting this tactic in the form of an *expediente* tax added to the 1892 tariff. This increased duties by as much as 60 percent and thus restored the competitive advantage of the home producer. Although the action was clearly against the spirit of the treaty, American merchants would have no grounds of complaint because the margin of their preferential privilege over foreign goods remained intact.

The critics of reciprocity were therefore effectively disarmed and the issue became much less politically controversial. Not only could Brazil apparently alter the arrangement to its own satisfaction, but it also became evident that Brazilians stood to gain more than the Americans. Within one year of the treaty's being put into effect, the *Rio News* asserted "that Brazil is thus far getting nearly all the benefits." The continuation of this trend was confirmed by Secretary of State Gresham's comment in 1894 that reciprocity had increased American purchases from Brazil by nearly $17 million while American exports to Brazil had risen by less than $500,000.[70]

The economic imbalance was annoying to American officials, but the treaty had substantial diplomatic compensations. John W. Foster suggested in November 1890 that the United States had concluded the agreement with Brazil for political as much as commercial reasons. It was intended as a gesture of American friendship and a means of strengthening the new republic. Moreover, the treaty played a significant role in the evolution of the Pan-American diplomacy of the Harrison administration. By guaranteeing adequate supplies of sugar, coffee, and hides to the American market, the arrangement with Brazil lent substance to Harrison's threat of retaliation against other raw material producers should they decline to enter into similar reciprocal arrangements. A British official summed up that Brazil's "surrender" had "crippled" the other Latin American governments.[71]

The United States subsequently signed similar treaties with the countries of Central America and with Britain and Spain in behalf of their Caribbean possessions. The flowering of the reciprocity policy was pleasing to the Harrison administration and beneficial to the American consumer, but it was a blow to Brazilian commercial calculations. Only with a large tariff advantage could Brazilian sugar producers hope to compete with their more efficient Caribbean competitors. To make matters worse, Brazilian protests to Washington were treated in a somewhat offhand and cavalier manner.

Despite the bruised feelings of Brazilian diplomats, the arrangement proved advantageous for Brazil. The expectation of dominating the American sugar market was dashed, but this was more than offset by a substantial increase in coffee sales to the United States so that total exports doubled from $59 million in 1890 to $118 million in 1892.[72] Salvador was therefore vindicated in his argument that Brazil's main objective should be to maintain and promote close links with the huge American market. The reciprocity treaty failed to halt the decline of the Brazilian sugar industry, but it gave a boost to coffee exports and thereby assisted the development of the fastest-growing sector of the Brazilian economy. "Free coffee" now replaced "free sugar" as the dominant issue in commercial relations between the two countries.

THE NAVAL REVOLT

In retrospect, the signing of the reciprocity arrangement in January 1891 marked a high point of cooperation between the United States and the new Brazilian republic. The results were disappointing to American merchants, but their discontent was diverted by the prospect of more profitable treaties with Cuba and Argentina. Moreover, as Brazil became wound up with its own internal political concerns and showed little desire to be involved actively in foreign affairs, it diminished in importance in the eyes of American policymakers. Events in other countries such as the Baring crisis, the *Baltimore* incident, and the Hawaiian revolution claimed the attention of officials and politicians in Washington.[73] Furthermore, by 1893 both Blaine and Harrison had departed from office. The incoming Cleveland administration was preoccupied with political appointments and seeking a means of carrying out its electoral mandate to reduce the tariff. In April a Democratic loyalist was duly selected to replace Conger. From the State Department's point of view, Brazilian affairs were in a state of limbo until the new minister, Thomas L. Thompson, took up his post. But Thompson delayed his arrival in Rio until late August 1893. Just as he was about to present his credentials a major political disturbance erupted.

Despite Deodoro's enforced resignation in November 1891, political peace had not materialized in Brazil. Vice President Floriano Peixoto succeeded to the presidency, but his hold on power remained precarious. A serious split emerged within the military as naval officers grew more and more resentful of the prestige and prominence accorded to the army since the fall of Dom Pedro. In April 1893 Admiral Custódio de Melo ostentatiously resigned his post as minister of the navy. On September 6, 1893, he took command of the navy in the harbor of Rio and demanded Floriano's resignation under threat of naval bombardment of the city.[74] Contrary to Custódio's expectation, Floriano refused to give way as Deodoro had done in almost identical circumstances only two years previously. The sphinxlike Floriano confounded contemporaries by skillfully exploiting rivalries between the army and the navy and among state politicians. Custódio found himself outmaneuvered and effectively deprived of local political support.[75]

A military stalemate prevailed in which Custódio commanded all the Brazilian ships in the bay while Floriano controlled the batteries on shore. What had been originally intended as no more than a brief political interlude became transformed into a prolonged siege lasting from September 1893 to March 1894. The revolt also assumed diplomatic significance because of its damaging effect upon trade within the harbor. The foreign powers were presented with the taxing questions of how to protect their commerce and whether belligerent rights should be granted to the rebels. For American officials there was the additional concern that the revolt might represent ulterior motives adverse to American interests. Allegations that foreign nations, especially Britian, were covertly supporting the rebels in order to restore the monarchy and bring an end to the reciprocity treaty were assiduously propagated in Washington by Salvador de Mendonça who called almost daily at Secretary of State Gresham's house during the revolt.[76] Officials in Washington were naturally suspicious of European intrigues in the New World, but State Department policy toward the Naval Revolt was pragmatic and emphasized legalistic rather than commercial or ideological considerations.

The wily Floriano also sought foreign assistance in a more direct form. Although it would take weeks or months before they could arrive, orders for warships were placed in the United States.[77] In the meantime, Floriano attempted to compensate for his lack of a navy by persuading the foreign powers to use their ships in the harbor against Custódio. At the beginning of the revolt he requested that all the foreign diplomats at the capital come to the presidential palace and discuss measures to safeguard merchant shipping. But the diplomatic corps were not so easily manipulated. Thompson joined with his European colleagues in refusing the invitation on the ground that compliance would be a departure from the instructions of their governments to observe strict neutrality.[78]

No favoritism was therefore shown to Floriano. Instead, the foreign representatives and their naval commanders decided among themselves to present a series of notes to both Floriano and Custódio stating that ships flying foreign flags should continue to go about their business in the bay and would be protected by their respective national warships. The policy was legally correct although its practicable enforcement would tend to restrict Custódio's operations and consequently favor the established government.[79] Approval came from Secretary of State Gresham who instructed Thompson that American goods should continue to be landed at Rio with naval assistance if necessary, provided that the lighter "in doing so does not cross or otherwise interfere with Mello's line of fire."[80]

The actual implementation of this guideline was the responsibility not of Thompson but the commander of the American naval squadron. No American warships were present at Rio when Custódio declared his revolt. "For many years now," observed the *Rio News,* "this port has been almost wholly abandoned by the naval forces of the United States."[81] In response to Thompson's request, the *Newark* and *Charleston* arrived in October. Shortly after entering the bay, Commodore Oscar Stanton ordered an exchange of salutes and visits with Custódio. This provoked a diplomatic furor in which Floriano accused the American commander of collusion with the rebels. Stanton was recalled by the Navy Department and the next ranking officer, Captain Henry Picking, was placed in temporary command.[82]

The relatively inexperienced Picking was confronted with an unenviable task. Although Custódio refrained from bombarding the city, the frequent outbreak of sporadic firing between the rebel ships and the harbor gun batteries made commercial operations extremely hazardous and at times impossible. Despite their earlier declaration that they would support their own merchant ships, all the foreign naval commanders adopted a passive role. Unless they were prepared to intervene actively, they could do little to prevent injury to their nationals and their property. The American commander was no exception. Complaints about lack of protection were frequent, but he defended his caution by pointing out that forceful action on his part must inevitably assist one side against the other and would be construed as a departure from the policy of noninterference in the domestic affairs of Brazil. No doubt, the example of Stanton's fate also convinced Picking to avoid taking any controversial initiative.[83]

Compounding the difficulties of the foreign officials on the spot was the continued uncertainty as to the exact legal status of the rebels. Initially, Custódio's declaration of revolt was regarded as little more than an attempted military coup. But the stalemate in the harbor persuaded him to seek to strengthen his position by forming an alliance with separatist forces already active in Rio Grande do Sul.[84] On October 24 Custódio announced the formation of a provisional rebel government at Destêrro in Santa Catarina. The foreign powers declined, however, to confer the desired recognition. Thompson's dispatches were particularly dismissive of the rebels. Two days before Custódio's announcement, the American minister had telegraphed Gresham that the position of the insurgents in the harbor at Rio was "becoming desperate." On October 24 he reported that the Uruguayan government had refused to receive a deputation sent by the rebels. On the basis of this information, Gresham judged that recognition by the United States of the provisional government was not justified.[85]

The sagging morale of the rebels was, however, given a considerable boost in early December when the head of the prestigious naval academy, Admiral Saldanha da Gama, joined their cause. Saldanha assumed command of the rebel fleet in the harbor and announced his intention of instituting a more vigorous prosecution of the siege. It now became extremely difficult for the foreign naval commanders to find a safe landing place for their merchant shipping. British merchants complained in particular of the inadequate protection afforded to them by their own naval commander. Saldanha's monarchist sympathies were well known and the fact that his entry into the struggle coincided with rumors of the withdrawal of naval protection by the British commander stirred American suspicions of British complicity in plots to restore the Brazilian monarchy.

The charge made by the Floriano government that the rebels intended to destroy the republic was designed to win support primarily within Brazil, but it was realized that this might also influence American policy. Thompson had little knowledge of Brazilian affairs and was quick to see the specter of monarchist plots. As early as October 3 he relayed official government statements that the true aim of the revolt was to bring back the monarchy. Two months later he informed Gresham that the Brazilian foreign minister claimed to possess proof that British naval forces were giving material support to the rebels.[86]

The secretary of state was not so easily persuaded by Brazilian government propaganda and his response was to seek clarification of these allegations from the American ambassador in London. Uppermost in Gresham's mind from December onward was not the question of monarchist intrigue but how to resolve the problems posed to American merchant shipping by Saldanha's much more energetic policy. Conditioned by his legal training and conservative instincts, the secretary of state could only suggest a continuation of the very same thing that the foreign diplomats and naval commanders had been trying to achieve since the beginning of the revolt. He instructed Thompson on January 9, 1894: "Cooperate with senior commander of our naval forces and others if possible in effort to induce insurgents to designate a place, if there be such a place, where neutral vessels may receive and discharge cargoes in safety without interference with military operations." The next day, Gresham informed his minister that unless all foreign shipping suffered common restrictions "no substantial interference with our vessels, however few, will be acquiesced in."[87]

Coincidental with the dispatch of these instructions, Admiral Andrew Benham arrived at Rio. The Department of the Navy had ordered three additional ships to Rio and wished an officer more senior than Captain Picking to be in command. Benham was therefore transferred from Caribbean waters in December to assume control of a squadron comprising five warships, the most powerful foreign fleet in the harbor. Moreover, the admiral's arrival came just at the time when Saldanha was attempting to prevent all articles of war from being landed. To achieve this the insurgents demanded the right to search all merchant vessels and seize any contraband goods that were found. If allowed, such action would mean the establishment of an effective blockade by the rebels and a consequent de facto recognition of their belligerent rights. After consultation with his foreign naval colleagues, Benham informed Saldanha on January 28 that he would not tolerate interference with American merchant shipping and would employ the force at his command to ensure the safety of American ships. On the following day shots were exchanged between American and rebel ships as Benham successfully escorted an American merchant vessel to the docks.[88]

Instead of attempting to keep American ships away from the line of fire between the harbor forts and the rebel ships, Benham was effectively asserting that American merchants should be allowed to proceed about their business unmolested unless firing was actually under way. Benham claimed to be neutral, but his intervention indicated a refusal to allow Saldanha to establish the very blockade that would secure recognition of the belligerent rights of the rebels. The admiral, no doubt, understood that his task was to open the harbor to American merchant shipping. This was achieved, although in doing so he inevitably assisted Floriano at the expense of Saldanha. That this was not the purpose of American diplomacy was evident in Gresham's frantically worded telegram sent to Thompson on January 30:

> Is the attitude of our naval forces towards Brazil and the insurgents same as when Picking commanded? If different in what respect and why? Wherein does Benham disagree with other commanders if at all? What are your relations with him and Brazilian government? What protection if any is accorded our merchant ships that was not accorded by Picking? Are insurgents enforcing or attempting to en-

force blockade? Report fully and speedily present situation, what has occurred at Rio and in harbor.[89]

While Benham's naval intervention resolved the immediate problem of the protection of neutral shipping in the bay, the rebel fleet still remained in the harbor. Furthermore, the news of military successes by the insurgents in southern Brazil suddenly gave the question of recognition added urgency and significance. Thompson once again raised the specter of British plots. The conspiracy theory of a European intrigue designed to restore the monarchy and overturn the reciprocity had plausibility and would later attract American converts.[90] But Gresham was skeptical. He outlined his views to Ambassador Bayard in January: "I do not believe Great Britain, or any other European Power, will attempt to re-establish the Monarchy in Brazil. The present state of things at Rio can not last much longer and I shall not be surprised at the result whatever it may be. I do not believe the Brazilian people are very patriotic. Perhaps a majority of them are indifferent to what is now going on."[91]

Gresham did not therefore see events at Rio as simply a struggle between republicans versus monarchists. They were not only much more complex, but also contained an element of tragedy. The Brazilian republic was in danger not from external forces but from its own lack of virtue and patriotism. American opinion had welcomed the creation of the republic in 1889, but reservations had always been expressed concerning the new type of government. These doubts were reinforced as Brazil seemed to lurch from one political crisis to another. The Naval Revolt appeared as yet another example of military infighting and one in which the Brazilian people were reluctant to give support to either faction. In October 1893 Captain Picking described Brazilians as showing "little interest" in the revolt.[92] Gresham's allusion to "indifference" three months later showed that the American perception of the Brazilian attitude was unchanged. In the circumstances the secretary of state adopted a policy identical to that of the European powers and stressed the principles of neutrality and noninterference in the domestic affairs of foreign states.

Even though there was some cooperation between American officials and their European colleagues at Rio, American independence of action was always emphasized. There was no formal attempt to concert policy with the European powers; when the intervention by Benham took place, it was executed in a unilateral fashion. Even officials in Washington were confused by events. Gresham was alarmed at unconfirmed reports of fighting involving American warships. His immediate anxiety was that the United States had been drawn into the conflict. He was reassured to learn that Benham's objective was not to maintain Floriano in power or to crush the insurgents but to assert the American right to carry out commercial operations without hindrance. In so doing, he was merely implementing the policy set down earlier by Gresham himself.

Moreover, the fact that the intervention took place in Brazil was merely incidental. This aspect was underlined in a report later presented by Secretary of the Navy Hilary Herbert that placed the whole matter in a much broader moral and legal context. Commending Benham's action as meeting with "universal approval," Herbert declared that it would "have a far-reaching and wholesome influence in quite a number of countries where revolutions are so frequent as to almost constantly imperil the rights of American citizens."[93]

Whatever his exact intention Benham had effectively demonstrated how the growing military power of the United States could be used to assert American rights in Latin America. Scant attention was given to local feelings. Indeed, the British minister at Rio reported that Benham's action had created "a very bad impression on shore" and added that Brazilians "dread the ascendancy of the United States which they think that power wishes to exercise over all American states."[94] Brazilian nationalist sensitivities were aroused by the audacious act of interference in their affairs, but little adverse comment surfaced because Benham had dealt a severe blow to the rebels for which the Floriano government was naturally very appreciative.[95] Thwarted in his attempt to establish an effective blockade, Saldanha's position became untenable and he withdrew from Rio in mid-March 1894. In retrospect, he had attached himself to a doomed cause much too late in the day. The ill-fated admiral joined the rebel forces in the South and eventually was killed in June 1895.[96]

Floriano's ultimate triumph owed much to the rivalries and divisions among his enemies and to his own stolid refusal to surrender power. Diplomacy was merely one of a number of instruments used to gain assistance against the rebels. Floriano never requested American military intervention, but he did seek the material and moral support of the United States. American officials were sympathetic but also cautious. Gresham stressed neutrality and sought to avoid entanglements. However, by its insistence on upholding the status quo, Gresham's legalistic approach actually assisted the established government. Benham's forceful action constituted interference in Brazilian domestic affairs, but it also had the fortuitous effect of strengthening diplomatic relations between the two countries. Floriano was so grateful that he ordered July 4, 1894, to be observed as a Brazilian national holiday.

THE REVIVAL OF RECIPROCITY

While American policy toward the Naval Revolt ultimately favored Floriano, this did not signify the emergence of a special understanding between the two governments. The departure of the rebel fleet led to the resumption of normal commercial activities at Rio, but this was of more immediate benefit to European rather than American merchants. At the end of Saldanha's siege, Thompson recalled there were only five ships in the harbor flying the American flag.

At the same time, he counted more than 100 British vessels. The American minister believed that American ships were similarly outnumbered throughout the hemisphere and he urged that "something should be done to meet this already dominating and rapidly increasing European influence in South and Central America."[97]

American political constraints frustrated diplomats in their pursuit of closer commercial relations. Republican congressmen traditionally favored financial subsidies to shipping lines. Democrats invariably adopted an opposing view. In the case of Brazil, a difference of opinion within the Republican party had delayed recognition of the republic and also hampered the negotiation of the reciprocity treaty. Relations between the two countries were similarly upset by the passage of the Wilson tariff in August 1894.

When the Cleveland administration came to office in 1893, its declared priority was to reverse the Republican policy of protection. A bill was prepared in Congress that proposed not only tariff reduction but also the abrogation of the various agreements made under the 1890 tariff, including the reciprocity arrangement with Brazil. Salvador informed the State Department that his government regarded the reciprocity arrangement as a formal treaty and that there were agreed-upon terms for its abrogation. Gresham devised a formula designed to accommodate the minister's objections by allowing time to terminate the treaty "in the proper manner." But Democratic congressmen were unsympathetic to such diplomatic niceties and refused to accept the proposed compromise. The secretary of state was therefore compelled to reject Brazil's contention that there was an agreed-upon procedure to terminate what he now described as a "so-called treaty."[98] It was clear that American diplomacy enjoyed a latitude of maneuver not permitted to Brazil. Three years previously Salvador's hints that his government might not ratify the arrangement had met with a brusque reply from President Harrison. In 1894 President Cleveland abrogated the controversial arrangement by the simple announcement that the U.S. Congress had passed a law to this effect.

Domestic politics rather than commercial calculation motivated the Wilson tariff. Democratic politicians had no ill will toward Brazil; in the main, they were indifferent. As ever, sugar proved a highly contentious issue. A concern for the welfare of American sugar producers sparked off a Democratic revolt in the Senate and ensured the reimposition of duty. No such political significance was attached to coffee so that this product remained on the free list. Before the 1894 tariff more than 99 percent of Brazilian goods entered the United States free of duty. Afterward, the figure dipped only slightly to around 95 percent. Consequently, there was little detrimental effect on Brazilian exports to the United States. In fact, American merchants stood to lose most as the abrogation of the reciprocity arrangement removed the preferential tariff advantages that they had enjoyed in Brazil. A London journal observed that British residents in Brazil were "greatly pleased" to learn of the demise of the treaty.[99]

Brazilian diplomats were annoyed at the way in which reciprocity was ended, but they no doubt welcomed the opportunity to put aside what had long been a controversial and disagreeable matter. Of more immediate importance for them was the eagerly awaited arbitration of the Misiones boundary dispute with Argentina. The failure to secure ratification of the 1891 settlement had resulted in the question going to the arbitration of the president of the United States. Aguiar de Andrade had been appointed to present Brazil's case at Washington, but died suddenly. His place was taken by José Maria de Silva Paranhos, who had been created baron de Rio Branco in 1888. The choice proved inspired. Despite his relative diplomatic obscurity at Paris, where he was serving as director of immigration at the Brazilian consulate, Rio Branco possessed impressive credentials. Not only had his many years at Liverpool given him fluency in the English language, but he had also personally toured the disputed area when his father had negotiated the peace settlement to the War of the Triple Alliance. These advantages proved useful in what became a personal battle between Rio Branco and Estanislau Zeballos, who represented Argentina. While Rio Branco approached his task with calmness and detachment, Zeballos was extroverted and ostentatious. It was a clash of opposites that soon developed into mutual antipathy.[100]

After months of painstaking preparation and research both ministers submitted their respective cases to Cleveland in February 1894. As the summer months passed by, the president's apparent delay in making his decision aroused growing apprehension in both Argentina and Brazil, but in February 1895 Brazilians were delighted by the announcement of an award that gave Brazil virtually all of the disputed territory. The result was regarded as a personal triumph for Rio Branco and marked the first of a series of brilliantly successful boundary settlements for his country. An overjoyed Brazil sang the praises of Rio Branco and of President Cleveland too. The annoyance over the 1894 tariff became a distant memory in the light of what was interpreted as a conclusive demonstration of American friendship for Brazil. It was not surprising therefore in December 1895 that the Brazilian Senate sent a message of congratulations to President Cleveland for his handling of the Venezuela boundary crisis. A few years later Brazil was notably the only Latin American country to sympathize publicly with the United States during the Spanish-American War. A conspicuously friendly attitude was adopted. Two warships were sold to the American navy and ships of the United States fleet were allowed to take on fuel and to refit in Brazilian ports.[101]

Such bold action was, however, uncharacteristic of Brazilian diplomacy during the late 1890s. A decided lack of interest prevailed in affairs beyond South America and was summed up by the decision not to attend The Hague peace conference in 1899. Of the Latin American countries, only Mexico and Brazil received invitations. The British minister at Rio observed: "Brazil has of late years unwisely allowed herself to drop out of international 'society.'"[102] Diplomatic business was monopolized by tedious financial matters usually involving complicated claims for compensation due to foreign nationals. An outwardly courteous but basically negative attitude was invariably adopted by the understaffed foreign office. "The Brazilian Government," remarked the British minister, "are masters in the art of temporisation," while his American colleague, Charles Page Bryan, later complained of "unreasonable delays" in obtaining replies from the Itamaraty.[103]

Brazilian diplomacy was more actively involved in South American affairs where the threat of conflict with Argentina was a constant concern. While the Misiones arbitration was pleasing to Brazil, it upset Argentina. Any aggressive Argentine designs were, however, restrained not so much out of respect for Brazil but by concern over how Chile might respond. The Brazilian republic appeared as a lesser partner, if not a pawn, in the diplomatic game currently played by its two powerful neighbors. For example, the negotiation of a commercial treaty between Brazil and Chile in 1897 prompted Argentina to demand an exchange of presidential visits as a prelude to the negotiation of a similar agreement between Rio and Buenos Aires. A treaty was not forthcoming, but Brazil consented to receive the Argentine president, Julio Roca, in 1899. This visit was duly returned by President Manuel Ferraz de Campos Sales in 1900. Brazil's diminished diplomatic importance was further underlined in 1902 when Argentina and Chile concluded their rapprochement known as the "Pactos de Mayo" without any reference to Brazil.[104]

Brazilian receptivity to Argentine and Chilean diplomatic initiatives was not an indication of Machiavellian calculation but more the reflection of a society suffering the effects of a decade of political turmoil. The external image of the republic was markedly improved in 1894 by the election of its first civilian president, Prudente de Morais e Barros. But the energies and resources of the federal government continued to be absorbed and dissipated by a succession of internal difficulties. Prudente narrowly escaped assassination in 1897. He also suffered a prolonged period of ill health, which prevented him from effectively asserting executive leadership. The alarming fragility of the republic was further highlighted by the rebellion of religious fanatics in the backlands of the Northeast. The devoted followers of Antônio Conselheiro defied federal authority and were suppressed only with great difficulty in 1897. The operation to destroy the rebel headquarters at Canudos was a considerable embarrassment to the Brazilian army and cost at least 5,000 casualties. A mood of pessimism and despair gripped the Brazilian elite. Despite the brave efforts to celebrate the fourth centennial of Cabral's discovery in May 1900 there was no disguising the fact that national pride was severely dented.[105]

Persistent financial crisis was also a feature of the 1890s. Rui Barbosa served only 14 months as the republic's first finance minister from November 1889 to January 1891, but his legacy was considerable. He sought to stimulate economic prosperity by allowing the printing of substantial quantities of paper money. The result was a short-lived boom followed by runaway inflation.[106] At the federal level, financial disorder was masked by buoyant income from import duties, which climbed to almost three-quarters of total revenue. The attitude of complacency, however, was severely jolted in 1896–1897 by a fall in world coffee prices and the resulting contraction of trade. By the time of the 1898 election the federal government faced a huge deficit. Declining revenues made the outlook appear extremely bleak and the republic's financial standing was reflected in the foreign exchange value of its currency. From its high point of 27 British pence at the end of the empire, the milréis plummeted to 5 pence. The only recourse was an appeal to Brazil's traditional creditors in Europe for a loan on virtually any terms. To avert imminent national bankruptcy President-elect Campos Sales traveled to Europe in April 1898. Led by the Rothschilds, the European bankers agreed to provide a funding loan of £10 million, which would be guaranteed by receipts from Brazil's customs revenues. Bankruptcy was avoided by consolidating and refinancing the foreign debt so that normal servicing would be suspended until 1911. In return, the Brazilian government undertook to pursue a policy of fiscal austerity and to raise the value of the milréis by reducing the amount of paper money in circulation.

American observers such as Thomas L. Thompson remarked that Brazil was steadily drifting into a state of "general demoralization."[107] While recognizing the need for financial discipline, they were also aware that the atmosphere of tension and insecurity encouraged an inward-looking mentality characterized by growing demands for economic protectionism and frequent outbursts of hostility toward foreigners. Most resentment was directed against Europeans, but Americans were not immune. Local disturbances at Rio in 1896 and 1897 prompted the American legation to request the protective presence of American warships. Anti-American feeling was especially aroused by reports that American business interests were intriguing to seize territory in the remote rubber-producing region of Acre. Ugly scenes occurred in 1899 when an angry mob attacked the American consulate at Manáus. The incident was provoked by the news that the American warship *Wilmington* had ignored local regulations and had sailed up the Amazon.[108]

The sensitive state of the diplomatic relationship between the United States and Brazil was further illustrated by the difficulties experienced in the renewed American attempt to gain tariff concessions. Once again the American political world was turned upside down, this time by Cleveland's electoral defeat in 1896. The Republican party returned to power and proceeded to pass the

1897 Dingley tariff. The new law included the reinstatement of the reciprocity provision. Like the McKinley tariff of 1890, it gave the president authority to negotiate reciprocal commercial arrangements and, at his discretion, to retaliate against those countries that pursued unfair practices against American goods.[109]

Republicans claimed that reciprocity would alleviate American economic discontent by stimulating agricultural exports to Latin America. It was especially applicable to Brazil because the balance of trade with that country was known to be notoriously adverse to the United States. In 1897 the difference was more than $50 million in Brazil's favor. This disparity was likely to grow larger as a result of the alarming displacement of American flour in Brazil by imports from Argentina. Up to 1880 flour made up more than 50 percent of American exports to Brazil. During the 1890s it declined to 27 percent. Baltimore merchants pointed out that more than 90 percent of their South American business was with Brazil. They argued that a reduction of the Brazilian tariff on flour was crucial for Baltimore's prosperity.[110]

Section 3 of the Dingley tariff specifically empowered the president to impose a three-cents duty upon each imported pound of coffee. This was the threat that provided American officials with a substantial bargaining leverage against Brazil. When discussions began in 1897 the American minister, Edwin Conger, advised: "I believe only a positive, imperative and authoritative request for fair treatment, emphasized by the imminency of an import duty on coffee, in return for our generous concessions already, will move them to any action."[111] In his official statement presented to the Brazilian government in March 1899 Secretary of State John Hay mentioned the "serious anxiety" of President McKinley on this question and hinted at the likelihood that a three-cents duty might be placed on every pound of Brazilian coffee.[112]

American policy stressed, however, a desire for fair commercial treatment and regarded retaliatory action as a threat only to be implemented after persuasion had failed. Confident in the unassailable nature of their case, officials in Washington expected quick results. A willingness to be reasonable and fair-minded highlighted Hay's instructions to the American minister at Rio, Charles Page Bryan. Hay pointed out that in 1898 the United States had imported more than $61 million of Brazilian products and that 95 percent of these were admitted free of duty. In return Brazil purchased American goods valued at only $13 million, out of which a mere 13 percent was admitted free. These "unequal conditions" greatly discouraged American trade and had led to demands for retaliation against Brazilian coffee. The secretary of state was, however, confident that the logic of his arguments would prevail. "It is due," he remarked, "to the cordial friendship of which this Government has given many proofs to Brazil, to inquire whether that Government will not make such reasonably adequate concessions to the exports of the United States as to justify the continuance of our present free market for the important products of Brazil."[113]

After the controversial experience of the earlier reciprocity agreement, it was hardly surprising that Brazil's response in 1897 was much less accommodating than in 1890. Prior to the passage of the tariff bill Salvador candidly informed the State Department that he could not see in the proposed measure "one single word which can attract Brazil." Despite his undeniable pro-American sympathies, Salvador's disillusionment was evident when he commented that the gains that reciprocity promised to Latin America were "illusory." In what appeared to be a deliberate attempt to avoid the mistakes of the recent past, he hosted a conference of Latin American ministers at the Brazilian legation in Washington. The ministers affirmed their common criticism of reciprocity and stated that they would not sign separate commercial agreements with the United States.[114]

Memories of the previous arrangement still rankled in Brazil too. Moreover, the timing of the reciprocity initiative was inopportune. In contrast to 1890, Brazilian officials could not perceive any obvious diplomatic or commercial advantages to be gained. Indeed, there was a disinclination to grant commercial concessions to the United States. The protectionist lobby in the Brazilian Congress backed by influential state politicians and industrialists urged an increase rather than a reduction in tariff levels.[115] This course of action was attractive to the federal government for whom import taxes contributed more than half of total government revenue. Any reduction of duty would inevitably result in a decrease of income at a time when the Brazilian economy was on the verge of bankruptcy. The American chargé at Rio, Thomas Dawson, confirmed in 1898 that the outgoing Prudente administration was "exceedingly averse to disturbing in any way the financial status quo." The negotiation of the 1898 funding loan in London and the implementation of fiscal austerity by Finance Minister Joaquim Murtinho brought temporary relief, but a severe banking crisis in 1900 indicated that the financial crisis had not been resolved. Dawson summed up in 1902 that the Campos Sales administration "can not bring itself to the point of giving up any revenue."[116]

The hostile attitude of foreign governments was an additional complication. The 1891 agreement had drawn protests from several European countries and these governments were unhappy that American goods might once again enjoy a preferential tariff. The issue also coincided with pressure from Argentina for a commercial treaty. During the 1890s Argentina had displaced the United States as Brazil's principal supplier of wheat and flour. Argentine merchants especially hoped to increase their exports of flour and were acutely aware that this was the product on which the Americans most wanted Brazilian concessions. In the opinion of the British minister at Rio, Brazilian commercial policy was "in an inextricable tangle in every direction."[117] Any concessions granted to the United States must inevitably provoke Argentine anger and vice versa. Indeed, the press of Buenos Aires reacted to rumors of the conclusion of an arrangement between Brazil and the United States in 1900 with bitter denunciations of Brazilian betrayal. The American minister at Rio judged, however, that this "menacing attitude" only consolidated Brazilian support for the measure.[118]

One reason for American patience with Brazil during the trying saga of reciprocity negotiations was the awareness of the many obstacles faced by that government in attempting to conclude a commercial agreement. "The difficulties now surrounding the Brazilian Government," wrote Secretary of State John Sherman in 1897, "deserve fair consideration and forbearance on the part of our Government."[119] Yet Sherman and his successor, John Hay, remained optimistic that an agreement would ultimately be reached. It was their opinion that Brazilian diplomats recognized the anomalous nature of trade relations between their respective countries and that they would proceed to rectify this out of a sense of fairness and justice. The stick of the retaliatory tax on coffee existed, but was held in reserve because its use would indicate diplomatic defeat. It was also a threat that was largely discounted in Brazil. "Almost the universal opinion among public men here," reported Dawson from Rio in 1901, "is that we have no such intention."[120] So long-standing and well established was the coffee trade that Brazilians were confident American consumers would continue to purchase substantial quantities no matter what the particular commercial policy pursued by the United States government.

On the other hand, Brazilian officials could never be completely sure that the threat would not be carried out. In June 1899 the new Brazilian minister at Washington, Joaquim Francisco de Assis Brasil, noted apprehensively that New York firms were buying up coffee stocks in anticipation of the imminent imposition of a retaliatory tax on the product.[121] Another source of pressure arose from the persistent and forceful presentation of the American case. Hay stressed fairness and reason, but his dispatches also talked of the United States "demanding" and "insisting" on reciprocal concessions. When he learned that the Brazilian Congress was considering an increase in the duty on flour, Hay telegraphed that "this Government would regard it as an act directed against our commerce and justifying countervailing action on our part."[122] Charles Page Bryan later revealed that during 1900 he had "urged" Brazil to grant tariff concessions "at nearly every weekly audience" with the Brazilian foreign minister.[123]

In general, Brazilian political and business opinion was averse to a new reciprocity treaty with the United States. But internal opposition had to be balanced with the diplomatic consideration that Brazil desired to maintain the goodwill and support of the United States. Moreover, at a time when overproduction contributed to fluctuating fortunes in the coffee trade,[124] Brazilian producers were desperate for export markets. Promotional displays were mounted at Brazilian consulates in Europe, but so long as the United States remained Brazil's largest single purchaser, it was crucial that Brazilian coffee retain free access to the American market.

Brazilian ambivalence was demonstrated by the decision to transfer Salvador from Washington to Lisbon in 1898. His successor, Assis Brasil, reflected the best traditions of the Brazilian diplomatic service in that he was cultured and widely traveled, but he could hardly hope to match his predecessor's intimate knowledge of American affairs.[125] The *Washington Post* regretted Salvador's departure and praised him for his "able and tactful diplomacy" and "unvarying friendship" for the United States. It was also noted, however, that the new minister was keen to increase commercial contact with the United States, thus confirming the suspicion that Salvador had been removed "to make room" for a man who would conclude a reciprocity treaty.[126]

The optimism proved ill-founded. It was not until late in 1900 that the Brazilian government responded reluctantly to American diplomatic pressure and undertook to grant tariff concessions on imports of American flour.[127] Hay believed that the agreement would be implemented immediately by executive action, but this proved unfounded as the Brazilian government sought unsuccessfully to obtain congressional approval.[128] In effect, the measure fell victim to unlucky timing. By 1901 the Campos Sales administration was fast becoming a lame duck. Its authority was diminishing as Brazilian politicians turned their attention to the forthcoming presidential election. Campos Sales no longer possessed the political influence to sway sufficient congressional votes. His financial policies earned the praise of European bankers but at a cost to his own personal popularity. Violent street demonstrations occurred in Rio during his last months in office and his departure from the presidency in November 1902 was accompanied by scenes of public derision.[129]

The Campos Sales administration simply could not deliver the reciprocity agreement. American retaliation was rumored, but did not materialize. A memorandum of 1906 disclosed:

> It was understood during the McKinley Administration that the threat to penalize Brazilian coffee would be carried out in the final refusal of Brazil to comply with our demands. This threat . . . was, however, not taken seriously by the Brazilian Government. The belief held at the Department was that if it had been carried out we should have been able to accomplish our object. . . . In 1901, however, when the question of actually imposing the penal duty on coffee called for immediate decision . . . the Secretary of State deeming such action unwise, declined to recommend its adoption to the President, remarking to me, on the occasion of the discussion of the matter, that we had tried to scare Brazil, but failed to do so, and that was the end of the matter. Threats were thereafter discontinued.[130]

Unlike 1890, the turn of the century was not a propitious time for the revival of reciprocity. In fact, Brazil's attitude was typical. With the exception of Ecuador, all of the South American countries refused to conclude treaties with the United States. The subject was notably given relatively little attention at the second Pan-American conference, held in Mexico City from October 1901 to January 1902. The American delegation had to be satisfied with the adoption of a token resolution reaffirming support for reciprocity treaties as a means of promoting international trade. The *Chicago Tribune* summed up that the delegates were "talking much but doing little."[131]

American officials concentrated their efforts on Brazil, but financial crisis, congressional opposition, and the growing political preoccupation with the 1902 presidential election compelled the Brazilian government to proceed with circumspection. Moreover, in the United States, the onset of economic prosperity after 1897 diminished the attractiveness of the reciprocity policy. The assassination of President McKinley in 1901 also removed its leading political exponent.[132] Hay confessed his inability to conclude an arrangement with Brazil, but this was only a temporary setback for American diplomacy. The importance of the commercial relationship with the northern republic was such that the Brazilian government would remain receptive and vulnerable to changes in American commercial policy. The potential for closer relations undoubtedly existed and only awaited new circumstances and new men.

CHAPTER 2

Years of Approximation, 1902–1912

A DISTINGUISHED SCHOLAR wrote at the beginning of the twentieth century that the United States had "assumed a new position among nations" and should now be considered "as one of the chief forces in international affairs."[1] American diplomatic interest in Europe and Asia was increasing, but most activity was still concentrated within the Western Hemisphere. The "splendid little" Spanish-American War had reawakened the sense of revolutionary mission and enhanced the strategic significance of the Caribbean area. The booming American economy was also eager to take advantage of commercial opportunities on its doorstep. Between 1900 and 1910 trade and investment with Latin America more than doubled and grew at a faster rate than with other regions of the world.[2]

The same period was marked by American military intervention in several of the countries of the Caribbean and Central America. This policy reflected not only America's new naval and economic power but also the influence of progressive ideas that advocated the imposition of political stability and financial rectitude in those republics considered guilty of wrongdoing. The progressive impulse extended to the reorganization of the American foreign service. The creation in 1909 of a separate Latin American Division underlined the importance attached to hemispheric affairs.[3]

The idealistic aspects of progressivism were belied by the frequent use of the "big stick." Throughout Latin America there was widespread concern about the apparently unquenchable American appetite for expansion.[4] Officials in Washington such as Secretary of State Elihu Root were aware of the growing anti-American sentiment and attempted to alleviate this by cultivating Latin American goodwill.

Foremost to benefit from this conciliatory attitude was Brazil, whose enhanced prestige was highlighted by the raising of diplomatic relations to ambassadorial level and the choice of Rio as the venue of the third Pan-American conference. Root personally attended the conference and suggested that the two countries "acting together, would form a single and eternal guarantee for the integrity of America."[5] The concept of an alliance was very appealing to Brazilian leaders, but it never emerged as a concrete proposal and remained only an item of press speculation.

By the time of the Rio conference the economic achievement of Brazil was undeniable and presented "incalculable" commercial opportunities.[6] The State Department sought to assist American merchants by continuing to demand "reciprocity" in the form of preferential tariff reductions on American goods imported into Brazil. But American exporters and investors were still reluctant to commit themselves to risky overseas expansion. Consequently, American products made up no more than one-eighth of Brazil's imports and remained "only a drop in the bucket."[7]

Diplomatic appointments to Brazil received similar limited consideration. The necessity of reorganizing European postings in 1902 enabled Charles Page Bryan to transfer to Switzerland. His successor, David Thompson, was a self-made businessman from Nebraska whose appointment was designed to please western politicians. The upgrading of the legation to embassy status and the task of preparing for the imminent Pan-American conference gave a new significance to the selection of Thompson's replacement in 1906. The post was offered to Lloyd Griscom, who hesitated to accept, but was soothed by Roosevelt's parting words: "You go down to Brazil and make Root's visit a success and you won't be there long." The president fulfilled his promise and within a year Griscom was rewarded with an ambassadorship to Rome. Suffering acutely from tropical fever he reacted to the news by exclaiming: "It was as though manna had fallen from Heaven." A successor was found by the simple expedient of transferring Irving Dudley from Lima to Rio. Dudley spent almost five years in Brazil before contracting a fatal disease that brought about his early retirement. The appointment of Edwin Morgan in 1912 indicated the desire of the Taft administration to place an experienced career diplomat in charge of the Brazilian mission.[8]

The British minister at Rio considered that the American ambassador "is the only representative here who has any influence."[9] The privileged status was derived from Brazil's dependence upon the American coffee market. The attempt to exploit this leverage by demanding preferential commercial treatment increasingly dominated diplomatic relations during the era of Rio Branco. Despite some Brazilian concessions in 1906, American diplomatic pressure was unrelenting.

Careful regard for Brazilian sensibilities was not a characteristic feature of American policy. Root's Pan-American initiative was more public rhetoric than a genuine change of policy. Certainly, officials in Washington took closer note of Latin American affairs, but "Latin America" meant the more narrowly defined area of the Caribbean and Central America.[10] Brazil's growth and potential were duly acknowledged, but it was still perceived as a remote region on the periphery of American concerns.

For Brazil the twentieth century began as a decade of order and progress. The political chaos of the 1890s was replaced by "the politics of the governors" in which stability was maintained by alliance between the two most powerful states of São Paulo and Minas Gerais. The London *Times* reported approvingly that "Brazil is more tranquil than at any period since the revolution against Dom Pedro II."[11]

After a spell of virtual diplomatic isolation Brazil once more became a continental power of significance and assumed an international role commensurate with its size. A remarkable element of continuity in the conduct of diplomacy was provided by the Baron do Rio Branco who served as foreign minister from December 1902 until his death in February 1912.[12] Under his leadership the Ministry of Foreign Relations, popularly known as the "Itamaraty," became synonymous with Brazil's foreign policy. The baron masterminded a conspicuous effort to promote the Brazilian image overseas. Several new missions were established so that by 1912 Brazil was represented in 39 countries. Of all the diplomatic appointments, the selection of Joaquim Nabuco as Brazil's first ambassador to the United States was undoubtedly the most successful.[13]

Diplomatic relations with Europe continued to be important, but Washington became Brazil's leading diplomatic post because Rio Branco considered the friendship and support of the United States crucial to the protection and achievement of Brazil's national interests. A foreign policy was formulated that sought to promote a confluence of interests and was popularly known as the strategy of "rapprochement" or "approximation." Claiming the support of the United States, Rio Branco asserted Brazil's hemispheric role as leader of the southern continent.[14]

Approximation was brilliantly promoted by Joaquim Nabuco in the United States. "Brazil's heartiest wishes," he told Theodore Roosevelt, "are for the increase of that vast moral influence that the United States exercises upon the march of civilization."[15] Dispatches from the American embassy at Rio confirmed the friendly feeling. Of all the South American countries, Griscom believed that "Brazil is most likely to respond quickly to our advances."[16]

Economic reasons also motivated the desire for close relations with the United States. The latter was the largest purchaser of Brazilian coffee and rubber. More American imports boosted government revenue and helped to offset Brazil's traditional dependence on European and Argentine suppliers. Although the tariff was technically a matter for the Ministério do Fazenda (Treasury), the fact that American representatives pursued reciprocity through diplomatic channels meant that the Itamaraty played a prominent role in commercial negotiations.

The controversy over reciprocity brought approximation directly into the political debate over the exact powers of the federal government. In 1904 Congress prevented the renewal of the tariff concessions granted earlier that year to American goods. The power of the protectionist lobby was demonstrated during the following year by the passage of a substantial increase in the tariff. Rio Branco personally favored a general reduction of duties, but he bowed to the force of congressional opinion.[17]

Rio Branco was genuinely friendly toward the United States, but disagreements could also occur. During the Second Peace Conference at The Hague, Brazil publicly opposed the views expressed by the American delegation. While anti-American feeling was less evident in Brazil than in Spanish America, Brazilian nationalism was easily provoked by sensationalized reports of American entrepreneurs searching for rubber in the Acre territory. Griscom warned of the constant need "to keep down the ever recrudescent suspicion that under our friendly attitude lies some ulterior motive."[18]

The pursuit of approximation had also to contend with the pro-European sympathies of Brazilian society. Brazilians felt honored by the visit of Elihu Root, but they were even more flattered when prominent Europeans such as Georges Clemenceau and Anatole France came to Brazil.[19] The ties with the Old World grew stronger rather than weaker as hundreds of thousands of immigrants annually poured in from Italy, Spain, and Portugal. By contrast only a few hundred Americans came to live and settle.[20]

The buildup of military power was another means by which Brazil sought to emulate Europe. But the decision to purchase British dreadnoughts only provoked an arms race with Argentina and revealed the inherent contradiction in Rio Branco's strategy. Approximation encouraged him to indulge his dream of Brazil as the leader of South America, but inevitably heightened tensions with Argentina. When Rio Branco looked to Washington for support, it was not forthcoming. After almost a decade of diplomatic effort he concluded sadly that approximation had resulted in few tangible benefits for Brazil.

THE ACRE TERRITORIAL DISPUTE

After his spectacular triumph at Washington in presenting Brazil's case concerning the Misiones arbitration, Rio Branco chose to return to Paris. Although the post of director of the Immigration Service appeared modest, its incumbent had the priceless advantage of residing in the city that Brazilians regarded as the cultural capital of the world. But Rio Branco's talents were not allowed to remain in obscurity. The reputation he had earned as an expert on territorial claims was soon utilized to prepare his country's submission in the dispute with France over the northern border region of Amapá. The decision given by the president of Switzerland in 1900 awarded more than 100,000 square miles to Brazil and was acclaimed as another outstanding success for the baron.

His reward was appointment in 1901 as minister at Berlin. Rio Branco admired Germany and was content with the promotion,[21] but such was the legend of skill and success now associated with his name that President-elect Francisco de Paula Rodrigues Alves offered him Brazil's top diplomatic post in 1902. The baron hesitated to accept. Since the beginning of the republic the authority of the foreign minister had been undermined by interference from politicians. Moreover, Rio Branco was conscious that his long residence overseas had effectively deprived him of political influence. Various excuses were expressed to justify his indecision such as concern about interrupting the education of his eldest daughter, the high cost of living in Rio, and the long, hot summers. In reality, he was seeking to negotiate the terms of office. When satisfactory assurances were forthcoming, he accepted the invitation to become foreign minister.[22] After an absence of 15 years, Rio Branco was given a hero's welcome on his return home in December 1902. Brazilian diplomacy would be under his personal direction for the next ten years.

The expertise in boundary matters proved invaluable when his first year as foreign minister became clouded by the difficult problem of the Acre territorial dispute. This remote area of forest and jungle adjoined Amazonas and marked the western limits of Brazilian expansion. During the 1890s it had suddenly acquired prominence as a result of the international demand for rubber. Reckoned to be the richest rubber region in the world, its ownership became a matter of considerable diplomatic interest. Indeed, the exact location of the territorial boundary had long been a matter of dispute between the governments of Brazil, Bolivia, and Peru. While Bolivia was acknowledged as possessing the strongest historical claim, its actual contact with the region was slight. Very few Bolivians resided in the territory, which had become mostly occupied by large numbers of Brazilian *seringueiros* (rubber latex extractors) seeking profits from the rubber trade.[23] These settlers not only gathered the rubber, but also transported it along tributaries of the Amazon to Manáus and Belém. The attempt by the Bolivian authorities to tax these shipments in 1899 sparked off violence and demands for independence. In what seemed to be an unmistakable prelude to annexation, the Campos Sales administration claimed that Acre belonged to Brazil.

Bolivia appeared powerless to resist its giant neighbor. It was all highly reminiscent of similar events in Texas half a century earlier. However, Brazil's contention that its de facto control should be given de jure recognition was threatened by reports of American support for Bolivia. These arose initially from the publication of a secret treaty allegedly concluded between the United States and Bolivia in the late 1890s. This scare coincided with the unauthorized voyage up the Amazon in 1899 by the American warship *Wilmington* and fueled Brazilian suspicions of collusion between Washington and La Paz. In 1902 anti-American sentiment became even more pronounced after it was learned that the Bolivian government had granted not only commercial rights but also virtual sovereign powers of administration in the disputed area to a syndicate of American capitalists.[24]

Only a few years earlier, Brazil had adopted a sympathetic attitude toward American intervention in Cuba. But no strategic interests had been involved on that occasion. The emergence of a direct threat to Brazil's own territory caused a marked change of opinion. "There is so general a distrust of the United States," lamented an American merchant, "that the people grasp eagerly at the chance to make mountains out of molehills."[25] The increasing outcry over what was called "the American danger"[26] provoked a swift and positive response from the Campos Sales administration. In July 1902 Foreign Minister Olinto de Magalhães informed Colonel Bryan that Brazil and all of South America objected to the "menacing precedent" of a foreign company assuming governmental functions on Latin American territory. He hoped that American capitalists would be "discouraged" from involvement in "an undertaking which was sure to result in financial disaster to themselves and in discord between nations."[27]

The State Department replied that the syndicate was a purely private venture and had no official backing. Brazilian diplomats, however, were not fully reassured by this disclaimer, as it was known that the list of investors included a cousin of President Roosevelt. American imperialist designs could not be ruled out especially when Assis Brasil reported his suspicion that Secretary of State John Hay was more personally interested in the matter than he wished it to appear. Despite the United States' proclaimed attitude of neutrality, the Brazilian minister noted ominously that the U.S. government always sought to protect and safeguard the interests of its citizens.[28]

A similar determination was also evident in Brazil. Shortly before leaving office in November 1902 Campos Sales ordered the closure of the River Amazon to foreign shipping. The action was intended to express his government's serious concern over the Acre question. It also effectively isolated the syndicate from its source of external supplies and underlined how much any exploitation of the rubber trade was dependent on Brazilian consent and assistance. Rio Branco was determined to avoid any show of weakness and resolved to continue this demonstration of Brazil's sovereign power despite protests from Britain, France, Germany, and the United States.

The United States claimed a particular interest because it had been the pioneering surveys by American naval officers such as Herndon, Gibbon, and Maury that had persuaded the imperial government to reconsider its traditional policy of exclusion and open the river to foreign shipping in 1867. The American consul-general at Rio, Eugene Seeger, interpreted the measure "as a thrust against the United States." He believed himself justified in protesting to Rio Branco that the United States government "has always considered the navigation of the Amazon through Brazil as being free to all nations." In fact, Seeger had little sympathy for Brazil's case and privately condemned the latter's intrusion into the Acre territory as "an act of modern piracy directed by politicians and speculators in Manáus and executed by the basest kind of adventurers and cut-throats."[29]

Officials at the State Department were guided by broader diplomatic considerations and were inclined to be more sympathetic than Seeger. They were sincerely pleased by Rio Branco's appointment as foreign minister and "agreeably recalled" his residence in Washington at the time of the Misiones arbitration.[30] The American minister at Rio, David Thompson, also confirmed that the baron was "most friendly." While he acknowledged that some Brazilians were suspicious of American motives, Thompson stressed that Rio Branco "does not court this feeling, and wants to feel faith in our good intentions."[31]

The mutual goodwill between the two foreign offices was carefully exploited by Rio Branco to help him gain his first diplomatic success as foreign minister. It was also an invaluable asset with which to counter the growing diplomatic involvement of Peru in the Acre dispute. Clearly worried by Brazilian expansion, Peru laid its own claim to part of the territory and also sought American support. Washington became a battle station for Brazilian diplomacy as Rio Branco attempted to persuade State Department officials to adopt a neutral attitude in the dispute. Such a stance would result in the diplomatic isolation of the American syndicate who would then be compelled to look for a means of abandoning the enterprise. Once this was achieved, Rio Branco reckoned that Bolivia and Peru would have to accept Brazil's possession of the disputed territory.

A strategy combining firmness with friendliness was pursued. Reports of disorder between settlers and Bolivian officials prompted the dispatch of Brazilian troops to the region. Assis Brasil was instructed to keep American officials fully informed of developments. The Brazilian minister argued that the syndicate was not a straightforward capitalistic enterprise and skillfully likened its activities to those of the "chartered companies" that had acquired imperial control of much of Africa and Asia. The interpretation of the venture as a danger to Latin American independence and a threat to the Monroe Doctrine made a visible impression at the State Department. Moreover, in contrast to Hay's ambivalence, Assis reported gratifyingly that President Roosevelt was personally sympathetic to the Brazilian case. Consequently, Assis felt able to state in February 1903 that the United States government would not now intervene in the dispute.[32]

Brazilian diplomacy, therefore, had effectively deprived the syndicate of outside supplies and any prospect of American diplomatic support. The closure of the Amazon was also extended to agents of the syndicate who were compelled to remain at Pará. Little new capital was forthcoming for an enterprise whose future looked decidedly gloomy. Frustrated in every direction, the syndicate gratefully took up Rio Branco's suggestion of a financial arrangement with the Brazilian government.[33] With the knowledge and approval of the State Department, negotiations commenced in Washington between Assis and representatives of the American syndicate.

In another astute move, the distinguished Republican diplomat and international lawyer, John Bassett Moore, was retained as Brazil's counsel. His support for Brazil's case was unequivocal. In January 1903 he described the contract between the syndicate and the Bolivian government as "mere irresponsible speculation, which no respectable tribunal could be expected to countenance." In his judgment, the disputed territory was "inhabited chiefly by Brazilians, who carry on the industries of the country" and Brazil should not consent to its transfer "to the control and government of an alien private company of uncertain nationality and destitute of international powers and obligations."[34]

By late February 1903 the syndicate agreed to renounce its contract in return for an indemnity of $550,000, to be paid by the Brazilian government. The arrangement was confirmed during the following month by which time the Amazon had been reopened to foreign shipping and the outline of a similar agreement was concluded between Brazil and Bolivia. Rio Branco had correctly judged that a helpless and solitary Bolivia would soon come to terms. By the treaty of Petrópolis, signed in November 1903, Bolivia formally recognized Brazil's possession of more than 70,000 square miles of the Acre territory. As part of the settlement, Brazil agreed to facilitate Bolivian access to the Amazonian river system by constructing a railroad from Madeira to Mamoré. Rio Branco had skillfully turned the "American danger" to Brazil's advantage. He had not only peacefully secured the further extension and consolidation of his country's national frontier, but also ensured Brazilian control over the booming profits of the Acre rubber trade.[35]

The boundary question, however, was not finally concluded because of Peru's annoyance at being excluded from the 1903 settlement. The Peruvian government responded by reaffirming its own territorial claims and stated that it would send troops to the area. Like Brazil, Peru was also well aware of the critical value of American influence and attempted to win Washington's goodwill by promptly recognizing the new republic of Panama in December 1903, ahead of similar action by Brazil and other South American countries. Rio Branco's Chief Diplomatic Secretary, Domício da Gama, informed the American chargé at Rio that Peru was intriguing "to procure the moral support of the United States in her boundary disputes with Chile and Ecuador."[36] He might have included the Acre dispute too!

Once again Rio Branco pursued a policy combining firmness with moderation. Army units were dispatched to the border as a signal of Brazil's determination to expel any attempted Peruvian military encroachment. At Washington, the State Department was kept fully abreast of events and was also encouraged to play an active diplomatic role. On this occasion American good offices were especially welcome, as official opinion had approved the arrangement with the syndicate and was believed to be clearly on the side of Brazil. The United States wanted a peaceful settlement of the dispute and used its influence to expedite negotiations to this end. Hay instructed the American minister at Rio to work for an outcome "mutually honorable and advantageous" to both countries.[37] In effect, American impartiality assisted Brazil because it enabled Rio Branco to insist on the maintenance of the territorial status quo. Peru was effectively isolated and looked for a face-saving formula. Thompson's mediation allowed the drawing up of a preliminary accord in 1904 that essentially represented a Brazilian victory, but whose verbal formula was acceptable to Peru. With the assistance of American diplomacy Rio Branco thereby secured Peruvian recognition of Brazil's undisputed legal title to the Acre territory.[38]

The Acre dispute demonstrated that the United States was no longer a distant and indifferent spectator of South American affairs. All interested parties saw Washington as the decisive focal point of their diplomatic maneuvers and each side competed to win American support. Rio Branco appreciated that American goodwill had already helped him achieve advantageous results in awkward boundary disagreements with Argentina over the Misiones and with France over Amapá. This experience impressed upon him the need to inform and persuade American officials of the justice of Brazil's case. Initially, the Itamaraty was uncertain and apprehensive as to the exact attitude of the State Department, but this anxiety proved to be misplaced when it became apparent that American officials were not prepared to back a financial enterprise whose intentions and legal title were dubious. The demonstration of Brazilian determination and power in closing the Amazon also underlined the futility of the venture. Once the dispute with the American syndicate was satisfactorily resolved, Rio Branco was proved correct in his belief that American goodwill for Brazil would assist a favorable settlement of the Acre question.

CONTINUED DISCUSSIONS OVER RECIPROCITY

Since the Pan-American conference of 1889–1890, relations between the United States and Brazil had been dominated by commercial negotiations. The Acre dispute provided merely a temporary diplomatic diversion. The area was rich in rubber, but the profits were unobtainable so long as access was denied by the Brazilians. State Department officials took a pragmatic view of the issue and were disinclined to promote risky business ventures in distant regions of

South America. What they wanted was a peaceful outcome so that they could concentrate on the task that had recommenced with the 1897 Dingley tariff: securing "reciprocity" in commercial relations with Brazil.

The basic goal remained to increase American exports in order to redress the adverse trade balance, which averaged more than $50 million annually at the beginning of the twentieth century. A cosmetic change was introduced by the abandonment of the terms "reciprocity" and "treaty," which were judged to have too many awkward political and legislative connotations. The aim of reducing the Brazilian tariff on imported American products was unchanged, although it was now described as seeking "preferential treatment." Whatever the terminology, the Brazilian response remained unyielding. The American chargé at Rio, Thomas Dawson, explained that the federal government simply could not afford to give up any revenue. Moreover, his instructions to press for a reduction in the duty on flour were particularly controversial because of the general fear "to take any action adverse to Argentina and the local flour mills." In Dawson's experience, requests for tariff changes met only with "evasion and delay."[39]

A more optimistic outlook was adopted by the American minister, Colonel Bryan, who was particularly encouraged by the election in 1902 of Rodrigues Alves. The new president possessed considerable experience of high governmental office and had served as finance minister under Floriano and Prudente before being elected governor of São Paulo in 1900. A mood of confidence in Brazil's prospects was clearly emerging. "The financial condition of the Government is more satisfactory than for some time past," remarked the London *Times*.[40] An article in the *Atlantic Monthly* by an American consul with long experience of Brazil predicted that the country was destined to become a larger market than any single European nation.[41] As the representative of the rising Paulista interests, Rodrigues Alves promised to place a welcome emphasis on economic expansion and breaking down the barriers to trade. Bryan reported gratifyingly that each member of the new cabinet had "at one time or another given public expression of their friendliness for the United States and of admiration for our institutions." He believed that there was a particular desire to expand trade with the United States and was confident of the "readiness to assist in our wishes for commercial reciprocity."[42]

Bryan's transfer to Switzerland meant, however, that it was his successor, David Thompson, who entered into commercial discussions with the new government on his arrival at Rio in March 1903. Thompson acknowledged that a desire existed to give concessions, but he encountered only delay and prevarication from the Itamaraty. In September he concluded gloomily that it would be "most difficult and most likely impossible" to persuade Brazil to alter its tariff unless the United States categorically declared that retaliation against Brazilian goods was imminent. So many threats had been made in the past, however, that American credibility was doubted. "I am confident," reported Thompson, "no one connected with the administration or congress here believes our administration will alter its present course no matter what is done here."[43]

An unexpected development occurred only a few weeks later and illustrated Thompson's lack of understanding of the inner working of Brazilian politics. As Bryan had predicted earlier, the new administration was keen to stimulate foreign trade and wished also to counter the trend toward protectionism.[44] In December 1903 Thompson disclosed with some surprise that the government intended to reduce the tariff in favor of American products. Domestic opposition would be circumvented by rushing through an amendment to the annual budget in the hectic closing days of the congressional session.[45] The American minister considered that the administration was "undertaking a difficult thing" and that "its willingness to resort to disguise and secrecy as it has done shows the sincerity of its purpose in this matter."[46] But Congress was not so easily deceived and the amendment was rejected.

In February 1904, however, the Rio press carried news from New York that tariff reductions had actually been granted to various American goods including varnishes, watches, clocks, condensed milk, and, more controversially, on flour. The British minister, Henry Dering, wrote from Rio that there was "a considerable sensation in commercial circles." He requested a statement from Rio Branco on the subject and received the reassuring answer that the report was inaccurate and would be officially contradicted.[47] However, the publication of a presidential decree on April 16 confirmed the authenticity of the earlier press report by stating that a 20 percent tariff reduction would go into effect until the end of the year. Domício da Gama attempted to explain that the reply given by the foreign minister to Dering in February was "at the time entirely justified," but that considerable American pressure had been subsequently exerted to drive Brazil "into a corner," thus forcing the grant of preferential concessions.[48]

An embarrassing incident was therefore clarified by blaming the Americans. The British minister needed little convincing of the machinations of his commercial rivals and reported to the Foreign Office that the "corner" referred to the Acre dispute. He suspected that the preferential tariff was either a quid pro quo for American support or, perhaps, a Brazilian surrender to an American threat to back Peru in the boundary dispute.[49] This analysis seemed especially plausible as the executive decree attracted virtually no support from political or commercial interests in Brazil. When reports of the preference first appeared in February 1904 Dawson remarked sadly that "no favorable editorials" were forthcoming in the Rio press. The northeastern states condemned the concession as a purely sectional measure designed to favor São Paulo and Minas Gerais.[50] Moreover, the use of an obscure law permitting the alteration of the tariff by executive action provoked a "storm of opposition." Thompson later commented that "it is said nothing since the revolution in this country has stirred up so much sentiment and caused so much complaint as the favors shown our commerce."[51]

The administration attempted to justify its action locally by pointing out that the United States was the largest importer of coffee and that the product entered that country free of duty. Confronted by a delegation of angry businessmen, President Rodrigues Alves explained that a "small sacrifice" was necessary "in order to promote and maintain the interests of Brazilian coffee."[52] Domício told the British minister that the United States government was about to impose a three-cents duty on each pound of coffee unless concessions were immediately forthcoming from Brazil.[53]

While the tariff reductions were primarily intended to improve Brazil's relations with the United States, they were also calculated to divert trade in certain products from European to American merchants.[54] The financial sums involved were small, but this failed to moderate the annoyance of the European suppliers of varnishes, watches, and clocks. The Rio press declared that the measure "will land this country into serious complications" because other nations would inevitably demand similar privileges. If these were granted, government revenue would be seriously depleted. Refusal might lead to retaliation against Brazilian goods.[55]

Official protests were lodged by France, Belgium and Switzerland, but it was the reaction of Argentina that most immediately troubled the Itamaraty. By the turn of the century more than 50 percent of Brazil's imports of flour came from Argentina. The granting of an exclusive preference to American flour threatened to disrupt this growing and profitable market and was regarded by the press of Buenos Aires as a virtual declaration of economic war. Rio Branco argued that the impact of the preference would only be marginal. He predicted that the cost of Argentine flour would still be cheaper because of the expensive freight rates from the United States and the relatively high price of American goods. Stressing a desire for good relations, the foreign minister sought to conciliate Argentine opinion by encouraging discussions about a possible commercial treaty between the two neighbors.[56]

Foreign representations were an awkward but scarcely unexpected consequence of the preferential decree. The Rodrigues Alves administration had braved considerable political and diplomatic controversy to effect the measure, and it must have been disconcerted to learn that even American officials were not completely satisfied. In 1890, John W. Foster had used the passage of the McKinley tariff to adopt a tougher bargaining stance. In similar fashion Secretary of State Hay regarded the 1904 concessions as merely a first installment and requested that the list of articles accorded preference be extended.[57] Rio Branco frankly explained to Thompson that any further concessions "might cause dissensions of a serious character." Nevertheless, throughout April and May the American minister pressed for the inclusion of additional items such as butter and still wines and eventually drew from Rio Branco a plea asking Hay to "moderate Thompson's zeal."[58]

The granting of tariff preference in 1904 illustrated the nature of United States–Brazilian relations at the beginning of the twentieth century. Dependence upon the American market for its exports of rubber and especially coffee made Brazil extremely sensitive to commercial pressure exerted by the United States. "The United States," Rio Branco noted in 1905, "are the principal market for our coffee and other products."[59] The Paulista interests that dominated the Rodrigues Alves administration needed little reminding of this fact and ensured that the question of preserving a thriving coffee industry received a high diplomatic priority.[60] But more than economic compulsion was required to persuade Brazil to give way. The anxiety over the Acre dispute and Rio Branco's unfolding strategy of approximation pointed to a desire for closer relations with the United States, of which the grant of commercial concessions was just one step. Nevertheless, the administration badly miscalculated the amount of internal dissent provoked by the tariff decree. Ironically, during the six months that the measure was in effect, the import of products given preferential reductions increased by a mere $130,000, and most of this was attributed to unusually large purchases of condensed milk.[61] Rio Branco confided later to the British minister that the 1904 preference was "not of sufficient importance to have raised the excitement which it actually did."[62] The concessions may have been marginal, but the slighting of Congress by the executive proved not to be such a small matter.

Indeed, the whole affair aroused so much controversy that the administration was probably relieved when the preferential lapsed at the end of the year and Congress passed a law to prevent its renewal. The political impasse temporarily muted the American minister. In July 1905, Thompson returned to the fray with the suggestion that congressional objections might be overcome by proposing a straightforward 20 percent reduction on all American goods coming into Brazil. Whereas previous measures had emphasized differential duties on a wide range of products, the simplicity of the new proposal was intended to disarm the critics. Rio Branco welcomed Thompson's suggestion and undertook to prepare a congressional bill.[63] It seemed a typical example of the Itamaraty's delaying tactics. Instead of quietly shelving the matter, however, a proposal to renew the concessions of the previous year was placed before Congress and secured its approval in December. The preferential treatment would come into effect on July 1, 1906. The explanation for this welcome turn of events lay not in the force of Thompson's arguments, but that the matter had assumed a much wider diplomatic dimension. A number of significant changes were taking place in the relationship between Brazil and

the United States that resulted in a desire for closer cooperation and friendliness. Instead of tedious correspondence over tariff scales, the stress was increasingly on broader matters affecting hemispheric diplomacy.

THE BEGINNING OF APPROXIMATION

As the political and financial disorders of the 1890s receded into the past, Brazil became much more conscious of its continental power and international
status. The desire of the Brazilian elite to improve the nation's image was illustrated by the beautification and "regeneration" of Rio. Wide publicity was
given to the construction of modern dock facilities and the completion in
November 1905 of the splendid Avenida Central. Linked to the latter was
the Avenida Beira Mar, which provided a picturesque boulevard stretching
for six miles along the bay. Even more famous was the successful campaign
organized by Dr. Osvaldo Cruz to rid the city of yellow fever. Many Cariocas
were critical of the destruction of the "old" city and the wholesale adoption
of European styles and fashions, extending even to the importation of marble
statues from Italy and sparrows from Paris. They were especially suspicious
of the program of compulsory vaccination. But visiting foreigners were greatly
impressed. "No nation can show a more conspicuous example of modern energy and enterprise than is seen in the new federal capital of Brazil," stated
an American visitor. "The marvellous changes in Rio" earned the praise of a
British journalist, and he added that the capital "is most beautiful and now
one of the cleanest cities in the world."[64]

The rebuilding of the capital according to European specifications was
matched by Rio Branco's similar reorganization of his country's foreign policy
establishment. The baron's exuberant personality invigorated the Brazilian
foreign service and provided a sharp contrast to the stifling influence exercized
for so long by Cabo Frio.[65] Administrative reforms resulted in a steady increase
in the number of diplomatic posts at home and overseas. The financial cost
was high, but Brazil was soon able to claim that it maintained diplomatic relations with the leading nations in all the continents of the world. The baron
also insisted that the buildings of the Itamaraty palace be extended and mod-
ernized so that foreign representatives would be received in a manner and style
worthy of an important nation.[66] The new look was particularly evident in
the appearance and deportment of the young men who were recruited to the
foreign service. Social background was still regarded as more important than
diplomatic experience. Wherever possible, Rio Branco selected men of culture
and "Aryan" civilization and insisted that Brazilian diplomats sent to Europe
should be "tall, well groomed, and personally attractive," and that their wives
should be, "if not always beautiful . . . white or near-white in appearance."[67]

Rio Branco's sensitivity to European opinion reflected the sense of racial and cultural inferiority that was typical of the Brazilian ruling class. The desire for the praise and approbation of the Old World was also mixed with fear of European imperialism. Large areas of Africa and Asia had recently been subjected to colonial status. Moreover, the inability of certain Latin American governments to pay their debts to European bondholders threatened a similar fate for Latin America. The danger became only too apparent in 1902–1903, when Britain, Italy, and Germany resorted to "gunboat diplomacy" in an attempt to coerce Venezuela. As a result of its scrupulous enforcement of the terms of the 1898 funding loan, Brazil was on excellent terms with its foreign creditors, but the recrudescence of the awkward boundary dispute with France over Guyana and rumors of German designs on southern Brazil nourished intense Brazilian suspicions of European plots. The German threat was a particular cause of concern, as it was linked to perennial doubts over the loyalty to the republic of the large German community in the south. In contrast to other immigrant groups, the Germans resisted assimilation and had made determined efforts to retain their own native language and attachment to the mother country. An attempt at secession could never be entirely ruled out.[68]

In Rio Branco's opinion, internal divisions prevented the Latin American nations from effectively uniting against the European danger. The obvious counterpoise was provided historically by the United States, who had checked European territorial ambitions in the Western Hemisphere by the Monroe Doctrine. "The great service given to the hemisphere by the Monroe Doctrine," wrote Rio Branco in 1905," is the liberty guaranteed to each nation to develop freely."[69] In contrast to most of his Spanish-American colleagues, Rio Branco regarded the United States as a benevolent guardian, and he even gave tacit approval to the Roosevelt Corollary that justified U.S. intervention to punish Latin American wrong-doing. Far from being a danger, the rising military power of the United States was a force for peace because it promoted stability and served as a restraint upon European aggression. Rio Branco argued logically that Latin America should look to Washington for protection against external interference.

Such views obviously reflected an element of Brazilian self-interest. The Misiones arbitration had demonstrated how American goodwill could assist the resolution of Brazil's boundaries. Commercial ties between Brazil and the United States were already substantial. Their further extension would increase Brazil's wealth and reduce financial dependence upon Europe. Relations with the great powers of the Old World would continue to be important and vital, but the friendship and support of the United States was now considered crucial to the achievement of Brazil's own national interests. Rio Branco reasoned that American assistance would be assured if Brazil aligned its own foreign policy as closely as possible to that pursued by the United States. As foreign minister, he was naturally seen as the instigator and architect of this policy, but it also attracted other distinguished advocates including Joaquim Nabuco and José Carlos Rodrigues, the editor of the influential *Jornal do commercio*.[70] Nor was the concept completely original. Similar ideas had been proposed during the 1890s by Quintino Bocaiúva and Salvador de Mendonça. The latter commented sarcastically that Rio Branco "always had the fate of breaking down open doors." But the baron's talk of shifting the "axis" of Brazil's foreign relations from Europe to the United States sounded different and justified the new description of his policy as the strategy of rapprochement, or approximation.[71]

The first tangible evidence that Washington had become diplomatically more important than London, Paris, or Berlin was the upgrading of relations between Brazil and the United States to ambassadorial rank in 1905. The alteration marked a significant success for Rio Branco's pursuit of enhanced diplomatic status for his country, but it was also more than merely a cosmetic change of title. During the Acre dispute Assis Brasil pointed out that Mexico was the only Latin American nation to enjoy embassy rank in Washington. The Mexican ambassador was therefore the sole Latin American representative to possess a standing equal to that of the European powers. This was a matter of some importance because ambassadors had the privilege to request direct access to the president whereas ministers had to confine their official dealings to the State Department. Assis judged that this had been detrimental to Brazilian interests because President Roosevelt was more sympathetic to Brazil over the Acre question than was Secretary of State Hay.[72]

For centuries the rank of ambassador had been the prerogative of the great European powers, and historical convention dictated that only they could confer the prestigious title upon the representatives of other nations. But the grip of tradition was significantly relaxed in 1893 when the United States abandoned its centurylong aversion to Old World protocol and exchanged ambassadors with Britain, France, Germany, and Italy. Ambassadorial rank was subsequently granted by the United States to Mexico in 1897, Austria-Hungary in 1902, and was under consideration with Japan. The time was therefore opportune for a Brazilian initiative to achieve the much-coveted status.

The change itself came about rather casually in December 1904, after Rio Branco adopted the advice of Assis Brasil and proposed that his replacement at Washington should assume the rank of ambassador and not that of minister. The American government quickly acquiesced and agreed to reciprocate in January 1905 by upgrading its own minister at Rio to ambassadorial rank. The decision attracted little discussion and was communicated by the State Department in a manner reminiscent of the treatment of Robert Adams over recognition in 1890. Thompson was aware of his impending promotion, but actually received news of its confirmation first from Rio Branco rather than from his own superiors in Washington. Although somewhat perplexed by the perfunctory behavior of the State Department, Rio Branco expressed his "great satisfaction" at the honor shown to his country.[73]

"As matters stood," Rio Branco informed the British minister, "any little South American Republic, which had a difference with Brazil, at once commenced to intrigue at Washington with a view to intervention in their favor."[74] Brazil had, however, now acquired a distinct diplomatic advantage over its rivals because the raising of rank gave its representative at Washington seniority over other South American ministers. This practical benefit was soon superseded by broader considerations. In Thompson's opinion, the request for the elevation of rank reflected Brazil's wish for "a closer relationship."[75] But this was not to imply a subordinate or inferior role for Brazil. At the formal exchange of ceremonies in March 1905, the *Jornal do commercio* exulted in the achievement of "diplomatic approximation."[76] Indeed, the special status accorded by the United States stimulated Brazilian ambitions to become the leader of South America. The two giants would form a partnership within the Western Hemisphere. "It is just," commented *O Paiz,* "that the United States should receive us from now on as equals in the guarding of the destinies of the American continent."[77]

The significance attached to Washington in Brazilian diplomacy was underlined by the choice of the celebrated orator and diplomat, Joaquim Nabuco, as Brazil's first ambassador to the United States. Nabuco initially disapproved of the elevation of rank, believing that "Brazil would gain nothing and would probably lose by it." He was persuaded, however, to accept the appointment when Rio Branco described Washington as "our most important post."[78] Nabuco's acquiescence was significant because his personal distinction helped to overcome the traditional reluctance of Congress to vote extra diplomatic appropriations. "An unjustifiable luxury" was how the *Jornal do Brasil* summed up the proposal. Indeed, Thompson observed that the wily Rio Branco was even seeking to quiet discontent "of which there is here not a little" by suggesting the idea had originated in the United States and that Brazil was merely following the American lead.[79]

Whereas the attempt to introduce a preferential tariff had aroused widespread political controversy, the question of embassy rank proved to be far less contentious. Rio Branco explained that it was a purely diplomatic matter and used his personal authority to stifle criticism. The complaint about unjustified expense was really partisan sniping designed to cause political embarrassment to the government. The embassy at Washington would inevitably mean increased expenditure, but its total complement of two diplomatic staff was unchanged and compared very favorably with the seven diplomats assigned to the Brazilian legation in Rome. While Congress claimed to be economy-minded, it also approved appropriations to send new ministers to Colombia and Ecuador in 1904 and additional representatives to seven Central American capitals in 1906. Indeed, the elevation of diplomatic status was generally welcomed as adding to Brazil's hemispheric and international prestige and soon came to be seen as an indispensable part of the Itamaraty's aim to pursue a more active role. The success of a similar initiative by Rio Branco in securing the pope's creation of Archbishop Joaquim Arcoverde of Rio as Latin America's first cardinal in December 1905 was also greeted with immense satisfaction by Brazilians and even overshadowed the upgrading of diplomatic relations with Washington.

Although he was always alert to opportunities to promote Brazil's image in Europe, Rio Branco argued that his country's diplomatic axis had shifted from the Old World to the rising power of the United States. An important adjunct to this was the constructive response of American officials, who were simultaneously reappraising their own attitudes and policies toward Latin America. The result was essentially a reaffirmation of the Pan-Americanism of the 1890s. What was novel was the deliberate emphasis on promoting an improved image of the United States throughout the hemisphere. By inclination and perceived strategic necessity the Roosevelt administration had developed an assertive and interventionist policy that had aroused considerable distrust and fear in Latin America. The administration wished to counteract these feelings and reassure Latin Americans that the United States harbored no selfish or aggressive designs and desired only peace and prosperity for all.

Despite his reputation for public bluster, President Theodore Roosevelt genuinely wished for friendly relations. As part of his instructions to the American delegates at the second Pan-American conference held at Mexico City in 1901, he stressed that they must avoid giving offense to the other delegations and, wherever possible, emphasize the desire of the United States to be "the friends of all the Latin-Americans republics."[80] But prejudices were also deeply ingrained. In private conversations, John Hay referred contemptuously to the "dagoes." A marked change, however, was brought about by the new secretary of state, Elihu Root, who assumed office in July 1905. Stressing the importance of personal relations and good manners, he urged officials at the State Department to show Latin American diplomats much more attention and consideration than they had experienced in the past.[81] He wrote in December 1905: "The South Americans now hate us, largely because they think we despise them and try to bully them. I really like them and intend to show it. I think their friendship is really important to the United States, and the best way to secure it is by treating them like gentlemen. If you want to make a man your friend, it does not pay to treat him like a yellow dog."[82]

Root's reference to "South Americans" was deliberate and reflected contemporary progressive ideas, which distinguished between different nations and placed them in an ascending order of merit. On this scale, Brazil appeared stable and prosperous, in sharp contrast to the less-developed republics of the

Caribbean area. After delivering a speech critical of the behavior of Latin American countries, Assistant Under Secretary of State Francis Loomis hastened to reassure the Brazilian chargé that none of his remarks were directed at Brazil. In his dispatches from Rio, Thompson expressed a similar sentiment when he complimented Brazilians as "the most peaceful, conservative and law-abiding people in South America."[83]

The timing of the "Root Doctrine" was fortunate in that it coincided almost exactly with Rio Branco's formulation of the policy of approximation. Moreover, Root's initiative in desiring to improve personal relations was fully reciprocated by Joaquim Nabuco. From his arrival in Washington in early 1905 the new ambassador worked assiduously to cultivate and charm American officials. He regarded Root as especially sympathetic and described the secretary of state as "a unique type in his interest in Latin America."[84] A press headline reported in November 1905 that the two men had "struck up a particularly warm friendship" and that "Washington pinched itself one night when it saw this diplomat as the guest of the secretary of state at the theater."[85] The honor shown Nabuco attracted notice because it was unusual. It was a personal tribute to the Brazilian statesman and also indicated the special American regard for the largest of the Latin American republics.

That something important was in the offing became apparent during the fall of 1905. Nabuco telegraphed Rio Branco the substance of a private conversation in which Root suggested an arrangement by which the United States, with the assistance of Mexico and Brazil, would take responsibility for affirming the Monroe Doctrine throughout the hemisphere. A few weeks later Nabuco added that President Roosevelt wished to see Brazil rather than Argentina or Chile exercise the preponderant influence in South America.[86] These unofficial soundings coincided with the choice of Rio instead of Caracas or Buenos Aires as the site for the 1906 Pan-American conference and the announcement in December 1905 that Root would personally head the American delegation. This would be the first time that a serving secretary of state had left the United States, and the American chargé at Rio remarked that the unprecedented decision emphasized "the predominance of Brazil among the nations of South America" and presented that country "a trump in the diplomatic sphere."[87]

The secretary of state's singular regard for Brazil was apparent in his private letter thanking the Brazilian ambassador for the invitation to attend the conference:

> The dignity and self-restraint with which the people of Brazil have conducted their political affairs, both under the Empire and during the trying times which accompanied the infancy of the Republic, have caused me to admire your people and to feel a strong desire to visit your beautiful capital and your wonderful coun-

try. Much more weighty, however, than any personal inclination is the convic-
tion which I feel that in those qualities of the Brazilian nation there is a poten-
tiality of influence for great good to all America and that the exercise of such
an influence ought to be encouraged in every way.[88]

The new significance accorded Brazil was also demonstrated by the appointment of Lloyd Griscom as ambassador to Rio in January 1906. Griscom
was not the typical party loyalist who was dispatched to be forgotten in some
remote overseas post. By contrast, he was a well-educated young man from
a wealthy eastern establishment background. His personal connections had
secured him entry to the foreign service and he had typically begun his diplomatic career with a post at London. Roosevelt now judged that Root's visit
to Brazil required the presence of an ambassador with Griscom's social prestige
and talents. Indeed, the president saw Griscom personally and explained that
his task in Brazil was to prepare for the visit and ensure its success.[89]

Immediately prior to Root's departure for Rio, the Washington *Evening
Star* predicted that the Roosevelt administration intended "to arrange an
informal – but none the less strong – alliance with Brazil, and to relegate to her
the policy of the Monroe doctrine in South America."[90] Nabuco was excited
by what he believed was a "unique opportunity" for the secretary of state and
his Brazilian counterpart to meet and perhaps establish an "entente" that one
day might become an "alliance."[91]

The ambassador's enthusiasm, however, was tempered by the surprising
and inexplicable delay of Rio Branco in replying to the dispatch reporting Root's
intended visit. Nabuco became apprehensive. Only a few weeks previously in
December, Rio Branco had pointedly instructed him to emphasize Brazil's independence of action in the *Panther* incident. The notorious German gunboat
had landed in southern Brazil to arrest a man alleged to be a German citizen.
Rio Branco protested this flagrant violation of Brazilian territory and secured
a prompt and full apology from Berlin. Alerted by Nabuco, Root privately
instructed the American embassy in Germany to assist Brazil. But Rio Branco
seemed displeased. He was concerned that Brazil suffer no derogation of its
sovereignty by appearing subordinate to the United States. He thanked Root
for his sympathetic consideration, but deliberately stressed that Brazil had settled
the incident independently without requesting American intervention.[92]

Nabuco even began to fear that a cold reception awaited Root in Brazil.
But this apprehension was soon dispelled as it became apparent that Root's
initiative fitted very well into Rio Branco's own diplomatic schemes. The new
American ambassador, Lloyd Griscom, was made to feel welcome on his arrival at Rio in June. "Everything connected with the Conference interests the
public," he reported.[93] The introduction only a few weeks later of a 20 percent tariff preference on American goods provided further convincing evidence

of Brazil's goodwill, especially as it was a concession taken on the initiative of the Brazilian executive and without significant pressure from the American embassy.

Rio Branco's ambivalent attitude toward the Pan-American conference was partly explained by his jealousy of Nabuco's personal success in Washington. This caused him particular concern because it was an open secret that President-elect Afonso Pena of Minas Gerais was eager to appoint his old personal friend, Joaquim Nabuco, as foreign minister.[94] Self-doubt also seemed to afflict the baron. He eagerly welcomed international meetings and was pleased with the success of the Third Latin American Scientific Congress, held at Rio in October 1905. The Pan-American conference was, however, a much-larger undertaking to organize, and its success was by no means certain. Although Root's presence would lend considerable prestige to the meeting, it would also highlight the policy of approximation between Brazil and the United States. Rio Branco suddenly became fearful that the very success of his strategy might be counterproductive for hemispheric relations. To avoid potential jealousies and rivalries the foreign minister suggested that after leaving Rio, Root should go on to Montevideo, Buenos Aires, and Santiago.[95]

The secretary of state had in fact already enlarged his itinerary. Not a keen traveler he had originally thought in terms of a limited journey with the sole object of attending the Pan-American conference. On reflection, however, he devised a virtual grand tour to please Latin American opinion in general. As the *New York Evening Post* noted, the trip "will go far toward convincing our southern neighbors that his motives are disinterested and his efforts to bring about a closer working agreement are absolutely sincere."[96]

Accompanied by his wife and daughter, Root left New York on July 4, 1906. His first stop was Pará, which he described as "this august city of the great empire which reaches from the Amazon to the Uruguay." At Recife he paid personal tribute to one of its favorite sons, Joaquim Nabuco. The next port of call was Bahia where Root's arrival dressed in a light sack suit and straw hat amazed his formally attired reception party of Brazilian dignitaries, but established the impression he sought of informality and friendliness. At the banquet held in his honor he praised "the charm and grace of living in Bahia." After alluding to popular views that Americans "work too hard" or were "too strenuous" in their lives, Root's sympathetic attitude shone through when he remarked: "We may give to you some added strength and strenuousness; you may give to us some of the beauty of life."[97]

The atmosphere awaiting the secretary of state in Rio was one of growing excitement and euphoria. "The people," observed Griscom, "are in a highly elated state."[98] Rio Branco's earlier doubts had been completely swept aside. The foreign minister was extremely flattered by Root's decision to stay longer in Brazil than in any other country on his itinerary. The conference was also attracting interest in Europe as an event of international significance, and Brazil basked in the unaccustomed and gratifying attention.[99] No expense was to be spared to make the visit a memorable success and to show off the "new" Rio to the world.

On July 27, Root and his family received a magnificent welcome as they entered Guanabara Bay. To take them ashore was the same state barge that had similarly transported Dom João of Portugal in 1808. According to Griscom, the following eight days "were a constant succession of luncheons and dinners, each of which entailed a speech." Carioca hospitality was exceedingly lavish and ornate; the furnishings at one banquet were reported to have been specially imported from Paris at a cost of $100,000. The conference itself took place in the newly constructed Senate building, which overlooked the bay and was brilliantly illuminated at night. As an honor to the United States and to his distinguished guest, Rio Branco declared that the building would become known as the "Monroe palace."[100]

Nineteen nations attended the conference. Nabuco was elected the permanent conference president and set the tone when he told delegates that their aim was "to promote harmony."[101] In contrast to the previous meetings at Washington and Mexico City less attention had been paid to preparing the agenda. The number of open sessions was deliberately limited and there was a conscious effort to avoid public disagreement. Several committees were appointed and reports were prepared on a variety of subjects ranging from arbitration to transportation. Pan-American goodwill exuded, but little substantive was achieved.[102]

As one American delegate noted, it was never the intention "to inaugurate sweeping policies or to attempt radical changes."[103] What brought the delegates to Rio was the visit of an American secretary of state. It was a historic occasion and so great was the desire to please the United States, that its delegates were initially given the chairmanship of all the committees. The gala event was the session on July 31 to honor the distinguished visitor from the United States. Root had previously delivered all his speeches extemporaneously, but this one was carefully prepared. It was designed to explain American policy toward South America and fix "a standard which the United States is bound to live up to."[104] He alluded to the idea of a common hemispheric consciousness and stressed the necessity of harmonious cooperation. One section from his speech soon resounded throughout Latin America: "We wish for no victories except those of peace. We wish for no territory except our own and no sovereignty except over ourselves. We neither claim nor desire any rights or privileges of power that we do not freely concede to every American republic."[105]

The high point of approximation was reached when Root left Brazil in August with the parting words that the two countries "acting together, would form a single and eternal guarantee for the integrity of America."[106] Elated by this apparent selection of Brazil as the preferred partner of the United States, Rio Branco was able to indulge his dreams of Brazilian leadership of the southern continent. The conference was now judged to have been an enormous triumph for Brazil. Rio Branco's strategy of approximation was fully vindicated and his continued tenure as foreign minister seemed assured, especially as Nabuco discouraged all suggestions of his own succession.[107]

The conference was also a personal success for Nabuco, but he was disappointed that the alliance, which he had so much hoped for, did not materialize. Certainly, the conference allowed Rio Branco and Root to become acquainted and to learn more about each other's policies. Root came away impressed and described the baron as "an exceedingly astute and capable man."[108] Except for various ambiguous public remarks, there appears, however, to be no evidence that an alliance was ever discussed. Root's decision to go on to the other capitals of South America pleased Rio Branco, but also indicated that the visit had taken on a broader perspective in which Brazil became merely one part of the itinerary.[109] Indeed, the British minister at Rio reported that "a far more magnificent reception" awaited Root in Buenos Aires where he could not conceal his admiration for Argentine wealth and progress.[110] Ironically, the encouragement given by Root to Brazilian diplomatic ambitions contained the seeds of future difficulty between Brazil and the United States and, as Rio Branco had anticipated, contributed to increased tension within South America itself.

THE HAGUE CONFERENCE

At the beginning of the twentieth century the movement for world peace attracted growing support from American progressives and political leaders. A peace conference had been held at The Hague in 1899, and the proposal to organize a second international meeting received emphatic endorsement from Roosevelt during his campaign for the presidency in 1904. The president's own peace efforts gained worldwide prominence during the following year when he mediated the Russo-Japanese War. The momentum was sustained by the announcement that a second international peace congress would convene at The Hague in 1906.

As part of his increasingly active interest in world affairs, Roosevelt regarded the conference at The Hague as a major event and wished that the Latin American nations be fully represented. The proposed timing was awkward because it would come so closely after the Pan-American conference scheduled for Rio. The likely agendas for both meetings were also very similar. The desire to provide a peaceful means to resolve disputes was an integral element of Pan-

Americanism and would be discussed at Rio. Consequently, the Latin American governments might justifiably argue that there was no reason to incur the expense of sending delegations to a European conference. Roosevelt asked therefore that the meeting at The Hague be delayed to allow time to persuade the Latin American nations to attend. In deference to American wishes, the European powers agreed to a postponement until 1907.[111]

The original purpose of the Pan-American initiative of the Roosevelt administration was to improve inter-American relations. Broader diplomatic considerations now interposed themselves as Root's journey to South America acquired the additional aim of persuading those countries to participate actively in the forthcoming peace conference. Unfortunately, it produced the one jarring note in what was an excellent public relations exercise conducted by the secretary of state. Several of the Latin American delegations were eager to discuss a common hemispheric stand on the issues of arbitration and the forcible collection of public debts. To their dismay, it became clear that their American colleagues regarded the sessions at Rio as merely providing a preliminary for further debate at The Hague. Root's speech at the Monroe palace emphasized the role of the whole hemisphere in the task of securing world peace: "Within a few months, for the first time, the recognized possessors of every foot of soil upon the American continents can be and I hope will be represented with the acknowledged rights of equal sovereign states in the great World Congress at The Hague."[112] Despite the open American pressure and calculation, the Latin American governments were attracted by the chance to have a voice in world affairs. Root's appeal did not therefore go unheeded. With the exception of Costa Rica and Honduras, all the Latin American countries agreed to attend the peace conference.

In 1899 the Campos Sales administration had demonstrated Brazil's lack of active interest in international affairs by declining to attend the first Hague Peace conference. By contrast, only a few years later the invitation to the second Peace conference was quickly accepted. Rio Branco eagerly grasped the opportunity for Brazil to make its debut on the international stage and appear as one of the powers contributing to the cause of world peace. A prominent role was envisaged; this prominence was underlined by the appointment of one of the largest delegations comprising twelve officials. At its head was the distinguished jurist and orator, Rui Barbosa.[113]

The question of status was vital and assumed added significance after Rio Branco's old rival, Estanislau Zeballos, became Argentine foreign minister in December 1906. Prior to the conference Rio Branco sought to utilize American goodwill by securing for Brazil some of the conference honors, most notably an honorary presidency. When it was learned in May 1907 that Argentina had made a similar request to the British foreign office, Nabuco journeyed to Root's home in Clinton, New York. He argued that Brazil's greater size and population gave it precedence over the other Latin American nations. Nabuco was confident that "the sincere friendship that binds Brazil and the United States" would result in Root's doing "his best." It was therefore especially pleasing when Rui was the only Latin American to be granted an honorary presidency; the Argentine delegate had to be satisfied with a vice-presidency.[114]

Nabuco reported from Washington that the American delegates would be under instructions to work closely with their Latin American colleagues at The Hague. The spirit of approximation was given a further boost when Root openly discussed with Nabuco the policy that the United States would pursue.[115] Root's desire for inter-American cooperation at The Hague was genuine, but his control over policy was significantly undermined from the beginning by the intervention of President Roosevelt. Unfortunately for the secretary of state, Latin American considerations were far from the president's thoughts. He took a personal interest in the conference and it was his wish that the former ambassador to Britain, Joseph Choate, lead the United States delegation. Since recalling Choate from London in 1905 Roosevelt had tried to persuade him to return to the diplomatic service. But the independently minded Choate turned down the chance to be the first American ambassador to Japan and also to head the delegation at the Algeciras conference in Morocco. Roosevelt was "delighted" when the eminent New England lawyer accepted appointment to The Hague.[116]

The second nomination was General Horace Porter, who had only recently been ambassador to Paris. The additional delegates were also men whose experience and sympathies lay predominantly in dealing with the statesmen and affairs of the Old World. When the names were announced, Root privately expressed concern at their lack of familiarity with Latin American affairs. To remedy this he secured the inclusion of William Buchanan, a former minister of Argentina who had performed a similar liaison function at the previous conferences in Mexico City and Rio. The latter's expertise proved useful, but in rank and influence he was decidedly inferior to the other American delegates. Root's misgivings were fully realized at The Hague as Choate deliberately avoided contact with the Latin Americans and adopted an independent and abrasive style that clearly departed from Root's original guideline.

When the conference opened in June 1907 the first contentious issue concerned the forcible collection of public debts. During the late nineteenth century increasing amounts of foreign investment were placed in Latin America. The servicing of these debts became so onerous that some governments were fearful of armed European intervention to enforce payment. The attempt at gunboat diplomacy by Britain, Germany, and Italy against Venezuela in 1902 provided a salutary warning and prompted the Argentine foreign minister, Luís M. Drago, to state that public debts should not be used as justification for the use of force in Latin America by European powers. While the Roosevelt administration never recognized the "Drago Doctrine," it was concerned that armed intervention by Europe would not only create instability in the hemisphere but also pose a threat to the Monroe Doctrine.

Root discouraged discussion of the Drago Doctrine at the Rio conference by stating that his government preferred to raise the issue at The Hague. The proposal put forward at the peace conference by General Porter stipulated, however, that force should only be renounced if arbitration was refused. By implicitly recognizing the right to use force, it fell a long way short of the Drago Doctrine. The Latin American delegates were unhappy, but Brazil notably endorsed the "Porter Resolution." Rio Branco instructed Rui to stress that Brazil historically welcomed foreign investment and conscientiously paid its debts.[117] The foreign minister's own sympathies lay with the Roosevelt Corollary rather than the Drago Doctrine: if countries misbehaved, he believed that they should suffer punishment. Nor should Latin America be exempt. Indeed, Rio Branco was particularly critical of the governments of Central America. "If those countries do not know how to govern themselves," he told an Argentine journalist in July 1906, "they do not have a right to exist."[118]

Brazil's support for the Porter Resolution was useful but hardly essential. The American delegation paid scant consideration to Latin American opinion and was much more concerned about winning the votes of the European powers. Indeed, the proposal had been deliberately expressed in "moderate" terms to win British and German acquiescence. After five anxious days of waiting the American delegation learned that Germany would give its support without reservations. Success was therefore guaranteed and the Porter Resolution was carried, with 39 votes in favor and 5 abstentions.[119] With the exception of Chile and Brazil, all the Latin American countries attached various reservations to their affirmative votes. Rui was known to be personally critical of the Porter Resolution, but his support for the proposal only confirmed the suspicions of the Latin American delegates that Brazil had made a prior agreement to give its unconditional backing to the United States.[120]

The apparent harmony proved, however, to be the lull before the storm. Disagreement between the American and Brazilian delegations soon emerged over compulsory arbitration, the creation of an international prize court and especially the nomination of judges to the proposed International Court of Justice. The debate over the latter exemplified the differences between the two countries. With its resemblance to the Supreme Court, the concept of an International Court of Justice had the enthusiastic endorsement of American progressives and was particularly favored by President Roosevelt. Choate's legal background also made him specially interested in this subject. With his assistant, James Brown Scott, he worked closely with the British and German delegates to formulate a proposal that would gain general acceptance. A particularly taxing question was the composition of the court. During secret committee discussions it was decided that it would be too unwieldly to extend membership to all nations. Choate argued instead that only the great powers should have permanent representation, while lesser nations such as Brazil should be relegated to temporary and rotating membership.

Bruised feelings were inevitable. But even before Choate's proposal was announced, growing disillusionment with the conference was already evident at the Itamaraty. Initial hopes had been high and had been buoyed by the granting of an honorary presidency to Rui. Moreover, considerable effort and expense had been directed toward publicizing Brazil's role. "Nothing," observed the American journalist William T. Stead, "came up to the Brazilian dinners for the good taste and magnificence of floral decoration, and the fascination of the combined effect of music, mirrors, lights, paintings, flowers, and foliage."[121]

While lavish hospitality brought gratifying acknowledgment of Brazil's culture and sophistication, it could not hide the lack of economic and military power. Choate's plan underlined this by consigning Brazil to the "third category" of nations, behind less-populated countries such as Turkey, Holland, and Spain. Rio Branco favored the idea of the court in principle, but was annoyed at being presented with what amounted to a fait accompli by the great powers on how the court should be organized. Brazil faced humiliation and Rio Branco resolved to save diplomatic face by a direct appeal to Root.

Unfortunately, Nabuco's personal influence was unavailable since the ambassador was ill and on leave in Europe. Instead, the chargé at Washington, Silvino Gurgel do Amaral, was instructed to propose that the size of the court be considerably enlarged. In this way, Brazil could have a permanent seat. Root showed some sympathy and agreed to communicate the proposal to The Hague. Choate, however, rudely dismissed the plan as "an impossibility." More tactfully but no less firmly, Root later explained to Rio Branco that "we must yield something to European views" in order to achieve "a practical result for the good of mankind."[122] In hemispheric terms, Brazil's status was substantial, but this was not transferred to world affairs.

Rio Branco allowed this setback to his quiet diplomacy in Washington to surface publicly at The Hague so that Choate met a much stiffer challenge from Rui Barbosa.[123] During the conference the Brazilian delegate gradually emerged as the spokesman and champion not only of his own country but of Latin America too. Rui's initial instructions were to work closely with the American delegation, but a divergence of national viewpoint was soon apparent. As the United States and the European powers sought to dominate the proceedings in their own interest, Rui took special satisfaction in reminding the American delegates of Root's recent remarks at Rio about the equality of all nations whether large or small. In a celebrated speech delivered in fluent French, Rui asserted the principle of equal representation and argued that each country possessed its own "great fortress" of sovereignty: "In this fortress of an equal right for all, and equally inviolable, inalienable, incontrovertible, each State, large or small, felt that it was so truly its own master and even as safe with regard to the rest, as the free citizen feels safe within the walls of his own house."[124]

Rui's oratorical brilliance made him the sensation of the conference. His determined if obstinate defense of the rights of small nations irritated Choate and many European diplomats, but pleased his Latin American colleagues. When Choate personally rebuked Rui for condemning any proposal but his own, it seemed a severe blow to the strategy of approximation. However, the British minister at Rio reported Brazilian delight that Rui was bringing their country into the forefront of world affairs. "There is no doubt," he believed, "that Dr. Barbosa will receive a most extravagant welcome on his return to this country, and be hailed as the vindicator of Brazil's national rights amongst the Powers."[125]

Rui was proclaimed "the eagle of The Hague" and regaled with a hero's welcome when he arrived in Rio at the close of 1907. Two weeks later a lavish though more subdued reception attended the visit to Guanabara bay of the American fleet en route to the Pacific Ocean. Despite the effusive speeches proclaiming the closeness of United States–Brazilian relations, a jarring note was introduced by Rui's refusal to attend the banquet held in honor of the American naval officers. In October 1907 the British minister stated that the discord at The Hague had "effaced" the effects of Root's visit. The acclaim shown to Rui only highlighted the pervasive strength of Brazilian nationalism and revealed the latent suspicions of the United States. "In reference to The Hague," Nabuco concluded regretfully, "it would have been better if there had not been a conference."[126]

BRAZILIAN RIVALRY WITH ARGENTINA

At The Hague, the Latin American delegates initially accused Brazil of colluding with the United States. Later, they cheered Rui when he clashed with Choate and emerged as the spokesman of Latin America. But suspicion and mistrust of Brazilian motives persisted. Despite repeated expressions of desire for friendly relations with all Spanish-American countries, Brazilian national pride and sense of apartness created tension. Rio Branco might be renowned for his consummate diplomatic skill, but Spanish-Americans also suspected that his real purpose was the extension of Brazil's power and influence at their expense. The American ambassador at Rio, David Thompson, considered that Rio Branco had "no little ill-feeling" for the other countries of South America with the possible exception of Chile. On one occasion he reported the private remarks of the foreign minister that "no Spanish speaking country is good, and no person of Spanish blood can be believed."[127]

What Brazilians most resented was the attitude of superiority adopted by Argentina. At the beginning of the twentieth century both countries vied with each other in a battle of statistics. Whenever comparisons were made, Brazil was proud to point out that it was almost three times the size of Argentina in both area and population. The press of Buenos Aires focused, however, on the greater per capita wealth of Argentina. Especially provocative were references to Brazil's racially mixed population and how this was responsible for Brazilian economic and cultural backwardness. Such insults stung Rio Branco's pride and he openly criticized his southern neighbor in conversation with the American minister: "Yes, in all the world she thinks she has no peer except in numbers, not even excepting your own great country; in South America she wishes to pose as dictator."[128]

Underneath the emotional rhetoric lay significant historical, strategic and economic differences. During the 1890s Brazil's internal disorders muted the traditional rivalry between the two South American giants, but the reemergence of a stable and prosperous Brazil disturbed the balance of power in the River Plate. Argentina was alarmed by the increase of Brazil's boundaries in the Acre region and by the extension of Brazilian influence into Uruguay and Paraguay.[129] Another cause of anxiety was the decision of the Rodrigues Alves administration to rebuild the Brazilian navy with powerful warships from Britain. Argentine sensitivity was further heightened by the policy of approximation between Brazil and the United States and particularly its impact in the form of the unilateral granting of tariff concessions on American goods. The preferential duty on flour aroused considerable bitterness because Brazil was Argentina's main market for that product. In the background, there was also the additional grievance that the generous American tariff treatment given to Brazilian exports was not similarly extended to Argentine products.[130]

The choice of Rio rather than Buenos Aires for the Pan-American conference gave Brazilians a signal opportunity to overshadow the Argentines. Despite Rio Branco's tactful efforts to allay mistrust and the inclusion of Buenos Aires on Root's itinerary, the pomp and circumstance accorded to the secretary of state in Brazil inevitably exacerbated Argentine jealousy. Relations were further strained in December 1906 by the return of Estanislau Zeballos to head the Argentine foreign office. The open personal enmity between Zeballos and Rio Branco originated during the Misiones arbitration and embittered relations to such a degree that war scares became frequent. A year after Root's historic visit, the American minister at Buenos Aires concluded that Argentine-Brazilian relations were "far from satisfactory" and that this unfortunate state of affairs was mainly due to Argentine suspicion of approximation.[131]

The ill-feeling aroused by approximation was absorbed into what briefly became an arms race between the two neighbors. During the 1890s Brazil's military weakness was painfully exposed by Benham's action and the humiliating Canudos expeditions. Writing from the vantage point of England, Rui Barbosa drew an alarming analogy with Turkey in which he described Brazil as "the sick man of South America" whose weakness inspired the greed of external aggressors and contributed to hemispheric instability.[132] Conscious of its huge territory, vast coastline, and inadequate defenses, Brazil felt increasingly insecure as international crises proliferated at the beginning of the twentieth century. In 1904 the Rodrigues Alves administration commenced a program of increased military spending designed to reorganize and modernize the army and navy. Recruitment and training were radically reformed. Equipment was improved and ambitious plans were unveiled for a huge military arsenal to be constructed in Rio. Particular emphasis was also put on replacing antiquated naval ships with purchases of the most modern warships from Britain.[133]

The military buildup was fully endorsed by Rio Branco; it complemented his plan to promote Brazil's international stature. But it also upset the existing South American balance of power in which Argentina enjoyed naval superiority over both Chile and Brazil. The Argentine press denounced Brazil's "warlike preparations."[134] The argument that powerful dreadnoughts were required for the purpose of protecting Brazil's long and vulnerable coastline provoked disbelief not only in Buenos Aires but also in Santiago. When Argentina threatened to retaliate against Brazil's plans for naval rearmament, the value of American support became highly significant. Rio Branco instructed Nabuco to inform Root of Argentina's bellicose attitude. The Brazilian ambassador reported reassuringly in January 1907 that Root had shown "visible sympathy" and had described the Argentines as "crazy" to think of going to war. Moreover, the secretary of state considered that Brazil had every right to build up its navy for defensive purposes without having to consult Argentina.[135]

Root was genuinely friendly toward Brazil, but he had no intention of interfering in the quarrel between the two neighbors. In fact, he had already received a different perspective of the arms race from Griscom, who regarded the alleged struggle for continental hegemony between Brazil and Argentina as "theoretical." Adopting a somewhat simplistic and haughty tone, the ambassador considered that both nations were fundamentally "bound by ties of race, customs, and practical identity of language." In his opinion, the possession of large navies could only be dangerous for "people so peculiarly sensitive as Latin-Americans."[136]

Rio Branco was not slow to realize that Washington's support against Argentina was uncertain. As early as January 1907 the British minister at Rio noted that there was already some disenchantment with the lack of tangible results from Root's visit and that a possible commercial treaty with Argentina was under discussion.[137] In March the former Argentine president, Julio Roca, was received in Rio on an "elaborate scale." Although he doubted that a commercial agreement would be forthcoming, the American chargé at Rio considered that Brazil "sincerely hopes for closer political relations with Argentina."[138] Furthermore, the festivities marking Roca's visit contrasted strikingly with the quiet reception given only a few days later to the new American ambassador. "The arrival of Mr. Dudley, commented the British minister, "has not been greeted with the same enthusiasm which attended Mr. Griscom's reception here, and this is regarded in many quarters as a sign that the wave of Pan-American feeling is receding a little."[139]

While Rio Branco sincerely wished to be on friendly terms with Argentina, he also desired to assert Brazil's leadership in South America. The inherent contradiction in these aims was temporarily masked by the baron's astute and tactful diplomacy. However, the naval arms race openly flaunted Brazil's aspirations and provoked Argentine retaliation. When the Argentine Congress voted large naval appropriations in 1908, relations took a decided turn for the worse. The personal antipathy between Rio Branco and Zeballos was publicly displayed as both foreign ministers accused each other of seeking war. "So long as they remain at the head of their respective foreign offices," lamented Dudley, "it may well be presumed that the establishment of better relations between the two countries will be impossible." A few weeks later the American ambassador faithfully reported the Itamaraty's wildest fear that Argentina aimed to restore the old colonial boundaries. He solemnly warned: "This would involve and means the annexation of Uruguay, Paraguay, and a portion of Bolivia."[140]

The American embassy at Rio was only one of the channels by which Rio Branco sought to keep Washington fully informed of his anxiety over Argentine intentions. Nabuco was also instructed to raise the matter frequently with Root. As the Roosevelt administration was drawing to a close, the secretary of state appeared more guarded and less sympathetic than formerly. While Root listened to Brazilian charges of Argentine aggression, he was also receiving reports from the American minister at Buenos Aires expressing local fears of an imminent attack from Brazil. These dispatches quoted the opinion of Argentine leaders that war would be "a calamity" and that "whatever desire there may be for war emanates from Brazil and not from this country." They desired a reassurance that the United States would not back Brazil in the event of war. "The Argentines have a strong impression that the U.S. shows a preferential friendship for Brazil," minuted Alvey A. Adee in October 1908. "Is there," he asked Root, "any way of convincing them that we love them just as much as the Brazilians?" The secretary of state instructed that an evenhanded attitude be displayed toward the two South American rivals.[141]

Ironically, Root's personal rapport with Nabuco gave him the confidence to exert direct diplomatic pressure upon Brazil. He told the ambassador of his anxiety over the escalating arms race in South America and suggested that Brazil could ease the tension by reducing its own naval establishment. On receiving this advice, Rio Branco confided to Nabuco that he was "very sad." In a somewhat petulant though accurate observation, the foreign minister remarked that the 1906 visit had been designed to suit Root's own selfish purposes and not especially to help Brazil. American policy began to change from the time that the secretary of state sailed from Santos to Buenos Aires where his speeches once again were full of praise for the host country, but this time that country was Argentina not Brazil.[142]

The policy of approximation upset the balance of power in South America and intensified the historic rivalry between Argentina and Brazil. While American flattery was gratifying to Brazilian pride, it conferred only slight if not false benefits. The idea of an alliance or partnership to maintain the Monroe Doctrine proved to be premature. The United States was confident of its ascendancy in the Caribbean and saw no need to become entangled in the affairs of South America. By its unwillingness to side with Brazil against Argentina, the United States government revealed the limits of approximation and thereby exposed the precariousness of Rio Branco's pretensions to South American leadership. Brazil found itself suddenly alone and facing diplomatic isolation.

In fact, the indifference and insensitivity of American attitudes led Brazil to assume the role of defending the rights of Latin America against the United States. "Brazil," considered the British minister at Rio, "has taken the place of the United States as herself the protector of the South American states."[143] The most obvious example was Rui Barbosa's clash with Choate at The Hague. In 1909 Rio Branco took the State Department to task for what he considered was its harsh treatment of Chile over the pressing of the financial grievances of an American mining company. In his opinion, the aggressive imposition of the claims raised "the most disagreeable impressions" throughout Latin America.[144] Only a few years previously, in what seemed a similar case, American officials had declined to support the Bolivian syndicate. However, Nabuco found the new secretary of state, Philander Knox, less sympathetic to his appeal that the United States desist from pressing the Chilean matter so vigorously.[145]

By contrast, the resignation of Zeballos as Argentine foreign minister in 1908 paved the way for an improvement in relations between Rio and Buenos Aires.[146] Progress was halted, however, by outbursts of public ill temper that flared when Argentines felt slighted at Brazil's failure to pay sufficient homage to their centennial celebrations of independence in 1910. News of the burning of the Brazilian flag at Rosario provoked demonstrations in Rio. Rio Branco affirmed his intention of reducing tensions between the two neighbors by personally intervening to calm the crowds. The tilt of policy toward Argentina was confirmed only a few weeks later in August 1910 when President-elect Roque Saenz Peña received an "exceptional" welcome at the Brazilian capital on his way home to Buenos Aires from Europe. Enthusiastic applause greeted the Argentine statesman whenever he concluded his speeches with the sentence: "Everything unites us; nothing separates us." Rio Branco confided in the American ambassador that "Brazil now counted with greatest satisfaction upon having a friend during the coming six years in the presidential chair at Buenos Aires."[147]

The selection of his loyal protégé, Domício da Gama, as minister to Buenos Aires gave further evidence of Rio Branco's desire for close relations with the new Argentine government. Indeed, beset by growing political and financial weakness, Brazil seemed to be falling under the diplomatic shadow of its more dynamic and prosperous neighbor. Domício remarked later that the legation in Buenos Aires was regarded as more important than the Washington embassy.[148] When political disturbances broke out in Paraguay, Rio Branco appeared keen to discuss the possibility of cooperation between Brazil and Argentina to restore order. The South American press even speculated that Rio Branco was positively seeking diplomatic allies and that Brazil would join Argentina and Chile in an "ABC" alliance allegedly designed to counter American imperialism.

State Department officials, however, took only a passing interest in these developments and were not impressed by speeches and "friendly after-dinner oratory." The countries of South America were regarded as too jealous of each other to form an alliance and Adee dismissed the prospect as "an illusion."[149] Despite the efforts of Rio Branco and Nabuco, the concept of approximation between Brazil and the United States had never taken root in Washington. The strategy simply had no equivalent in the United States. When it came to relations with Brazil, American diplomats were more concerned about extracting tariff concessions and exploiting commercial opportunities than assisting Brazilian aspirations to live up to its giant status.

DOLLAR DIPLOMACY

Another item to cause disquiet in Brazilian–United States relations was the continuation of forceful American diplomatic pressure to increase tariff concessions. Although Root displayed a more sympathetic attitude to Latin America than Hay, he was no less keen to expand American trade and made deliberate use of the State Department to achieve this. Employing his administrative experience and organizational flair, Root emphasized the need for greater efficiency and professionalism. In particular, he sought to utilize the specialist abilities available within the department. Commercial skills were improved by the passage of the Lodge bill in 1906, which led to a reform of recruitment and salary structure throughout the consular service. Although it was outside the jurisdiction of the State Department, the provision of business information was also improved in 1903 by the incorporation of the Bureau of Foreign Commerce into the Department of Commerce and Labor. In 1912 it was renamed the Bureau of Foreign and Domestic Commerce.[150]

Root singled out Latin America as a most promising area for commercial expansion and was especially impressed by Brazil, which he described as "that wonderful continent."[151] Economic motives were clearly present in his decision to attend the Pan-American conference at Rio. Indeed, Root was especially encouraged to learn during the winter of 1905 that Rio Branco would ask Congress to agree to a renewal of the preferential concessions granted to the United States during the previous year. This measure was important because it would help increase American exports and thereby correct the prevailing adverse trade balance between the two countries. The theme was mentioned in many of the speeches delivered by Root during his visit to Brazil in 1906. At Santos, he reminded his audience of the official statistics for 1905, which revealed that Americans bought goods valued at $99 million from Brazil while selling only $11 million in return. "I should like to see the trade more even," he concluded laconically.[152]

Root's diplomatic initiative created a disposition in Brazil to please the United States. It also presented the Rodrigues Alves administration with welcome ammunition in its battle against the protectionist lobby. In fact, the issue aroused little controversy and the necessary authority to renew the preference was voted by Congress in December.[153] The government underlined the political significance of the concession when it announced that the reductions on American goods would come into effect on July 1 so as to exert a maximum favorable impression on the American delegation scheduled to arrive only a few weeks later.

The preference given to American goods in 1906 was condemned by European diplomats at Rio as unfair and unjust. Protests were unavailing as the Brazilian government was determined to increase its commercial ties with the United States. The subsequent increase in American exports, however, was relatively modest and did little to upset the European domination of the Brazilian market in most products. The granting of a preferential tariff on American flour continued to attract adverse comment, but foreign and local milling made only a token protest. Imports were currently static and the American share of the market was known to be declining. A 20 percent preferential was worth 30 cents a barrel and would do little to outweigh the 75 cents it cost to ship the same barrel of flour from the United States. Indeed, the American practice of packing flour in barrels not only increased overall costs, but was also disadvantageous because the southern ports of Brazil were accustomed to dealing in sacks. Most American flour was therefore directed to northern Brazil. From 1906 to 1909 sales of flour increased only slightly and the American share of the market rose from 18 to 23 percent. The British minister concluded that the tariff advantage "only operates within a certain distance from American ports and that its total effect is very small."[154]

Even at the height of Pan-American enthusiasm in 1906, the *New York Times* noted perceptively: "When a letter may very probably take six weeks to reach New York from Rio, and when a Brazilian traveler bound for New York finds that he gains in comfort and scarcely loses in time by crossing and recrossing the Atlantic, it seems idle to expect a diversion north and south of the commerce now carried east and west."[155] In their official report the American delegation to the 1906 conference contrasted unfavorably the "meager service" offered by American shipping lines with the "constant coming and going of the splendid passenger ships" of the European companies.[156] Speaking to the Trans-Mississippi Commercial Congress at Kansas City in November 1906 Root took up the same theme when he pointed out that, of the more than three thousand foreign ships that had docked at Rio during the previous year, only seven sailed under the American flag and two of these entered in distress.[157]

The need to strengthen American shipping appeared obvious, but the issue remained entangled in partisan politics. Despite the efforts of the Roosevelt administration, Congress rejected the merchant marine bill in 1907.[158] An American consul explained that the failure to expand economic ties simply reflected the "rock of indifference" shown by American society toward Brazil.[159] Diplomacy sought to help, but could only achieve so much. "I am well aware," stressed Root, "that the course of trade cannot be controlled by sentiment or by governments." In the circumstances, Root's best advice to the American merchant was to learn what the South Americans wanted and to conform the product to those wants.[160] The American consul-general at Rio stressed that there were "bright prospects" for increasing trade "if manufacturers would push their goods." "In general," summed up a State Department official, "we cannot be said to have got much farther than the incipient stage of development as a nation manufacturing for export."[161]

The task of promoting American trade in countries like Brazil, however, was not so straightforward. The first problem was where to begin. Lloyd Griscom found the country enormous. He was mystified by its decentralized political structure and could only liken it to the Chinese empire. Of more immediate concern were the many personal irritants. "The high cost of living here," complained Griscom, "is about the same as in the Klondike." Despite the improvements in public health, the terror of yellow fever persisted so that the diplomatic corps were "huddled at Petrópolis" and nobody "would have spent a night in Rio at any price."[162] Not surprisingly, all foreign diplomats were annoyed by Rio Branco's growing habit of moving frequently and without warning between Rio and Petrópolis.[163] As the baron became notoriously elusive to contact, it seemed that he was seeking deliberately to tease and frustrate foreign diplomats. Despite almost a decade of diplomatic service in South America, Irving Dudley told his British colleague that he could not recall "the discourteous treatment which he had encountered here in the studied neglect to reply to his communications."[164]

Although Rio Branco preferred to direct his energies to such prestigious matters as his country's role at The Hague or plans for the state visit to Brazil of the king of Portugal in 1908,[165] he could not escape the unrelenting pressure from the American embassy for increased tariff concessions. The 1906 reductions had only been in effect for a short time before Griscom declared them "worthless." The price of American flour was still deemed to be uncompetitive, prompting the ambassador to resort to the old tactic of threatening a retaliatory tax on coffee in order to gain "more important tariff concessions." The British minister commented disapprovingly that Griscom was acting "in just the manner that a concession monger does."[166] Because the preference came up for renewal annually, American ministers were not only required but eager to exploit the opportunity of keeping the question very much in the forefront of their dealings with the Itamaraty. They stressed that American exports to Brazil were less than one-third the value of Brazilian sales to the United States. A stream of personal interviews, letters, and memoranda requested that this imbalance be partially rectified by increasing the preference to at least 40 percent. Although the existing 20 percent advantage was maintained, representations for change met with polite refusal. "There is," summed up Irving Dudley in 1909, "still a lack on the part of Brazil of reciprocity in her trade relations with the United States."[167]

Dudley's sense of frustration was understandable, but his interpretation ignored the fact that the preference had never been intended to give American goods such an overwhelming tariff advantage that they would flood the Brazilian market. Moreover, his criticism failed to take account of the complexities of Brazilian politics. The Afonso Pena administration, which assumed office in November 1906, was not so overtly friendly to the United States as its predecessor. Pena had deliberately avoided seeing Root during the early stages of his visit to Rio, and suspicions lingered that the Mineiro president distrusted the policy of approximation.[168] His financial policy guided by Minister of Finance David Campista sought to increase government revenue from customs duties and was therefore less inclined to favor a reduction of the tariff. On the other hand, the Afonso Pena administration was in no doubt about the crucial importance of American goodwill, especially when a bumper coffee crop was imminent. An increase in the preferential would clearly please the United States, but it would also anger Argentina at a time when the press talked of the possibility of war. Moreover, it would only cause further annoyance to European diplomats who were already complaining that Americans were seeking not "fair treatment" but "a monopoly."[169]

At this juncture, a change of administration occurred in the United States. In March 1909 Roosevelt and Root were replaced by William H. Taft and Philander Knox. The Republican party remained in control of the White House so that a basic continuity of foreign policy was maintained. Where the new administration differed from its predecessor was in formulating a more structured approach to overseas commercial expansion, especially in Latin America and China. A distinct emphasis was placed on using American capital investment to create bigger overseas markets and to tie them commercially to the United States. This assertiveness became popularly known as "dollar diplomacy."

At the State Department, Taft decided to promote Francis Huntington-Wilson to the post of assistant secretary of state. Huntington-Wilson rapidly implemented what was described as the most thorough reform of the department in half a century. He had already worked with Root to create in 1908 the Far Eastern Division. In November 1909 he persuaded Knox to set up a similar desk for Latin American affairs. This was followed later in the year by separate sections for Western Europe and the Near East. The reorganization showed the new emphasis on efficiency and specialist skills. "The day is past," summed up Knox, "when a man representing this country shall simply wear a silk hat and ride around in an automobile."[170]

The new administration proclaimed its desire for close and friendly relations with Latin America. In contrast to Root, however, both Knox and Huntington-Wilson displayed little affinity with diplomats from south of the Rio Grande. "We are simply very different in tastes, psychology, sense of values, standards, customs, and outlook on life," remarked Huntington-Wilson.[171] The note of condescension was reflected in drawing qualitative distinctions between the countries of the South and insisting that they must act "respectably" in their management of financial affairs. Although Taft and Knox stressed their intention to emphasize "dollars" rather than "bullets," Huntington-Wilson considered that they adopted "a much stricter" approach to Latin America than their predecessors.[172] The result was frequent American intervention in the Caribbean area. Brazil was never in danger of military or political interference, but dollar diplomacy affected relations by giving additional impetus to what had already been more than a decade of persistent American pressure to win tariff concessions.

Throughout his presidency Theodore Roosevelt had carefully avoided the controversial tariff issue. But Taft promised tariff revision during the 1908 election and resolved to carry out his pledge. Consequently, his administration's commercial policy toward Latin America during its first year of office was in a state of limbo as it awaited the outcome of the congressional tariff debate. Throughout 1909 a battle between the House and Senate over the Payne-Aldrich bill threatened to lead to increased duties on a large number of items including coffee. The Itamaraty carefully monitored events and was relieved when coffee was retained on the free list.[173] But the new law also invigorated the reciprocity issue by instructing the State Department to negotiate trade concessions for tariff favors. A harassed Brazilian government agreed tactfully to add a small number of extra American goods such as cement, dried fruits, and school furniture to the 1910 preferential list. In 1911 the concession on flour was increased to 30 percent.

The changes were marginal and aroused minor local interest. As the British minister noted, they also reflected the growing influence of Dudley who, after an inauspicious beginning, had gradually developed a cordial relationship with Rio Branco.[174] However, when Dudley left Rio in 1911, George Rives assumed the post of acting minister. The inexperienced chargé embarked upon a vigorous and at times tactless prosecution of dollar diplomacy more reminiscent of nineteenth-century bluster than twentieth-century professionalism.[175] The formerly friendly tone of the exchanges between the American embassy and the Itamaraty soon deteriorated. Writing in November 1911, Rives condescendingly reminded Rio Branco:

> The Government of Brazil, with a far-sighted grasp of the principles which govern the trade of nations, has, in consideration of the unusually generous treatment accorded by the United States to her exports, wisely made some small concessions to American imports. . . . My Government, while appreciating at their full value the reductions already decreed, is persuaded that . . . in justice to the obligations still clearly existing, the present preferential list should be very considerably extended.[176]

Added to the insistence for an extension of commercial preference was similar diplomatic pressure exerted directly on behalf of American business. The Taft administration strongly supported the expansion of trade with Latin America and was especially desirous of assisting American companies to win contracts for warships and armaments. Brazil's desire to rebuild its navy was well known and presented a particularly "encouraging" market. "It is scarcely necessary to reiterate," stated Huntington-Wilson, "that the Department of State is prepared to give its energetic support to such efforts on the part of American shipbuilders."[177] Official assistance was considered necessary to break into what had long been a European monopoly and to enable American businessmen to compete on equal terms with their heavily subsidised foreign rivals. For example, the Niles-Bement-Pond Company of New York received the co-operation of the State Department in its attempt to secure a contract for a huge marine arsenal to be built near Rio. Huntington-Wilson believed that British and German diplomats were making vigorous efforts on behalf of their own citizens, but he was confident that similar lobbying by the American ambassador "will without question have a strong influence in turning the order to this country."[178]

Moreover, the stakes extended beyond Brazil. If Americans won this prize, Knox predicted, "it would probably be instrumental in bringing other South American business of a similar character here." The American embassy was therefore instructed: "You will, whenever in your judgment, the occasion is opportune, bend every effort to procure the award of this contract."[179] Identical guidelines were given Rives to support the Electric Boat Company of Connecticut in its bid for an order to construct submarines. The chargé was told of the State Department's "keenest interest" in the progress of the bid and was directed to give "all possible aid" to the agents of the company.[180]

The policy was unequivocally to back American businessmen to the hilt and Rives followed his orders to the letter. He personally accompanied and introduced the representatives of the Electric Boat Company to officials at the Navy Ministry and made "strong representations" as soon as it appeared that the contract would not be awarded to the American company. But the State Department was alarmed when it learned of a disagreeable exchange of notes between Rives and Rio Branco. The chargé had insisted that Brazil was bound by a previous undertaking and that his government would "be greatly and justly annoyed should the repeated promises to award the contract to American builders not be kept." The result was a "caustic" reply from Rio Branco: "With regard to the acquisition of material for national defence, we understand it to be our perfect right to proceed always with the same liberty of action and selection with which we have proceeded up to the present time from the first days of our independence."[181]

Contrary to the chargé's expectations, his superiors in Washington were not sympathetic. Officials such as Thomas C. Dawson in the new Latin American Division had personal experience of serving in Brazil and understood very clearly the dangers posed by the "too controversial" tone of the correspondence. It was acknowledged that the Brazilian government "was unquestionably within its right in awarding this contract as it pleased, to whomsoever it pleased." One official sadly observed that such "unwelcome and unauthorized representations" could only have "a harmful influence" upon American attempts to win Brazilian contracts.[182]

Nevertheless, State Department officials could themselves be guilty of similar tactless behavior. Huntington-Wilson's arrogance was a byword and once provoked a British diplomat into calling him "that pestilential beast." The assistant secretary of state was renowned for trying to gain the best of any bargain and his diplomatic interventions often resembled attempts to tout for trade.[183] For example, in January 1912 he wrote directly to the Brazilian ambassador at Washington, Domício da Gama, on the question of the proposed naval arsenal. Pointing out that the American consumer was a "large purchaser" of Brazilian goods and that American firms "have never in the past figured on the list of foreign concerns to which the Brazilian Government contracts have been awarded," he hoped that Brazil would "give special consideration" to bids placed by American companies for the construction of the arsenal.[184] Domício politely replied that he would attempt to ensure that his government "give this matter all the consideration it merits." He envisaged a "favorable" reception and stressed that his country always welcomed the entry of American firms into the bidding for contracts.[185] In his report to Rio Branco, however, Domício openly condemned the exercise of "imprudent" official interference in specific business matters and declared that such pressure could only be "counterproductive."[186]

Domício's comments were written at a time when the Itamaraty was itself most offended by American tactics. "Mr. Rives has been very zealous," commented the British minister at Rio, "with the result that he had made himself disliked by the authorities here."[187] The forceful dollar diplomacy of the Taft administration was resented because it undermined Brazil's sovereignty and status. Despite his wish for increased commercial relations with the United States, Rio Branco recognized that Europe supplied most of Brazil's trade and investment. Moreover, contrary to American belief, he informed Rives that European governments did not request special favors in the awarding of armaments contracts. Matters of national defense were separate from those of commerce and required "the greatest delicacy and responsibility." In a statement worthy of Rui Barbosa, Rio Branco insisted that "each country has the right to choose freely" and should be guided only by its own national interest.[188]

When Rio Branco died in February 1912, the strategy of approximation appeard to be in ruins. In his obituary of the baron, the British minister concluded:

> His one aim was to place his country at the head of South American states. . . . The mainspring of this policy was to induce the United States to back Brazil against Argentina, or at least to make the other South American states believe that they would do so. In the latter he succeeded, at all events to a certain extent; in the former I do not think he got further than the attitude of subjection which would, he hoped, bring its reward. Oddly enough, what it did bring during His Excellency's lifetime were demands from the United States for preferential customs treatment of so wide a character and pressed in so peremptory a manner that he was compelled to resent them, and thus the first rift in the lute appeared shortly before his death.[189]

Joaquim Nabuco had died two years previously in 1910 and therefore escaped the unhappy experiences that caused Rio Branco to doubt the feasibility of approximation. In retrospect the euphoria of 1906 had been short-lived. Root's visit brought international prestige, but only to a modest degree as the conference at The Hague demonstrated when Brazil was firmly assigned to the category of minor nations. Approximation contributed to Brazil's sense of national security, but it also encouraged Brazilian diplomatic ambitions. It soon became painfully apparent, however, that Brazil lacked the resources to lead the southern continent. The hollowness of this pretension was exposed in 1909–1910 by what seemed like a return to the chaos of the early years of the republic. The emergence of Deodoro's nephew, Hermes da Fonseca, as a leading presidential candidate evoked fears of "militarism" and persuaded Rui Barbosa to challenge the "politics of the governors." Despite a brilliant campaign, Rui could not prevent the oligarchy from securing victory for Hermes.

The Hermes era began disastrously. Only days after the new president assumed office in November 1910, the sailors of the navy's two largest warships *Minas Gerais* and *São Paulo* mutinied at Rio. The city was terrified of bombardment and the new government felt compelled to grant an amnesty to the mutineers. The mutiny of the ships, which were regarded as the pride of the Brazilian navy, followed by the capitulation of the government represented a humiliating setback to Rio Branco's attempts to portray Brazil as a model of stability and progress. The American ambassador confirmed that the baron was "very pessimistic" and that the events were "a bitter experience" for the government.[190]

Just as Brazil's prestige was declining, Argentina enjoyed the glory of hosting the Pan-American conference in 1910, followed shortly by elaborate celebrations to mark the centenary of Argentine independence. The gloom and pessimism of the Brazilian elite was heightened as the world praised their rival's achievements and proclaimed Buenos Aires "the Paris of South America."[191] Even more alarming for the Itamaraty was the increasing evidence of friendly relations between Argentina and the United States. This had become evident at the beginning of Taft's administration when a close friend of the president, Charles H. Sherrill, was appointed minister to Buenos Aires. Sherrill made strenuous efforts to persuade the Argentine navy to purchase American warships and eventually secured an order for two large battleships in January 1910.[192]

The State Department appeared oblivious of the growing speculation in South America that it was assisting Argentina against Brazil and contributing directly to the arms race. Officials naively believed that they were simply responding to the forces of the marketplace. The chastening experience of the 1910 naval mutiny and current financial difficulties meant that the Brazilian government was not seeking to purchase warships. On the other hand, Argentina was in the market for battleships, and these were available from American shipbuilders. The aim of American policy was to help American businessmen to grasp whatever commercial opportunities presented themselves. There was no intention of becoming involved in South American domestic affairs. A few years previously, Griscom had expressed alarm over the "incalculable harm" likely to arise from the naval arms race between Brazil and Argentina. Adee minuted on the dispatch: "Rather unimportant."[193] Officials in Washington considered the arms race to be motivated by intense jealousy, and that any diplomatic interference by the United States would thus be counterproductive. The correct and sensible policy was evenhandedness. When Sherrill was asked whether his government favored Brazil above Argentina, he told the Argentine foreign minister that its attitude was one of "absolute impartiality."[194]

American diplomats retained, however, a friendly regard for Brazil. Prior to the Pan-American conference at Buenos Aires, Sherrill singled out Brazil and observed that "we can safely count upon the friendly cooperation of the Brazilian delegates."[195] When Nabuco died at Washington in January 1910, Taft paid the signal tribute of providing an American warship to take the ambassador's body back home to Brazil. But the "Root Doctrine" had passed away too, and the diplomatic atmosphere in Washington was no longer so receptive to Brazil. This was evident in the initial experiences of Nabuco's successor, Domício da Gama. The latter had once been selected by Griscom along with Rio Branco and Nabuco as particularly pro-American. It was soon apparent, however, that Domício's personal taste of life at the American capital was leading to a change of opinion. Whereas Nabuco had written admiringly about American society,[196] arrogance and brashness were the characteristics that most struck Domício. Moreover, the new ambassador was especially resentful of how American diplomacy continually used the "blackmail" of threatening to tax coffee in order to extract commercial privileges from Brazil.[197] No doubt, his anxiety over coffee was also a response to the growing American criticism that held Brazil responsible for rising prices. As the era of Rio Branco came to an end it seemed that United States–Brazilian relations had reached their lowest point in decades.

CHAPTER 3
Conflict and Conformity, 1912–1920

WOODROW WILSON dominated American politics during the second decade of the twentieth century. On assuming the presidency in 1913 Wilson announced his intention to concentrate on the pursuit of progressive reform at home. Contrary to his expectations he found himself increasingly entangled in the complexities of foreign affairs. Military intervention in Mexico was followed by a period of awkward neutrality toward the world war. Eventually the United States entered the conflict and thereby assumed a leading place in the councils of the great powers.

Although Wilson initially expressed little personal interest in foreign affairs, it was evident that he wished to reverse the aggressive foreign policies associated with his Republican predecessors. Instead of pursuing dollar diplomacy, the United States sought a relationship with its "sister republics" of Latin America that was firmly based upon reason and trust.[1]

Wilsonian idealism interacted, however, with more pragmatic considerations. The opening of the Panama Canal in 1914 created a new and vital security obligation for the United States. Latin America, as ever, remained a particularly inviting commercial market. Moreover, World War I provided substantial incentives for American business to expand at the expense of the European powers. American exports to the region tripled during the decade and by 1920 amounted to more than 40 percent of all South American imports. American businessmen directed more attention to Argentina rather than Brazil. Economic activities were hampered, however, by the shortage of credit and merchant shipping. Moreover, the outbreak of war brought a boom in American trade with Britain and France. Compared to the vast European market, Latin America was of considerably less value.[2]

Indifference bordering on arrogance continued to be expressed in official attitudes toward Latin America. Although the United States government publicly affirmed the rights of all neutral nations in its response to the European war, Wilson preferred to deal unilaterally with the belligerent powers. The various proposals to maintain "continental solidarity" made by Latin American statesmen were politely ignored. When the United States joined the war against Germany in 1917 there was no prior consultation with the Latin American governments.

Wilson's views were highly significant; the impact of war encouraged active presidential involvement in the making of American foreign policy. The president's strong character clashed with those of successive secretaries of state and forced the resignations of Bryan in 1915 and Lansing in 1920. Moreover, the State Department's customary supremacy in the conduct of diplomacy was challenged by other departments of the federal government. The Treasury Department actively participated in the formulation of economic policy toward Latin America. Another rival was the Department of Commerce, whose Bureau of Foreign and Domestic Commerce created its own Latin American Division in 1914.[3]

Relations with Brazil were affected by interdepartmental rivalry. For example, the awkward controversy over the valorization of coffee was initiated by the Justice Department. The wider requirements of the war effort defeated Ambassador Morgan's recommendation that the Navy department maintain a sizable squadron of American warships in Brazilian waters. Similarly, the demands of departmental protocol frustrated his desire for speedy action to purchase the ex-German ships from Brazil.

Like Roosevelt and Taft, Wilson was conscious of the relatively greater importance of the leading nations of South America. On taking office Wilson and Bryan seized the chance to end the valorization dispute and thereby give a practical example of their desire to improve relations with Brazil. An awareness of the significance of Brazil's friendly disposition and diplomatic influence was evident in attempts to resolve the Mexican crisis and to secure a Pan-American arbitration treaty. But American officials also sought Argentine diplomatic cooperation and thereby refused to recognize Brazil's claim to special status.

The retention of Edwin Morgan as ambassador to Rio helped give continuity to American policy toward Brazil. But Morgan was frequently disappointed with the indifference to his advice and recommendations shown by his superiors in Washington. While the war years stimulated increased American economic interest in Brazil, other forms of contact remained minimal. Theodore Roosevelt praised the "astonishing progress" made by the republic,[4] but the published account of his "expedition" in 1913–1914 confirmed the image of Brazil as a frontier society replete with poisonous snakes and Indians. Americans still knew so little about the country that it was not surprising the leading role in the "Girl from Brazil" should be presented on the New York stage as a Spanish-speaking Carmen.[5] The cultural gulf separating both societies remained as wide as ever.

As Europe was overwhelmed by war in 1914, the Brazilian republic celebrated its 25th anniversary. The apparent political order was, however, superficial. There was no leader of the stature of Woodrow Wilson. The disarray precipitated in 1910 by the election of Hermes da Fonseca persisted and was dramatically illustrated in 1915 by the assassination of the powerful *gaúcho* senator, Pinheiro Machado. Hermes's term of office was marked by increasing unpopularity and public derision. His successor, Venceslau Brás, reacted to a series of strikes and regional revolts by declaring a state of siege. The sudden death of newly elected President Rodrigues Alves in 1919 and the infirmity of Vice President Delfim Moreira revealed the collapse of the Paulista-Mineiro alliance as the presidency passed by virtual default of Epitácio Pessoa, an "outsider" from the tiny northern state of Paraíba.

The war was also economically damaging to Brazil. Overseas trade was severely restricted by the fall in demand for luxury products such as coffee, the shortage of merchant shipping, and the determination of Britain to impose virtual economic isolation upon the Central Powers. The result was a marked decline in Brazil's foreign commerce. For the Brazilian people and especially those living in cities, the direct consequences were inflation, a sharp fall in their standard of living, and a growing social unrest that expressed itself in strikes and political protest.[6]

Like the United States, Brazil proclaimed a policy of neutrality in 1914, but this did not ensure immunity from the effects of war. Bordering the Atlantic and possessing large international trading interests, Brazil could not avoid becoming involved in the controversy over maritime rights. The issue was of such national importance that the making of foreign policy became subject to increasing political interference. This was facilitated by the fact that no foreign minister after 1912 enjoyed the prestige and authority of Rio Branco. His successor, Lauro Müller, lacked diplomatic experience. His effectiveness was also undermined by frequent illness and the political controversy arising from his personal presidential ambitions. Eventually, Müller was compelled to resign in 1917 and was replaced by an undisguised political appointment in Nilo Peçanha, a former president of the republic and governor of Rio de Janeiro. The transfer of Domício da Gama from Washington in November 1918 put a professional diplomat once more in charge of the Itamaraty, but political machinations again predominated during the following year as President Epitácio Pessoa outmaneuvered Domício and secured his replacement with Azevedo Marques.

Events in Europe shocked and perplexed Brazilian leaders. Brazil enjoyed friendly relations with all the belligerents. Nevertheless, Brazilian opinion was outraged by the German invasion of Belgium. This unprovoked attack upon a small, neutral nation drew an immediate vote of condemnation from the

Brazilian Senate. Indeed, from the beginning of the war it was evident that the mass of Brazilians sympathized with Britain and France, especially the latter.

The ultimatum delivered by Germany in January 1917 to enforce unrestricted submarine warfare resulted in the sinking of four Brazilian merchant ships. It was, however, not until October that Brazil formally decided to enter the war. By joining the Allies in order to uphold maritime rights and the sanctity of treaties, Brazil was able to pose as the champion and leader of South America. Furthermore, by becoming a belligerent, Brazil gained the prospect of financial and military support from the United States and the Allies.

The wartime association of Brazil with the United States revived speculation that a special relationship existed between the two countries. After the euphoria of the 1906 conference the strategy of approximation had gradually receded into the background; it received a major jolt during Müller's first year in office when he was confronted with the disagreeable dispute over the valorization of coffee. Although Müller fully recognized the power and influence of the United States, he publicly stressed the importance of simultaneously developing close relations with Argentina and Chile.

The emergence of the ABC demonstrated Brazil's independence of diplomatic action, but was not meant to imply the formation of an anti-American alliance. Müller wished above all to be on good terms with the United States and was delighted to make two visits to that country in 1913 and 1916. Similarly, Ambassador Domício da Gama was initially critical of the United States, but his views gradually changed so much so that State Department officials welcomed his appointment as foreign minister in 1918.

Although Edwin Morgan was pleased to observe that the war had increased Brazilian awareness and admiration of the United States, he also observed that the Brazilian mind was still "not habituated" to news of American affairs. He concluded sadly that the country's "drift has rather been toward France and England than toward ourselves."[7] In fact, the war deflected attention away from internal difficulties and inspired a reaffirmation of Brazilian nationality. Elated by victory, the Brazilian elite acquired a new confidence and looked forward to opportunities to enhance their country's hemispheric and international prestige.[8]

THE VALORIZATION CONTROVERSY

The passing away of Rio Branco and Nabuco exposed the fragility of approximation. Despite the finely worded American obituaries accorded the two statesmen, Brazil possessed no special influence in Washington. The bequest of embassy status proved meaningless as Domício da Gama signally failed to establish the personal esteem and influence enjoyed by Joaquim Nabuco. Instead, the new Brazilian ambassador felt slighted and complained that Knox pointedly avoided discussing Latin American affairs with him.[9] Knox later grumbled that he would prefer to deal with an ambassador more receptive to "the Anglo-Saxon spirit."[10] Rumors of their personal friction circulated in Rio, causing the British minister to speculate that Domício "is not so popular in society in Washington where 'coloured gentlemen' are at a discount."[11]

Prejudices of a different sort were aroused by the selection of Lauro Müller as Brazil's new foreign minister. Whereas State Department officials had welcomed the appointment of Rio Branco as foreign minister, they were uncertain of his successor. Müller was known to be an influential political figure from Santa Catarina who had served as state governor and federal senator. Under Rodrigues Alves he had been an effective Minister of Transport and Public Works and was directly associated in supervising the rebuilding of Rio. He possessed no formal diplomatic qualifications, however, and appeared to regard the post of foreign minister primarily as a stepping-stone to the presidency.[12]

Müller's political ambitions, however, were incidental. Of more concern to the State Department were his Germanic surname and reported predilection for the Old World. The foreign minister's parents were immigrants from Germany who had settled in southern Brazil. Although Lauro was born and raised in Brazil, his desire to maintain links with the fatherland was demonstrated by two recent visits to Europe. Excellent hospitality had greeted him in Germany, where he was invited to dine with the Kaiser and attend military maneuvers. On returning to Brazil, Müller fully supported the proposal of the Hermes da Fonseca administration to appoint German military instructors to assist the modernization of the Brazilian army. The scheme was effectively frustrated by Brazilian financial difficulties, but German hopes were renewed by Lauro's appointment as foreign minister. The American chargé at Rio reported reassuringly that Müller was personally affable and "friendly" to American interests. He had even expressed a wish to visit the United States. Nevertheless, Rives also confirmed that the new head of the Itamaraty was "decidedly pro-German in his sympathies."[13]

Like Quintino Bocaiúva in 1889 and Rio Branco in 1902, Müller's immediate preoccupation was with South American affairs. The matter of gravest concern was Paraguay, where political violence had spread across the border into Argentina and threatened to provoke imminent Argentine military intervention. Brazil's confusion and weakness was symbolized by President Hermes da Fonseca, whose indecisiveness soon made him a figure of political ridicule. But his new foreign minister possessed a shrewd understanding of the realities of hemispheric power politics. After barely a week in office Müller looked for guidance to Washington and telegraphed Domício to ascertain "the views of the American government with whom we wish always to work in accord."

A startled Domício replied that Brazil's policy should not depend upon "the approval of the American cabinet." The essential thing was to maintain "complete freedom of action," and this could be best secured by reaffirming friendly relations with all neighboring countries including Argentina.[14]

The advice was consistent with Rio Branco's own policy of seeking Argentine cooperation to resolve the disturbances in Paraguay. Ironically, the baron's death had improved the diplomatic climate by removing the man whom many Argentines regarded as dedicated to the promotion of Brazil's "hegemony" at the expense of Argentina. In contrast to the aristocratic Rio Branco, Argentines could readily identify with Müller's ethnic background; they recognized that he represented the region of Brazil most similar to Argentina. Moreover, the new foreign minister acted decisively to take advantage of what the Buenos Aires press described as the opening of "a new era" in diplomatic relations. In a personal interview intended for publication in *La Nación* he repeated the slogan used by President Saenz Peña during his visit to Rio in August 1910: "Everything unites us; nothing separates us."[15] As a further gesture of good feelings, ex-President Campos Sales was nominated in March 1912 as special minister to Buenos Aires. Argentina reciprocated by sending Julio Roca on a state visit to Rio in July.[16] The lavish reception accorded the Argentine ex-president contrasted strikingly with the lukewarm welcome given to Edwin Morgan only a few weeks earlier. The British minister commented that his American colleague "has had to take a back seat and is indeed comparatively ignored."[17]

The American minister at Uruguay considered that Müller's "quick change of front" had obviated any need for Argentine intervention in Paraguay.[18] By contributing to a reduction of tension in South America, the diplomatic rapprochement between Brazil and Argentina should have pleased State Department officials. But it had also resulted in rumors of a commercial treaty between the two countries. Such a development would undermine American hopes for a further extension of the preferential tariff. The British minister, William Haggard, noted Müller's desire to improve relations with Argentina and concluded that this must lead to a reduction of American influence in Brazil. Indeed, the various European diplomats at Rio were eager to seize what they perceived as an opportunity to reverse the pro-American commercial policy of the Rio Branco era. Their efforts appeared to be gaining some success as it became clear that the new American ambassador, Edwin Morgan, who had arrived in May 1912, was unable to achieve his proclaimed intention of persuading the Brazilian government to alter its attitude on the tariff question.[19]

What upset Morgan's plan was not so much the intricacies of South American politics or European intrigue, but the emerging controversy over coffee. Brazil was truly "the land of coffee" and produced more than 80 percent of the world's supply. During the 1880s Brazil's output averaged five million bags per year. By the close of the nineteenth century this output had risen to ten million bags. At the beginning of the 1890s the average contract price of coffee at New York was 19 cents a pound. Good prices resulted in high profits and encouraged further production. By 1900 the state of São Paulo alone was reckoned to possess more than 500 million coffee trees under cultivation. But abundant supplies inevitably depressed both prices and profits. A bumper crop of 16 million bags in 1901 contributed to a collapse in price to just over five cents.[20]

The prospect of another massive crop in 1906 prompted the state governors of Rio de Janeiro, Minas Gerais, and São Paulo to hold a convention at Taubaté. Discussion centered upon how to reverse the trend of falling prices. The government of São Paulo formally proposed the purchase and storage of coffee in order to withhold supplies from the world market. In this way coffee would be increased in value or "valorized." The idea aroused little initial enthusiasm from the other states and foreign bankers; it was regarded as not only enormously expensive, but also as designed primarily to serve the sectional interests of the Paulistas. Nonetheless, as the largest coffee producer, the state of São Paulo felt compelled to implement the valorization plan on its own. The purchase of coffee was to be financed by loans and the imposition of a state export surtax of three French francs on each bag of coffee. The state government was, however, soon saddled with large debts and huge stocks of coffee, amounting to more than eight million bags in 1908. State bankruptcy was only forestalled by federal intervention. So important was the welfare of the coffee trade to the national economy that the federal government was persuaded to guarantee foreign loans contracted by São Paulo for the purpose of valorization.[21]

A financial arrangement was subsequently reached in 1908 between São Paulo and a group of foreign financiers and merchants, including most prominently the ruthless and abrasive "king" of the coffee trade, Herman Sielcken, who headed the firm of Crossman, Sielcken of New York.[22] Under Sielcken's direction, these merchants formed a valorization committee and agreed to assist the scheme by accepting supplies of coffee from São Paulo as security for a $75 million loan to that state. The valorized coffee would be stockpiled in New York and various European ports and only gradually released for sale.

Sielcken's plan worked extremely well and enabled São Paulo to reduce its surplus stocks. Brazilian coffee exports to the United States markedly increased in value from £10 million in 1908 to £16 million in 1911 and to a record £19 million in 1912.[23] The stated aim of valorization was to avoid damaging fluctuations of price and supply. In practice, however, the withholding of supplies encouraged the price of coffee to rise. While this was highly profitable for the producer and merchants, it was to the disadvantage of the consumer, most noticeably in the United States where prices increased from seven cents per pound in 1909 to more than fourteen cents in 1912. Consequently, valorization attracted unfavorable comment, including the scrutiny of progressive politicians who condemned the operation as yet another glaring example of a "trust" employing unfair and restrictive practices to force prices to artificially high levels. In the spring of 1911 the Brazilian chargé at Washington revealed that the matter was under investigation by the Justice Department; he drew attention to an article in the *Washington Post* describing valorization as "the new contrivance to squeeze all mankind."[24]

The delayed enquiry into valorization was explained by the fact that the scheme contained substantial financial advantages for certain American banking and coffee interests. In fact, the $75 million loan to São Paulo included $10 million provided by the National City Bank of New York. The loan was guaranteed by the federal government of Brazil and was virtually risk-free. Similar security was attached to the operations of the valorization committee. Overabundant supplies were also ruled out by São Paulo's willingness to increase its export surtax to five francs per bag of coffee. Consequently, Brazilian production fell back from more than 20 million bags in 1906 to 15 million bags four years later. Moreover, the placing of large amounts of valorized coffee under the control of Herman Sielcken allowed the "king" and his associates to manipulate the market by withholding coffee from the New York Coffee Exchange. A "corner" was created to drive prices up and to ensure high profits for insider dealing.[25]

Indeed, it was not criticism of Brazil but growing resentment at Sielcken's questionable activities that fueled demands in the United States for official investigation. A report prepared by William T. Chantland of the Justice Department and published toward the end of 1911 described the actions of the valorization committee as the "unconscionable, open, high-handed, continuous, and bold violation of law for the express and only purpose . . . of gouging the consuming public of this country." Chantland estimated that each increase of one cent in the price of a pound of coffee cost American consumers an additional $9.5 million per year. The report recommended that action be taken under the antitrust laws to release the large supplies of coffee known to be withheld in New York by American members of the valorization committee.[26]

Domício da Gama was not surprised by the report's conclusion, as it was common knowledge that Attorney General George W. Wickersham believed that the antitrust laws were being violated. But Wickersham was also known to be reluctant to proceed with what was likely to be a sensitive issue involving a foreign government. On May 18, 1912, however, the ambassador's comforting assessment was overturned when the Justice Department suddenly took the initiative and filed a suit in the New York district court requesting that Herman Sielcken and the New York Dock Company be prevented from either removing or disposing of stocks of "valorized" coffee currently held in their possession. The action was specifically directed at Sielcken as he was the only American member of the valorization committee.[27]

Domício was taken aback by what he regarded as a demeaning of São Paulo's right to enter into overseas contractual agreements. He was also annoyed not to have been forewarned of the legal action and only to have learned of the development from the newspapers. His resulting protest must have struck a responsive chord in the State Department; Knox had been similarly left in the dark and was compelled to request the attorney general to "be good enough to give me the necessary information."[28] Poor communications remained a persistent complaint throughout the dispute. Because Domício could only act within diplomatic channels, the State Department assumed the responsibility for communicating between the Brazilian embassy and the Justice Department. The resulting triangle did little to mollify the ambassador, whose frequent visits to the State Department indicated the serious turn of events. "This is the first time," observed the *Washington Post*, "that a foreign state has been concerned in the alleged violation of the Sherman law."[29]

The Brazilian embassy attempted to bypass the State Department by appealing directly to President Taft. Domício used his ambassadorial rank to secure a personal interview with the president. Assistance was also sought from Elihu Root. The former secretary of state, now a United States senator, confirmed his old friendship by visiting the White House to speak on Brazil's behalf.[30] Legal arguments were prepared for use in court by Crammond Kennedy, who had replaced John B. Moore as the embassy's legal counsel.[31] To the embarrassment of the Justice Department, Kennedy pointed out that the coffee named in the action was still legally the property of the state of São Paulo. He concluded therefore that the controversy was "of diplomatic cognizance and not justiciable in the courts."[32] Because the antitrust laws could not be applied against foreign governments, he advised Domício to await judicial developments and, for the moment, remain content with having lodged a protest to the State Department. The advice proved sound when the New York court on May 31 withdrew its temporary restraining order and instructed that a trial was necessary to determine the facts of the case. This would however have to be delayed until after the annual summer recess.

A few days prior to the court's decision, Domício's irritation could hold back no longer and he gave vent to his feelings at a banquet held in New York to celebrate the first meeting of the Pan-American Society. The declared aim of the new organization was to foster closer relations and understanding between the United States and Latin America, and Domício took the opportunity of following Knox's opening address with what was described as "a bomb."[33] In a speech disapproving of the sharp practices employed by American businessmen, the Brazilian ambassador indicted the supportive role played by the United States government. Referring to the coffee dispute he added:

> And the United States seems disposed to enforce it even at the sacrifice of a long standing international friendship. In their eagerness to establish their right to meddle with the property of a foreign state certain officials of this government went so far as to proclaim before an American court of justice the forfeiture of the sovereignty of that foreign state and this with an unthoughtfulness for the consideration due to a friendly state which borders on international discourtesy.

The rebuke was intended to apply to more than just the coffee question and represented also a direct condemnation of the Taft administration's pursuit of dollar diplomacy in Latin America. Domício was reported to have directed a sarcastic smile at Knox as he concluded his speech with the words: "South Americans have still as much to learn of North American ways in dealing with foreign countries as Americans have still to learn of the way to our own hearts." While the North Americans felt distinctly ill at ease, the Latin Americans in the audience received the speech with enthusiastic applause.[34]

Knox was an unfortunate victim for Domício's anger as he was known to have disagreed with Wickersham over taking the matter to the courts. His own preference had been to avoid acrimony and to settle the question through diplomatic channels. But personal and national pride had been injured. Huntington-Wilson later described Domício's speech as an "outrageous and insulting attack upon this Government."[35] It was uncertain, however, whether Domício's remarks had been delivered with or without the approval of his government. Tactfully, the United States government chose to take no official notice of them. The State Department's response was confined to telegraphing its new ambassador at Rio, Edwin Morgan, to send information clarifying the exact position of the Brazilian government.[36]

Like Thompson in 1893, Morgan had only been in Rio a matter of days when he was suddenly confronted with a crisis. But the new ambassador was hardly a diplomatic or political novice. His family background was steeped in the Republican politics of upstate New York and included a relative who had served as state governor during the Civil War. After graduating from Harvard with a degree in history, Morgan entered the foreign service and represented the new breed of career diplomats. A period of service as American minister in Korea gave him a reputation as an expert on Far Eastern affairs, but after 1905 he was assigned to a succession of Latin capitals beginning with Havana, followed by Montevideo, Lisbon, and finally Rio in May 1912.[37]

It was no secret that Morgan was ambitious and regarded Brazil as just another step up the ladder to a choice European posting. But it was also evident that the new ambassador sought to earn his promotion. "He is very active and takes his work extremely seriously, and is determined to make a success of mission here," noted the British minister.[38] In contrast to his predecessors, Morgan was a man of considerable personal wealth and culture. Like the most affluent Brazilians, he made regular visits to France. Indeed, his gregarious personality, lavish hospitality, and love of the arts soon endeared him to the Brazilian elite.[39] His obvious sincerity was both gratifying and disarming and in time would earn him the tribute of being described as the "most Brazilian of Americans."[40]

The new ambassador showed political astuteness by flattering Brazil's achievements and sense of international status. One of his first and most appreciated public acts was to place a wreath at Rio Branco's tomb. Favorable press coverage was ensured by his friendship with José Carlos Rodrigues, whose *Jornal do commercio* duly reported that the ambassador had "conquered the hearts of the Brazilian people." Morgan was also dismayed to discover that the American embassy was located in Petrópolis. Despite the improvements to Rio, the foreign diplomatic corps had obstinately remained in Petrópolis. This comfortable state of affairs was abruptly brought to an end by Morgan who simply ordered his own staff to settle permanently in Rio and, by so doing, compelled the European diplomats reluctantly to follow suit.[41]

Morgan spoke of promoting Pan-Americanism and hoped to secure tariff reductions for American products. His whirlwind activity received, however, an unlucky check in that it coincided with growing Brazilian fury over the valorization controversy. The state of São Paulo had incurred a massive debt to finance the scheme and was desperate for its success. The Paulistas were supported by politicians from other regions who were very sensitive about anything that affected the nation's most valuable export. There was also a growing sense of anger at what was interpreted as a calculated attack upon Brazilian interests by the United States government. Suspicion already abounded that "Yankee speculators" were responsible for the recent and sudden collapse of rubber prices. The legal suit against Sielcken was seen as another American conspiracy to drive prices down and a continuation of unrelenting American pressure to use threats against coffee as a means of forcing tariff concessions.[42]

Not only did the Itamaraty have to contend with the formidable political pressure exerted by the government of São Paulo, but it was also annoyed that the Justice Department was indifferent to the possibly damaging diplomatic consequences arising from its impulsive action. Lauro Müller was particularly concerned by the effects that the dispute might have upon Brazil's commercial relations with other countries. Germany was a case of special anxiety. That nation was the second-largest importer of Brazilian coffee and might be tempted to adopt the same aggressive tactics as the United States should the Americans secure any concessions.[43] Moreover, any changes in the Brazilian tariff would also annoy Argentina and, consequently, upset Müller's desire to improve relations with that country.

State Department officials were kept fully informed of Müller's views by Morgan rather than Domício. The Brazilian ambassador had once complained that he felt slighted by Knox. The outburst at the Pan-American banquet, however, did little to improve his personal relationship with the secretary of state. Moreover, it was also evident that the speech had so annoyed Müller that Domício's diplomatic career appeared in jeopardy, and rumors persisted of his imminent recall.[44] By contrast, Edwin Morgan had made an extremely favorable impression in Rio where his frequent meetings with Müller gave rise to rumors that he had "captivated" the foreign minister.[45] Indeed, Müller virtually ignored Domício preferring instead to confide in Morgan and to use the latter as a sympathetic and efficient channel of communication with Washington.[46]

The American embassy seemed to become the mouthpiece of the Itamaraty as Morgan's telegrams and dispatches consistently presented Brazilian policy in a very favorable light. Morgan, however, willingly adopted the role of conciliator because he believed that a continuation of the valorization dispute could only be harmful to American interests. Moreover, he was convinced that Müller genuinely wished to maintain close relations with the United States. Knox was told that the foreign minister desired a speedy end to what was considered a troublesome matter, one that threatened to spoil his chances of securing the presidency in 1914. Morgan also reported reassuringly that too much emphasis had been placed on Müller's German antecedents. In fact, the foreign minister was unable to speak German fluently and preferred to converse with the diplomatic corps in French. He had also repeated his desire for a visit to the United States in 1913. Morgan enthusiastically welcomed the idea of a personal meeting between Müller and State Department officials and suggested in August 1912 that an invitation issued by the United States government would lead to a marked improvement in relations.[47]

It was not necessary to act upon Morgan's suggestion because prospects looked promising for an out-of-court settlement satisfactory to both Knox and Müller.[48] A tentative agreement was reached during the summer between the Justice Department and Crammond Kennedy in which Sielcken undertook to dispose of the valorized coffee by sales on the open American market. But the chance of success was soon hindered by the emergence of adverse political forces from within the United States itself. Quite independently of the Justice Department, Congressman George W. Norris of Nebraska had also taken up the question and had placed a bill in the House of Representatives designed to eliminate alleged ambiguities in the existing antitrust laws. By allowing for the forfeit of goods transported from a foreign country, the Norris bill would remove the major obstacle that prevented legal action against the valorization committee. The Nebraskan steadfastly refused to be deflected by diplomatic technicalities. "We ought," he declared, "to be just as careful to protect our citizens against monopoly if the promoters of such monopoly are sovereign states as though the affairs were accomplished by our citizens alone."[49] The mood in Congress was receptive and the bill quickly passed the House in June 1912. Rather than an attack upon any particular government, the measure was seen as simply one among several actions against "trusts" that allegedly pervaded the American economy.

Indeed, the Taft administration was itself committed to "trust busting," and confirmation of this appeared in September when it was rumored in Rio that the Justice Department intended to resume the legal case against the New York Dock Company. Morgan reported Müller's irritation at this setback to the policy of quiet diplomacy. He warned that the foreign minister was under strong political pressure to stand firm and, if necessary, to threaten commercial retaliation against American products. The tough stance was followed by a softer approach in October as Müller informed Morgan that the valorization committee would meet at New York during January and dispose of all the existing stocks of coffee. Morgan recommended that the State Department agree to this. Approval was forthcoming, though Attorney General Wickersham insisted on assurances that the coffee would actually be sold on the open market and not simply apportioned among a group of "insiders." His doubts were heightened at the end of the year when the government of São Paulo announced that it could not complete the sale by January and asked for an extension of the original time limit.[50]

Governor Rodrigues Alves of São Paulo argued that the enforced sale at short notice of almost one million bags of coffee was stimulating bearish speculation, which would entail heavy financial loss for his state. In private, he complained that São Paulo was the victim of Wickersham's "insolence." During his presidential administration, Rodrigues Alves had endorsed the strategy of approximation with the United States. He now told Müller, however, that he was "beginning to doubt the wisdom of our direction in international affairs."[51] Herman Sielcken was even more publicly outspoken; shortly before leaving for Europe in December 1912, he made a series of statements to the press accusing Justice Department officials of deliberately frustrating a settlement. Wickersham was furious at this slur upon the integrity of his department. Huntington-Wilson agreed that Sielcken's behavior was "astonishing" and summoned Domício to the State Department. The interview was inconclusive because the Brazilian ambassador did not regard either himself or his government as responsible for Sielcken's interviews with the press. Huntington-Wilson evidently could not understand that the Brazilians were unable to control the millionaire "king" of the coffee trade. He petulantly complained to Morgan that Domício was "neither conciliatory nor agreeable in the matter."[52]

Morgan needed little reminding of the growth of anti-American feeling among Brazilians. Paulista politicians were especially prominent in advocating that Brazil show its displeasure at American policy. Morgan responded by presenting the annual request for the continuance of the preferential tariff in much more moderate language than that submitted by Rives only a year previously.[53] Nevertheless, Morgan's apprehensions were realized when the Brazilian Congress announced in December 1912 that preference would only be accorded those nations that granted Brazil not only tariff concessions but also "commercial facilities." The term was deliberately vague, but it was interpreted to mean American agreement to adopt a more accommodating attitude toward the sale of valorized coffee. In effect, this implied the temporary suspension of the preferential tariff on American goods. Anticipating that his government might retaliate and refuse São Paulo's request for additional time to sell its valorized coffee, Morgan attempted to place the matter in a more statesman-like perspective:

> The Embassy is convinced that the Foreign Minister's political position will be shaken unless the wishes of the powerful state of Sao Páulo are satisfied and believes that it would be permanently beneficial to our general interests in Brazil to support his political situation by coming to his rescue on this occasion. Not only would our preferentials for the present year be assured and the solution of the several important questions now pending between the two Governments be facilitated but we would secure as a friend the most permanently influential statesman of today if it should be found practicable to grant the requested favor.[54]

Knox was sympathetic, but the decision did not rest with the State Department alone. The secretary of state recommended "a magnanimous postponement" of legal proceedings and advised Wickersham that refusal to grant the extension "would have a most unfortunate influence upon our general interests in Brazil." But this met firm resistance from the attorney general, who regarded any further delay as "utterly inadmissible."[55] However, while American officials were pondering the Brazilian request, it was suddenly revealed in mid-January that the valorization committee had already met in London and claimed to have disposed of its stocks of coffee stored in the United States. In a manner reminiscent of Gresham's surprise at Benham's action in 1894, a bewildered Knox telegraphed Rio for information. Wickersham found himself, like Knox and Domício in the previous May, being informed of events from the newspapers. What he found even more infuriating was the obvious contradiction between the pleas from the Paulistas for additional time while they were simultaneously and furtively disposing of the coffee. His conclusion was that the episode seemed "one of distinct bad faith" on the part of the Brazilian government.[56]

The involvement of the Justice Department in the dispute was originally motivated by the determination to expose insider dealing in the coffee trade. The secrecy and element of mystery surrounding the sale in London made the transaction appear highly suspect, and Wickersham demanded that Brazilian officials provide proof of its authenticity. While Wickersham regarded his own attitude as one of reasonableness, Brazilians took a different view and complained bitterly of his insolence and self-righteousness. "The United States position here," wrote the British minister from Rio in January 1913, "is at this moment weaker than it has ever been during my six years stay here."[57] Moreover, Knox and Wickersham seemed oblivious to the fact that their prestige and authority had been diminished by Taft's defeat in the 1912 elections. Indeed, Domício believed that he had friends among the Democrats and welcomed their victory as beneficial for his own country's interests. His advice to Müller was to stand firm on the coffee question and to fight the matter in the American courts if necessary.[58]

The news in January 1913 that the Norris bill was about to come before the United States Senate injected an additional complication into the controversy. Müller viewed the measure as "antagonistic" and designed to deny "commercial facilities" to Brazil. He hinted ominously that its passage would "disturb" existing trade relations. At the State Department, Huntington-Wilson told Knox that he understood that the "real purpose" of the bill "is to hit the Brazilian coffee valorization." Choosing his words carefully, Knox instructed Morgan to explain that the bill "simply amends" sections of the 1894 tariff and "appears not to be directed against the commercial policy of any country." The secretary of state, however, firmly dismissed the notion of "commercial facilities." Brazilian products entering the United States were favored with "exceptional tariff treatment," entitling American goods to preferential treatment in return. "The Government of the United States," he told Morgan, "will not submit indefinitely to having the preferentials used as a club for first one privilege and then another." The ambassador was to stress the efforts of the State Department to resolve the controversy in a manner satisfactory to Brazil but at the same time he was to inform the Itamaraty that "the next manifestation of good feeling, which without doubt exists between the two countries, should come from Brazil."[59]

A virtual impasse had now been created that continued through the last weeks of the Taft administration. Although he was reported to be "very discouraged" by the turn of events, Morgan faithfully pursued his conciliatory role. He relayed information from Müller that the state government of São Paulo had informed the federal government of the successful disposal of all the valorized coffee "in the legitimate market." It was revealed that 80 American merchants representing 33 cities had participated in the sale. The ambassador also reiterated Müller's desire to visit the United States and noted the "thoroughly amicable spirit" that the foreign minister would bring to discussions of Pan-American questions.[60]

A distinctly cool attitude prevailed, however, in the State Department. Indeed, officials appeared oblivious to the fact that coffee prices were finally beginning to fall. At issue, however, was not so much the valorization of coffee as the whole subject of commercial relations between the two countries. Huntington-Wilson felt especially aggrieved and urged some plain speaking to Brazil. In his opinion, the United States generously provided Brazil's largest market and had received ony "insignificant commercial advantages" in return. He dismissed Brazilian criticism of American commercial policy as both "ridiculous" and "captious." While his recommendation to threaten a tax on imports of coffee was not adopted, it was decided to remind the Brazilian government that the dispute was far from being settled. Prompted by Wickersham, who ensured that the issue was discussed at a meeting of the cabinet, Knox agreed that the evidence presented so far of the reported sale of valorized coffee was "mere hearsay." He insisted that the Brazilian government provide detailed assurances of the bona fides, including names of the American dealers involved in the transaction.[61]

It seemed that Knox's demand might also be followed by the renewal of the legal suit against the valorization committee. From a constitutional point of view the administration was simply fulfilling its function of executing the laws of Congress but to the Brazilians this was just another example of ruthless dollar diplomacy. In fact, the suit was not revived, but the departure of Taft and Knox from office in March provided little immediate comfort for Brazil as the declared priority of the incoming administration of Woodrow Wilson was a tariff bill that provisionally included the ominous prospect of a tax on coffee to make up for reductions in duty on other products. Well might Müller deplore what he interpreted as the American "crusade" against his country's most important export.[62]

The new Democratic regime signified, however, changes in personnel at the State Department. Huntington-Wilson was replaced by John Osborne, while a businessman from New Mexico, Boaz Long, was appointed chief of the division of Latin American affairs.[63] Shortly before his own impending retirement, Acting Chief Seth Low Pierrepont prepared a memorandum to explain and justify the division's Brazilian policy. His general opinion was "that Brazil had acted badly in this whole matter." The United States accorded Brazil "exceptional tariff advantages" and had been "meagerly compensated" in return. The pent-up frustration of officials was evident in the comment that "Brazil has awarded no important contract to American firms" and that "many American enterprises in Brazil have been badly treated." Indeed, the threat by Brazil to withdraw the tariff preference was regarded as a blatant attempt at intimidation that had to be strongly resisted. The proposal before Congress to place a duty on coffee was therefore warmly welcomed because it could only strengthen American policy. Pierrepont recommended that the new administration "should preserve a firm attitude even if such a course should result in the loss of the preferential tariff reductions."[64]

Secretary of State William Jennings Bryan showed little immediate inclination to delve into the intricacies of foreign affairs and did not see this memorandum until late May. In the meantime the special session of Congress called by Wilson had already allayed Brazilian fears by deciding not to levy a direct tax on imports of coffee. Sensing the change of political mood, American merchants engaged in the Brazilian trade pointed out that the loss of the preference would seriously affect exports.[65] Indeed, the Wilson administration had publicly proclaimed its desire for a fresh relationship with Latin America, thus fulfilling expectations that the return of the Democrats to the White House would mean a reversal of the Republican policy of dollar diplomacy. Domício da Gama had already indicated this at the time of the November elections. An additional cause of Brazilian optimism was the fact that the new secretary of state had actually visited Brazil in 1910.

The way was opened for a honorable end to the controversy when Domício conveyed to Bryan in late March the formal assurances of his government that all American stockpiles of the valorized coffee had been legitimately disposed of and that the valorization committee no longer functioned in the United States.[66] In dispatches from Rio, Morgan emphasized Müller's "predisposition toward a closer approximation" between Brazil and the United States and advised the removal of "all impediments" to the foreign minister's forthcoming visit to Washington.[67]

Rumors that the legal suit would be dropped aroused the alarm of George Norris. "To my mind," he wrote Bryan, "this is one of the most obnoxious, gigantic, conscienceless and corrupt combinations that has ever bid defiance to our anti-trust laws."[68] The progressive rhetoric was powerful and persuasive, but the Wilson administration was more inclined to rid itself of an awkward inheritance from its Republican predecessor. For legal guidance Bryan sought the opinion of the Justice Department. The new attorney general, James C. McReynolds, believed that the statement of the Brazilian government to the effect that the coffee had been legitimately sold was sufficient cause to withdraw the legal action. On the other hand, he underlined that this did not mean a modification or suspension of the law in favor of Brazil. Consequently, any future attempt to repeat valorization would result in prosecution. These views were communicated to Rio and provided the basis for a speedy resolution of the coffee dispute.[69] The legal suit was abandoned; in return it was privately understood that the valorization scheme would not be applied to the United States. Within weeks the tariff preferences on American goods were restored in Brazil, and it was announced that Lauro Müller would visit the United States during June.

Both sides appeared satisfied with the outcome. The understaffed and overworked officials of the Justice Department enjoyed few outright victories over the giant American corporations. Wickersham could, however, claim success in so far as the scheme to "corner" the coffee market had been defeated and the American valorization committee had been disbanded. But the Brazilian government could also justifiably argue that its firmness had compelled the withdrawal of the legal action. In fact, the gradual reduction of coffee production in São Paulo caused by the imposition of the export surtax meant that valorization was no longer necessary by 1913. The scheme had brought considerable profits to São Paulo in the form of increased exports to the United States and sufficient revenue to pay off the 1908 loan within seven years. For the state's partners in the world of banking and the coffee trade, the operation had also proved financially rewarding. The only outright loser was the American consumer, who bore the brunt of high coffee prices.[70]

By regulating supplies, the policy of valorization brought stability to the coffee trade and averted the damaging effects of massive overproduction. From the Brazilian point of view, valorization was perceived as an undoubted success. The intervention of the United States government was therefore a cause of bitterness and ill feeling. Ironically, both Knox and Müller wished a speedy end to the dispute, but they exercised limited influence over the actions of Wickersham, Sielcken, and the government of São Paulo. The fact that the dispute could not be effectively contained also underlined the absence of the spirit of approximation. Brazilian irritation and obduracy was easily provoked and stung American leaders into a high-handed and unsympathetic response. The crucial voice of conciliation came from Edwin Morgan, who constantly reminded both sides of their mutual desire for friendly relations. Finally, the election of a new American administration presented a welcome opportunity of escape from what was fast becoming a disagreeable and sterile exchange of correspondence.

THE ABC

Despite his preoccupation with the valorization dispute Müller continued to maintain an active interest in South American diplomatic affairs. The initiation of legal action against Sielcken coincided with speeches in Buenos Aires by Campos Sales stressing his country's desire for "approximation" between the ABC powers. As the coffee controversy erupted again in September 1912, ex-Foreign Minister Luís Drago publicly endorsed "the policy of approximation" between Argentina and Brazil.[71] The moral backing of Argentina may have stiffened Müller's resolve, but there is no evidence that he sought that country's support during the dispute with Washington. The foreign minister astutely sought to avoid any implication of dependence on Argentina by stressing his desire for closer relations not only among the ABC nations but also "for the complete alphabet." The United States was not excluded. In an interview with Rubén Darío scheduled for publication in the leading Argentine daily, *La Nación,* Müller even expressed his dissatisfaction with Domício's speech at the Pan-American banquet and stated that Brazil sought a policy of "entente" with all hemispheric nations "beginning with the United States."[72]

Nor did Müller request European assistance. On one occasion he told the British minister, William Haggard, that the United States "had a perfect right" to tax coffee if they so wished. He was not afraid of this "bugbear" because the tax would fall upon the American consumer and not the producer. When the German minister encouraged talk of combined European diplomatic assistance for Brazil, Müller remarked to the French minister that "if the United States were to put pressure on Brazil, neither England, France nor Germany would raise a hand to protect her." In a similar vein, Müller mischievously replied to Haggard's criticism that too much deference was shown to the United States by saying that Brazil was only imitating the attitude accorded by Europe to that country.[73]

Despite these brave words, Haggard believed that the foreign minister had a "dread" of the United States. While Müller did not fully subscribe to Rio Branco's strategy of approximation, the British minister observed that he was surrounded at the Itamaraty by the baron's "retainers."[74] Especially influential was Enéas Martins, who had taken a prominent role in promoting the tariff preferential and now held the newly created post of Under Secretary for Foreign Affairs.[75] Martins assumed virtual administrative control of the Itamaraty as Müller began to detach himself from routine diplomatic business in order to concentrate on his own presidential candidacy. By early 1913 Haggard was complaining that Müller was "a political adventurer" who "rarely receives foreign representatives and appears to know nothing about the various matters presented to him or to take any interest in these."[76]

Part of Müller's campaign strategy included a trip to the United States. He first suggested the idea on assuming the office of foreign minister and ostensibly justified it as a return for Root's attendance at the 1906 Rio conference. In the midst of the valorization dispute, however, the prospect of an official visit attracted little enthusiasm either in Washington or Brazil. The Argentine press warned Müller to beware of appearing to pay "commercial homage."[77] However, as the Brazilian political process moved closer to selecting its presidential nomination for 1914, Haggard described the visit as "a good political move." Such a trip might achieve little of substance, but it would provide a boost to Brazilian morale. "Brazilian vanity is tickled with the idea that their Minister for Foreign Affairs is going to pay a visit to a big country in a big ship," reported the British minister.[78]

The most enthusiastic support for the visit came from Edwin Morgan; he referred to it frequently in his dispatches to Washington. Rio Branco habitually discouraged such invitations and President-elect Hermes da Fonseca had refused to include the United States on his itinerary in 1910. In Morgan's opinion, Müller's proposal presented therefore a rare opportunity for personal contact between Brazilian and American government ministers.[79] The end of the squabble over valorization finally allowed the visit to proceed in late May 1913. Müller sailed for the United States in the *Minas Gerais* and was accompanied by Morgan as far north as Bahia.[80] Arriving at Hampton Roads on June 10, 1913, Müller was met by Secretary of State Bryan. The party traveled to Washington where the foreign minister was given a private meeting with President Wilson at the White House. A brief stay in New York was then followed by an extensive railroad tour of the United States from New York to San Francisco. The final event was a banquet in New York organized appropriately by the coffee merchants and attended by Secretary of State Bryan. On his return home in August Müller spoke in glowing terms of his admiration for the northern republic.[81]

Unfortunately, Müller's political calculations had misfired. During his absence, the political bosses had chosen Venceslau Brás Pereira Gomes of Minas Gerais as the next president. Nevertheless, the visit brought diplomatic benefits and confirmed the improved state of relations between the two countries. If only briefly, Brazil became an object of American public interest. The *New York Times* welcomed its visitor from "the great republic of the South, whose Government and whose general political aims are in substantial harmony with our own."[82] The coverage given by the American press to the tour flattered and soothed Brazilian feelings ruffled by the coffee controversy. Müller was able to meet not only President Wilson and leading politicians but also numerous American bankers and businessmen. Shortly before his departure home he told American journalists: "The isolation of the two great divisions of the American continent, one from the other is not . . . only unnatural, but unwise and absurd."[83]

The attention paid to Müller's visit demonstrated the genuine desire of the Wilson administration to establish closer and more friendly relations with Latin America. A prominent feature of Woodrow Wilson's electoral campaign in 1912 had been the condemnation of Taft's practice of dollar diplomacy. "One of the chief objects of my administration," announced Wilson on becoming president, "will be to cultivate the friendship and deserve the confidence of our sister republics of Central and South America."[84] The choice of the "great commoner," William Jennings Bryan, as secretary of state served to symbolize the commitment to a new and idealistic foreign policy. Bryan made known his desire to promote the cause of international peace by emphasizing the conclusion of arbitration agreements that would settle disputes between nations quickly and amicably. The scheme was intended to be worldwide, but it also fully complemented Wilson's broad vision of a peaceful and prosperous hemisphere in which the spirit of Pan-Americanism would be reaffirmed by a relationship firmly based upon reason and trust.

By nature and background, however, Woodrow Wilson had little personal interest in foreign policy. His priority was the legislative enactment of the domestic program known as the "New Freedom." Müller was welcomed and treated with generous hospitality befitting a visiting statesman, but Latin American affairs were low on the agenda of the new administration. The interest that prevailed in the region during the spring of 1913 arose mainly from the machinations of spoils politics. The Democratic party had been denied the fruits of political victory for 16 years. Despite its proclaimed idealism the Wilson administration faithfully distributed federal jobs, including diplomatic offices, among "deserving Democrats." Of the senior officials appointed to Latin American posts by Taft, only two were retained–Henry Fletcher at Santiago and Edwin Morgan at Rio. This was hardly a tribute to the importance of either Chile or Brazil but to the fact that both men could count on influential supporters in the White House. Morgan was extremely fortunate in being personally known to Colonel House, the president's friend and closest confidant.[85]

The blatant pursuit of spoils politics undermined the morale and expertise of the foreign service.[86] This proved damaging when, contrary to his initial expectations, Woodrow Wilson became dominated and sometimes bemused by a series of intractable diplomatic problems. The first difficulty arose in Mexico, where General Victoriano Huerta had staged a military coup that resulted in the murder of President Francisco Madero in February 1913. Wilson condemned the assassination of the legally elected president and refused to recognize the new military government, which he declared was "stained by blood."[87] The State Department was bypassed as Wilson progressively took personal charge of policy. Frustrated in his efforts to drive Huerta from office, the president's antipathy toward the Mexican general eventually resulted in unilateral American military intervention at Vera Cruz in April 1914.

In marked contrast to the Spanish-American republics, Brazil was traditionally much less critical of forceful American diplomacy in Central America and the Caribbean region. This acceptance was partly explained by the fact that Brazil had little political or economic contact with the area. Consequently, the events culminating in the Mexican Revolution had been of minor concern to the Itamaraty. Indeed, the Brazilian legation at Mexico City had not been permanently established until 1906. The Vera Cruz crisis served, however, to heighten Brazil's diplomatic standing in the hemisphere and gave Lauro Müller an opportunity to confirm his desire for friendly relations with Washington. As the likelihood of war loomed, the United States government requested Brazil to look after its embassy's affairs in Mexico City. Domício da Gama proudly explained that Brazil was chosen because it was the "most important American nation" represented at the Mexican capital.[88] Müller complied with the request and publicly endorsed Wilson's policy by refusing to grant diplomatic recognition to Huerta. In doing so, Müller was rejecting the recommendation of the Brazilian minister at Mexico City, Cardoso de

Oliveira. Adverse comment was also forthcoming from sections of the Brazilian Congress and press, who complained of their government's implicit approval of armed American intervention in the internal affairs of a Latin American state.[89]

Müller effectively allayed criticism by adopting a statesmanlike role. He stressed that his sole aim was to assist the peaceful resolution of a grave hemispheric crisis. While wishing to maintain Brazil's tradition of friendly relations with the United States, the foreign minister was careful to point out that at no time had Brazil consented to the use of force by the United States. It was regrettable that fighting had occurred at Vera Cruz. In fact, the Brazilian government sought to exert a moderating influence upon both the United States and Mexico by joining with Argentina and Chile to propose their joint mediation of the dispute. The implicit abandonment of Brazil's pretensions to a special relationship with the United States was not a cause of concern. Müller described the ABC initiative, not as a criticism of Yankee aggression, but as a sincere and necessary attempt to prevent the Mexican crisis from escalating into a war that would be harmful to all the Americas.[90]

The offer of mediation was speedily accepted by President Wilson. While this reflected his awareness of the influence of the leading South American nations, he was also motivated by personal dismay at the moral consequences of American armed intervention and his surprise at the unfavorable response it had evoked both at home and abroad. The action of the ABC countries served the immediate and useful purpose of restraining any further extension of hostilities, but it did not deflect Wilson from his central objective of driving Huerta from the Mexican presidency. This determination was underlined by Wilson's initial refusal to withdraw American troops from Vera Cruz and his undisguised efforts to manipulate the peace conference held at Niagara Falls in May–June 1914 so as to exert additional diplomatic pressure upon Huerta.[91]

Even though Wilson successfully achieved Huerta's downfall in July 1914, this failed to bring an end to the violent struggle among the various revolutionary factions in Mexico. The president's displeasure was now transferred to the new Mexican leader, Venustiano Carranza; and in an attempt to oust the latter, a second peace conference was scheduled to be held in New York during the late summer of 1915. In addition to the ABC ambassadors, the State Department also extended invitations to the ministers from Bolivia, Uruguay, and Guatemala.[92] Only a year earlier, the United States government had asked Brazil to look after its affairs in Mexico City. Now Brazil had lost that special status and was regarded as simply one of a large group of Latin American countries. Müller was uncertain of the value of the proposed meeting, but he believed it was important that Brazil continue to support American policy for the sake of maintaining collective agreement. This sensible and accommodating approach received a severe jolt between conference sessions when it appeared that Wilson's views had undergone a radical change. Instead of criticizing Carranza, the new secretary of state, Robert Lansing, suddenly began to press for the latter's de facto recognition.

Like Rui Barbosa at The Hague, Domício da Gama openly bridled at the blatant pressure to turn the meeting into a rubber stamp for American policy. The Brazilian ambassador understood the importance of maintaining close relations with the United States, but he worried that the Latin American countries were being treated as "virtual satellites."[93] Seeking to correct this impression, Domício stressed his government's view that the ultimate solution to the Mexican crisis must have the support of the Mexicans themselves and should not be imposed from outside. The sentiments were admirable, but Domício's action threatened to destroy the diplomatic harmony for which he and Müller had been striving so long. Lansing misinterpreted Brazil's spirited show of independence by believing that Domício was "apparently opposed to all the revolutionary factions in Mexico to the extent that he is unwilling to be in any way responsible for the recognition of any of them." A potentially contentious debate was only avoided because of events in Mexico itself where Carranza had already clearly established his military ascendancy over his rivals. Consequently, Domício felt able to join his colleagues and comply with American wishes to recognize Carranza and thereby assist in bringing an end to a turbulent era in Mexican diplomatic history.[94]

The characteristically unilateral style of American diplomacy that annoyed Domício at the New York Peace conference had also been illustrated some months earlier in the reaction to the outbreak of war in Europe. President Wilson's initial proclamations of neutrality in August 1914 inspired similar declarations from the nations of Latin America, including Brazil. The show of unity was deceiving: the American government had made no attempt at prior consultation and during the months that followed showed little sympathy for the Latin American desire for a common policy.[95] However, in formulating his response to the problems posed by the war, Wilson's thoughts were directed by his personal adviser, Colonel House, to the importance of exhibiting hemispheric unity and political cooperation. Particular concern was expressed over reports of German threats to South America and especially to Brazil, which House regarded as apparently "the main object of Germany's desires."[96]

In December 1914 the president's enthusiasm was "excited" by the colonel's proposal to reaffirm the Monroe Doctrine by seeking a Pan-American treaty that would guarantee the political independence and territorial integrity of all the American nations. The concept was typically vague and idealistic. Later Wilson would inform Congress that the nations of the hemisphere were "not hostile rivals but cooperating friends" whose "growing sense of community of interests . . . is likely to give them a new significance as factors in international affairs and in the political history of the world."[97] The diplomatic initiative seemed to imply that the war was stirring the Wilson administration into urging Pan-American solidarity and self-defense. In reality, the desire to exert influence on events in Europe was the primary motivation. House described the treaty to Wilson "as a model for the European nations when peace is at last brought about." Bryan commented revealingly in May 1915: "The sooner we can get this before the public the better, for the influence it may have across the Atlantic."[98]

From the very outset the treaty's progress was hampered by internal American diplomatic rivalries. Wilson retained a close personal interest in the matter and instructed House to begin preliminary discussions. Secretary of State Bryan was not informed until early January 1915. Bryan's own scheme for arbitration agreements was conveniently forgotten. The emphasis on confidentiality was explained by Wilson's desire to go before the Senate only with a completed treaty. For similar practical reasons he also stressed the importance of securing the agreement of the three leading South American powers prior to publicizing the treaty. Initial soundings were therefore deliberately limited to private meetings between House and the ABC ambassadors in Washington. State Department officials were kept in ignorance of events. The American ambassador at Santiago, Henry Fletcher, only learned of the treaty from the Chilean foreign minister.[99]

Late in January 1915 Colonel House left for Europe to offer American mediation in the war. Bryan was therefore given charge of negotiations. It was hardly an enviable task as House continued to exercise a proprietary interest in what he regarded as his own personal project. On his return to the United States in June, House gleefully noted Bryan's failure to make progress. "Mr. Bryan had never done any serious work in his life," he told Wilson.[100] Nor did Bryan's successor, Robert Lansing, escape the colonel's scrutiny. The latter's influence at the White House was such that Lansing anxiously wrote him: "I hope I can see you in a few days in regard to the South American matter, in which the President is so much interested, and concerning which I am not as familiar as I wish I was. I have no doubt that a talk with you would help very much."[101]

The diplomatic impasse was made all the more galling for Bryan and Lansing and frustrating for Wilson because House's proposal had initially enjoyed spectacular success. In December 1914 the colonel had informally sounded out each of the ABC ambassadors and apparently gained their approval. "The President congratulated me warmly upon the day's work and said I had done a consummate piece of business," House proudly recorded in his diary. But American optimism was misplaced. In reality, House had merely elicited from the ABC ambassadors an endorsement of unobjectionable Pan-American aims that they promised to communicate to their foreign offices. The Argentine ambassador had warned that the Chilean government was fearful of external interference in its dispute with Peru over Tacna and Arica. Its studied silence was predictable and effectively prevented House from achieving his aim of quickly "buttoning up" the treaty.[102]

The response of Brazil was much more pleasing. Although House had chosen to visit the Argentine ambassador before seeing Domício, he found the Brazilian "easy of conquest." Indeed, Brazil was the first of the ABC governments to send an official reply agreeing to begin formal discussion of what it flatteringly described as "an epoch making negotiation." The Itamaraty was keen to assist the cause of hemispheric peace and, at the same time, cultivate closer relations with the United States. Nonetheless, although the idea of the Pan-American treaty was welcomed in principle, a certain amount of caution was also expressed. Not surprisingly for a country that bordered all of the South American nations, Brazil later announced various reservations over the proposal to include compulsory time limits for the arbitration of boundary disputes.[103]

An additional complication arose in that the launching of the Pan-American treaty coincided with a similar initiative taken by the ABC countries to devise their own arbitration arrangement independently of the United States. The concerted diplomatic action evident during the mediation of the Mexican crisis had been continued in further consultations about how the three governments should face the common difficulties emerging from the European war. In October 1914 the Chilean minister at Rio and Lauro Müller suggested an agreement to provide for military cooperation by the ABC nations in the event of external aggression. The scheme also included an arrangement to settle disputes that was broadly based on the formula contained in Bryan's arbitration treaties.[104]

Taking advantage of the cancellation of the fifth Pan-American conference, scheduled to be held at Santiago in late 1914, the Chilean government proposed that a meeting of the ABC foreign ministers be organized instead. In 1915 the three diplomats came together first in Buenos Aires and then at Santiago where in May a treaty was signed providing procedures for the investigation and arbitration of disputes. The British minister at Rio observed that the event was "much to the dissatisfaction of Mr. Morgan." In the American press there was speculation that the ABC treaty was directed against the United States, although Bryan dispelled such reports as "absurd."[105]

In fact, Bryan had scrupulously avoided any form of interference so as not to hinder the making of the agreement. He welcomed the treaty as very much in keeping with his own ideas and plans for hemispheric peace and cooperation. "We are sure," he wrote the American chargé in Uruguay, "that Brazil, Argentina and Chile would not enter into any treaty which could by any possibility be construed as antagonistic to the United States or detrimental to any other country in the Western Hemisphere."[106] Moreover, the Chilean government had kept Bryan informed of the ABC treaty from its inception. But Wilson was uneasy and seemed to feel that a conflict of interest might be present. Shortly before the meeting of the foreign ministers at Santiago, he asked Bryan: "Are you fully convinced that there is nothing in the proposed arrangement among the A.B.C. that will stand in the way of or embarrass our own American plan?"[107]

Wilson's apprehension was justified. While the Chilean government actively sought a treaty with its two neighbors, it adopted a negative attitude toward the Pan-American proposal. Desultory discussions continued until 1917, but the Pan-American treaty was effectively doomed by Chilean intransigence and American diplomatic ineptitude. Far from promoting hemispheric unity, House's initiative appeared to have provoked discord. In fact, the British minister at Rio interpreted the meeting of the ABC foreign ministers as a sign of waning American influence. Ambassador Morgan remarked reassuringly, however, that the event had aroused only "a lukewarm interest" in Brazil. In Morgan's opinion, Müller regarded it as primarily a public relations exercise designed to enhance his own presidential ambitions.[108] This assessment was confirmed later when the ABC treaty failed to secure ratification by both Brazilian and Argentine legislatures. Nevertheless, the growing unpopularity provoked throughout Latin America by Wilson's meddling in the affairs of Mexico and the Caribbean encouraged a belief that the ABC treaty was designed to oppose American aggression. Müller disavowed any such intention. His friendship for the United States had been underlined by his visit to that country and his support for American policy during the Mexican crisis. However, his adherence to the ABC agreement while at the same time tacitly consenting to Chile's efforts to hold up the progress of the Pan-American treaty indicated Brazil's capacity for independent diplomatic maneuver and the desire for closer relations with its South American neighbors. Keeping on friendly terms with the complete alphabet of nations was an admirable aim, but it proved more and more impossible as the impact of the world war stimulated the rise of conflicting national self-interests.

THE RESPONSE TO WORLD WAR

The attempt to conclude arbitration arrangements was influenced and eventually overshadowed by the impact of the European war. Initially, all the countries of the Western Hemisphere sought to avoid involvement in the conflict. Indeed, the crisis elevated the importance of Pan-American solidarity and thereby tested Wilson's proclaimed intention to cultivate more cooperative relations with Latin America. "The sentiment," noted Bryan in December 1914, "is unanimous among the South American countries that something ought to be done to protect the neutral nations if the war is to continue." But Latin American suggestions that the president call a conference of neutral nations at Washington were dismissed by State Department officials as "undesirable and inexpedient."[109] In characteristic fashion, the declaration of neutrality by the United States government in August 1914 had been a unilateral act. Until 1917, Wilson proved unwilling to provide the positive leadership that would facilitate the formulation of a common hemispheric policy. The period of neutrality was therefore marked largely by diplomatic indecision and confusion.

The economic dislocation caused by the war provided, however, a signal opportunity for the extension of United States commercial influence throughout Latin America. Secretary of the Treasury William McAdoo was enthusiastic about the opportunity: "The South Americans were like the customers of a store that has burned down, they were looking around for a place to spend their money."[110] Already alarmed by the likelihood of a severe contraction of trade with Europe, the Wilson administration was eager to support the search for alternative markets in Latin America. A sense of common purpose infused the activities of businessmen, politicians and government officials. It had taken more than a year to complete arrangements for the 1889 Washington conference. In marked contrast, less than two months after the passage of its congressional appropriation the Pan-American Financial conference speedily assembled at Washington in May 1915. A product of the initiative and energy of McAdoo, the meeting brought together diplomats, finance ministers, and businessmen.[111]

The "rediscovery" of Latin America was accompanied by a rehashing of the usual commercial arguments. On account of its large population and geographical proximity, Brazil was once again acclaimed as a particularly enticing market. It was important also to take full advantage of Europe's commercial disarray. Indeed, the sudden shortage of European goods gave American merchants a competitive advantage that made redundant the diplomatic strategy of seeking preferential tariff treatment. Ambassador Morgan viewed the outbreak of war as a "propitious" moment for Americans to increase their exports to Brazil and thereby reduce the long-standing trade imbalance. In April 1915 the British minister at Rio reported that "the United States are making great efforts." He jealously noted the frequent arrival of commercial missions, the opening of an American branch bank in the capital, and the proposal to establish a direct steamship line with New York.[112]

The challenge to Britain's economic influence was most vividly illustrated by the coal trade. Prior to 1914 Brazil was dependent upon British imports. The impact of war brought about a complete reversal of market share so that by 1916 American sales of coal were four times those from Britain.[113] But American economic advances in other products were much more modest. Indeed, despite the enthusiastic commercial rhetoric, the existing pattern of economic relations was not radically altered. While the amount of Brazilian exports to the United States held up fairly steadily throughout the period of neutrality, the value of American exports to Brazil actually declined from 1913 to 1916.[114] The resulting sense of frustration and disappointment produced the familiar complaint that American exports were unfairly hampered by Brazil's tariff restrictions.[115]

What militated most against a sustained boom in trade and investment was not so much Brazilian protectionist attitudes but the lack of American shipping and credit facilities.[116] Moreover, in the particular case of Brazil, American commercial optimism was soon tempered by the realization that the country was experiencing a period of general financial instability. "Brazil is passing through a crisis," noted the London *Times* in March 1914, "of which it is not easy yet to see the outcome." Morgan stressed the need for cuts in government expenditure, warning, "or national bankruptcy will follow." Earlier he had reported the continued fall in price of Brazil's staple exports, and he predicted that "the present credit crisis will grow disastrous" unless a "large foreign loan" was soon forthcoming.[117]

The outbreak of war in Europe savagely compounded the existing financial disorder in Brazil by shutting off the traditional source of foreign capital. The urgently needed loan that had been confidently anticipated in July 1914 was shelved. In addition the federal deficit was further increased by the contraction of trade with Europe caused by the growing shortage of merchant shipping. Moreover, British naval power gradually curtailed economic contact with the Central Powers of Germany and Austria, thus depriving Brazil of its second largest coffee market. As the war continued, further obstacles were placed in the way of trade by the imposition of Allied wartime regulations prohibiting British and French commercial dealings with allegedly pro-German Brazilian firms. The result was a drastic decline in Brazilian exports from £65 million in 1913 to £46 million in 1914. The collapse of the import trade was even more striking. "Never before, not even during the worst period of the previous great crisis in 1901," remarked the British consul-general at Rio, "has the value of imports into this country fallen so low as at the present time." Business revived in 1915, owing to increased Allied orders, but it was not until the postwar boom of 1919 that total Brazilian overseas trade recovered to its 1913 levels.[118]

American merchants wished to sell, but Brazilians lacked the funds to buy. While Morgan called on his countrymen to seize economic opportunities, he also warned that they "should use the utmost caution in granting credits." Brazil remained on the verge of bankruptcy until 1916 at which time, impressed by the success of the federal government's policy of financial retrenchment, Morgan became more optimistic and began to urge American bankers to invest in Brazil. In particular, he strongly recommended that the American International Corporation accede to a request from the minister of finance for a $25 million loan to the Brazilian government. Such a loan would free Brazil from its traditional dependence upon Europe; Morgan argued persuasively that it "would have important political consequences, would consolidate American influence, and would place her under obligation to us." Despite State Department lobbying in favor of the loan, American bankers were not swayed by political arguments and declined the proposal "on account of existing economic conditions." The American International Corporation was more interested in investing in Belgium and Russia.[119] Economic opportunities undoubtedly existed in Brazil, but the market was new and relatively unknown. The frequent reports of political and economic instability merely reinforced American financial conservatism and caution. One American visitor described American investment as "timid" and concluded that "North America has done remarkably little for Brazil."[120]

Ironically, the information services of the State Department and especially the Commerce Department ensured that American businessmen had never been better informed about commercial opportunities in Brazil. Morgan expressed concern, however, that Americans still displayed widespread ignorance of Brazilian ways of doing business. Shortcomings were evident at all levels of economic activity. Noting that "a medical man and a New England lawyer" had been sent to Brazil as agents of the American International Corporation, the ambassador pointed out that neither "has experience in international finance nor shows much capacity for it."[121] A similar criticism was made by the Brazilian delegate at the Pan-American Financial conference. Amaro Cavalcanti acknowledged and welcomed the enthusiastic interest of American businessmen, but he also stated that they possessed " a very confused idea of trade and commerce in Brazil."[122] Moreover, the personal quality of their northern visitors was frequently a matter of adverse comment in Brazil itself. The American consul-general at Rio, Alfred Gottschalk, echoed this complaint when he observed that the representatives of the National City Bank "have been childishly unfit for any work of representation on foreign soil" and that their behavior had "at times offended people here."[123]

The passage of the 1913 Federal Reserve Act permitted American banks to establish overseas branches for the first time. Although the National City Bank of New York had opened three offices in Brazil by 1915, the bank's first branch in Latin America was located in Buenos Aires and not Rio.[124] Indeed, it seemed that American economic and diplomatic efforts were directed more and more to Argentina than to Brazil. The latter's special diplomatic status at Washington was ended in 1914 when relations between the United States and Argentina were upgraded to ambassadorial level. It soon became evident that the Argentine ambassador, Rómulo S. Naón, enjoyed greater personal influence with the Wilson administration than did Domício da Gama. "He is one of our most devoted friends," Bryan informed Wilson about the Argentine, "and no one is more interested in everything that concerns Pan-America."[125] It was therefore no coincidence that Naón was the first of the Latin American ambassadors to be approached by House in the matter of the Pan-American treaty. A further indication of Argentina's importance was the choice made by the Pan-American Financial conference to establish the new International High Commission at Buenos Aires. In contrast to Root in 1906, McAdoo made the Argentine capital his main stop on his official journey to attend the first meeting of the commission in 1916. Indeed, American trade had expanded so rapidly with Argentina that by 1917 the United States was not only selling more to Argentina but also importing more from that country than from Brazil.[126]

The financial prosperity of Argentina was galling to Brazil, but it was not a subject of concern at the Itamaraty. Although the war stimulated closer commercial contact between Latin America and the United States, the diplomatic consequences were much harder to evaluate. The Latin American nations showed no desire to become embroiled in the European conflict and looked to the United States to direct the defense of neutral rights during time of war. President Wilson publicly championed these rights, but, in practice, took little account of Latin American views in his own discussions with the Allies and the Central Powers. As the role of the world's peacemaker came to absorb the president's attention, the various suggestions for inter-American action made from time to time by Latin American statesmen were either politely rejected or studiously ignored.[127] With the exception of the controversial Pan-American treaty, Wilson appeared indifferent to South American affairs and left those nations to evolve their own policies toward the war.[128]

Consequently, there was minimal diplomatic consultation and cooperation between Brazil and the United States. This lack of interaction was surprising as both hemispheric giants faced virtually identical problems and formulated very similar responses. Not unlike opinion in the United States, the Brazilian elite had reacted with shock and sadness to the dramatic train of events in Europe. "The general public in Brazil," the British consul, Ernest Hambloch, later summed up, "had no defined views on the rights and wrongs of the questions which suddenly plunged Europe into war in August 1914."[129] Brazilian politicians preferred to concentrate their attention on the inauguration of a new presidential administration and the celebration of the republic's first quarter-century. Unfortunately, the war was not the brief affair that contemporaries expected. The conflict could not be limited to the battlefields of continental Europe and soon spread to the oceans of the world. By its possession of a vast seaboard, a large merchant marine and international trading interests, Brazil could not therefore escape diplomatic involvement.

Within days of the outbreak of war in Europe, the Brazilian government declared a policy of neutrality and nonintervention and closed its ports to the warships of the belligerent nations. The action was strikingly similar to that taken by the Wilson administration, but it was not done at American bidding or prompting. Although Brazil claimed to pursue an independent course of action, military weakness dictated that it could hardly do otherwise than follow the example of the United States. In contrast to the latter, however, Brazil did not feel completely secure from aggression by the belligerent powers. After the holding of military maneuvers in 1916, Morgan concluded that the Brazilian army was "in serious need of instruction" and was inferior to those of Argentina and Chile.[130] It was widely acknowledged that the navy was scarcely better prepared. "The Brazilian Government is apprehensive lest it may be unable to maintain the neutrality of its waters," reported Morgan.[131] Moreover, the election of Venceslau Brás meant that Brazil faced the world crisis with a new head of government whom Morgan initially considered "of mediocre ability and of inconspicuous public service."[132] The fact that Müller was unexpectedly retained as foreign minister suggested that Venceslau would maintain the continuity of foreign policy. In reality, however, the open rivalry between the president and foreign minister introduced further uncertainty into the conduct of diplomacy.

By its very nature the pursuit of a truly neutral policy was inherently difficult. Brazil had long enjoyed a close relationship with Britain and France, but relations with Germany were also extremely cordial at the beginning of the war. Trade with the latter had grown considerably during the preceding quarter-century, so much so that Hamburg ranked second only to New York in its share of the Brazilian coffee trade. President-elect Hermes da Fonseca accompanied by Lauro Müller had been favorably impressed during an official visit to Germany in 1910. Hermes later made no secret of his interest in appointing a German military mission to instruct the Brazilian army.[133] Moreover, Müller's own political prominence pointed to the success of the German immigrant community in Brazil. There were several hundred thousand people of German extraction, mostly located in southern Brazil, and their power to threaten rebellion or even declare their independence was not discounted by politicians in Rio.[134] Furthermore, almost two million bags of valorized coffee originating from São Paulo were stored in German ports at the beginning of the war. The sale of this coffee was quickly completed, but the proceeds amounting to £6 million were held by the Bleischroeder bank of Berlin. The release of this money became a preoccupation of Brazilian diplomacy and provided a powerful argument for adopting a circumspect and conciliatory attitude toward Germany.[135]

The German cause was also assisted by Brazilian annoyance over the maritime restrictions imposed by the Allies. The right of search claimed by the British navy, and the introduction of the "black list" prohibiting trade with suspected "German" companies, were particularly resented.[136] However, with the notable exception of Dunshee de Abranches, few Brazilian writers were openly sympathetic to Germany.[137] Although Brazilian opinion was perplexed as to the reason for the fighting in Europe, it felt outrage at the German invasion of Belgium. This unprovoked and callous attack upon the sovereignty of a neutral nation was regarded as indefensible. No country, not even Brazil, could feel safe from German aggression. Moreover, the image of German barbarism was reinforced in the Brazilian mind by British and French propaganda. Effectively exploiting their control of telegraphic communication from Europe, the Allies assiduously disseminated accounts of German atrocities against civilians. "The prospect of German domination was not, of course, liked, and no one wished to see Germany become the sole arbiter of the destinies of the world," remarked the British minister at Rio, "consequently, sympathy with the Allies grew stronger as every month passed by."[138]

In fact, from the outset of the war it was evident that the mass of Brazilians sympathized with the Allies and especially with France. "Brazil is a latin country with a great admiration and friendship for France," noted a British report, "and this is at the root of her partiality."[139] Historical and cultural ties with Europe were also stirred by the entry of Italy into the war on the Allied side in May 1915. Less than a year later the similar decision by Portugal had an even greater impact. In fact, public sentiment in favor of the Allies was more marked in Brazil than the United States and was energetically promoted by the League for the Allies founded as early as March 1915. The league's president and most prominent spokesman was Rui Barbosa; in the same way that he had gained the world's attention at The Hague in 1907, Rui once again preached the rights of small nations and the sanctity of international agreements. Condemning the argument that the strong should dominate the weak, he declared that the neutral nations, and especially President Wilson, had made a serious error in not vigorously denouncing German ruthlessness:

> None can be an indifferent spectator in this world-tragedy. Neutrality entails obligations. Between those who destroy the law and those who uphold it, neutrality is not permissible. Neutrality does not mean impassibility; it means impartiality between right and justice on the one hand and crime on the other. To demand the observance of these precepts on which the conscience of nations reposes, to demand respect for treaties is not to break neutrality but to respect it.[140]

Rui therefore rejected the example of neutrality set by the United States. The logic of his argument was that Brazil should enter the war on the side of the Allies. This was a view that was gaining support, but it also provoked influential nationalist critics such as Alberto Tôrres and Oliveira Lima, who feared that joining the conflict would only increase the nation's dependence on the foreign powers. Within the Venceslau administration, indecision reigned. When a Brazilian merchant ship, the *Rio Branco,* was sunk by a German submarine in May 1916, the government lodged a firm protest and received a conciliatory reply from Berlin. The image of German reasonableness was further reinforced by that government's active propaganda emphasizing the illegality and ulterior motive of British commercial regulations such as the "black list."[141]

Brazil's quandary over the issue of maritime rights aroused little interest from the Wilson administration. In April 1916, Lansing politely declined Müller's suggestion that the leading American nations meet at Washington to discuss how to respond to the threat of submarine warfare.[142] Wilson privately made known his opposition to a conference that included only the United States and the ABC. On the other hand, he refused to countenance a larger meeting in which the United States possessed only one vote out of twenty. This refusal was purported not to arise from selfish national interest; Wilson explained that the other nations would be motivated by "national considerations," but America's vote would be cast "in the interest of mankind." In the president's opinion, "on this side of the water, we are the only nation that has this position of independence of judgment and of interest."[143]

It was recognized, however, that Brazil might contribute to the cause of world peace by using its diplomatic influence to persuade Chile to sign the Pan-American treaty. "Chile and Brazil have always walked hand in hand," observed Fletcher. When Brazil appeared to hesitate, Lansing suspected that German influence was at work.[144] Ambassador Morgan, however, was dismissive of the effects of German propaganda. Despite Müller's allegedly pro-German bias, Morgan never doubted that the foreign minister was friendly to American interests. A markedly different view was taken of Rui's activities, which Morgan believed were an embarrassment to the Brazilian government. "The Brazilians have an emotional nature," he commented, "and are readily affected by oratory, as are most men of the Latin race." According to Morgan, the "more thoughtful Brazilians" fully agreed with the "just and wise" policy of neutrality pursued by the Venceslau administration.[145] The British minister at Rio, Arthur Peel, regarded Morgan's views as "unsatisfactory" and implied a more sinister explanation for his colleague's behavior: "Whatever his opinions may be, he certainly never responded to the general desire of his countrymen to associate himself with the Allies. In fact before the United States declared war on Germany, his attitude was so singularly neutral that he was strongly suspected by them of being pro-German in sympathy."[146]

The ambiguity surrounding Morgan arose from his being thoroughly pro-American in his attitudes and policies. He approved Brazil's neutral course because it accorded with that pursued by his own government. What concerned Morgan most was not so much the intricacies of wartime diplomacy but the international struggle for economic preeminence in Brazil. The war gave Americans a tremendous opportunity to extend their influence in Brazil at the expense of the European powers. Gains had been made, but these were placed in jeopardy by the efforts of politicians such as Rui who advocated active support for the Allies. In his report on Rui's speeches, the war became a marginal issue as Morgan anxiously observed the decision of the French government to move its legation from Petrópolis to Rio and to buy propaganda space in the *Carioca* press.[147]

Morgan's enigmatic attitude may also have reflected his lack of personal influence with the leading members of the Wilson administration. In contrast to Henry Fletcher, Morgan was excluded from an active role in the negotiations over the Pan-American treaty. On occasion, communications became badly tangled. When Müller took sick leave in May 1916, Morgan gratifyingly reported that the foreign minister would make a private visit to the hot springs of French Lick, Indiana. Consul-General Gottschalk speculated, however, that Müller saw the trip as an electioneering exercise and hoped to negotiate a substantial American loan. The Latin American Division was puzzled. Gottschalk's information was discounted on the grounds that it had not been corroborated by Morgan.[148] But White House officials were under the very different impression that Müller's purpose in coming to the United States was to sign the Pan-American treaty. The origin of this belief seems to have come not from Brazilian or American diplomatic sources but via the Argentine ambassador, Rómulo Naón.[149] Domício learned of the rumor from his Chilean colleague and decided not to ask for confirmation from the State Department because this would reveal his own ignorance of the matter.[150] When Müller arrived in July he dismayed American officials by remaining noncommittal about the treaty.[151] Not for the first time, the diplomatic skill of the White House was brought into question, and its optimism was proved to have been seriously misplaced.

The deviation from normal diplomatic channels meant that American officials were not aware that Müller's negative attitude reflected his declining influence within the Venceslau administration.[152] The foreign minister's German ancestry had changed from a possible advantage to an increasing liability as it became evident that his conciliatory policy toward Germany had conspicuously failed to persuade that government to release the coffee money owed to the state of São Paulo. Indeed, the tide of opinion in Brazil was clearly running in favor of the Allied cause and against Germany. On Müller's return from the United States, British dispatches from Rio observed a marked change of official mood and attributed this to the growing awareness that the war might shortly end in an Allied victory. Initially, Brazilian leaders had been awed by the success of the German military machine. But the effective resistance of the

Allies to the German advance in France pointed the way to a realization that Germany might not be victorious after all. A new concern arose as to how neutral nations such as Brazil would be treated in the postwar world. It was feared that the victorious Allies might react to what they perceived as a lack of support during the war to justify a denial of capital and trade, thereby placing neutral countries in a position of "economic isolation."[153] The United States was rarely mentioned in this unfolding debate. Except for the customary show of public courtesy, Brazilians reacted to Wilson's reelection in 1916 with indifference. Some weeks later Wilson remarked that Argentina was "the only one of the A.B.C. Powers working cordially with us."[154] The traditional Brazilian attachment to Europe was evidently reasserting itself. By failing to provide positive hemispheric leadership, the United States stood to lose the economic gains it had made in Brazil during the period of neutrality.

WARTIME ALLIES

Events in Europe took a dramatic turn in January 1917 when the German government declared its intention of enforcing unrestricted submarine warfare in the war zone around the British Isles. This ultimatum signified the withdrawal of Germany's pledge to allow the safe passage of unarmed merchant ships from neutral nations. The nations of Latin America reacted with apprehension and naturally feared for the continuance of their commerce with Europe. Should the United States be drawn into the war, the economic consequences were likely to be catastrophic. Domício da Gama alarmingly observed that "a war in American waters" would entail "complete paralyzation of our external trade."[155] The whole of Latin America anxiously awaited Woodrow Wilson's response to the submarine threat.

The Latin American governments, however, were spectators rather than participants in Wilson's agonizing reappraisal of American policy. It was a role to which they were long accustomed. In his efforts to mediate the war, Wilson had preferred to deal directly with the European belligerents. Domício summed up that the president's mediation efforts were "sympathetically humane, though still perhaps impracticable."[156] His description reflected the detached attitude that most Latin American diplomats had adopted toward a peace process from which they were effectively excluded. But complacency turned to concern when the submarine controversy erupted. Led by Naón, the Latin American representatives at Washington lobbied for the maintenance of "continental solidarity." Domício joined this effort and informed Lansing that Brazil hoped "the United States will not leave the ranks of the neutrals."[157]

On February 3 Wilson decided to break off diplomatic relations with Germany. Hoping that the Latin American nations would follow suit, American officials suddenly showed a new interest in the attitude of their southern neighbors toward the war. The views of Brazil quickly acquired considerable importance and received regular coverage in the New York press. Shortly after the rupture of relations with Germany, a headline in the *New York Tribune* asserted that "Brazil will back U.S. to the limit."[158] The American chargé at Rio, Alexander Benson, confirmed Brazil's support for American policy, but he also reported Müller's statement that "Pan America must stand together." In fact, the foreign minister was known to be conducting separate discussions with "certain South American powers."[159] This later transpired to be connected with the proposal made by Argentine President Irigoyen to hold a peace conference of Latin American nations at Buenos Aires. American officials regarded this idea with considerable suspicion and were no doubt relieved to learn that Brazil was unlikely to attend.[160]

Nonetheless, Brazil had declined to follow America's lead even though Müller realized that the United States and Germany were inexorably moving to war.[161] Prevarication was understandable in the circumstances, but action could not be deferred indefinitely; the German declaration of unrestricted submarine warfare directly challenged Brazil's own sovereignty and threatened to close off all trade with Europe. The required official reply was delivered on February 9. Reiterating the protest lodged the previous year during the *Rio Branco* incident, the Brazilian government announced that it would hold Germany responsible "for all events which may happen to Brazilian citizens, merchandise or ships as a result of the abandonment of the principles recognized by international law, or by the conventions to which Brazil and Germany are parties." There was some local press criticism that the note was too mild, but the onus was now clearly placed on Berlin.[162] For almost two months the policy of moderation appeared to be vindicated. However, the fateful crisis occurred on April 5, 1917, when the *Paraná*, a Brazilian freighter loaded with coffee, was sunk without warning by a German submarine off the coast of France.

Anti-German demonstrations immediately erupted in Brazil, and there were demands from the League for the Allies for a declaration of war.[163] Despite the evident public anger against Germany, Müller hoped that a warning to Berlin would suffice and that drastic retaliatory measures might be avoided. What made the continuance of a moderate policy impossible was not so much the ugly mood of public opinion but the impact of decisions already taken in London and Washington. For some weeks before the sinking of the *Paraná*, Brazilian leaders had been reeling from the shock caused by Britain's announcement of an embargo on coffee imports. The specter of economic disaster came even closer on April 6 when the United States Congress recognized a state of war with Germany. The submarine crisis therefore became part of a wider Brazilian anxiety over the future of the coffee industry and the desire to prevent the American war effort from monopolizing scarce economic resources such as ships, coal, and wheat. Without ships there could be no foreign trade. Supplies of coal were crucial to operate railways, steamships and factories. Shortages of wheat would stimulate inflation and provoke social unrest.

In a mood of panic mixed with opportunism, Brazilian diplomacy turned to the United States and revived the strategy of approximation. The importance of close commercial relations between the two countries was vigorously reaffirmed. Particular emphasis was placed on Brazil's need for increased supplies of coal, wheat, and merchant shipping. In return, Brazilian officials indicated their country's willingness to step up its export of strategic materials such as manganese to the United States.[164] A further inducement was offered on April 7 when Domício startled the State Department with the announcement that his government was prepared to sign the Pan-American treaty.[165] On April 11 the Brazilian government broke off diplomatic relations with Germany. It seemed that Brazil was faithfully following the American lead. "It was only when the United States resolved to oppose the German submarine menace and appealed to all the states on this continent for solidarity," remarked the British minister at Rio, "that Brazil took the step of venturing to hold Germany responsible for any infraction of her sovereign rights."[166]

In fact, Brazil's diplomatic initiative enjoyed only minimal success. State Department officials acknowledged "the very friendly attitude of Brazil."[167] They were eager to secure supplies of Brazilian manganese, but were reluctant to discuss other substantive economic issues.[168] Most diplomatic attention was directed instead to the Pan-American treaty, largely because of Wilson's personal interest in the matter. Ironically, the president's inclination "to go forward" was hardly designed to satisfy Brazil's diplomatic or commercial aims. Since German influence was held to be stronger in Brazil than anywhere else in Latin America, Wilson believed that Brazil's adhesion to the treaty would deal a severe blow to German prestige. Similarly, relations with Brazil were very far from the president's mind when he observed that the signing of the treaty at this juncture "might turn out to be the psychological moment" to exert maximum impact upon the Europeans in favor of peace.[169]

However, White House enthusiasm for a speedy conclusion of the treaty was once again frustrated by internal bureaucratic rivalry. Secretary of State Lansing expressed concern that precipitate action would lead to embarrassing diplomatic difficulties with other Latin American nations, especially Argentina and Mexico. Wilson replied curtly that he "would be very much obliged" if Lansing would expedite negotiations "as promptly as possible."[170] What might have become an awkward matter between Wilson and Lansing was rendered academic by the unexpected presentation of an additional Brazilian protocol to the proposed treaty. The Brazilian government wished to uphold the sovereign rights of the signatories by stipulating that intervention to enforce the treaty would only take place after a formal request had been made. A disappointed Wilson termed this "a virtual repudiation of the Monroe Doctrine." In effect, the president was affirming that the United States refused to recognize the Latin American nations as equal partners. Unintentionally, Brazil had exposed the flaw that had frustrated the scheme from its very inception.[171]

State Department officials, however, were not unhappy to see the demise of the Pan-American treaty. The question of more immediate importance for them was whether Brazil would join the war. By doing so, Brazil would help to defend the principle of neutral rights for which the United States was fighting and would also provide a decisive example for the other Latin American countries to follow.[172] Although there were frequent reports in the American press that Brazil was on the point of declaring a state of war with Germany,[173] the attitude of the Brazilian government remained enigmatic. The breaking of diplomatic relations on April 11 had been followed two days later by the assumption of protective custody over the 43 German ships interned in Brazilian ports since August 1914. On the other hand, the German minister was allowed to depart from his post in leisurely fashion. Even more puzzling was the proclamation on April 25 of Brazilian neutrality in the war between the United States and Germany. This measure prohibited the warships of both belligerents from using Brazilian harbors.[174]

Beset by political, economic, and diplomatic crisis, confusion reigned in Rio. As the tide of anti-German sentiment increased, it was evident that Lauro Müller could not long hold on to office. The American chargé, Alexander Benson, complained of "the most astonishing delays" in transacting diplomatic business. He judged the Itamaraty to be in "a state of utter demoralization," which he attributed to the "selfish, shifty and utterly unscrupulous" foreign minister. Müller's intrigues and pro-German sympathies were not the only reason for Brazil's lack of diplomatic resolution. The American chargé was also critical of the indecisiveness of President Venceslau Brás. Instead of the hoped-for speech in favor of belligerency, Benson was disappointed to report the delivery of the president's "quite colorless" message at the opening of Congress in early May.[175]

Just at that moment, however, events took a decisive turn when Müller suddenly resigned on May 3.[176] His successor, Nilo Peçanha, was described by Benson as "strongly pro-Ally" and an advocate of "Brazilian approximation towards the United States."[177] Domício was instructed to renew his efforts to obtain guarantees of American economic and political support. Lansing was amenable. "My own view," he informed Wilson, "is that it would have a decided influence on Argentina and Chile if Brazil declared war, as it would on other American Republics."[178] Specific guarantees were not forthcoming, but Domício was able to telegraph assurances on May 18 that the United States would "stand by" Brazil.[179] The timing was propitious: five days later, news reached Rio of the sinking of the steamer *Tijuca* by a German submarine off the coast of Brittany. On June 1 the Brazilian Congress revoked Brazil's state of neutrality in the war between the United States and Germany.

The revocation of the neutrality proclamation allowed American war-ships—but not those of Germany—extended use of Brazilian harbors. As a re-sult, the United States South Atlantic squadron, consisting of four armored cruisers under the command of Admiral William B. Caperton, was dispatched to Brazilian waters.[180] The local excitement aroused first in Bahia and then at Rio by Admiral Caperton's June visit encouraged hopes in Washington that Brazil would soon formally declare war on Germany and thereby set an ex-ample to the uncommitted South American nations, especially Argentina and Chile. The *New York Tribune* observed that "Brazilian diplomacy is at work among the Latin-American republics, promoting the spirit of American unity and heartily seconding the course taken by the United States in its war with Germany."[181]

The optimistic American mood was reminiscent of the early stages of the abortive Pan-American treaty. However, beyond its obvious public relations value, the exact role to be undertaken by Brazil in the war effort was unclear. Shortly after taking office as foreign minister, Nilo Peçanha informed Benson that his country "was not in a position to take any active part in the war."[182] When interviewed by the American press in April, Edwin Morgan stressed that Brazil's greatest contribution would be a moral one, and he cited "her sense of international justice and right" and "sympathy for the underlying prin-ciples upon which humanity and civilizations are founded."[183] At the British Foreign Office a harsher realism was applied. "Brazil can render us best naval service by adopting general attitude of friendliness," stated one report in July 1917 and concluded that, "on the whole, it would be preferable that Brazil should not enter state of war with Central Powers."[184]

In fact, participating in the war was not the uppermost question in the minds of Brazilian leaders during the winter of 1917. The inadequacy of the army and navy to undertake overseas missions was freely acknowledged. The presence of Caperton's squadron was gladly welcomed because it provided protection against German naval raids in the South Atlantic and possible plots inspired by pro-German or Argentine factions in southern Brazil. Released from immediate military anxieties, the Brazilian government concentrated its atten-tion on reaching advantageous economic arrangements not only with the United States but also with Britain and France. The evenhanded approach was exem-plified on June 29, when Brazil revoked its state of neutrality in respect of the Allied powers.[185]

The war stimulated Brazilian exports of foodstuffs and raw materials such as sugar, beans, dried meat, and manganese. But the overriding priority re-mained the selling of coffee while securing supplies of coal. It was hardly a position of economic strength. Brazil desperately needed coal for the smooth running of its railways and factories. On the other hand, there was a world-wide glut of coffee. The expectation of a bumper coffee crop in 1917–1918 had already prompted the revival of a valorization scheme to assist the planters of São Paulo. The stark reality was that coffee was a luxury product whose demand had been drastically reduced by the war. For example, the British government justified its embargo on the ground that it possessed stocks equivalent to more than five years of normal consumption.[186]

A new factor emerged, however, to tilt the economic balance toward Brazil. At the beginning of the war Brazil had interned 43 German ships then in Brazilian ports. Despite the desperate wartime shortage of merchant shipping, the ships were left unmolested, in order not to provoke Germany into aggressive measures. Another consideration was the desire to safeguard the proceeds from Brazilian coffee sales that remained frozen in German banks. After the break of diplomatic relations in April 1917, the ships were taken into protective custody. There was some fear of German retaliatory measures, but this proved groundless. Comforted by assurances of American diplomatic support, the Brazilian government formally requisitioned the ships on June 1 and thereby finally came into possession of a valuable asset.

As early as May 1917 Morgan had suggested that the United States offer to buy the ships. He believed that such timely action would have "great persuasive force" in overcoming the hesitation of the Venceslau administration to join the war.[187] But the opportunity was allowed to pass. The matter fell into abeyance as the Brazilian government spent the following weeks debating whether the ships should be incorporated into Brazil's own merchant fleet or leased to a foreign power. During August, negotiations were commenced with several governments including Britain, France, Belgium, Italy, and the United States. Brazil was flattered by the high degree of interest and perceived an opportunity to dispose of surplus coffee stocks and acquire valuable foreign exchange. The determination to exact a high price provoked complaints of Brazilian selfishness. Only France was willing to contemplate a deal that involved a substantial cash payment plus the purchase of at least two million bags of coffee.[188]

In Morgan's opinion, the issue involved much more than maritime transportation. He wrote in October 1917: "The influence on Brazil of the United States during the war would be consolidated if we should unite with her in the employment of German shipping. Whatever power does so will obtain a dominating position."[189] The State Department was "keenly interested" in acquiring the ships for use by the United States, but was not prepared to negotiate on Brazil's terms. From the vantage point of Washington, the pressing need was not the battle for international prestige in Brazil but utilizing the ships in the transatlantic trade as soon as possible. If France could achieve this, the United States would not object. In fact, State Department officials were embarrassingly handicapped by having given an initial disclaimer of interest when the matter was first raised in Washington by the French ambassador. Moreover, the chief officers of the United States Shipping Board had informed the ambassador that they also had no objection to the ships going to France. Tied by these statements, there was no recourse but to instruct Morgan to allow the French negotiators a virtually free field.[190]

A more pleasing development for American officials was Brazil's recognition on October 26, 1917, that a state of war existed with Germany. For some months the Wilson administration had sought just this outcome, but the decision was not the direct result of American pressure. When diplomatic relations were broken with Germany in April Morgan had pointed out that this was not a simple imitation of the example of the United States. "She did not follow because we led," he stated, "her senses were shocked by German procedure just as ours were."[191] Similarly, the declaration of belligerency in October came three days after a German submarine had sunk the Brazilian steamer, *Macao,* off the coast of Spain. In his message to Congress, President Venceslau Brás declared that Brazil must act "in order to maintain the dignity of the nation." Joining the war simply affirmed the nation's traditional principles of respect for the sanctity of treaties and neutral rights.[192]

Brazilian sovereignty was also underlined by the fact that it became a cobelligerent and not a formal ally of the United States. Nonetheless, Brazil's course of action contrasted markedly with that of Argentina, who preferred to maintain normal diplomatic relations with Germany and continued to pursue the idea of hosting a Latin American peace conference from which belligerent powers such as the United States would be pointedly excluded. Brazil's cool response to the Argentine initiative and later its decision to go to war effectively sabotaged the conference and consequently rekindled the traditional suspicion and rivalry between the two countries. For a decade Rio Branco and Müller had sought closer diplomatic cooperation with Argentina. The process had culminated in the signing of the ABC treaty in 1915. This particular strategy was now abandoned. With the apparent blessing of the United States, Brazil renewed its claim to be the leader and spokesman of South America. "It was her proud boast," observed the British minister at Rio, "that she was the first among the Latin American republics to support the United States."[193]

While this was no doubt flattering to Brazilians, it was not exactly in accordance with the objectives of American policy. Officials in Washington were disturbed by Argentina's attitude and were not unhappy to see the gradual demise of the proposed peace conference. But there was no intention to punish or to isolate Argentina. The Wilson administration wished to bring in as many of the South American nations into the war as possible and thereby present "a solid front against the autocratic Government of the Kaiser."[194] Brazil was important, but so was Argentina. The significance attached by Washington to the latter was illustrated by the sending of Caperton's squadron south to Buenos Aires in July 1917 and the calculated publication of the "Luxburg Letters" in September.[195]

In believing that Brazil's action would be imitated by Argentina and Chile, American officials revealed a characteristic misunderstanding of South American politics. Far from promoting unity, Brazil's decision to join the war only provoked division. The British Foreign Office pointed out that Brazil would naturally seek to build up its military forces and consequently disturb the existing balance of power in South America.[196] Moreover, so long as Argentina and Chile obstinately remained neutral, Brazil felt justified in requesting military equipment from the United States to counter not only reports of German-inspired plots in southern Brazil but also rumors of the movement of Argentine troops to the border area.[197] Secretary of the Navy Josephus Daniels regretted that the emergence of "trouble" between Argentina and Brazil only served "to weaken the very end the United States is working towards."[198]

It was therefore more by circumstance than deliberate design that the bonds of wartime alliance brought the United States and Brazil closer together than at any time since the 1906 Rio conference. "An entente with the United States," declared the pro-government *Jornal do commercio,* "has always been the basic principle of our international policy."[199] But the British minister, Arthur Peel, had a different view. He recalled that the Venceslau administration had always stressed its independence of action during the submarine controversy. "The chief leaders of public opinion in Brazil, whatever may be their political tenets," argued Peel, "have been unanimous in repelling the idea of any form of protectorate on the part of the United States."[200] While the American press praised Nilo Peçanha's friendly attitude, Morgan privately regarded the foreign minister as "decidedly pro-British" and possessing no personal interest in developing relations with the United States.[201] In a broader context Morgan presented a similar conclusion when he wrote in April 1918:

> The Brazilian public is not vitally interested in the war. They wish its speedy termination and the end of the inconvenience it is causing. They are not yet prepared to make any national or personal sacrifices and they are even less interested in the principles behind the struggle than were the people of the United States previous to the loss of the *Lusitania.* Outside of a few persons who are impressed by the outrages against international law and humanity committed by the Central Powers there is no disposition to force the Government to take active measures in behalf of the Allied cause. Had the Brazilian merchantmen not been attacked by German torpedoes it is doubtful whether Brazil would have broken with Germany unless for the purpose of following an opposite course from that of Argentina and of attempting to obtain a leadership in South America through her identification with the interests of the larger powers of Europe and America.

While the American ambassador did not doubt that the war had increased Brazilian admiration for the United States, he was also conscious that Brazil's "drift has rather been toward France and England than toward ourselves."[202]

By joining the war Brazil had reawakened European interest in its affairs. "If the territory which was gained while the United States was a neutral nation is not conscientiously tilled," Morgan warned American diplomats and businessmen, "our commercial rivals will again obtain the upper hand."[203] But the ambassador was frequently dismayed by the complacency shown by his countrymen. The transfer of the ex-German ships to France particularly rankled. Peel confirmed that his American colleague was so upset that he "betrayed his mortification . . . in such diplomatic language that he gave very grave offence."[204] It must have been of little consolation to Morgan that his efforts had been frustrated not so much by Brazilian or French deviousness but by the blunders of his own superiors in Washington.[205]

A similar story unfolded in the diplomatic battle over the appointment of foreign military advisers. Shortly after entering the war, the Brazilian government announced its intention to appoint foreign advisory missions to modernize the Brazilian army and navy. The initial aim was simply to obtain instructors, but it was evident that substantial purchases of arms and equipment were also contemplated. Though he did not attempt to disguise his country's interest, Morgan did not try very actively to secure the army mission; sentimental and historical links made France the strong favorite for this contract. While gaining this contract would undoubtedly enhance French prestige in Brazil, Morgan recognized that the French "would probably accomplish more rapid results than any other nationality."[206]

This dismissive attitude reflected the traditional aversion of Americans toward standing armies. The naval question aroused much less complacency. The United States possessed a great navy and the extension of its influence was a matter of considerable strategic and commercial importance. But Britain posed a formidable obstacle. Brazilians were conditioned to believe that "Britain ruled the waves" and had traditionally maintained a close association with the British navy. The war had, however, created an opening for American influence when the shortage of British naval instructors forced Brazil to turn to the United States. In 1914 Captain Philip Williams secured an appointment at the newly formed Naval War College. Morgan was gratified to report that the quality of Williams's teaching ability and his popular personality had considerably raised the prestige of the United States navy among Brazilian officers.[207]

The prospect of a full naval mission presented a significant opportunity to build on what Williams had begun. Fierce competition was expected from Britain. Should a British naval mission be selected, Morgan predicted: "The United States may be surprised one day to find the new Brazilian navy being wholly constructed in English yards and upon English designs."[208] Only a few weeks after sending the above warning to Washington, Morgan learned to his dismay that Secretary of the Navy Daniels had informed the State Department that he had no objection to the choice of a British mission. This statement if true, was diametrically opposed to all that Morgan was working for in Brazil. It was also highly reminiscent of the crossed communications that had so recently allowed France to acquire the ex-German ships. The ambassador wrote to the State Department for reassurance in January 1918: "This office has understood that it was a basic principle of our South American policy that all American navies as much as possible should be brought under the influence of the navy of the United States. No more practicable method could probably be devised than by accrediting American naval missions to the navies of the leading South American powers."[209]

The alarm proved misplaced. The Navy Department's apparent acceptance of a British mission was based upon a broad strategic view that considered any improvement in the Brazilian navy a benefit to the common war effort. Indeed, the reasoning was virtually identical to Morgan's own rationale for approving the choice of French instructors for the Brazilian army. Nevertheless, Daniels had no desire to become involved in a quarrel with the State Department and quickly issued a clarification of his earlier opinion. "I appreciate fully," he informed Lansing, "the importance of military and naval commissions to South American states on account of the marked political and commercial effect that these commissions have produced in the interest of nations sending them in the past and which they may well produce in the future." In late February Lansing was therefore able to reply to Morgan: "Your understanding that it is a basic principle of our South American policy that all American navies as much as possible shall be brought under the influence of the navy of the United States is correct."[210]

As expected, the army contract was granted to France. The appointment of a naval mission, however, was deferred by budgetary difficulties and the surfacing of internal rivalries among Brazilian naval officers and the Navy Ministry. An opportunity did arise to continue Captain Williams's work of introducing American naval methods and ideas when an alternative project emerged to appoint five foreign instructors, two to teach at the Naval War College and three who would serve as fire control officers. British personnel were not available because of the war in Europe; thus, Morgan was able to secure the appointments for the United States. Five officers commanded by Captain Carl T. Vogelgesang were dispatched to Rio for this purpose in 1918.[211]

Despite Morgan's persistent prompting to seize and exploit the wartime opportunities to promote American influence in Brazil, the response emanating from Washington, though sympathetic, was also ambivalent and sometimes even operated adversely to the ambassador's advice. The State Department exercised primary responsibility for the conduct of relations with Brazil, but all decisions were subordinate to the wider requirements of the war effort. For example, although Morgan perceptively argued the political and commercial value of maintaining a sizable presence of American warships in Brazilian waters, the Navy Department had other priorities and insisted that ships could not be spared from the European war zone. Moreover, the threat of German submarine raids in the South Atlantic failed to materialize so that the area rapidly diminished in strategic significance. Consequently, Caperton's squadron was viewed as an unnecessary diversion of scarce naval resources. Within six months of its visit to Rio, the squadron had been reduced from four armored cruisers to one. To add insult to injury, the first replacement vessel to arrive was the *Raleigh*, an old cruiser that had taken part in the Battle of Manila Bay. But even this ship was soon transferred to other duties. By June 1918 Caperton commanded only his flagship, the *Pittsburgh*.[212] The United States had reverted to its traditional policy of maintaining only a token naval presence in the South Atlantic.

Another frustrating episode for Morgan concerned the direction of Brazilian naval operations. Brazil possessed a small but potentially useful navy, consisting of four destroyers and two cruisers. The exact contribution of these warships to the war effort was, however, a matter of prolonged discussion between the Brazilian and Allied governments. While Morgan believed that Brazilians were inclined to "dread service in the North Atlantic," he feared that they might comply with British requests to send the warships to Europe. Such a decision, in Morgan's opinion, "would undermine our naval and political position in this country." Not for the first time, the Navy Department in Washington failed to share Morgan's parochial view. It stressed the necessity of having as many ships as possible in European waters and urged the dispatch of Brazilian ships even if they were placed under British command. A small squadron was eventually equipped, but not sent out until August 1918. The signing of the armistice intervened before the ships reached Gibraltar, with the result that they were not able to experience active wartime service. The squadron did, however, pay a visit to Britain. Morgan gloomily observed that this "will not prove advantageous to our political and commercial interests."[213]

The local difficulties faced by Morgan in Brazil were replicated in Washington, where the decision to enter the war had stimulated the creation of a massive bureaucracy to manage the war effort. In overall control was the Council for National Defense, an inner-cabinet group headed by President Wilson. Ranked below were numerous departments and agencies whose areas of jurisdiction and responsibility not only proliferated but frequently came into conflict with each other. The State Department sought to retain its control over diplomatic and consular affairs, but was increasingly challenged by other departments. The heightened public and governmental awareness of Latin America arising from the war made that region a focal point of bureaucratic rivalry.

State Department officials regarded the Department of Commerce as their greatest threat. Secretary of Commerce William Redfield was especially interested in exploiting the commercial opportunities opening up in Latin America. Under his leadership, the Bureau of Foreign and Domestic Commerce established a network of permanent commercial attachés based throughout the world, including the leading Latin American capitals. The primary task of these officials was to provide commercial information for publication in the department's *Daily Consular and Trade Reports*.[214] An American journalist later described the commercial attachés as "the field commanders of the American army of trade promotion which scours the world."[215]

The battle, however, was not just against foreign competitors. The active involvement of the Commerce Department in the promotion of foreign trade provoked increasing conflict with the State Department. Brazil was only one of several countries that became entangled in the bureaucratic infighting. In 1916, for example, Secretary of Commerce William Redfield complained that the refusal of the State Department to divulge information quickly enough had prevented the successful conclusion of a loan to the Brazilian government. "I realize of course that there may have been some reason why you thought it best not to have the loan made," noted Redfield. At the same time he reminded the rival department: "Foreign loans are, however, so essential a part of our own financial stability in the near future that we desire to encourage them within due reason." Stung by this blatant encroachment upon the State Department's prerogative, Herbert Stabler minuted that "matters of foreign loans which involve political questions as well as commercial, should be handled entirely by the Department of State."[216]

While the State Department vigorously resisted interference from the Commerce Department, it could not prevent the Treasury from exercising its own prerogative to scrutinize the financial details of proposed foreign loans. Secretary of the Treasury McAdoo was Wilson's son-in-law and a powerful political figure. He was not averse to making known his opinion that the State Department was "deplorably weak so far as Latin America is concerned." His own personal interest in hemispheric affairs reflected the growing incidence of Treasury involvement in the discussion of important financial matters affecting Latin America.[217] Treasury officials, however, stressed financial considerations and were less sensitive to diplomatic nuances than their State Department colleagues. In April 1918, during preliminary discussions concerning a $50 million loan, Domício told Treasury officials that his government required the credit for "military preparations." Not satisfied with this explanation, the Treasury pressed for more specific information. Although the assistant secretary of the Treasury stated that the request was merely in accordance with regular departmental policy, this failed to mollify the Brazilian ambassador, who abruptly broke off the talks. A State Department memorandum attributed this to the sensitivity of the Brazilian government "at any inquiry which they may have considered as too personal."[218]

On occasion, the bureaucratic maze in Washington provoked a hostile reaction from Brazil. For much of 1917 the Venceslau administration had pleaded with the State Department to ensure sufficient supplies of coal. But American officials argued that their own country's needs came first and steadfastly refused to give the commercial guarantees that the Brazilian government so desperately wanted. Moreover, the desire to assist a wartime ally had to be balanced with the necessary of securing the cooperation and agreement of the War Trade Board, the Fuel Administration, and the Shipping Board. It was hardly surprising that the resulting shipments were subject to numerous delays and were regarded by Brazil as inadequate in both quality and quantity. In December the Itamaraty informed Domício that stocks were so low that Brazil faced possible economic "paralyzation." While the ambassador awaited the State Department's reply to his request to purchase 600,000 tons, the Shipping Board suddenly announced a reassignment of merchant shipping that effectively ruled out the transport of extra supplies of coal to Brazil. The Brazilian government was so angry that it retaliated by imposing a temporary suspension of manganese exports to the United States.[219]

Morgan was incensed and condemned Brazil's action as "a lack of international courtesy and of loyalty to the Allies which in an experience of some years I have rarely seen equalled."[220] Relations between the Itamaraty and the American embassy became so strained that Arthur Peel believed "general opinion out here is decidedly unanimous in thinking that the United States Government would be well advised to recall Mr. Morgan."[221] In June the ambassador was summoned before President Venceslau Brás to hear complaints that American restrictions limiting the import of coffee and rubber "were choking the economic life of Brazil and were creating resentment." By contrast, American trade with Argentina was booming. The president went so far as to accuse the United States of treating Argentina – a non-ally – with more consideration than Brazil.[222]

It was evident that Brazil expected the wartime alliance with the United States to produce substantial economic and military benefits. But American officials refused to grant any special favors. Insulated within Washington, their information on Brazil was limited and suggested that the people were only halfheartedly committed to the war. According to one American diplomat, the State Department believed it had Brazil "in its pocket."[223] The great battles were being fought in Europe, and American plans for victory did not include diverting shipping and important strategic materials to countries like Brazil. Coal was made available not to please the Brazilian government but to ensure that the Brazilian railways were able to transport manganese for export to the United States.

The concentration of American priorities on the prosecution of the war effort in Europe was further underlined in September, when the Brazilian government was told that imports of coffee into the United States must be reduced. Domício feared that the United States was reviving its traditional weapon to force economic concessions from Brazil. He informed the State Department that such a step would "seriously jeopardize" relations. Lansing was aware of the likely diplomatic difficulties, but could only answer that the restrictions would apply equally to all Latin American countries.[224] Despite Brazilian objections, a complete embargo on coffee was introduced in October. It was a brutal reminder of the disparity of power between the two countries. The only consolation for Brazil was that the restriction remained in force only a few days. Its termination, however, owed more to the sudden military collapse of Germany and the consequent ending of hostilities rather than to any particular desire to conciliate Brazil.

Ironically, the decision to embargo coffee was taken by the new joint United States–Allied committee, which had been established in June 1918 with the aim of coordinating policy so that Brazil would be treated, according to Lansing, "as a most valued associate of the countries at war against the Central Powers." In reality, the creation of the committee and its deliberate location in Washington marked an overt attempt to consolidate American influence in Brazil and counter the efforts of the European Allies to regain their former hold of the Brazilian market.[225] Throughout 1918 Morgan reported the arrival of successive British, French, and Italian commercial missions. Particular alarm was occasioned in May 1918 by the visit of Sir Maurice de Bunsen, which Morgan viewed as a striking example of "the intensity, directness and persistence of the present British drive." An argument in favor of setting up the inter-Allied committee was that it would provide a means of "destroying" the impact of de Bunsen's mission.[226]

The plan to divert Allied discussions involving Brazil to Washington could do little more than blunt the determined European attempts to regain their share of Brazilian trade. Morgan appeared to take fright at the prospect of a resurgence of international trade rivalry in the Brazilian market. As early as December 1917 he warned American businessmen not to relax; otherwise, their recently won commercial gains would be "ephemeral."[227] Such strictures, however, seemed unnecessary as the lifting of wartime restrictions precipitated a trading boom in which the United States was the best-placed nation to take advantage. Brazilian coffee exports to the United States in 1919 tripled in value over those of the previous year. The value of American products imported into Brazil more than doubled from £19 million in 1918 to over £37 million in 1919 so that American merchants enjoyed more than 40 percent of total Brazilian overseas trade.[228]

The market was literally flooded with American manufactures, and the response was not always welcoming. Peel reported "serious complaint" about the quality of American goods and considered "that American traders have a reputation for being deficient in reliability and good faith and ability to gain over South American sympathy." The British consul, Ernest Hambloch, also mentioned the "dismal reputation" acquired in Brazil by American bankers; he concluded that they "have lost a golden opportunity to establish and consolidate their commercial position here."[229] From 1914 onward American trade and investment had made significant inroads into Brazil. Lucrative export markets had been developed in coal, petroleum, and automobiles. Substantial investments were also evident in Brazilian cable communications and the new meat-packing industry. Although the basis for American economic preeminence was firmly established, it was impossible for contemporaries to conceive that the United States could really have established supremacy over its European rivals in such a short space of time. Edwin Morgan was typical in projecting the past into the future when he observed pessimistically: "American trade has increased principally because trade with Europe has been curtailed. How much of this trade will remain after the war is problematical. Brazilian merchants will probably buy in the cheapest markets and where they can obtain the best credits irrespective of whether that market is allied or German."[230] Morgan had already noted Brazil's "drift" to the Allies, and he was fully conscious of the powerful ties with Europe. He wrote in March 1919: "Although Brazil and other South American countries entered the war because the United States did so the effect of their participation has been to enhance their appreciation of Europe and to tighten rather than weaken the bonds of race, language, habits, and customs, that unite them to the civilization of the old world."[231]

Shortly after the war ended, the British minister at Rio speculated that, unless American diplomacy was "applied with tact and discretion," the newly acquired Brazilian sense of importance and self-awareness would conflict with "the smooth working of Pan American principles." The minister optimistically referred to a long-standing Brazilian sentiment when he remarked: "there is no real ground for the often expressed sense of solidarity between Brazil and the United States because there ever exists a latent suspicion that the United States have views and intentions of exercising indirectly a policy of protection which is offensive to the feelings of this very susceptible people."[232] Indeed, the dramatic rise of American power and influence had aroused mounting disquiet among Brazilian nationalists. Echoing the familiar theme of "the yankee peril," writers such as Alberto Tôrres denounced Pan-Americanism as "the creation of imagination." British dispatches confirmed the existence of an "undercurrent of anti-American feeling" in the Rio press. With the lifting of censorship, America was about to be repaid for its failure to give preferential economic treatment to Brazil during the war. "We must be prepared," concluded Morgan, "to have the policies of our government and the acts of both American public officials and private individuals attacked, with an audacity and venom which has never before been witnessed."[233]

The evolving mood of national assertiveness also extended to diplomatic affairs. Morgan was particularly irritated by the anti-American content of some of the speeches and writings of Rui Barbosa. The Brazilian statesman eloquently argued: "Let us lay aside the stupid conception which places Brazil under the exclusive seal of the United States of America and which would accustom us to the idea that we depend on them more than on France or Great Britain when the truth is that we require equally the friendship of all these three great nations."[234] Rui's provocative outbursts were intended to promote his own presidential ambitions, but they also reflected the revival of the views associated with Rio Branco that Brazil should be diplomatically active and ought to make its mark on international affairs. The tortuous diplomacy that had preceded Brazil's decision to enter the conflict in October 1917 was now forgotten. Elated by victory, the Brazilian elite looked forward to the exciting prospect of Brazil's inclusion in a great peace congress that would change the world.

THE VERSAILLES CONFERENCE

On November 18, 1918, Woodrow Wilson astounded opinion at home and overseas by announcing his intention to head the American delegation at the forthcoming Versailles peace conference. A month later the man who had promised "peace without victory" was greeted by enormous public interest and enthusiasm on his arrival in Europe. Throughout Latin America too, Wilson was acclaimed a hero and a great peacemaker. But Latin American diplomatic opinion was inclined to be more cautious. Wilson's image as a peacemaker was tarnished by his military interventions in Mexico, Central America, and the Caribbean. He had also rejected Latin American proposals to hold a conference of neutral nations and clearly preferred only to assemble meetings he could personally control and manipulate. There was no reason to believe that Wilson had altered his views. Despite his grand rhetoric, he had little to say about the role of Latin America at Versailles. Indeed, invitations to the preliminary peace conference were pointedly reserved for the great powers. Although State Department officials made known their support for Latin American representation at the actual peace congress, they underlined that this would only apply to those nations that had actually joined the war.[235]

Brazil stood to gain most from this distinction. In fact, British foreign office officials considered that the advance of American prestige and influence was more evident in Brazil than any other part of South America. In their view, "the burning question of Brazilian politics" was whether that country would maintain its traditionally close relations with Britain and France or whether it would fall more and more under the sway of the United States. Despite the appearance in Brazil of local anti-American sentiment and complaints over the commercial methods of American businessmen, the British consul, Ernest Hambloch, observed: "It would be a mistake to think that the United States, as a country is unpopular here."[236] Moreover, the prospects of diplomatic harmony were heightened by the election of Rodrigues Alves to succeed Venceslau Brás in 1918. In Morgan's opinion, Rodrigues Alves was "a strong Pan-Americanist" who "believes in continental solidarity and in the influence which the United States should and does exercise over the American continent." The ambassador was confident that the new president would continue the pro-American policy associated with his first administration.[237] The common perception of shared mutual interest between American and Brazilian leaders was soon evident at the Versailles conference where the United States proved to be Brazil's foremost friend.

Brazil looked forward to the conference, but the story of its participation was one of increasing irritation and bruised feelings. The first difficulty actually predated the conference and concerned the extent of Brazilian representation. As the only South American nation to enter the war, Brazil confidently anticipated a position of some distinction at the conference table. This expectation was reinforced by the flattering attentions recently paid to Brazil by European governments, especially the upgrading of diplomatic relations to ambassadorial level in London and Rome. Moreover, the question acquired added domestic political significance when it sparked off a clash between Rui Barbosa and the newly appointed foreign minister, Domício da Gama. Rui was the nation's most renowned statesman and could hardly be denied the honor of leading the Brazilian delegation at Versailles. Domício feared, however, that Rui's selection would diminish his own authority as foreign minister. After a brief but unpleasant struggle, Rui declared his intention not to go to Paris.[238] Shortly afterward, a delegation of four was appointed. It was headed by Epitácio da Silva Pessoa and included Raul Fernandes, João Pandiá Calógeras, and Olinto de Magalhães. But Domício's triumph was short-lived. The arrangement had hardly been made when news was received from Europe that Brazil was designated not as a "belligerent great power" but a "belligerent power with a special interest" on a par with Belgium, Greece, and Portugal. Consequently, much to Domício's embarrassment, Brazil would be allowed only one or perhaps at the most, two representatives.[239]

In his hour of distress, Domício appealed for assistance to the State Department. Counselor Frank Polk wired Secretary of State Lansing in Paris, advising that Brazil be given "most favored treatment." If the contents of Polk's telegram had been published, they would surely have brought joy to Brazilian hearts. In contrast to the days of the valorization controversy and the Mexican crisis, Domício was now considered a most friendly and dependable ally, whose return to Rio was seen as considerably strengthening the pro-American element in the Brazilian government. Not only did Polk wish to avoid political humiliation for the foreign minister, but he was also concerned that a blow to Brazil's prestige "would be a source of gratification" to Argentina and Chile who had stayed out of the war. "Brazil," he noted, "has stood loyally by us in practically every question that has come up in South America." Moreover, it was "the only power in South America that really declared war promptly and also was of material assistance in the war by active cooperation, such as sending ships." Polk was even prepared to acknowledge that "Brazil is the greatest power in South America" and thereby entitled "to a fair representation on account of its geographic position."[240]

Woodrow Wilson had concurred in the original decision to enhance the role of the great powers at the conference. Nevertheless, he was sympathetic to Brazil's case and was prepared to debate the matter at the first meeting of the Supreme Council.[241] He argued that, as the largest of the Latin American nations, with a population in excess of 30 million, Brazil should be granted "an exceptional position." By denying Brazil adequate representation, the great European powers were attempting to mute the voice of the Americas. Betraying a naive understanding of Brazilian society, Wilson also expressed concern over the influential German element in Brazil and the fear that "in another generation this country might have become wholly Germanised." It was therefore imperative that Brazil be kept attached "to our own interests" by being given three representatives instead of the two delegates allotted to "powers with a special interest." The proposed concession appeared modest, but it aroused criticism from the British prime minister, Lloyd George, who suspected an ulterior motive to increase the voting power of the American nations. Objecting that "a preponderating position" was being sought for Brazil, the wily British statesman requested additional representation for the British Empire. The particular merits of Brazil's own case were therefore lost sight of as the country became a pawn in the game of great power politics. A compromise emerged in which the British Dominions were each granted two delegates. It was agreed that Brazil would have three delegates, although the same privilege was also extended to Belgium and Serbia.[242]

In Brazil, Wilson's intervention was adjudged a complete success. The government was delighted and Domício's political standing was temporarily boosted. Although the official delegation was limited to three, face was saved by allowing the fourth delegate, Olinto de Magalhães, to travel to Paris in an unofficial capacity. But the concept of a "preponderating position" was illusory so long as the world remained strictly divided into greater and lesser powers. Without exception, all the smaller nations found themselves treated with little consideration as the "Big Four" of Britain, France, Italy, and the United States dominated the conference proceedings and reserved the important committee appointments for themselves. Far from enjoying a position of honor and influence, Brazil had to be content with a place on the commission assigned to draw up the covenant of the League of Nations. Though dominated by the great powers Brazil made a useful, if limited contribution to the discussions. "A people as idealistic as the Brazilians," correctly predicted Morgan, "do not aspire to the aggrandisement of their native country . . . nor are they hostile to an endeavor to establish a super-national authority such as the League of Nations."[243]

Brazil was keen to participate in the new world organization, but the question was completely overshadowed by other more pressing matters. At one stage it seemed as if Brazil was actually being punished for having entered the war. A particular cause of irritation concerned the amount of financial compensation due on payment of the coffee money that had been frozen in German banks during the war. While this had long been a vital question for Brazil, the Allies gave it an extremely low priority as they sought to press their own much larger claims for reparations upon Germany. The conference committee on finance eventually recommended that Germany should pay compensation but that this should be in marks at the prevailing rate of exchange. Since the mark had greatly depreciated during the intervening five years, Brazil stood to lose a substantial sum.[244] Another decision by the same committee proposed that the various merchant ships confiscated from Germany be allocated to the victors in proportion to maritime losses suffered during the war. This plan was clearly designed to benefit the great maritime powers and had little attraction to countries like Brazil that had experienced relatively minor losses. It would also be extremely detrimental to Brazilian interests because the recommendation would allow France to retain the ex-German ships chartered from Brazil in 1917.[245]

Instead of expounding on international and hemispheric issues as Rui had done at The Hague in 1907, the Brazilian delegation at Versailles became preoccupied with what appeared to be a mercenary assertion of national interest. For example, the question of the coffee money was vigorously pursued and ultimately degenerated into a squabble over interest percentage points. Brazilian diplomats insisted that the amount due from Germany be assessed at 1914 rates of exchange and should also include an additional charge for annual interest of 5 percent. The fact that world coffee prices were currently rising to record levels only served to enhance the image of Brazilian selfishness. In order to rid itself of a trivial and irritating issue, the Supreme Council eventually assented to Brazil's demands. After the conference was over, the haggling still continued when Germany protested and secured a reduction in the interest rate to 4.5 percent.[246]

The matter of the ex-German ships was even more contentious. The recommendation of the committee that compensation should correspond to the amount of tonnage lost during the war would result in Brazil receiving no more than 25,000 tons. Should the scheme not be implemented, Brazil would retain the ex-German ships and thereby gain more than 200,000 tons of shipping. A major complication, however, was the fact that France was currently in possession of most of the ships in question. Moreover, it was evident that the European powers had little sympathy for Brazil. Lloyd George was unhappy that a country that had done so little in the war "would profit enormously."[247] The French government was convinced that it had already paid an excessive amount to lease the ships. In fact, the contract was due to expire on March 31, 1919, and it hardly seemed coincidental that the method of allocation proposed by the committee on finance offered not only a timely means of exerting diplomatic pressure on Brazil but also held out the possibility that France might keep the ships without having to renew the lease.

Epitácio Pessoa responded by declaring that his country had seized the ships as enemy property in June 1917 and consequently possessed the title to ownership. They had therefore become Brazilian property that Brazil could do with as it pleased. The argument was plausible, but some doubt existed over whether Brazil had actually stated at the time of requisition that it was dispossessing the German owners. Whatever the legal technicalities, Epitácio's version of events also gave ammunition to those critics who suspected that Brazil had always regarded the ships purely as a source of profit. Such criticism was ignored by Epitácio who pointed out that Brazil's legal title had been recognized in the arrangement transferring the ships to France. When the French government refused to endorse his contention, Epitácio remarked that he had not expected "such unjust treatment from our noble ally and friend."[248]

Once again, it was American diplomatic intervention that came to Brazil's aid. At Wilson's insistence, the Allies had agreed to exclude the United States from the allocation plan and to permit that country to retain the German ships it had seized during the war. Epitácio simply claimed the same right for Brazil and personally appealed to Wilson for support. The legal officers of the State Department had reservations about Brazil's claim to own the ships, but Wilson could hardly contradict the principle he had already fought for. "It is needless to say," he replied to Epitácio, "that the United States would never do anything intentionally or conscientiously that could injure Brazil's interests." The American president personally raised Brazil's protests at the Supreme Council. The issues posed were annoying but also expendable so that Britain and France tactfully gave way and assented in principle to compensation settlements that were acceptable to Brazil.[249] In June 1919 diplomatic relations between Brazil and France were upgraded to ambassadorial level. This was followed a year later by the conclusion of a financial arrangement in which France recognized the ex-German ships as "the permanent property of Brazil."[250]

The diplomatic support of the United States was crucial to Brazil overcoming European objections at Versailles. Although Wilson's interventions on Brazil's behalf deservedly gained public attention,[251] Domício was even more appreciative of the assistance of Secretary of State Lansing. In marked contrast to the way he had chastised another American secretary of state seven years earlier, Domício wrote to Lansing: "your attitude towards us has been most gratifying as one effective manifestation of our old mutual friendship. . . . I only wish to thank you for being our friend at the Conference and say this is known here and makes for a stronger inter-American friendship, that is shown in acts."[252] Of special value also to the Brazilian delegation was Herbert Stabler, the chief of the Latin American division of the State Department. During the conference Stabler had "placed himself entirely at Pessoa's disposal," and the Brazilian diplomat was so appreciative that he insisted on Stabler's remaining with the official Brazilian party when it visited the United States en route home to Rio. Alvey Adee remarked that Epitácio "realizes that the European nations did not assist him in getting what Brazil desired at the Peace Conference and that the United States was a friend indeed, this he has expressed very openly."[253]

The choice of Epitácio Pessoa to head Brazil's delegation at Versailles had been a fortunate one for the United States. Like Rui Barbosa, Epitácio was also a distinguished orator and jurist. While he could be as vain and awkward as Rui, he was not anti-American or so strongly in favor of Britain and France.[254] In fact, he welcomed closer contact with the United States. The calculated American efforts to cultivate Epitácio acquired extra significance when he suddenly emerged as the probable successor to Rodrigues Alves after the latter's death in January 1919. Three months later Epitácio defeated Rui in a special presidential election. To American delight, Epitácio agreed to make a brief stop in June at New York and Washington en route home from the conference. It was a break with precedent and reflected the growing significance of the United States in the Brazilian mind. Lavish entertainment regaled the first Brazilian president-elect to visit the United States. An excursion was organized to Niagara Falls, but there was no time for the customary deluxe railroad tour. Instead, the State Department arranged meetings with prominent American bankers and businessmen. Epitácio pleased his audiences by making frequent reference to the need for closer economic relations between Brazil and the United States. "It is believed," reported Adee, "that he was greatly impressed by the United States and its power and energy and it is hoped that upon his return to Brazil it may be possible to continue this excellent effect upon him."[255]

The hopes were initially fulfilled. In his financial report for 1920 the British consul, Ernest Hambloch recorded: "The Americans have turned their attention to things Brazilian with much greater confidence during the last year, as though they were well assured of receiving whatever backing they required in Brazilian government circles." By 1922, however, Hambloch was observing that the United States "have lost ground."[256] Epitácio had returned to a booming economy enjoying the benefits of high coffee prices and an appreciating milréis. But financial crisis soon reasserted itself in 1921 as coffee prices fell and the milréis sharply depreciated. Total trade between Brazil and the United States slumped from £96 million in 1920 to only £40 million in 1921. From an annual average of almost £50 million in 1919–1920, American exports collapsed dramatically to £21 million in 1921.[257] The onset of economic recession also made Brazil appear less attractive to American bankers. In August 1920 the State Department advised that it was "a most inopportune time" for Brazil to seek a loan in the American money market.[258]

The very commercial success of American merchants suddenly became a disadvantage. "The Americans," stated the British minister at Rio in December 1920, "are at the moment very unpopular in this country, as, rightly or wrongly, the recent fall in exchange and consequent financial crisis is laid at their door."[259] Ironically, this dispatch coincided with a belated diplomatic maneuver by the Wilson administration calculated to improve the American image in Latin America. The initiative was surprising because Washington had shown little interest in hemispheric affairs since the end of the war. Moreover, the morale and efficiency of the State Department was hampered by President Wilson's illness and his personal friction with Lansing that brought about the secretary of state's resignation in February 1920.[260] It was evident, however, that America's espousal of freedom and self-determination was contradicted by its military occupation of such countries as Haiti and the Dominican Republic. In an attempt to improve hemispheric understanding it was decided to send the new secretary of state, Bainbridge Colby, on a goodwill mission to Brazil, Uruguay, and Argentina.[261]

Brazil was chosen because an official visit to that country had been under discussion since 1917 and was intended to be in return for Müller's two trips and Epitácio's short stay in 1919. The stop at Montevideo was also meant to reciprocate a visit made to the United States by the Uruguayan foreign minister. A desire existed to express American appreciation of Brazil's participation in the war, but any suggestion of a special relationship was dispelled by the deliberate inclusion of Buenos Aires on Colby's itinerary. Ambassador Stimson was instructed to inform the Argentine president "that there does not exist now nor has there at any time . . . any trace of resentment because of the policy pursued by the Argentine Government during the war."[262] Colby's desire to appear friendly and evenhanded toward the South American rivals was understandable, but it was also an implicit vindication of Argentina's wartime neutrality and a blow to Brazil's aspirations to continental leadership.

Colby arrived in Rio on December 21, 1920 and left four days later. He visited the president and made several speeches including an address to Congress. In his farewell message he stressed: "There is a strong bond between the United States and its sister republic of Brazil. . . . The roots lie in a similarity of our histories, in the logic of events, in the parallelism of our national aims and destinies."[263] Edwin Morgan reported reassuringly that the secretary of state's "agreeable personality and rhetorical gifts" had created "an excellent impression." The British minister noted, however, that Morgan had not even invited Colby to a meal and, in his opinion, the visit had "excited practically no interest at all."[264]

Both the American ambassador and Colby's Brazilian hosts were fully aware that their visitor was the representative of a lame-duck and "discredited" administration.[265] The visit served little purpose. It was arranged rather hurriedly and smacked too much of a public relations exercise. The Brazilian elite had a high regard for President Wilson and the United States. The effusive speeches that greeted Colby were full of Pan-American sentiment, but they could not disguise the fact that the record of Wilson's policy toward Latin America was uneven and disappointing. The Wilsonian era was drawing to a close, and America was about to face a new decade of Republican leadership. The diplomatic ties with Brazil were also beginning to slacken. Although the pro-American sympathies of President Epitácio Pessoa were not in doubt, his administration subscribed, however, to a foreign policy whose direction and purpose were more consonant with Brazilian nationalism than any particular desire to please the United States. As the latter withdrew into normalcy and isolationism, Brazil chose instead to become a member of the Council of the League of Nations and to embark upon an ambitious strategy designed to assert Brazilian influence not only in the Western Hemisphere but in the wider world.

CHAPTER 4

Misunderstandings and

Bruised Feelings, 1921–1928

B Y 1919 the era of progressivism was drawing to a close in the United States. In its place came a yearning for a return to normalcy, which was translated into a decade of Republican political ascendancy. The administrations of Warren G. Harding and Calvin Coolidge stressed economy and efficiency; for the majority of Americans the result was a time of unprecedented affluence. In foreign affairs an inward-looking, isolationist mentality prevailed, symbolized by the decision not to join the League of Nations. But the apparent aloofness from international relations was superficial. Suspicion of overseas entanglements was balanced by awareness that the United States was a great power with worldwide interests.[1]

The tangible power of the United States was most evident in the Western Hemisphere where the war had further boosted its already substantial economic and political influence. No longer fearful of European challenge to the Monroe Doctrine or threats to the Panama canal, officials in Washington regarded the region as securely within their sphere of influence. The nations of Latin America were accorded little military or diplomatic significance and were pointedly not invited to the naval disarmament conferences nor included among the initial signatories to the Kellogg-Briand Peace Pact.

During the 1920s American diplomacy was less subject to outside political and public pressures. Both secretaries of state were strong personalities and each enjoyed full presidential support. Charles Evans Hughes was noted for his stern and legalistic attitude. He had a low opinion of Latin American governments and showed no great interest in their affairs. His successor, Frank Kellogg, displayed a similar attitude even though he had served as a member of the American delegation at the 1923 Santiago Pan-American conference and claimed therefore a personal familiarity with the southern republics.[2]

In contrast to the war years, there was a reduction in overt rivalry between government departments. In part this reflected the noncontroversial nature of most Latin American questions and the existence of broad unanimity of opinion among cabinet officers. Moreover, the strong leadership of Hughes enhanced the prestige of the State Department and affirmed its primacy in dealing with political matters affecting foreign governments. A challenge was posed by the vigorous efforts of Herbert Hoover at the Department of Commerce to promote American trade and investment in Latin America.[3] As the coffee dispute with Brazil demonstrated, Hoover's interference was not always helpful.

During the 1920s the diplomatic and consular establishment in Brazil was supplemented by attachés from the Commerce, War, and Navy departments.[4] However, the retention of Edwin Morgan as ambassador to Rio ensured the preeminence of the State Department in the conduct of relations with Brazil. Morgan's influence became almost legendary. The British ambassador jealously noted "the comfortable new American Embassy at Rio" in which his American colleague entertained Brazilian society "with some brilliance." So intimate was Morgan's knowledge of Brazilian affairs that he was described as possessing "the local habit of getting things done rather by indirect means than through the usual diplomatic channels."[5] But Morgan's skills were not used to their best advantage. His frequently frustrating experiences with officials in Washington show that he was regarded more as an expert adviser rather than a maker of policy.[6]

Another illustration of the advance of American influence in Brazil was the establishment of regular steamship service from New York, which reduced sailing time from three weeks to twelve days.[7] The image of Brazil as a land of unlimited opportunity still wove its spell. "No territory in the world," stated the *Wall Street Journal* "is better worth exploitation than Brazil's."[8] By 1929 American businessmen boasted a larger share of the export market than their British rivals. Moreover, New York had replaced London as the major source of new capital investment. Nevertheless, American trade and investment with Brazil grew at a relatively slower rate than with the rest of South America. The economic prospects of Argentina continued to be more alluring so that, out of total American investment in the region, the proportion held by Brazil actually fell from 29 to 20 percent during the decade.[9]

American diplomatic interest in Brazil showed a similar ambivalence. Despite his well-known reluctance to embark on overseas trips, Hughes visited Rio to attend the 1922 centennial exposition and to complete the final details of the contract establishing an American naval mission in Brazil. In Ambassador Morgan's view, the importance of winning the contract against strong British competition lay in its potentially lucrative benefits for American business. But when the orders for ships and naval equipment materialized, an unexpected response was forthcoming from Washington. The divergence of opinion between Hughes and the Rio embassy pointed not only to poor diplomatic communications but also to a basic lack of sympathy shown by officials toward Brazil. A briefing prepared for Hughes's visit accurately noted the political dominance of São Paulo and Minas Gerais. However, it also described the ruling elite as "self centered lovers of power and pleasure" and stressed that "many of the natives are negroes or of mixed breeds with negro predominating." Even Edwin Morgan contributed to the stereotyped view of Brazil as a wild, almost savage society when his political reports mentioned that the *gaúchos* of the South "pass their lives on horseback and have inherited traditions of guerrilla warfare" or that the poverty in the Amazon region was so extreme "that in localities slightly removed from the centers of population civilized life has been abandoned."[10]

The American public was hardly better informed. The Brazilian ambassador at Washington bemoaned the only too evident lack of interest in his country and remarked that news about Brazil was "scarce" in the press.[11] All too often whatever was reported proved to be unflattering and sensational. Disease was still so prevalent that one traveler stressed that "Brazil is one vast hospital."[12] An account of the search for rubber in the Amazon described how the expedition "met all of the deadly terrors of the jungle; saw-toothed fish attacked them; many of the places where they were forced to live were infested with poisonous snakes; insects made their lives one long torture."[13] After searching for background reading material one professor concluded: "The American reader looks in vain for a comprehensive treatment of the country."[14]

The American public's neglect of Brazil was reflected in diplomatic attitudes. The Republican administrations of the 1920s wished to maintain the predominant influence of the United States in Latin America, but the countries that gave most concern were still Mexico and the Caribbean republics. Relatively little attention was paid to South America. Indeed, American diplomats were sometimes accused of failing to differentiate between Brazil and the Spanish American countries.[15] Brazil was traditionally regarded as a friendly nation and tended to be taken for granted. Ironically, this merely presented an excuse for diplomatic indifference and inertia. "Besides, Brazil can usually be counted upon to support us," explained Henry Fletcher in 1927.[16]

After noting the "community of political ideals" shared by the United States and Brazil, the *Washington Post* acclaimed Brazil's centennial exhibition in 1922 as marking a "century of achievement." Four years later the orderly inauguration of President Washington Luís prompted the *New York Herald Tribune* to describe Brazil as the "colossus of the South."[17] The celebrations masked, however, a decade of considerable political unrest punctuated by a series of military rebellions. The presidential administrations of Epitácio Pessoa and Artur Bernardes maintained public order with difficulty. Morgan reported in 1925 that Bernardes had "lost his grip" and might be deposed at any moment.[18] Nevertheless, Bernardes survived for his full term and thereby ensured that "the politics of the governors" was effectively reasserted in 1926. His successor, Washington Luís, instituted a period of deceptive political calm that remained unbroken until the final year of his presidency.

During the 1920s Brazil also experienced frequent economic instability. The sudden collapse of the postwar boom in 1920 precipitated a financial crisis that persisted throughout the decade, manifesting itself in rising inflation and a fluctuating foreign exchange value of the milréis. The federal government stressed the achievement of a balanced budget, but the pursuit of fiscal stability was seriously hampered by the decentralized nature of the republic and its many competing political pressures. For example, coffee planters favored an expansion of the export sector while industrialists urged the retention of high protective tariffs. Another contentious issue was the import of foreign capital. Foreign loans were needed to finance industrial development and also provide a valuable means of funding federal deficits and stabilizing the milréis. Nevertheless, nationalist sentiments were stirred by alarmist reports that foreign capitalists sought to exercise control over large areas of national territory.[19]

The upsurge of nationalism stimulated by the war found further expression during the decade in the formation of nationalist organizations and the holding of the celebrated Modern Art Week at São Paulo.[20] Nevertheless, foreign ideas and models still possessed considerable influence. Awareness of the United States was growing, although the Brazilian elite still retained its cultural fascination with Europe. "For every Argentine, Chilean or Brazilian who visits the United States, a thousand go to Paris," noted an American journalist.[21] Moreover, the domination of the European news agencies ensured that American affairs were inadequately reported in the Brazilian press.[22] On the other hand, the advent of motion pictures provided Brazilians with a new window to gaze upon America and its society.[23] The impact was considerable, but it was also highly confusing. One Brazilian diplomat listed his immediate impressions of America: "dollars, skyscrapers, tremendous dimensions, not only as regards cities, but everything else, moving pictures, jazz bands, prizefights, victrolas, pianolas, radios, typewriters, expensive cars, ice cream soda and new methods for forgetting cocktails." He could not help wondering, however, whether "this jumble of confused impressions" hindered rather than developed a better understanding between the peoples of North and South America.[24] Indeed, movies did not always promote harmony. Certainly, the portrayal of Rio as a "squalid Spanish town" in the Hollywood movie "The Girl From Rio" provoked an outburst of Brazilian anger against the American producers.[25]

Suspicion of foreigners also existed at the diplomatic level. Both Epitácio Pessoa and Artur Bernardes were regarded as staunch nationalists. While Washington Luís proved more moderate, he exhibited little personal enthusiasm for close diplomatic contact with foreign countries. In fact, domestic political considerations frequently intruded upon the making of foreign policy and directly influenced the appointment of foreign ministers. Epitácio's personal friction with Domício da Gama resulted in the latter's transfer to London and his replacement by the more pliable Azevedo Marques. Similarly, the selection of Otávio Mangabeira as foreign minister in 1926 was interpreted as a sign that Washington Luís intended to dictate the formulation of foreign policy. The most politically powerful foreign minister was Félix Pacheco who served under Bernardes from 1922 to 1926. But Pacheco's own prominence also made him a figure of keen political controversy. Morgan considered his tenure of office as "disastrous to Brazilian interests both at home and abroad."[26] In fact, Brazil could boast no statesmen of the stature or authority of Rio Branco or Joaquim Nabuco. Both Pacheco and Mangabeira came to office with no formal diplomatic experience. Azevedo Marques was considered to be amiable but "very weak."[27] In the United States, Augusto Cochrane de Alencar served as ambassador from 1920 to 1924 and Silvino Gurgel do Amaral from 1925 to 1930. Neither diplomat achieved, however, the prominence or influence enjoyed in the American capital by Nabuco or Domício da Gama.

Despite the background of political unrest and financial stringency, Brazil's ruling elite attempted to put into effect a vigorous policy of national defense and diplomatic assertiveness. Membership on the Council of the League of Nations was prized so highly that the securing of a permanent seat became an obsession of Brazilian diplomacy. A policy of military preparedness was also pursued by the federal government. Foreign military missions were contracted to modernize the army and navy. In 1924 Bernardes announced a substantial program designed to replace Brazil's obsolete warships.

Brazil's lack of diplomatic finesse was apparent as Argentina and Chile coldly received the argument that naval armament was intended purely for defensive purposes. Moreover, the maneuvering for a permanent seat on the League Council further estranged Latin American governments and led to accusations of Brazilian selfishness and overbearing ambition. The expenditure of diplomatic effort at Geneva proved ultimately futile and ended in the decision to withdraw from the League in 1926.

Confronted by internal unrest and fearful of the dangers of diplomatic isolation within South America, Brazil frequently looked to the United States for aid and sympathy throughout the 1920s. The outward show of friendliness concealed, however, a good deal of misunderstanding and friction. For example, American diplomacy was scarcely of any value to Brazil either at the Santiago conference or at Geneva. Nor was the Itamaraty always amenable to American wishes. Brazil refused to conclude a most-favored-nation commercial treaty and would not sign the Peace Pact. Nevertheless, the British embassy at Rio continued to deplore "the definite American bias" of the Itamaraty. Even though Mangabeira declared that Brazil was determined to assert its autonomy in foreign affairs, British officials had no doubt that approximation with the United States remained a cardinal principle of Brazilian diplomacy.[28]

THE NAVAL MISSION

Despite its symbolic rejection of membership of the League of Nations, the Harding administration did not intend to pursue a purely passive international role. This became evident within weeks of Harding's assuming office, when he announced America's determination to work for world peace by concentrating on naval disarmament.[29] A conference to limit the size of the navies of the great powers was held later at Washington in November 1921. The meeting revealed, however, that the primary concern of American officials was to achieve a reduction of force levels in the Pacific Ocean. The South Atlantic was accorded only a passing mention. Consequently, all the nations of Latin America found themselves ignored and pointedly excluded from the conference. It was apparent that the Harding administration intended to continue the traditional American diplomatic strategy of acting unilaterally and taking little account of Latin America.

The course of events was also painfully reminiscent of the treatment meted out by the great powers to Latin America at the Versailles conference. On that occasion the United States had exercised a moderating influence and had shown particular concern toward Brazil. In 1921, however, the Harding administration signified no such disposition even though the Brazilian government made little secret of its desire to attend the conference. Ambassador Augusto Cochrane de Alencar was informed by the State Department that Brazil's participation was ruled out because it would necessitate bringing in similar-sized powers like Belgium and Spain. President Harding was described as "intransigent" in his opposition to any enlargement of the conference. While the Itamaraty understood only too well that the great powers would seek to monopolize the proceedings, it was perplexed to learn that an invitation had been issued to Portugal. When Cochrane de Alencar raised this in Washington, he was left in no doubt that the matter should not be pressed further. In return the State Department gave an assurance that nothing would happen at the conference prejudicial to Brazil's interests.[30]

This well-meaning though blunt reminder of Brazil's international powerlessness was hardly reassuring to the government of Epitácio Pessoa. Just a year earlier the minister of war, João Pandiá Calógeras, had stated: "Nobody respects or seeks the solidarity of the weak."[31] At Versailles the great powers had sought to enhance their own naval strength at the expense of the smaller nations. The belief persisted in Brazil that they would use the Washington conference for the same purpose.[32] Moreover, while Brazil might approve the concept of world disarmament in principle, it could not ignore the fact that the war had exposed the country's military inadequacy especially in relation to the growing power of Argentina. This had resulted in a determined effort to increase the nation's armed strength ranging from the introduction of compulsory military service to the contracting in 1919 of a French mission to train and modernize the army.

The military buildup was seriously hampered by financial constraints and the reluctance of young men to serve in an army and navy both notorious for their harsh discipline and bad conditions.[33] In consequence the balance of power in South America shifted even further in favor of Argentina and Chile and against Brazil. Although priority was given to remedying the deficiencies of the army, growing concern arose over the plight of the navy, especially when its sole battleships, the *Minas Gerais* and the *São Paulo* had to be humiliatingly taken out of service to undergo extensive repairs in the United States during 1920–1921. The American chargé at Rio, Sheldon Crosby, believed that Brazil possessed no territorial ambitions or "aggressive intentions" toward the rest of South America. On the other hand, he acknowledged that Brazil had "no up-to-date ships" and was "clearly inferior" to its two neighbors.[34] Despite the concern of the United States and the European powers to secure naval disarmament, reasons of national pride and security compelled Brazil to consider ways of strengthening its own navy. As the conference at Washington drew to a close in early 1922, the Brazilian government independently revived the idea of appointing a foreign naval mission.

The decision lifted the sense of tedious routine that had settled upon diplomatic relations between Brazil and the United States since the Versailles conference. Only a short time before, it had been rumored in Rio that Edwin Morgan was seeking a transfer to a European post and that he was disappointed not to have succeeded.[35] The ambassador's spirits were revived, however, by the prospect of a diplomatic battle between Britain and the United States to win the contract for the naval mission. Fundamental strategic, political, and commercial questions were held to be at stake. "Our naval prestige would be seriously lowered if mission should be British instead of American," Morgan stated in March 1922, "and there would be slight possibility of American firms securing contracts for dry-dock, arsenal and new naval units which would be established upon the advice of the mission head."[36]

The ultimate decision was not easily arrived at. The tradition that "Britain rules the waves" exercised a powerful influence, and a good deal of sentiment in favor of a British mission persisted among senior Brazilian naval officers.[37] Nonetheless, it had not gone unnoticed that Britain had withdrawn its South American naval squadron in 1919 and that the contracts to repair and refit the *Minas Gerais* and *São Paulo* had been placed with American companies. Brazilians had come to regard the United States as a great naval power almost on a par with Britain. Indeed, Morgan believed that his country possessed distinct advantages over its rival. One cause of his optimism was the establishment of an important precedent when the unavailability of British personnel during the war had persuaded Brazil for the first time to request the American navy to supply specialist instructors. In addition, the State Department's policy of cultivating the goodwill of Epitácio Pessoa promised now to reap substantial benefits. The president dominated his ministers and insisted on retaining the final decision in all executive matters for himself. Not only was Epitácio a sincere friend of the United States, but he had also personally confided in Morgan his preference for a mission headed by Captain Carl T. Vogelgesang. The latter was a much-admired American officer who had served in Brazil at the end of the war. In Morgan's opinion, the appointment of Vogelgesang would clinch the contract for the United States.[38]

As on previous occasions involving naval matters, Morgan's recommendation for positive action was not implemented by his superiors. Hughes gave his approval for an American mission, but then routinely passed the matter to the Navy Department. Indeed, a misunderstanding between officials in Washington and the American embassy at Rio nearly resulted in diplomatic disaster. This arose from the Navy Department's initial response, declaring that Vogelgesang was unavailable but that another "distinguished officer" might be sent in his place. When the information was relayed to the Rio embassy, it was interpreted by Morgan as implying that Washington was prepared to send merely one officer and not a full mission comprising of at least 20 to 30 men of all ranks.[39]

The Brazilian government was most disappointed by what it considered to be an apparent display of American apathy. Epitácio retaliated by hinting ominously to Morgan of the "insistent" pressure of the British ambassador to win the mission for Britain.[40] It was evident that the president personally favored an American mission, but the American naval attaché at Rio, Captain Sparrow, became so disturbed by the turn of events that he predicted first, the likelihood of a joint Anglo-American mission and then, pessimistically, the award of the contract exclusively to the British. "Of course, I presume that our Government is very indifferent to whether we maintain relations of the character of military missions with other powers," lamented Sparrow. He added: "Unless a miracle happens, the British will get the mission, and the big contract which will later be given." The naval attaché gloomily concluded that he hoped all American naval personnel currently stationed in Brazil would be allowed to leave before the humiliating but inevitable decision favoring Britain was publicly announced.[41]

Contributing to the mood of local despondency was the emergence of a similar misunderstanding surrounding the American attitude toward the centennial celebration of Brazilian independence scheduled to be held in Rio during September 1922. The Brazilian press carried reports that the American Congress had objected to the appropriation of funds requested by the executive to send an American commission to the centennial. With a certain amount of understatement, Crosby observed in May 1922 that this news had created an "unfavorable impression."[42] In fact, the Harding administration was not indifferent. Although he gave little consideration to its historic or cultural significance, Secretary of State Hughes regarded the occasion as an important opportunity to promote American economic influence in Latin America. During the previous August he had urged Senator Henry Cabot Lodge of Massachusetts to exert his influence as chairman of the Senate Foreign Relations Committee to ensure that Congress vote one million dollars so that the United States could mount a "creditable exhibit." In a period of financial stringency, Lodge was not confident that such a large amount would be approved. Congressmen were well disposed toward Brazil, but queries were raised whether public funds should be used to promote private business interests at overseas expositions. Nevertheless, Lodge and his supporters in both the Senate and the House were able to prevail over critics wishing cuts in the appropriation. To the acute embarrassment of both Lodge and Hughes, it was then discovered that the appropriation was not strictly a foreign relations matter and should have been brought in the first instance before the House Committee on Industrial Arts and Expositions. The enforced wait for a favorable report from that particular committee introduced further delay and formed the basis for the press notices of American indifference toward the centennial.[43]

Indeed, the evident lack of cooperation between government departments on the question of relations with Brazil had attracted cabinet discussion during April 1922. It soon became evident, however, that the difficulties had arisen over means rather than ends. Both Secretary of State Hughes and Secretary of the Navy Denby found themselves in agreement on the desirability of winning the naval contract for the United States. Their direct involvement ensured that the matter received a high priority and that a coordinated strategy was put into effect. First, the Navy Department announced the release of Vogelgesang for overseas duty. At the same time Hughes was made aware of the misunderstanding with the Rio embassy and immediately telegraphed the government's willingness to dispatch a full mission and not just one officer. The secretary of state also linked the mission with Brazil's centennial exposition and believed that an "excellent effect" would be produced if someone of international prominence was appointed to head the American delegation. Who that person would be was uncertain, but the United States government decided in June to confirm publicly that it would be sending a distinguished commission. A few weeks later it was announced that Hughes would personally lead the special commission. "When the exhibition opens," summed up the British ambassador at Rio, the United States hope to carry everything before them."[44]

The positive attitude displayed by officials at Washington achieved its desired aim toward the end of July when the Brazilian government stated officially that the naval contract was to go to the United States. It was a decision received with obvious disappointment in Britain. The London *Times* declared that the outcome was a historical watershed marking the "waning of British prestige" in the Brazilian navy. The British ambassador, Sir John Tilley, reluctantly shared this opinion and dated the decline as starting from his country's wartime inability to provide naval instructors to Brazil. On that occasion, the Americans had more than competently filled the gap. A question of propriety arose in that the Brazilian government could hardly now reject American instructors and thereby commit "the insult of supplanting them after making use of them for several years." Tilley also believed that insufficient weight had been given to the feelings of gratitude that President Epitácio still retained as a result of American diplomatic assistance at Versailles.[45]

As Hughes set sail for Brazil in late August, the former director of the Pan American Union, John Barrett, described the secretary of state as the "envoy of new Pan-Americanism."[46] At the centennial exposition itself American businessmen displayed the latest technological marvels such as large models of electric light bulbs and stimulated a "radiophone craze" by mounting a broadcasting station on Corcovado.[47] Two American battleships were in attendance and their crews performed flying displays and a series of drill demonstrations. Although local visitors were duly impressed, the British ambassador reckoned that "the results do not seem to have been commensurate with the efforts made."[48] Partly responsible for this was the fact that the Brazilians welcomed the whole world to their centennial and were unable to give special attention to their American guests. Consequently, there was no attempt to create the public relations fanfare associated with Root's trip in 1906.[49] Moreover, in contrast to Root and Colby, Hughes appeared stiff and reserved in manner. The British ambassador remarked that he stayed "a very short time" and gave "the idea of being conscientiously civil to people whom he despised." Much more local attention was attracted by the presence of a commission from revolutionary Mexico and by the visit and eloquent speeches of the president of Portugal. "My instinct at present," commented Tilley, "is that the United States have weakened rather than strengthened their position."[50]

Nevertheless, the reversal of the decision over Vogelgesang's availability and Hughes's own presence at the centennial celebrations signified the importance attached by the Harding administration to winning the naval contract. Prominent among the members of the American commission was Captain Vogelgesang, whose purpose was to assist Hughes in completing the final details of the naval contract. Indeed, State Department officials pressed for speedy ratification. They were conscious that Epitácio Pessoa was scheduled to leave office in mid-November 1922 and would be replaced by Artur da Silva Bernardes, who was unlikely to be so sympathetic to the United States. Ratification was duly achieved by the executive action of both governments so that the contract was signed and binding on both countries for at least two years. By the close of 1922 American naval personnel had assembled in Rio and were ready to undertake their duties.[51]

The winning of the contract in face of British competition reflected a diplomatic triumph for the United States but one that Morgan had no wish to flaunt. He saw the mission's presence as "certain to arouse jealousy" and believed it would be best if it received "as little public notice as possible."[52] Moreover, the response of the new Bernardes administration remained uncertain. Morgan was particularly struck by the failure of the new navy minister, Admiral Alexandrino de Alencar, to make even a passing reference to the American mission in his speech on taking office. While the American ambassador attributed this omission to the minister's advanced age, he frankly admitted that considerable sentiment in favor of Britain still prevailed among the officers of the Brazilian navy.[53]

In fact, the most outspoken criticism came not so much from within Brazil or Europe but from Argentina. The Argentine government had already expressed disquiet earlier in the year over the proposals made by the French military mission to increase the size of the Brazilian army and to conduct military maneuvers in Rio Grande do Sul. At the head of Argentina's foreign office was Estanislau Zeballos, who rekindled the traditional antagonism between the two countries by publicly describing Brazil as a "serious menace."[54] Argentine sensitivity and concern were further heightened by the negotiation of the naval contract and the fact that its terms were not made public. The background of secrecy naturally encouraged speculation in Buenos Aires that the United States had pledged its support for Brazilian militaristic ambitions. These allegations were categorically rejected by Hughes, who privately reassured the Argentine government in December 1922 that the mission neither marked a new departure in American policy nor did it signify a desire for special relations with any particular South American country. He emphasized that the mission had been sent purely at the request of the Brazilian government for assistance in the modernization of its naval forces and that a similar arrangement was already in existence between the United States and Peru, thus demonstrating Washington's evenhanded approach in South America.[55]

Although Hughes sincerely wished to allay Argentine apprehensions, Morgan perceived the beneficial aspect of Argentine criticism in that it helped offset Brazilian misgivings against the mission. "The Brazilian admiralty," he observed, "is likely to think more rather than less of the mission because it is unpopular in Buenos Aires."[56] But the two continental rivals were far from set on a collision course. While the Brazilian government was worried by the military threat constantly posed by Argentina throughout the 1920s, it also desired friendly relations with its South American neighbor and did not wish to appear as militaristic. The Brazilian ambassador at Washington, Cochrane de Alencar, repeated on a number of occasions to Hughes that his government was not embarked upon a program of major rearmament and wished merely to reorganize its military forces for defensive purposes. Moreover, only a few days before Hughes arrived at Rio in 1922, a warm welcome had attended the visit of President-elect Marcello Alvear of Argentina. The friendly state of Argentine-Brazilian relations was also underlined by the decision of both countries to raise their diplomatic representatives to ambassadorial rank.[57]

The whole question was further complicated, however, by the decision of the Pan American Union in 1922 to revive the Pan-American conference system. The last meeting had been scheduled for Santiago de Chile in 1914, but had been canceled by the European war. It would now take place at the Chilean capital in March 1923. The Brazilian government publicly welcomed the development as a step toward Pan-American harmony, but was privately disturbed at the inclusion of the reduction of armaments as one of the most prominent items on the agenda. The new head of the Itamaraty, José Félix Alves Pacheco, feared that the Spanish-speaking nations intended to thwart his country's expressed desire to build up its military forces. Pacheco's journalistic background and lack of diplomatic experience inclined him to resort to bold and somewhat imprudent action.[58] Seeking to take advantage of the recent improvement in Argentine-Brazilian relations, he startled the foreign offices of South America in December 1922 by proposing a preliminary meeting of the ABC countries to discuss specifically the question of disarmament.[59]

Mindful of the value of American support, Pacheco instructed Cochrane de Alencar to sound out the views of the State Department. The ambassador gratifyingly reported from Washington that Hughes had no objection to the initiative and, in fact, favored any development that would promote naval disarmament.[60] Pacheco's proposal, however, received short shrift in both Buenos Aires and Santiago where it was condemned for being vague and hastily conceived.[61] Argentina had no desire to be seen as following Pacheco's lead and seized the opportunity to accuse him of seeking to circumvent the interests of the other Latin American nations in order to pursue Brazil's own selfish militaristic aims. Nor could Brazil rely any longer upon the friendly diplomatic assistance of Chile. The latter's suspicions of the United States had been heightened by the Washington naval conference. The British ambassador at Santiago believed that the Chilean government saw in Pacheco's proposal "the hand of the United States directed towards securing her ascendancy in the naval and military affairs of South America."[62]

Pacheco was chastened and retaliated by declaring that he would not attend the Pan-American conference. Confronted by Spanish-American hostility, he sought a sympathetic hearing in the United States. Assurances were sent to Hughes stating that Brazil had no aggressive designs and was practically disarmed already. In Pacheco's opinion, so long as the Brazilian navy was inferior to those of its neighbors the continuance of the status quo could only be to the advantage of Argentina and Chile.[63] An article in *O Jornal* articulately expressed the Brazilian viewpoint: "Standing in the way of limitation of armament in South America is the difficulty of an understanding between Brazil and Argentina. . . . If it is true that we do not possess sufficient military resources to meet a South American crisis, which is our most simple and possible problem, we are not yet in a position to consider limitation of armament. We cannot limit that of which we have too little."[64]

While American officials looked with favor on proposals to promote disarmament, they displayed no inclination to take any hemispheric initiative on this question or to become entangled in the internal politics of the ABC. "The tension between the Argentine and Brazil will make the U.S. Government cautious," wrote a British diplomat.[65] Indeed, the Harding administration approached the forthcoming Santiago conference with little enthusiasm. The agenda was held to contain too many potentially controversial political items, including a Uruguayan project to set up a Pan-American League of Nations. President Harding did attach significance to the conference and wanted Hughes to attend. However, it was quite evident that the secretary of state's sympathies and priorities lay elsewhere. Replying to the president that he "had no love whatever for speechmaking trips," Hughes declined to undertake another journey to South America so soon after his visit to Brazil's centennial. Instead, the experienced diplomat, Henry P. Fletcher, was appointed to head the United States delegation.[66]

Hughes's decision not only diminished the importance of the conference, but also encouraged Pacheco to stand firm in his refusal to go to Santiago. Nevertheless, despite its show of pique the Brazilian government eventually decided to attend. This was only publicly confirmed, however, after a secret understanding had been made with Chile stipulating that both their delegations would avoid discussion of the disarmament question.[67] The various delegates assembled on schedule in March 1923, and for the ensuing five to six weeks the conference provided little more than the usual forum for Pan-American rhetoric. In general, the proceedings attracted little comment in the Brazilian press. Nevertheless, both Pacheco and President Bernardes carefully followed events. The foreign minister still smarted from the way Argentina had taken advantage of his attempt at "open diplomacy," and he feared that the meeting at Santiago might cause further embarrassment.[68]

Consequently, the Brazilian delegation endured not only Spanish-American suspicion but also close supervision from Rio. What was described as a "hard task"[69] was fortunately eased by the similar desire of the Harding administration to steer clear of controversial issues. The American delegates had instructions to "bear in mind that the present Conference has not been called to sit in judgment on the conduct of any nation or to attempt to redress alleged wrongs." They were also told to expect "less hostility" from Brazil than any of the other Latin American nations.[70] Indeed, Morgan had reported earlier that the Brazilian delegates "will be able to work satisfactorily" with those of the United States.[71] His judgment was confirmed, although Brazilian dispatches complained privately that Fletcher appeared to hold the opinion that Brazil was seeking more armament than was necessary.[72] As chairman of the committee on armaments, the American diplomat possessed substantial influence, but he carefully avoided taking sides and preferred to confine his role to that of an intermediary trying to assist improved relations among the ABC powers.

The lack of American leadership was pleasing to Brazil because it effectively ensured that little progress could be made on the question of armaments. The British minister at Rio summed up the mood as the conference closed: "The main purpose, as far as Brazil is concerned is that the nightmare of Santiago is now over and that she has emerged with her hands free. . . . Still the fact remains that Brazil has come out of the conference giving the impression to the outside world that she is the one intransigent South American country in the matter of armaments."[73] At the last moment Fletcher privately invited the ABC governments to a further meeting to be held in Washington. This offer was courteously received, but not acted upon when the Itamaraty learned that Harding and Hughes did not regard the idea with favor.[74] However, as it became evident that the conference had only drawn Argentina and Brazil further apart, the State Department took fright that the United States would be blamed for this unwelcome development. A press communiqué was hastily issued, expressing the hope of the United States government that "notwithstanding the inherent difficulties, a satisfactory formula may be found."[75] In what must have appeared as an empty gesture to the diplomats who had participated in the conference, the United States publicly declared its readiness to act as an honest broker.

The following months saw no real change in the diplomatic deadlock. Despite reports of various high-level ABC meetings, Morgan doubted whether anything tangible would materialize. "The jealousy of Brazil and Argentina in regard to military and naval programs is still active," he observed in January 1924.[76] American policy in the shape of the naval mission merely contributed to this tension, even though the mission soon encountered its own local difficulties and frustrations. In December 1923 the British ambassador at Rio reported rumors of Vogelgesang's intention to "abandon the task" because he was irritated that his advice was ignored.[77] While the American chargé, Sheldon Crosby, was outwardly optimistic, he admitted "that at times it is very difficult and discouraging to get Brazilian officers to take a sufficient interest and initiative in the work which has been planned for them."[78] Moreover, the nationalistic tone of the Bernardes administration made the political atmosphere much less favorable to the United States than under Epitácio Pessoa; by mid-1924, speculation was rife that the mission might be withdrawn after only two years of duty. The British ambassador later analyzed the difficulties facing the Americans: "They have found the work of an uphill nature due to the indolent character of the Brazilians, the worn-out condition of the ships and the lack of money for training and upkeep."[79]

Just as relations appeared to reach their nadir, the foresight and perseverance of the mission's staff and its advocates at both Rio and Washington seemed suddenly about to be vindicated in June 1924, when Bernardes announced an ambitious naval program involving the prospect of substantial purchases of new ships and equipment. Two replacement battleships were envisaged, and the size of the fleet would be more than doubled to 200,000 tons. Vogelgesang's influence had finally taken effect, and it was confidently expected by the Rio embassy that the forthcoming naval orders would be placed in the United States. Events, however, took a surprising turn.

Morgan's advocacy of an American naval mission from 1917 onward had been predicated not only on its strategic and political value but also on its benefits for American business. Lansing endorsed this view, and that Hughes similarly approved and wanted an American mission in Brazil implied the continuity of American policy. In reality, the strategic imperatives resulting from the war were no longer pertinent. This became evident when Crosby's disclosure of Brazil's naval-rebuilding plan, far from pleasing Hughes, brought about a most unexpected rebuke. The secretary of state was highly critical of "a program on the scale proposed." He demanded an explanation from Vogelgesang and placed the admiral in a position of virtual disgrace.[80]

Citing the example of the activities of the French military advisers in successfully securing army contracts for their own manufacturers, Crosby replied to Hughes that, if another nation had gained the naval mission, it would have sought to exploit the resulting commercial advantages. "It may be natural to suppose," he argued, "that the representatives of American firms may have expected that preference would have been given to their products where naval construction was concerned." The chargé also noted disingenuously that the proposed program emphasized the much-needed replacement of out-of-date ships rather than the addition of purely new warships. While Hughes acknowledged that the Brazilian navy was inferior in strength to those of Argentina and Chile, he believed that the proposed program would lead not to equality but Brazilian superiority. "Such a result," he declared, "would be most unfortunate and would bring about a condition of armaments rivalry in this hemisphere which has happily up to now not existed." Crosby was curtly informed: "The Department feels so strongly about the matter that it would recall the Naval Mission rather than assume the responsibility for the naval program proposed by it."[81]

Brazil's legitimate security needs therefore fell victim to the determination of the Harding and Coolidge administrations to maintain the naval status quo in South America. The perceived role of the naval mission was dramatically clarified. Contrary to some Spanish-American fears, the mission was not designed to assist Brazilian militarism. Nor was it the agent of American business imperialism. Morgan, Crosby, and Vogelgesang were bluntly disabused by Hughes of any notion that it was their particular function to tout business for American armaments manufacturers. Similarly, when representatives of Bethlehem Steel visited the State Department in May 1924 they were informed that the department would help them to obtain equality of opportunity with foreign companies in competing for export orders in Brazil, but "it had never been the practice of this Government to send military missions to foreign countries in order to obtain contracts for American armaments manufacturers."[82] From the outset Hughes had conceived of the mission in a limited and technical sense and fully compatible with America's goal of achieving world peace by disarmament. This had been underlined in his description of the mission's activities conveyed to the Argentine government in December 1922: "The purpose of the Mission is merely to cooperate with the Brazilian Minister of Marine and with the officers of the Brazilian Navy to secure a good organization of the Brazilian Navy ashore and afloat; improving the methods of work and in training and instructing the personnel and in drawing up and executing plans for the improvement of the Navy."[83] If the United States had not complied with Brazil's request, Hughes argued that another power would have secured the contract, which could only have intensified the naval arms race in South America. Moreover, in the discussion over the terms of the contract, the State Department had required the inclusion of a proviso allowing the immediate termination of the mission should Brazil go to war. The mission represented, therefore, a moderating and not a warlike influence. The sincerity of American policy statements was later confirmed by Hughes's insistence that he would rather see the withdrawal of the mission than the United States held responsible for causing a buildup of armaments.[84]

Despite Crosby's forebodings, the commercial damage to American interests was slight. Only a few weeks after their announcement, Brazil's naval plans were suspended in July 1924 as armed revolt erupted in São Paulo against the federal government. For several weeks the Bernardes administration became totally preoccupied with defeating the rebels and ensuring the survival of the federal union. By the end of the month the rebels had been forced to evacuate the city of São Paulo and to withdraw into the interior. Bernardes had triumphed, but the ensuing stability appeared very precarious. "Although another military outbreak is unlikely to occur in the immediate future," noted Morgan in August 1924, "the political situation is far from calm and will continue to be disturbed until the termination of the Bernardes administration in 1926."[85]

The São Paulo revolt underlined the military deficiencies of the federal government and justified its desire to strengthen the nation's armed forces. But the attitude of the State Department remained unsympathetic. Late in 1924 the *New York Times* reported that Brazil was planning to revive its naval ambitions. Hughes immediately telegraphed the Rio embassy for clarification. Morgan could not deny the authenticity of the information, but he stressed apologetically that the naval mission was "in no wise responsible." Only a few months earlier Morgan had eagerly awaited the prospect of naval orders. Now he emphasized the precarious economic condition of government finances and sought to reassure Hughes with the statement: "Unlikely that national resources will make it possible to carry out any such program."[86]

The same guarded tone was evident in the embassy's appraisal of the mission's work as Vogelgesang's two-year tour of duty came to an end. Morgan believed that the admiral had approached a difficult task with tact and sound judgment. "The country was in financial straits, the Mission was expensive," explained Morgan, "and there was no money for effecting reorganization." Matters were, however, hardly improved by Vogelgesang's departure, for his successor could not achieve similar popularity. In fact, the British ambassador commented that Brazilian naval officers were "jealous" of the special financial terms and privileges of rank enjoyed by the Americans and hinted that the contract would not be extended when it came up for renewal in November 1926. So concerned was Morgan that he asked as early as March 1926 whether Washington wished an extension. In order to counter a possibly negative reply, he emphasized that the mission was popular in Brazil. Moreover, he considered that a unilateral American decision to withdraw would "be scarcely loyal" to the Brazilians, especially when it would abruptly end a task of instruction that had only just begun. The ambassador also reminded Washington that if the mission left, it would almost certainly be replaced by a British one with consequent loss of American influence and prestige.[87]

Such cogent arguments had little impact in Washington. State Department officials knew that Bernardes was scheduled to leave office in November, but they hardly regarded the mission's future as a matter of urgency or priority. "I think our policy," minuted Assistant Secretary of State Francis White, "should be to continue the Mission if Brazil wants it but not to try to force its continuance if Brazil doesn't want it."[88] Fortunately for Morgan, the Bernardes administration remained eager to strengthen the forces of the state against civil disorder and requested the renewal of the contract for another four years. This was agreed by both governments in July 1926. Like Epitácio Pessoa four years previously, Bernardes was tying the hands of his successor. But the issue was not controversial. Brazilian politics appeared to be marking time until the new president, Washington Luís Pereira de Sousa, assumed office in November.

A general expectation existed that Washington Luís would inaugurate a period of much-needed political and financial stability. Morgan shared this optimism and predicted the possibility of "a considerable number of orders" for the navy. No doubt, with the memory of the 1924 rebuke in mind, he also remarked that American companies could expect to obtain no more than "their fair share of these orders."[89] This laissez-faire approach faithfully reflected the thinking of the State Department. In December 1926 the continued ascendancy of these ideas was confirmed by a memorandum replying to public queries about the exact purpose of the naval mission. The memorandum stated that the mission merely illustrated the desire of the United States government "to lend its good offices when asked to do so by other governments wishing the services of American experts in various fields. These experts, it should be noted, serve under contracts or agreements which clearly define their status. There are no grounds for the allegation that through them the Government of the United States is trying to dominate the Government of any other country."[90]

Despite Spanish-American suspicions and any imagined Brazilian pretensions, the naval mission did not mark a special relationship or militaristic conspiracy between Brazil and the United States. Indeed, from the inception of the mission in 1922, officials at Washington had consistently downgraded its importance. This attitude appeared to confirm that the primary motivation of the Harding administration had been to prevent the contract falling into the hands of Britain. Once this was achieved, the State Department began to lose interest. Consequently, the American embassy at Rio was compelled to abandon the ambitious commercial strategy initially associated with the mission. The winning of the naval contract represented a notable diplomatic success for the United States and established a crucial foundation for future extension of American influence over the training, operational procedures, and strategy of the Brazilian navy. American instructors worked hard to improve naval organization and efficiency. However, a later report concluded that "results were in no way commensurate with the efforts being expended."[91] Far from strengthening relations between the two countries, the naval mission served only to further misunderstanding and frustration.

ECONOMIC RELATIONS

After a brief postwar economic boom Brazil experienced growing financial instability during the first half of the 1920s. The budget of the federal government swung into deficit; inflation soared to record levels; and the milréis began a downward spiral, losing half its value in two years. Consequently, the terms of international trade moved adversely against Brazil. While the weak milréis made foreign goods more expensive, it did little to assist Brazilian exports because of the sharp fall in world demand for products such as cotton, meat, and manganese. The slump in commodity prices extended to coffee whose price collapsed from almost 24 cents per pound in 1919 to just over 9 cents in 1921. After reaching a peak of £128 million in 1919, Brazilian exports fell to £58 million in 1921. The Old Republic actually suffered a deficit in its visible balance of trade in 1920 and 1921.[92]

Both the Epitácio Pessoa and Bernardes administrations responded to the severe financial crisis by adopting orthodox policies of fiscal austerity. A firm emphasis was placed on balancing the federal budget and restricting the circulation of money in order to bring about an appreciating milréis.[93] Financial stability was ultimately achieved by the middle of the decade but at the cost of economic stagnation and considerable political and social discontent. Epitácio Pessoa and Bernardes bore the brunt of public criticism, but foreigners, including Americans, also incurred blame. Nationalist sentiment was particularly alarmed by the large increase in the foreign debt and fearful that overseas interests were buying up substantial amounts of national territory and economic resources. The schemes of the American entrepreneur, Percival Farquhar, to exploit the vast iron-ore deposits located at Itabira in Minas Gerais excited particular suspicion.[94] In 1926 the Brazilian Congress passed a constitutional amendment nationalizing all mineral deposits located on federal land. Despite its desire to attract foreign capital to reduce the deficit and stabilize the milréis, the federal government did not disavow these nationalist suspicions. Epitácio Pessoa was in favor of increased economic contact with foreign countries, but he was also a staunch nationalist. British diplomatic dispatches described his successor, Artur Bernardes, as an "open xenophobe." The American chargé, Sheldon Crosby, reckoned that Bernardes opposed foreign investment because of his inordinate anxiety that foreigners would "control" Brazil's resources and assets.[95]

On the other hand, the growth of economic nationalism was moderated by the traditional desire of the Brazilian elite to maintain close contact with the world economy and especially with the United States. Of the foreign nations, the latter had made the most striking economic advance in Brazil during the war. In 1913 it had accounted for almost one-quarter of Brazil's foreign trade. By 1919 that amount had virtually doubled. Underpinning these figures was the remarkable rise in value of American exports, whose share of the Brazilian market increased from 15 to 48 percent. At long last, American merchants appeared to have established economic ascendancy over their European rivals. However, the wartime gains were soon challenged by the revival of strong European competition, especially from Britain. From a peak of $156 million in 1920, American exports slumped to just one-third of this figure in the following year. Although America's share of the Brazilian market was reduced to 25 percent during the early 1920s, the decline was not irreversible. By the second half of the decade American exports once again exceeded $100 million and surpassed in value those from Britain. It was evident that a new pattern of trade, in which the United States was preeminent, was establishing itself. Whereas Britain's trade dominance had been based on coal and textiles, Brazil looked to the United States to supply the new products of the twentieth century such as automobiles, films, petroleum products, and electrical goods. The demand for these items was constantly growing and was restrained only by Brazil's financial inability to buy.[96]

Trade from Brazil to the United States experienced similar statistical fluctuations during the 1920s. Brazilian exports peaked in 1919 at $233 million and then fell to $96 million in 1921. A slow recovery began until exports were in excess of $200 million by the middle of the decade. However, in marked contrast to the pattern of American exports, Brazil had no new products to sell. Indeed, the long-standing importance attached to coffee increased rather than decreased. In 1925 it was estimated that coffee accounted for 87 percent of Brazil's earnings from sales to the United States. Consequently, the latter remained Brazil's single biggest market, with purchases ranging from 42 to 47 percent of Brazil's total annual exports. The dependent economic relationship excited little adverse comment in Brazil. To sell coffee was considered an end in itself and vital for national prosperity. Moreover, the balance of trade remained in favor of Brazil. Americans could hardly be criticized for being not only Brazil's best customers but also for purchasing more from Brazil than they sold. "We buy from the people who buy most from us," summed up the *Jornal do commercio*, "these are precisely the great people of the United States who represent the world's greatest consuming market."[97]

The war also witnessed the emergence of Wall Street as the world's leading money market and financial center. American investments flooded the world and substantial sums were directed toward Latin America. Prior to 1914 there had been relatively little American financial involvement in Brazil. While American investment amounted to scarcely $50 million, British loans were in excess of $1 billion. During the war American banks and financial institutions steadily increased their interest in Brazil. In 1921 and 1922 large sums amounting to more than $150 million were placed mainly in railroads, utilities, and state and municipal bonds. However, the amount lent in 1923 declined precipitately to a low point of just over $2 million. The default by a number of state governments was particularly damaging to Brazilian credit. Nevertheless, a recovery followed during the middle of the decade so that by 1929 total American investment in Brazil reached almost $500 million. Although this was only one-third of the corresponding British figure, American investment had grown at a faster rate than that of Britain during the decade and constituted a larger proportion of new capital issues.[98]

Stocks and bonds, however, were only part of America's economic success story. In its ever-widening search for markets and raw materials, American business invested directly in Brazil to finance the acquisition and establishment of local subsidiary companies. British and foreign competitors found themselves overwhelmed by the financial resources available to the giant American corporations.[99] The latter included Armour, Ford, General Electric, General Motors, Standard Oil, Swift, United States Steel, and Westinghouse. Corporate investment brought cash for new factories and jobs. It also spread American business skills and cultural values. One American traveler reported in 1925 that General Electric operated "the only factory in Brazil where the women wear shoes."[100] The building of "outposts of Yankee enterprise" was most vividly symbolized by Henry Ford and his Ford Motor Company. At its São Paulo plant in 1919, the company assembled just over 2,000 automobiles. In 1925 production had increased to the same figure per month with an annual capacity of 45,000. Model Ts, Fordson trucks, and tractors became a regular sight on the roads of Brazil. By 1928 the Ford Motor company had authorized 700 agencies and more than 2,000 garages all over Brazil to market, distribute, and repair its products. Henry Ford's ambitions knew no bounds. Acquiring a concession of territory almost the size of Connecticut, he ordered work to commence in 1928 on his ultimately ill-fated scheme to create a prosperous rubber plantation in the Amazon jungle.[101]

American economic expansion in Brazil during the 1920s was largely the achievement of private individuals, financial institutions, and industrial corporations. The United States government played an important though essentially supportive role. Officials in Washington and Rio were keen to promote American trade and investment, but the task was complicated by the misunderstandings that seemed all too frequently to affect their commercial dealings with the Brazilian government. One obvious example had been the ill feeling arising from the persistent American demands for preferential reductions in the Brazilian tariff. Although this particular cause of annoyance lapsed after the settlement of the valorization dispute, it assumed another form as a result of America's startling economic transformation during the war. No longer so fearful of foreign competition, the United States abandoned the pursuit of special tariff concessions and sought equality of commercial treatment. The aim was equal access or the "open door" to the markets of the world. The new commercial strategy was contained in a proviso of the 1922 Tariff Act, which ruled that existing tariff preferences should be terminated and replaced by treaties containing a most-favored-nation clause. In contrast to the 1894 tariff, these agreements were to be achieved by negotiation rather than by unilateral abrogation.[102]

The intention of the tariff proviso was to conclude a large number of new trade treaties, especially with European nations. Existing commercial arrangements were regarded as expendable. In the case of Brazil, State Department officials would have to overturn an arrangement that was evidently satisfactory on both sides because it had been renewed annually for the past decade. Without any trace of embarrassment the State Department informed the Brazilian government in December 1922 that it no longer wished the continuation of the annual grant of preferences to imports of American goods and requested that this be replaced by a treaty extending most-favored-nation treatment to the United States.[103]

The initiative was ill timed: the Bernardes administration had only recently taken office and was preoccupied with formulating its policies toward the forthcoming Pan-American conference at Santiago. Conscious of the financial crisis facing the nation, the new president desired stability and was inclined therefore to defer taking action on an issue as politically and economically divisive as the tariff. Only three years previously the Epitácio Pessoa administration had attempted to reduce tariff levels and had suffered a rebuff from Congress.[104] The American request threatened to reopen the controversy and thereby upset the complex web of interstate business relationships that made up Brazilian commercial policy.

Moreover, beyond the bland prediction from Secretary of State Hughes that "in the long run this policy offers larger advantages of amity and trade," there was no apparent incentive for Brazil to conclude a new commercial treaty.[105] Indeed, Bernardes was concerned that the most-favored-nation concept would severely restrict his government's latitude of commercial maneuver. So long as the vast majority of Brazilian products were imported into the United States free of duty, Brazil had nothing to gain from acquiring "most-favored-nation" status. On the other hand, the United States would be entitled as a "most-favored-nation" to receive whatever tariff advantages Brazil might grant to other nations. This would apply to existing arrangements such as the one concluded by Brazil with Belgium in 1920 and any treaty which might be negotiated in the future. In fact, the arrangement with Belgium had already prompted Britain to press the Itamaraty for a similar commercial agreement. The Brazilian government feared that the American proposal would only encourage further international pressure for trade concessions which, if granted by Brazil, must also be given to the United States.[106]

The one American diplomat to appreciate Brazil's difficulties was Edwin Morgan. Instead of submitting the customary request for renewal of the preferential duties, the ambassador found himself advocating a type of treaty his government had always firmly resisted. In his dispatches to Washington Morgan pointed out that the preferential policy was an American creation and arose as a result of Brazil being "educated by the United States." He considered it somewhat invidious for his government to insist on reversing a policy it had itself originally inspired. Such arguments, however, carried little weight at the State Department where officials simply reaffirmed that "it is the policy of the United States to offer to all countries and to seek from them unconditional most-favored-nation treatment."[107]

Like the majority of foreign governments, Brazil was not greatly interested in taking up the offer. Discussions could not be avoided, but little substantive progress was made.[108] By the summer of 1923 American officials acknowledged that a formal treaty was impossible to achieve and agreed to a compromise that effectively reaffirmed the status quo. To mollify the Americans, Brazil agreed that the treaty negotiations had only been temporarily deferred. A "modus vivendi" was drawn up in October 1923, stipulating that the existing tariff advantages were not only to be retained but were also to be extended to other American products. Significantly, the advantages were redefined as most-favored-nation concessions and were no longer to be known as "preferences." The United States had failed to secure a treaty, but the letter of the 1922 tariff law had been met. The Bernardes administration was relieved to have prevented an unwelcome issue from acquiring domestic and international complications.[109]

As the tariff question diminished in importance, American diplomats found more of their time and energy being directed to promoting the export of American capital. During the war the United States government had encouraged the efforts of American businessmen to displace the previously well-established European interests in Latin America. Brazil attracted particular interest, and various financial schemes were proposed which, if implemented, would have resulted in significant American influence over that country's economic affairs. One ambitious plan even envisaged Brazil depositing its gold reserves with the Federal Reserve Bank.[110] Immediately after the close of the war, officials were also active in cultivating the goodwill of leading Brazilian politicians such as President Epitácio Pessoa and assisting American companies to gain control of commercially and strategically important communications facilities such as telegraph cables and radio.[111]

The conduct of foreign economic policy was hampered, however, by bureaucratic constraints and rivalries. The State Department had long considered itself the premier institution, with responsibility for relations with foreign countries including matters of trade and investment. During the war years this preeminence was challenged by the Treasury and the Commerce Department. However, with the lifting of wartime financial regulations the interest of the Treasury in loans noticeably diminished. Moreover, an economy-minded Congress instituted cuts in appropriations for the Commerce Department on the grounds that there was too much needless duplication of the commercial activities of the State Department.[112] But the latter's triumph was short-lived. Interdepartmental rivalry between State and Commerce was renewed after Herbert Hoover became secretary of commerce in March 1921. Under Hoover's dynamic leadership the Commerce Department claimed the commanding role in the promotion of the foreign trade of the United States and encroached directly upon the State Department's traditional control of foreign economic policy.[113]

The most immediate clash arose over the question of loans to Latin America. An element of uncertainty existed in American financial circles after 1919 as to whether the federal government would continue its wartime practice of supervising these loans. The perceptive Hoover saw an opportunity for administrative aggrandizement. Expressing concern that his department was too frequently bypassed whenever there was discussion of loans to Latin America, he wrote a personal letter to Harding in January 1922 noting that "there is no one particular department that has the responsibility in this matter." In Hoover's opinion, foreign loans were an essential means of boosting exports and directly affected "commercial" questions in the United States such as employment, the movement of commodities, and provision of credit. These "commercial" aspects were "constant" and required the attention of the Commerce Department.[114]

Under the guise of how best to further the national interest, a fierce bureaucratic struggle ensued in Washington. Hoover argued in favor of a systematic policy to control foreign loans. He was adept at public relations and enjoyed considerable political support from Congress. But Hoover faced a formidable antagonist in Secretary of State Hughes. While the State Department tacitly acknowledged that it should avoid competition with the Commerce Department on purely commercial questions, it was determined to assert its prerogative on "political" aspects. On March 3, 1922 the State Department shrewdly outmaneuvered Hoover by issuing the "Statement on Loans." This document emphasized that the State Department was responsible for the conduct of foreign relations and requested that bankers inform the department in advance of their loans. The Treasury and the Commerce Department would be asked to examine the financial and commercial details while State Department officials would review the political implications and determine whether any objection should be made.[115]

The public declaration of the State Department's administrative powers was not intended to signal a governmental policy of formally controlling foreign loans. A degree of supervision was considered necessary in the national interest, but the cooperation of the financial community was invited rather than insisted upon. State Department officials also invariably pointed out that a statement of "no objection" to a loan was not to be interpreted as a government guarantee. This was underlined by the insertion of the following disclaimer in the "Statement on Loans": "The Department of State does not pass upon the merits of foreign loans as business propositions nor assume any responsibility in connection with such transactions, also that no reference to the attitude of this Government should be made in any prospectus or otherwise."[116]

This cautious approach was applied to dealings with all Latin American countries. Brazil enjoyed no exemption or special attention. In 1920 the Brazilian ambassador at Washington requested the State Department to use its good offices to persuade American bankers to take up a loan on behalf of the Brazilian federal government. Alvey Adee replied that the department could only "advise" bankers and that they must make their own specific arrangements with foreign governments.[117] A similar attitude was conveyed in 1924 by Assistant Secretary of State Joseph Grew. When asked whether political disturbances in Brazil would affect the security of a proposed loan, he told a group of New York bankers that this was "a matter of business judgment as to which this Department can assume no responsibility.[118] By the same token Grew realized that government supervision could only go so far. In response to a complaint from Hoover that American banks were "evading" guidelines on loans to Brazil, he noted:

> I do not see that there is anything effective that we could do about this. The importation and sale of these bonds is entirely legal. In these matters we must rely on the cooperation of bankers to carry out the spirit as well as the letter of such indications of policy as we may make to them. If an American firm, knowing the policy of the Government will openly try to evade that policy, I do not believe the firm would regard a suggestion from the Government, that it act differently in the matter.[119]

On the understanding that the United States government would not enter into particular financial commitments or entanglements, the Harding and Coolidge administrations were eager to encourage American investment in Latin America. No objection was made to the large number of Brazilian loans floated in 1921 and 1922. Brazil was also eager to attract funds from Wall Street and saw this as a means of reducing the country's irksome dependence on European money markets. But diplomacy could hinder as well as help the flow of investment, as became evident when divergent attitudes arose once again between the governments of Brazil and the United States over the question of coffee.

In 1922 memories of the earlier controversy over valorization were reawakened when the Brazilian federal government reacted to the dramatic slump in coffee prices by reinstituting a policy of directly purchasing substantial quantities of coffee so as to regulate supply and thereby maintain, if not raise, prices to higher levels. On this occasion, the term "valorization" was scrupulously avoided in favor of the less emotive description "the permanent defense of coffee."[120] The deliberate use of the word "permanent" underlined the desire to evolve a long-term strategy that entailed not only the purchase and storage of surpluses but also the financing and supervision of future crops. In a further attempt to escape the difficulties associated with the first valorization scheme, control over stocks was maintained by Brazilians and not assigned to foreign bankers or valorization committees. The policy promised to be highly costly and attracted only halfhearted support from the economy-minded Bernardes administration. Moreover, the Mineiro president was reluctant to raise foreign loans that were designed predominantly to assist Paulista coffee interests. The growing disenchantment with federal policy persuaded the state of São Paulo to establish its own Defense Institute in December 1924. São Paulo was joined later by the other coffee-producing states after the federal government virtually abandoned its purchases of coffee in 1927. Despite the internal dissensions, the overall strategy was successful inasmuch as coffee prices rose in 1924 to a level 50 percent higher than the preceding year.[121]

The policy of defense, however, was on such a large scale that it could not be conducted in a vacuum. Overseas assistance and cooperation were indispensable for its continued success. Because Brazilian financial resources were inadequate to fund its effective operation, the program required substantial foreign loans. In 1922, £9 million was raised from British and American banks for this purpose. Indeed, foreign bankers were initially very ready to participate in a scheme that held out the prospect of relatively high returns and attractive rates of commission.[122] More problematic was the reaction of foreign consumers and their governments to the deliberate effort of Brazilian federal and state authorities to manipulate market forces and thereby dictate the level of coffee prices. In this sense, the response of the United States was crucial and proved a dominant theme in the unfolding of "the coffee question" during the 1920s.

Officials at both the Departments of State and Commerce in Washington were well aware of the attempts to influence coffee prices. It was not considered, however, a matter for either diplomatic protest or discussion at government level. There was no discernible evidence of the existence in the United States of a coffee "king" or "trust" whose operations were likely to provoke legal investigation and adverse political comment. Indeed, with coffee selling for as little as ten cents per pound in 1922, American officials regarded Brazilian efforts as skillful and even necessary to alleviate the damaging effects of overproduction. Moreover, the experience of wartime emergency measures had altered American attitudes toward state intervention in the economy. For example, Grosvenor Jones of the Commerce Department sympathetically compared Brazil's action to the assistance that the War Finance Corporation had given to American copper producers.[123]

Nevertheless, the frustrating lessons of previous coffee conflicts were not easily discarded. American officials appeared unwilling to distinguish between "defense" and "valorization" and invariably insisted on using the latter, more pejorative term. William Manning of the State Department summed up in August 1922: "If that country wishes to manipulate the market and charge 'all that the traffic will bear,' it is probably useless for this country or the rest of the world to prevent it, except in so far as it can be done by retaliatory threats or practices." Manning's note of alarm was tempered, however, by his belief that Brazil was "treading on dangerous ground" and might "suffer the natural economic penalty" caused by stimulating other nations to increase their own production so that they might also profit from rising prices. While more competition might be detrimental to Brazil, it could only be to the benefit of the United States.[124] Indeed, as sales of Colombian coffee climbed to more than 15 percent of the American market, it appeared that Manning's prediction was already beginning to materialize.[125]

Just as in the previous valorization dispute, the rise in coffee prices after 1922 aroused pleasure in Brazil but growing displeasure in the United States. One group of American coffee importers represented by the National Coffee Roasters Association was especially critical.[126] Because the matter was not one of diplomatic dispute between governments, the coffee roasters directed their protests to the Commerce Department. While this underlined the growing prestige of the latter and its success in establishing close relations with the business world, Commerce Department officials were unable to act on these complaints. Precluded from dealing directly with foreign governments, they passed the relevant correspondence on to the State Department for action via diplomatic channels. Morgan was informed, but regarded the matter of coffee prices as less important than the arrival of the American naval mission and the requirement to conclude a new commercial treaty arising from the 1922 tariff. After conferring with the commercial attaché, William Schurz, he reported in December 1922 that the embassy would "watch the situation but shall not take action."[127]

The Commerce Department was not so inclined to adopt the passive role envisaged for it by Morgan and the State Department. As Director of the Bureau of Foreign and Domestic Commerce, Julius Klein maintained a keen interest in developments. The Harvard-trained economic historian was personally hostile to the concept of valorization and instructed Schurz to exert informal pressure upon the Brazilian government. For example, in July 1923 Klein recommended that "our people" convey a protest "tactfully to the appropriate Brazilian authorities." Almost a year later he noted that "our office in Rio has long been serving as a friendly intermediary" between the Brazilian government and American coffee importers. However, Klein was alarmed by the drift of events in 1924 and warned Herbert Hoover that "the situation may again come to a head."[128] In December, at the same time that the Defense Institute was being established in São Paulo, the National Coffee Roasters Association met with the secretary of commerce and presented a petition asking for government assistance to reduce the price of coffee.

Hoover's economic views were already well known and virtually guaranteed the roasters a favorable response. The "rugged individualist" firmly believed in a "free" economy both at home and abroad and was acutely suspicious of attempts by foreign governments to establish monopolies over raw materials. In his first annual report as secretary of commerce he had listed nine commodities that were considered particularly vulnerable: cotton, camphor, coffee, iodine, nitrates, potash, mercury, rubber, and sisal. The one that initially most concerned him was rubber, and he soon became involved in a battle against the alleged British monopoly in this product.[129] The other commodities were left alone until 1925 when Hoover suddenly widened the struggle to include coffee.

For the following 18 months the coffee question revolved around Herbert Hoover, who acted as the virtual "economic president" of the United States.[130] Moreover, his ability to influence foreign economic policy was enhanced by the retirement of Hughes in January 1925. It was a most opportune time for the Commerce Department to seize the initiative. Consequently, the new secretary of state, Frank Kellogg, found himself relegated to a subordinate role as Hoover launched a public relations campaign against the Brazilian coffee cartel. Although Hoover claimed to represent "the administration," he astutely avoided assuming direct diplomatic responsibilities. He refrained from attacking or dealing directly with the federal government of Brazil or the state government of São Paulo. His wrath was directed instead at "the São Paulo coffee speculators,"[131] whom he accused of conducting a "trade war" against the consumer in which the price of coffee had been deliberately driven up from 13 cents a pound in the spring of 1924 to more than 30 cents during 1925. A report prepared by Commerce Department officials estimated that Americans were being overcharged more than $80 million a year for their coffee. Having alerted the public to what was going on, Hoover planned to encourage the formation of a countercartel of American buyers that would employ its own market power to force a reduction of price.[132]

In addition, Hoover sought to strike at the heart of Brazil's valorization policy by persuading American bankers not to finance the Paulista Defense Institute. The timing was both deliberate and opportune: the Paulistas were eager to raise money in the American market after failing to secure a loan in London. But Hoover's strategy could only be effected indirectly. According to the provisions of the 1922 "Statement on Loans," bankers initially approached the State Department about foreign loans. Kellogg, however, had no disagreement on policy with Hoover and was quite ready to cooperate. Officials at the Latin American Division were instructed to scrutinize carefully all proposed financial arrangements with São Paulo.[133] The one that caused the most trouble related to Speyer and Company of New York. In March 1925, a representative of Speyer and Company told the State Department that the government of São Paulo wished to borrow $15 million to modernize the Sorocabana railroad. Assistant Secretary of State Leland Harrison pressed for further information and immediately telephoned news of his meeting to

Hoover's personal assistant. Commerce Department officials were suspicious, but agreed not to object to the loan on condition that the bankers give written assurances that none of the proceeds would be used to assist valorization.[134] Despite the granting of these assurances, it quickly became evident that part of the loan had been diverted to purchase coffee. William Manning was so annoyed that he recommended in June what would have amounted to a government embargo on American loans not only to the state of São Paulo but extending even to the federal government of Brazil.[135]

In contrast to Hoover's adversarial stance, the Paulista coffee interests displayed a desire for discussion and compromise. During the early months of 1925 their case was ably presented by the Brazilian consul-general at New York, João Carlos Muñiz. In a series of unofficial speeches, which were reprinted in the press, he sought to explain the policy of defense to American audiences. He stressed that Brazil wished a stable market in coffee and did not want to drive away customers. Muñiz attributed the increase in price not to the machinations of his country but to the recent fall in coffee cultivation. In addition, the Defense Institute had to contend with factors beyond its control such as the rising cost of production in Brazil and the fluctuating value of the milréis.[136]

A sympathetic response was forthcoming from American coffee merchants and importers. Unlike the consumer, their major concern was to secure a reliable and regular supply of coffee. Price was a lesser consideration. Consequently, Hoover's hopes for an effective cartel of buyers were dashed as prominent figures such as Felix Coste of the National Coffee Roasters Association and Berent Friele of the National Chain Store Grocers Association broke ranks. During June and July 1925 meetings between representatives of American coffee interests and officials of the Defense Institute were held in São Paulo. Both sides found much in common. Mindful of the likelihood of bumper coffee crops in 1926–1927 they fully appreciated the need for cooperation and portrayed the policy of defense as necessary to regulate supply. American representatives concurred that substantial financial assistance to the newly formed Defense Institute was essential and undertook to present this view to officials in Washington.[137]

The State Department was ignored as Coste and Friele concentrated their efforts on Hoover. From late August onward they presented the Paulista case in writing and by personal interviews. The prospects for success, however, were hardly helped by the fact that the same individuals had advocated an opposite course of action less than a year previously. Hoover listened, but could see no reason to approve the use of American funds to finance a scheme that led directly to higher prices for the defenseless American consumer. He implied that there was too much profiteering by the Defense Institute and stated that the price of coffee was too high and must be reduced. To the argument that

São Paulo might go bankrupt, he replied that such an outcome would be "the result of their own folly." In Hoover's view, the manipulation of prices led to the twin evils of underconsumption and overproduction, which would spell inevitable ruin for the Paulista coffee industry. The only logical course of action was to abandon valorization.[138]

The new Brazilian ambassador at Washington, Silvino Gurgel do Amaral, cynically remarked that "the Americans easily forget their own trusts." After a meeting with the secretary of commerce, he described Hoover's attitude as "hostile." Although personally dismayed, the ambassador was not surprised when Hoover launched a public tirade against Brazilian coffee policy beginning with a speech at Erie, Pennsylvania, on October 31, 1925.[139] Silvino's dispatches to Rio privately described Hoover as "truculent and arrogant." Annoyed at the way in which a cabinet officer openly conducted a public campaign against a friendly country, the ambassador could only believe that Hoover was deliberately playing politics with his eyes on the next presidential election.[140] If so, Brazil's leading industry was the victim of one man's personal political ambitions.

Hoover nursed presidential hopes, but there is no documentary evidence to show that he sought to use the coffee question as a springboard to the White House. He had embarked on a battle against the coffee monopoly as part of the campaign for free access to the world's raw materials. In this struggle Hoover regarded the support of American public opinion as crucially important. The value he placed on public opinion was revealed by his concern to gauge press reaction to the demand that American loans be withheld from the Defense Institute. The analysis prepared by his personal staff in November 1925 showed that ten newspapers approved while six were opposed.[141] It was hardly conclusive evidence of overwhelming public approval. Moreover, Wall Street was not the only source of capital for foreign loans. Indeed, on the same day as the Erie speech, Kellogg dispatched a letter informing him that the Paulistas might turn to the London money market for a loan. "It appears possible," noted the secretary of state, "that financial pressure on our part might not indefinitely be effective." However, the hint that the United States should relax its policy of financial supervision received the uncompromising retort from Hoover that loaning money was "merely a method of pouring credit into the coffee speculation."[142]

Contributing to the State Department's sense of unease was the argument of certain American bankers that restrictions upon loans would only antagonize Latin America and hinder the expansion of United States influence. Advice from Washington was acceptable, but dictation was resented. In a personal letter to Leland Harrison, James Speyer complained of the government's "parental" attitude that prevented his company participating in "safe and profitable transactions" such as the $35 million loan currently being sought by São Paulo. "In the long run," he predicted, "this will help Great Britain and work a disadvantage for the U.S.A."[143] It was a cogent point of view and one that State Department officials preferred to gloss over. Their embarrassing lack of control over current policy was reflected in Harrison's formal reply to Speyer. While reiterating government support for American loans to overseas countries, he reminded the banker of the "strong feeling on the part of leading members of the administration that American credits to foreign combinations engaged in fixing prices to American consumers should be discouraged."[144]

A further cause of concern to the State Department was the report in the New York press that Hoover's public statements had produced "a considerable outburst of criticism in Brazil." Dispatches from Edwin Morgan confirmed that the "hostile action" of the United States government had provoked "unfavorable reaction toward American interests in São Paulo."[145] Hoover had always been careful in his speeches and correspondence to avoid any expression of hostility toward the government of Brazil or its people. But he was alert to possible charges that his actions were damaging to United States–Brazilian relations. By requesting William Schurz to assess local reaction to his Erie speech, Hoover demonstrated his understanding of how to prepare the ground to outmaneuver political opponents. Seizing upon Schurz's brief but reassuring report, Hoover effectively muzzled the State Department by informing Kellogg: "there was no hostile reaction in Brazil towards Americans or American trade as the result of the administration's policy. . . . I might add that there had been some criticism in Sao Paulo but it has been merely local and that the rest of Brazil, as near as I can make out, is entirely in favor of our activities."[146]

In a similar blunt fashion, Hoover also dismissed press criticism that he was overzealous or too forceful. Lengthy explanations were not even necessary. It was quite sufficient for Hoover to declare that monopolies were illegal in the United States and ultimately damaging to world peace and harmony. In a private letter he noted:

> No one wishes to maintain the good will of foreign nations more than I do, but I would be serving the American people badly if I did not bespeak their interest as consumers against the monstrous imposition which has been imposed upon them in many directions. Furthermore, unless the growth of foreign monopolies directed against consuming countries can be halted, we shall be confronted with an era of international friction such as we have never hitherto conceived.[147]

Like the battle against the British rubber cartel, the coffee question was presented not as an isolated and obscure economic issue but one that directly affected world peace. It also involved an everyday commodity enjoyed by the large majority of Americans. Not surprisingly, some emotions were highly aroused. "Don't let the Powers down you in your effort to help the people," wrote one admiring supporter. A letter from a Minnesotan housewife urged Hoover to "remember the Boston Tea Party."[148] Moreover, Hoover's spirited stand against the foreign monopolists appeared to achieve tangible results. By the end of 1925 coffee prices had fallen to 22 cents per pound. Hoover noted gratifyingly that this difference meant an annual saving to the American consumer of $50 million.[149]

On the other hand, the government of São Paulo had refused to abandon the policy of defense or to desist from seeking an American loan. Wisely avoiding a direct confrontation with the most powerful political figure in America, it relied on the efforts of sympathetic American coffee merchants and bankers to bring about a change in government policy. The pressure was stepped up in December 1925 when Coste informed Hoover "that a strong unfavorable feeling towards this country exists" in Brazil. Hoover also received a personal letter from James Speyer expressing concern that "too close restrictions" would cause the United States to lose the São Paulo loan and "the financial leadership and prestige that goes with it."[150] In a similar vein, Morgan reported the irritation felt by Paulista officials and urged the desirability of "some sign of friendly disposition" on the part of the United States government.[151]

Even before Morgan's dispatch reached Washington, American officials had realized the need for a conciliatory gesture. Worried by the prospect of a Brazilian backlash against American trade, Klein informed Shurz that "any sound program for agricultural banking or other solution will be given strongest support provided valorization be eliminated."[152] In December an attempt was made to soothe Brazilian feelings by offering "no objection" to two small loans floated in New York for the construction of waterworks and sanitation projects in São Paulo. On Christmas Eve, Hoover issued a statement to the press denying reports that his household had switched from coffee to tea. "Nothing of the sort has been done or suggested," he declared.[153]

The holiday season had barely ended when it was announced that the Paulistas had successfully raised a loan of £5 million in London. This represented a considerable boost for the Defense Institute, which was now able to proceed with its plan for substantial coffee purchases. Speyer's forebodings were fulfilled as Schurz observed that the loan "has greatly strengthened the British position in São Paulo and has correspondingly reduced our prestige in that field."[154] Moreover, Hoover's assessment of Brazilian opinion as well disposed was contradicted by Morgan's report that Brazilians were jubilantly contrasting "the rebuke" in Wall Street to "the apparent warm welcome" of the London money market.[155] "The Americans," concluded *O Jornal*, "showed again that they do not possess the same thorough psychological knowledge of foreign peoples as the English."[156]

Despite his best efforts, Hoover had not been able either to organize an effective boycott of coffee at home or to prevent São Paulo from raising a loan in the international money market.[157] On Capitol Hill there was talk of reprisal against Brazil, but Hoover appeared before a congressional committee to argue that retaliation would only "aggravate" the problem. According to the *New York Times*, the secretary of commerce was acting like "a man trying to put out a fire which he himself had started."[158] The Commerce Department maintained its opposition to foreign governmental monopolies, but the public campaign against the Defense Institute was suddenly wound down, and a desire was signaled to mend fences. In April 1926 Hoover gave an interview designed for publication in the leading Paulista daily newspaper, the *Estado de São Paulo*. He skirted the issue of foreign loans and simply stated the administration's desire "to offer any proper and acceptable aid." However, he gladly seized the opportunity to praise "the great sister republic of the South," expressing his "clearest sympathy" with the coffee industry of São Paulo and "warmest concern for its continued prosperity." Schurz reported reassuringly from Rio that "the interview caused an excellent impression with everybody."[159]

In the meantime a little flurry of diplomatic activity had occurred. The fact that the question had never been deemed to be an issue between governments had relegated the diplomats to a subordinate role. Like Domício da Gama in 1912, Silvino Gurgel do Amaral could not repress his frustration indefinitely. In February 1926 he decided to aim an indirect swipe at Hoover by complaining officially of biased statements made by his second-in-command, Julius Klein. Citing an article in the *Washington Star*, Silvino presented the following protest to the State Department: "the Ambassador of Brazil feels that he must express his regret at public declarations of a responsible high official, the effect of which on the sentiment of the country without an abundance of proof, may cause injury to the credit of a State of the Union which devotes its life to the most legitimate defense of its commercial and financial interests."[160] While privately disapproving of the interviews given by Klein to the press, Kellogg replied that Klein was an official of another department and that he had therefore no authority over his activities. No doubt, to conciliate the ambassador, Kellogg also stressed that the State Department had not made any criticism of valorization and did not assume the right to make any representations in matters that "pertained solely to the domestic affairs of another country." Despite the hint of dissatisfaction with his role as intermediary for the Commerce Department, Kellogg remained steadfast in his support for Hoover. Although the secretary of state did not contest the right of the state of São Paulo to take action in protection of its own interests, he also reminded the ambassador in words taken from a memorandum by Klein "that it is not always expedient for a state to do all that it may have a right to do from a strictly legal standpoint. If the Brazilian authorities, therefore, insist upon their rights in this matter, they in turn will not, I am sure, question the equal right of the American consumer to demand the help of his government in taking such measures as seem expedient in the defense of his interests."[161]

In effect, neither side wished to prolong the controversy. Silvino chose not to reply and appeared content to have made his own point against the policies of Hoover and Klein. Kellogg was merely reiterating the attitude adopted by the State Department throughout the coffee question. The secretary of state had always remained loyal to Hoover despite disturbing reports from Morgan that the Paulista authorities did not take kindly to American interference with their coffee policy. But Hoover had insisted on applying financial pressure and seemed to believe that the Paulistas must succumb to the inescapable force of economic logic. However, as other American administrations had discovered in past dealings with Brazil, the coffee question was a most complex and sensitive issue, one in which American demands stimulated Brazilian resistance rather than compliance. Though he might claim credit for bringing down coffee prices to acceptable levels, Hoover's intervention had plainly backfired. He had annoyed the American banking community and had caused ill feeling in Brazil. By compelling São Paulo to resort to a European loan he had hindered the strengthening of American economic links with Brazil. The Brazilian demand for American goods and capital was so strong during the late 1920s that this setback would prove only temporary. Nevertheless, the intrusion of the Commerce Department into the making and conducting of American foreign policy had proved an unhappy experience. The British ambassador at Rio summed up that Hoover "has just been taught a hard lesson."[162]

DIPLOMATIC PITFALLS

In Brazil the dominant diplomatic issue during the mid-1920s was not Herbert Hoover and the coffee question, but whether Brazil would remain in the League of Nations. As a founding member of the League, Brazil had been accorded one of the four nonpermanent seats on the League Council in 1920. The distinction was regarded as a reward for Brazil's active involvement in World War I and helped to alleviate the frustrations aroused by the Versailles conference. The Brazilian elite was immensely flattered at the attention bestowed by Europe upon their country and showed no disposition to follow America's retreat into isolationism. Indeed, Brazil's sense of international status and influence was enhanced by the decision of the United States to remain outside the League. As the only Latin American nation initially represented on the Council, Brazil outshone Argentina and irritated the latter by claiming the leadership of the American continent.[163]

In substantive terms, the association with the new world organization had little relevance for Brazil and its people. Nevertheless, the opportunity to act the role of the South American giant was eagerly grasped by the Itamaraty. "Now, we have become a nation," one diplomat proudly boasted, "that reaches beyond its continent to take part and be heard in the deliberations that concern the world."[164] A fond belief even existed that Brazil was helping to achieve Canning's dictum of "calling in the New World to redress the balance of the Old World."[165] Officials busied themselves traveling between the network of Brazilian embassies located in Lisbon, London, Paris, Rome, and Brussels.[166] In 1924 this network was extended to include Brazil's representative at Geneva. These activities did not go entirely unnoticed in international diplomatic circles. At the League of Nations itself, Ambassador Afrânio de Melo Franco was appointed as an ex-officio vice president of the League Assembly. The Brazilian delegate, Raul Fernandes, also attracted considerable praise for his legal skills and erudition.[167] But the sinews of power did not reside in holding ceremonial offices or attending splendid diplomatic conferences. The yearning to be accepted within the inner sanctum of international affairs was negated by the League's becoming more and more an instrument under the control of and for the sole benefit of the great European powers. Lesser nations such as Brazil enjoyed an equal status only in theory and not in practice.

This was not particularly galling to the Bernardes administration, which showed little desire to become closely involved in the affairs of the League.[168] The Mineiro president considered such matters as European boundary disputes and the fate of German minorities to be peripheral to Brazilian interests. Nor was there any disposition to exploit the absence of the United States and use Geneva as a forum for the discussion of Latin American issues. The League was not regarded as an alternative to the Pan-American conference system. From the point of view of Bernardes and Pacheco, its principal value lay in Brazil's membership on the Council. This was a place of signal honor that more than compensated for the country's evident lack of tangible diplomatic influence. But Brazil's seat was nonpermanent and subject to election by the Assembly. It was not surprising therefore that Brazil should strive to secure permanent status. According to Edwin Morgan, this soon became "the principal aspiration" of the Itamaraty.[169]

Although the great European powers wished to broaden membership of the Council, their thoughts centered on bringing in the United States, Germany, Poland, or Spain. The aspirations of other countries were brusquely dismissed as thinking "worthy of Alice in Wonderland."[170] Consequently, scant consideration was given to the arguments of Félix Pacheco that Brazil "has a right to a prominent place" and should be allowed to assume the permanent seat left vacant by the United States.[171] However, the claim could not go completely unheeded; it coincided with similar pressure exerted by the other Latin

American members for some sort of additional representation. It was decided, therefore, to enlarge the Council in 1923 by including a second Latin American country. But both seats were still classified as nonpermanent and would be subject to reelection every three years. The Assembly subsequently elected Brazil and Uruguay to these places.

The setback delivered to Brazil's desire for a permanent seat was not entirely due to the insensitivity of the great European powers. In fact, the idea of a special status for Brazil had never been acceptable to the other Latin American governments. Mutual suspicions were heightened by the Pan-American conference at Santiago and Brazil's evident determination to build up its navy. In 1925 the Spanish-American members of the League proposed that the two Council seats reserved for the hemisphere should rotate annually among all the Latin American countries. The adoption of this scheme was clearly intended to deprive Brazil of the Council seat it had uninterruptedly held since 1920. Nevertheless, such was the weight of Latin American opinion and voting power that the Bernardes administration felt forced to assent in principle to the proposal. Moreover, even in Brazil itself, there was a growing undercurrent of opinion that the government was pursuing a misguided policy that only contributed to further hemispheric misunderstanding and division. "We are looked upon with suspicion by our neighbors," reported *O Jornal* in September 1925 and added that "around us there has grown up the absurd legend that we are an ambitious and capricious people who are trying to assume the leadership of the continent."[172]

The dilemma was highlighted toward the close of 1925 when the great powers successfully concluded the Locarno negotiations. The agreement resolved various outstanding territorial disputes arising from the world war, but the terms were not to be effected until such time as Germany was admitted to permanent membership of both the League and Council. The consequent reopening of the question of Council membership presented the Bernardes administration with the opportunity of pressing once again for Brazil's own permanent seat. If successful, Brazil would not be affected by the Latin American scheme to rotate membership of the Council. The granting of a permanent seat would also reflect valuable political credit upon a beleaguered and unpopular administration.

The diplomatic maneuver provoked only indignation and ridicule in Europe. Brazil was accused of selfishly sabotaging the Locarno agreement. Diplomats at Geneva were also mindful of the political instability prevailing in Brazil and that only as recently as July 1924 the city of São Paulo had fallen under the control of a dissident military faction opposed to the federal government. The image prevailing of Brazil was summed up by the British ambassador's sarcastic comment in 1925 that "the country is hardly being governed at all."[173] But Bernardes refused to be deflected from the course he had undertaken. To demonstrate to the European governments how important the matter was regarded at home, he threatened the use of Brazil's veto to block Germany's membership on the Council.[174] From Geneva, Ambassador Melo Franco advised caution. Bernardes impatiently brushed aside the fears of the professional diplomats and informed Melo Franco in March 1926 that Brazil was facing "a question of national dignity that must be preserved no matter what sacrifice was entailed."[175] Presidential intervention had determined that the stakes would be set very high.

Britain and France acted quickly to put Brazil firmly in its place. They secured an adjournment of the Council until September and announced arrangements for the election of nonpermanent members. The implication was that Brazil would not be reelected to the Council. At the final meeting of the Council on March 17 an unhappy and tearful Melo Franco faithfully carried out his instructions to veto Germany's membership.[176] The news from Geneva resulted in a massive demonstration at Rio on March 21 in which Bernardes made a rare public appearance to outline his government's case.[177] The president stressed the fact that Brazil was a signatory of the treaty of Versailles and a founding member of the League of Nations. He reminded his audience that their government did not object to the admission of European members; its protest was against "the inequality of the treatment accorded to the nations of the Old and New World." Bernardes summed up: "It was inconceivable that the Brazilian Government should not view with favor Germany's entry to League and Council, but it was their duty not to vote for her otherwise than on condition that she should not enter alone to permanent membership and that the aspirations of Brazil should not be prejudiced."[178]

The virtually unprecedented invocation of public opinion illustrated the extent to which the Bernardes administration had become preoccupied with the League issue. But public demonstrations in Rio were hardly likely to influence the behavior of European and Latin American governments. Like Domício da Gama only a few years earlier, Pacheco felt it necessary to appeal to the United States for diplomatic assistance. The foreign minister requested that American ambassadors in European capitals place "a discreet word" on Brazil's behalf. The act smacked of desperation because relations between Rio and Washington were currently clouded by the coffee question. Moreover, the United States government had maintained a curiously detached attitude toward the League ever since its foundation. In fact, Hughes had refused a similar appeal from Pacheco when the matter of a permanent seat for Brazil had first been raised in 1923.

Secretary of State Kellogg was similarly unmoved in 1926 and explained to the Brazilian ambassador, Silvino Gurgel do Amaral, that the League was "a most delicate" subject for his government. Although he appeared outwardly sympathetic, Kellogg was also openly critical of Brazil's diplomatic brinkmanship. He predicted that Germany would almost certainly join the Council and that this might compel Brazil to withdraw from Geneva. The secretary of state also informed Silvino that his government's position was considerably weakened by evidence that Chile was secretly opposing Brazil's continued membership on the Council. In fact, it was already common knowledge that the Spanish-American governments favored the creation of a third nonpermanent seat for Latin America rather than a permanent place for Brazil.[179]

The likelihood of American diplomatic intervention had always been a forlorn hope. Of more immediate concern were the intrigues of the Spanish-American representatives at Geneva. Melo Franco sadly observed "the treacherous game of our friends and cousins."[180] But the same charges of selfishness and insensitivity that Brazil directed at its critics soon rebounded upon itself. The British government was particularly disapproving and stated that Brazil was embarked on a course that could only lead to "suicide in international life."[181] The Bernardes administration was furious. In May 1926 it retaliated against the unyielding British attitude by deliberately placing a $30 million loan in New York rather than London. The British ambassador at Rio noted that Bernardes had personally requested an American loan and was especially insistent that it be contracted quickly so as to exert maximum influence on the League issue. The renewal of the contract for the American naval mission on May 20 also indicated Brazil's intention to exploit Anglo-American rivalry. "If Brazil leaves the League," predicted the British ambassador, "the blame will be centered on Great Britain.[182]

Brazil's insistence that it be treated on a par with Germany proved unacceptable to the European powers. The country was demonstrably not a great power and was accused of desiring merely to play "a showy part."[183] The policy of obstructive diplomacy employed by Bernardes and Pacheco further isolated Brazil and alienated possible supporters. Not only was a permanent seat on the Council definitely ruled out, but Brazil faced the prospect of not even being reelected. It was painfully apparent that the Bernardes administration had badly miscalculated. The president's tough style might impress his domestic opponents, but overseas opinion judged him naive and ridiculous. Rather than face open diplomatic humiliation when the Council reconvened in September, Brazil announced on June 11, 1926 that it would formally leave the Council and the League.[184]

British officials suspected the hand of Edwin Morgan, who was known to be a longtime critic of the League. According to the *Diario Oficial* the ambassador had visited the Catete palace on June 11 to congratulate Bernardes for deciding to leave the League. "The action of Brazil," a British diplomat later minuted, "was largely due to American edging at the psychological moment."[185] The actual role of the United States was hardly so decisive. The *New York World* reported the suspicion that "it is to Rio's advantage to create an

impression among South Americans that the United States approved and ap-
plauded the withdrawal."[186] In fact, the State Department immediately disavowed the report that Morgan had congratulated Bernardes and sought to
distance itself from any semblance of complicity in the course of events at
Geneva. "American diplomatic officials made swift and emphatic denial to-
day," stated the *New York Times* on June 17, 1926, "that they had been involved even indirectly in the League of Nations controversy which resulted
recently in Brazil's withdrawal as a League member."[187] While Kellogg's refusal
to intercede in Europe on Brazil's behalf had made the ultimate decision to
withdraw more likely, this was a negative rather than a positive influence. Bernardes had sought to gain diplomatic advantages by playing off the Americans
against the British, but his government had also carefully avoided claiming
American support for its position in contrast to the frequent allusion to backing from other countries.

The attitude of officials in Washington toward the League remained curious. Their lack of willingness to assist Brazilian pretensions at Geneva was
not meant to undermine the League. If anything, American diplomats were
critical of Brazil's immature international behavior and appeared to wish that
Brazil remain a member of the Council. This view was reflected in several press
articles. The *New York World* remarked that Brazil "has not been ill-treated
by the League" and that the organization "loses little by Brazil's withdrawal,
but Brazil loses a real voice in world affairs." While the argument that the League
had become a purely European instrument was not disputed, it was considered
that the Bernardes administration had forced the issue to the point where Brazil felt compelled to withdraw. The *Philadelphia Public Ledger* bluntly summed
up: "It was Brazil that raised the question and Brazil that pushed the answer
to its extreme."[188]

The trend of events at Geneva had resulted in diplomatic humiliation for
Brazil. Ever since the Versailles conference Brazil had affected the role of a
world power, but the illusion could be sustained no longer. By seeking a loan
in New York, Bernardes not only delivered a calculated snub to Britain but
also illustrated his decision to turn away from Europe. Even though the State
Department had been studiously unhelpful over the League issue, the president confided to Morgan in June that Brazil planned "to return to the orbit
of her continental relations" and especially to cooperate closely with the United
States. The British ambassador at Rio confirmed that the government was di-
recting the press to "miss no opportunity of emphasising the solidarity of the
sister republics of the American continent."[189]

The development appeared propitious for American diplomacy in that it
coincided with the State Department's renewed effort to negotiate most-favored-
nation commercial treaties. This particular policy had so far enjoyed precious
little success. Of the Latin American countries, only Panama had agreed to

conclude a treaty. The sudden revival of American interest during 1926 was prompted not by what had occurred at the League of Nations but by reports of Spanish attempts to negotiate separate preferential commercial arrangements with Latin American governments. The Rio embassy, however, could find no evidence that any such discussions had taken place between Brazil and Spain. Nonetheless, although American exports to Brazil continued to enjoy tariff privileges according to the "modus vivendi" of 1923, the conclusion of a formal treaty was still regarded by the State Department as a desirable end in itself. As ever, American officials appeared optimistic that success was within their grasp. In reviewing the past history of commercial relations between the two countries, Assistant Secretary of State Leland Harrison considered it a matter of regret that the 1828 treaty of friendship, navigation, and commerce had lapsed in 1841. Glossing over almost half a century of contentious correspondence, he simplistically recommended the urgent need for "a comprehensive modern agreement." Harrison's confident approach was shared by Secretary of State Kellogg who believed that the proposed arrangement would be of "special advantage" to Brazil. Moreover, the American chargé at Rio, Thomas L. Daniels, reported a "readiness" to enter into discussions and attributed this to the prevailing despondency over the League debacle. The chargé comfortingly observed that the Bernardes administration was "particularly interested in fortifying its relations with the United States."[190]

Despite the proclaimed desire for closer contact with Washington, the Bernardes administration failed to conclude the commercial treaty that the State Department so eagerly wanted. The Itamaraty resorted to the old delaying tactics so familiar to veterans of the struggle for commercial reciprocity. Daniels would receive an encouraging response from Pacheco, only to be told that the matter was not purely a diplomatic question and consequently required the assent of other cabinet ministers. Inevitably, these ministers requested additional time for study and reflection. In short, Brazil was satisfied with the 1923 modus vivendi and saw no political or commercial reason to enter into a formal treaty. Moreover, Bernardes was due to leave office in November and would not be hurried into precipitate action. Notwithstanding his recent statements emphasizing hemispheric cooperation and solidarity, Bernardes was strongly nationalistic and the disinclination to negotiate the treaty was consistent with this attitude. In this respect the election of Washington Luís as the new president was a hopeful sign. Daniels described the president-elect as "friendly to the United States" and reckoned that his prospective cabinet was similarly minded.[191]

The new president promised firm and authoritative government. He also pledged to continue the economic policies of his predecessor by stressing sound fiscal orthodoxy and a strong currency.[192] While Washington Luís wanted good relations with all countries and especially with the United States, his preoccupation remained fixed on domestic politics. An invitation to visit Washington was politely rejected so that the weeks preceding his inauguration could be spent touring Brazil, mending political fences, and consulting with local bosses. The results were evident in the selection of cabinet ministers, most of whom were politicians directly recruited from Congress. "Care has been taken to divide cabinet posts among the most important states," noted the American chargé.[193] Despite rumors that Brazil might return to the League and would require therefore a professional diplomat like Melo Franco to head the Itamaraty, spoils politics dictated the appointment of Otávio Mangabeira as foreign minister. Mangabeira was a civil engineer by training. He was regarded as a shrewd politician and had risen to be leader of the Bahian state delegation in the Chamber of Deputies. Speculation abounded that he would be offered the post of minister of agriculture. His selection as foreign minister was a surprise; he possessed no experience in foreign affairs and was reputed to have made only one journey outside Brazil.[194] O Jornal later concluded that Washington Luís preferred a policy of "splendid isolation" and that his object "is clearly to let sleeping dogs lie as regards all dangerous questions of foreign affairs."[195]

Contrary to the prediction of the American chargé, the new administration showed no serious interest in discussing a commercial treaty.[196] On the other hand, a friendly disposition toward the United States undoubtedly existed. Indeed, Brazilians markedly refrained from adopting the anti-American attitudes that were so common in the rest of Latin America. For example, the execution in 1927 of the Italian-born anarchists, Sacco and Vanzetti, excited little adverse comment in Brazil. Morgan reported that "the amount of annoyance which American officials have received has been considerably less than elsewhere."[197] Sections of the Brazilian press were even kindly disposed toward American intervention in Nicaragua. O Jornal stated in December 1926 that "an unjust outcry" had been raised against the dispatch of American marines. In its opinion, Latin America was reacting with "much exaggeration and hasty judgment." The Jornal do commercio sympathetically remarked that American influence "will always be employed for upholding equity and justice" while the Gazeta de Notícias predicted that the intervention in Nicaragua would have "a benificent result."[198]

The desire for close diplomatic cooperation with Washington surfaced most visibly at the Havana Pan-American conference in 1928, where Brazil's friendly attitude contrasted markedly with the anti-American mood of many of the other Latin American delegations. Several months before the conference assembled, Kellogg had written apprehensively to Henry Fletcher:

> The next meeting of the Pan American Conference is going to be more important and probably more difficult than any we have had in many years. . . . There is no use disguising the fact that there are liable to be elements going to the next

Conference purely for the purpose of making trouble for the United States. You know how difficult it was to suppress some of this even at Santiago, where there was a much better feeling toward us than there is now.[199]

In order to impress the Latin Americans it was decided to schedule a brief visit by President Coolidge to the opening ceremonies at Havana. At the head of the American delegation was the country's most distinguished statesman, Charles Evans Hughes. An influential position was also reserved for Henry Fletcher, whose service at the Santiago conference had made him an automatic choice for Havana.

For once Edwin Morgan was seriously considered for appointment to the American delegation. As the department's most senior diplomat in Latin America, he obviously possessed strong credentials. However, Morgan's career had marked time ever since he had taken charge of the Rio embassy in 1912. By contrast his younger colleague, Henry Fletcher, had steadily advanced from being minister at Santiago to more prestigious postings in Asia, Europe, and Washington. In 1927 Fletcher served as American ambassador to Rome, the very post that Morgan had coveted only a few years earlier. When Secretary of State Kellogg wished to discuss the composition of the American delegation at Havana, he turned to Fletcher for advice. The latter had never displayed much sympathy for either Morgan or Brazil. In somewhat parochial fashion he expressed concern that there was a danger of including too many ambassadors. Diplomatic propriety compelled the selection of the American ambassador to Cuba. Political factors also favored the appointment of Dwight Morrow, the American ambassador to Mexico. Morgan was therefore redundant. If there had ever been any prospect of his appointment, it was effectively dashed by Kellogg's personal worry that the choice of the ambassador to Brazil might provoke jealousy from Argentina and Chile. Fletcher agreed and added: "Besides, Brazil can usually be counted upon to support us." It was evident that neither Morgan nor Brazil carried much weight in Washington. In fact, the legacy of approximation actually worked against Brazilian interests by providing a rationale for excluding Morgan from the Havana conference.[200]

On the other hand, Fletcher's presumptuousness was not misplaced. Brazil's pronounced pro-Americanism was confirmed by Morgan in late September 1927. Without any prompting from his government, he stated that the Brazilian delegation at Havana would be instructed to discourage discussion of "controversial subjects or matters of a political nature which the American Government does not believe appropriate." When the delegates later assembled in Rio prior to leaving for Cuba, Morgan reported that Otávio Mangabeira had personally stressed the importance of cooperating fully with the views of the American delegation. The American ambassador explained: "This country never forgets that it is of Portuguese and not of Spanish origin. . . . An attachment to the United States is fundamentally based upon the fact that both she and ourselves are built upon a non-Spanish foundation and derive none of our force or power from a Spanish source."[201]

Still reeling from the shock of the debacle of Geneva, Brazilian diplomacy turned instinctively to the policy of approximation with the United States. But the League crisis had also painfully underlined Brazil's isolation within Latin America and pointed to the urgent need to rebuild relations with its neighbors. Just as Rio Branco had reacted to the setback at The Hague almost 20 years earlier, Otávio Mangabeira similarly sought a closer diplomatic understanding with Argentina. The foreign minister also followed the example of the baron by engaging in unpublicized but fruitful discussions with neighboring governments that led to the conclusion of a number of agreements demarcating their respective territorial boundaries with Brazil.[202] Another feature of this continental strategy was an improvement in pay and conditions at South American postings plus the upgrading of Brazil's missions in Colombia and Venezuela to ambassadorial rank. "The proposal," commented the American chargé at Rio, "is an indication of a desire of the Brazilian Government to strengthen its relations in this hemisphere."[203]

The good neighbor policy was laudable and sensible, but it contained the perpetual dilemma for Brazilian diplomacy of how to be on good terms simultaneously with both the United States and Argentina. The problem loomed acutely at the Havana conference, which was scheduled to meet in January 1928. From the Brazilian embassy at Buenos Aires came reports that Argentine public opinion was "frankly hostile to the United States" and that the Argentine government would instruct its delegation to condemn American imperialism in Nicaragua.[204] A further complication resulted from the selection of Honório Pueyrredón to head the Argentine delegation at Havana. Pueyrredón currently served as his country's ambassador at Washington, where he had made no secret of his resentment of American intervention in Central America. He was also an avowed critic of Brazil. Silvino Gurgel do Amaral remarked that American officials expected the worst and were prepared to endure whatever ill feeling emerged at the conference. In his view, the United States government was "putting its cards on the table" and would now discover who its friends were. He considered that the wisest course for Brazil was "silence."[205]

At Havana, Pueyrredón seized his chance to castigate American imperialism. Telegrams from the Brazilian ambassador at Buenos Aires suggested, however, that the Argentine had exceeded if not mistaken his original instructions.[206] But the Itamaraty chose not to meddle, believing that any attempt to moderate Argentine policy would be regarded as an impertinence and could only be counterproductive. This passivity, far from incurring criticism, was considered to be sensible and made a favorable impression not only in Argentina but also in the United States. "Brazil's silence when contrasted with [the] flamboyance of Pueyrredon," remarked Silvino, "is to Brazil's advantage."[207]

American policy was under such severe attack at Havana that it was generally held that the Pan-American conference system had come to an end. However, the American delegation was not entirely lacking in friends and allies. Indeed, Brazil's statesmanlike posture proved invaluable and helped to prevent the proceedings from becoming totally one-sided. After the conference had ended in February 1928, Silvino gratifyingly reported the compliment from Kellogg that "Brazil has been a tower of strength to us." The ambassador added jubilantly that "the Government of the United States would never forget the work of the Brazilian delegates" and that the conference had "considerably strengthened the friendship between the two countries."[208] In its annual report on Brazil for 1928, the British embassy at Rio confirmed "the definite American bias" of the Itamaraty. "Throughout the conference," observed the British ambassador, "the Brazilian delegates, by their negative attitude, were of the greatest assistance to the United States."[209]

Brazil had approached the Pan-American conference intent on avoiding controversy and maintaining friendly relations with both the United States and Argentina.[210] However, the desire for consensus was defeated by the open hostility between the American and Argentine delegations. Brazilian diplomacy was consequently placed in a quandary. By refusing to join the general condemnation of American interventionism, the Brazilian delegation inevitably came to be seen as siding with the United States. So long starved of tangible diplomatic successes, Brazilians could not resist the temptation to boast that a special understanding existed between the two non-Spanish powers. Morgan cited an editorial from *O Jornal* that stated that "not since Domicio da Gama vacated the Brazilian Embassy at Washington had there been such effective cooperation between the United States and Brazil as marked the recent conference at Havana."[211]

Brazilian joy, however, was brief: hopes of a privileged relationship with Washington were rudely shattered by the conclusion of the Kellogg-Briand Anti-War Peace Pact. Although the United States had attached considerable importance to the Havana conference, it was also aware that its great power role extended beyond the hemisphere. Ever since the hosting of the Washington naval conference in 1921 Republican administrations had particularly stressed the desirability of preserving world peace. Throughout 1928 Kellogg worked closely with his French counterpart, Aristide Briand, to devise a treaty to outlaw war. Amid a fanfare of international celebration, the Peace Pact was signed at Paris in August 1928 by the American secretary of state and the foreign ministers of the leading European powers.[212]

The initial announcement in June 1928 of the pact's conclusion came as a surprise to the governments of Latin America because the State Department had neglected to inform them of developments. Morgan reported that Mangabeira was "embarrassed" by the fact that Brazilian newspapers apparently knew more than the Itamaraty. Moreover, the foreign minister was clearly unhappy that Brazil had not been invited to the signing ceremony at Paris while "minor" nations such as Czechoslovakia and Poland had been included.[213] Kellogg explained that the necessity of expediting negotiations had compelled this exclusion. "The present fear of war is principally in Europe," he noted, "and it was deemed most important to get the leading powers there to sign the treaty."[214]

The explanation smacked too much of the great powers looking down upon their smaller brethren. Brazil's disappointment at not being an initial signatory was eloquently expressed by the *Jornal do Brasil:*

> The omission really signifies disdain, either because Brazil's participation is valueless or because in reality we have little to do with warring disputes. In the first instance, the feeling of national dignity should lead us to refuse our adherence to a treaty with which Brazil's cooperation may be dispensed. In the second instance, as we also have little to do with the warlike preoccupations of the world it is natural that we should not participate in that which does not concern us. . . . A treaty which might be injured by our cooperation in the preparation of its text is also one which we will advance nothing by our posthumous adherence.[215]

It was evident that Morgan faced an unenviable task in soothing Brazilian feelings, especially as the demeaning of Brazil's status was attributed directly to action by the United States and not the European powers. Only a few days before the Paris conference Morgan recorded the foreign minister's "considerable annoyance" at Brazil not being given "special consideration" in view "of the services which the Brazilian delegation to the Pan American Congress of Habana rendered to the United States." The anxious tone of the ambassador's dispatch betrayed his own concern that officials in Washington had forgotten the special characteristics of Brazil: "there are always people ready to suggest that the United States is unduly inclined to group Brazil with the South American Powers of Spanish origin and does not differentiate Brazil's peculiar position in view of her racial and linguistic origin and her special economic relations arising from the fact that the United States is the principal consumer of her chief agricultural product."[216]

The State Department was mindful of the turn of events and, if somewhat belatedly, sought to reassure the Brazilian ambassador at Washington that the United States was sincerely friendly to Brazil. Fortunately, Silvino was in a receptive mood and faithfully reported Kellogg's worry that other countries, particularly Argentina, would be angry if any special preference was shown to Brazil. He also informed the Itamaraty that some consideration had been given to the idea of inviting Brazil as an initial signatory on the grounds that Brazil had been a full participant in World War I. This was rejected, however, when it was pointed out that other belligerents such as Cuba and Peru would raise objections unless they were similarly included.[217]

These conciliatory gestures had little effect because the Brazilian government had already decided not to adhere to the Peace Pact. At the close of August 1928 Mangabeira declared Brazil's approval of the aims contained in the pact and stated disarmingly that his country did not need to sign the document because those same principles renouncing war were already a part of the 1891 Brazilian constitution. Morgan was struck by the favorable local reception given to the foreign minister's note and saw this as further proof of Brazil's "annoyance" at not being consulted during the preliminary negotiations. The American ambassador tactfully advised:

> The imagined wound to national "amour propre" which resulted from her exclusion from the group of first signatories will gradually heal, and the more quickly if we do not importune her to accept the Pact at once but will allow her an opportunity to realize in full that its principles, which are those which she takes pride in stating, were incorporated into her Constitution nearly 40 years ago and practiced by her consistently ever since.[218]

For officials in Washington the Peace Pact was an agreement primarily between the United States and the great European powers. It was always intended and assumed that the other nations of the world should join, but the matter had been complicated by the need to secure speedy agreement during the final phase of negotiations and the general wish to exclude Bolshevist Russia from the pact.[219] Consequently, the Latin American countries became once again the victims of great power politics. Moreover, as State Department officials explained to Silvino, the nations of the Western Hemisphere presented their own particular diplomatic complexities. If Brazil received special attention, this could only incur Argentine resentment. To Silvino's dismay, Americans appeared to show much greater interest in the deliberations taking place in Buenos Aires than in Rio. Indeed, Brazilian sensitivities were acutely stung when an article appeared in the *Washington Post* stating that Brazil was waiting on Argentina's lead. By suggesting that the report originated within the State Department, Silvino inadvertently shocked the Itamaraty. He was soon in receipt of a telegram from Rio spelling out the independent stance taken by Brazil at the Havana conference and the government's determination to maintain "its autonomy in foreign affairs." Silvino contritely replied that the article did not reflect the official view in Washington and that no credence was given to the idea that Brazil was under Argentine influence.[220]

Since the announcement in August 1927 that he would not be a presidential candidate in 1928, President Coolidge had presided over a lame-duck administration. The conclusion of the Peace Pact not only raised morale but its ratification also provided a tangible and worthy objective for the administration's last months of office. By mid-September the process began of asking foreign governments formally to sign the pact. A State Department memorandum observed that "it is important to play up to the South Americans particularly."[221] In a manner reminiscent of earlier discussions over the Pan-American treaty, it was also believed that Brazil might exercise an important influence over its neighbors. Morgan was instructed to inform Mangabeira

> that the Secretary of State of the United States is greatly pleased at the tenor of your note and particularly at your assurance that the purpose of the treaty so fully accords with the spirit of the Brazilian Constitution. This leads him to believe that Brazil will desire to be one of the first formally to adhere to the Treaty. . . . I may add that such adherence will give particular satisfaction to my Government because of the unbroken tradition of cordial and understanding friendship between our two nations.[222]

Contrary to the expectation of officials in Washington, their appeal was rejected. Now that the United States sought an answer from Brazil, the Itamaraty seized the opportunity to show its annoyance by adopting an attitude of deliberate awkwardness bordering on intransigence. Mangabeira curtly informed Morgan that Brazil's adherence required the authorization of Congress and that this "was not likely to be given during the present parliamentary session."[223]

The Itamaraty's negative response disturbed American composure. Soon Kellogg was confiding his dismay to Morgan:

> I am, as you know, very anxious to have all countries of the world adhere or definitely state their intention of adhering to the Multilateral Treaty before it is submitted to the Senate when it meets on December 3. . . . The only other countries that have not done so are Brazil, Argentina, Chile, Colombia, Ecuador and Paraguay. Do you think that you could by discreet conversations with the proper Brazilian authorities find out the intentions of Brazil and discreetly urge Brazil's adhesion?[224]

Kellogg's uncertainty in dealing with Brazil had not gone unnoticed by Silvino. Indeed, the ambassador advised the Itamaraty to maintain "a certain reserve" in the face of American pressure. This tactic soon began to pay dividends. In October he wrote that Brazil's "resentment" was keenly appreciated in Washington, but that, ironically, this resentment had actually increased his country's diplomatic prestige. The Havana conference was now agreeably recalled and Kellogg commented privately on how much he had valued Brazil's support in contrast to the hostility shown by Argentina. The secretary of state also acted promptly to conciliate Silvino after the latter had complained of further articles in the American press implying that Brazil and the other South American countries were waiting to see what Argentina was going to do about signing the pact. At his next press conference, Kellogg went so far as to insert the statement that "each country is examining the matter independently."[225]

Despite these accommodating gestures, Morgan could still only report from Rio that Brazilian compliance "appears to be unlikely." The Brazilian Congress was said to be fully occupied at present and would not be able to discuss any additional business before Kellogg's own congressional deadline of December 3. The ambassador confirmed in November that the Brazilian attitude was unchanged. In what seemed like a reproof to his colleagues in Washington for ignoring his advice to treat Brazil considerately, Morgan admitted that a "non-Latin mind" would be perplexed by Brazil's attitude. The diplomatic reality, however, was that Brazil's "amour propre" had been wounded and could only be healed "with the passage of time."[226]

Brazil's intransigence was disappointing to American officials, but it was not initially an item of overwhelming concern. In fact, the discussions were overshadowed by the immediate priority of securing ratification of the Peace Pact by the United States Senate. This was eventually achieved by a comfortable majority in mid-January 1929. The Coolidge administration then redoubled its efforts to secure adherence to the pact of the remaining foreign governments before it left office in March 1929. Of these countries, Brazil and Argentina were accorded special attention. On January 31 Kellogg met with Silvino at the State Department. In what he described as a very useful meeting, Kellogg told the ambassador that "Brazil's adherence would have a good deal of influence."[227] The secretary of state thereupon telegraphed Morgan: "I am particularly anxious to get the Brazilian Government to adhere. . . . I do not wish to unduly press Brazil so that she will resent our suggestions but if you feel as though you could do so, I should be pleased for you to have further conversation with the Minister for Foreign Affairs."[228] Hopes of a favorable response were quickly dashed when Morgan sent back Mangabeira's comment that "it would not be fitting" for Brazil to assent to something already written into the country's constitution. The American ambassador pessimistically concluded that "it is improbable that the views expressed above will be altered in the immediate future."[229]

No doubt only too well aware that Kellogg was within days of leaving office, Mangabeira informed Silvino that he knew the secretary of state was "unhappy," but that Brazil was a "friend" and not "a servile follower" of the United States. He repeated this comment to the British ambassador and stressed that, because of the lack of consultation, Brazil was "under no obligation to follow slavishly the lead of the northern continent." The foreign minister affirmed "the necessity for Brazil . . . to follow an American policy. This had become all the more imperative as a result of the Conference at Havana; but the advent of the Kellogg Pact and the pressure exercised by the United States to adhere to it had given this country the opportunity, of which they had gladly availed themselves, to assert their independence of the North American continent."[230] Two years after withdrawing from the League of Nations, Brazil had once again adopted a proud and unyielding attitude that appeared to obstruct diplomatic efforts to promote world peace. The consequence was a certain amount of international opprobium for Brazil and a renewed compulsion for that country to look for support and sympathy from its South American neighbors. Close relations with Argentina were desired,[231] but the endemic rivalry between the two countries was exemplified by Silvino's protests over press reports that his government was subordinating itself to Argentina's diplomatic direction. The Havana conference had rekindled the Itamaraty's dreams of a special relationship with Washington, but these had been dispelled by the unedifying saga of the Peace Pact. Despite Morgan's tactful warnings the State Department too often acted insensitively. The Brazilian ambassador at Washington concluded, "sadly it has been the tendency of Republican administrations to have dealings with Europe at the expense of the Americas."[232] No longer "a tower of strength," Brazil retaliated by becoming awkward and uncooperative. However, so long as Argentina remained an unreliable ally and a potential enemy, diplomatic fences would have to be mended with the United States. The Coolidge administration left office in March 1929, but the new president was none other than Herbert Hoover, the man whose record was one of hostility to Brazil. After a decade in which diplomatic relations between the United States and Brazil had been characterized as much by friction than harmony, Hoover's election was hardly the happiest of omens for the future.

CHAPTER 5

Demise of an Era, 1928–1930

FOR THE AMERICAN people Herbert Hoover's landslide victory in 1928 held out the promise of four more years of Republican prosperity. "Work is Life" was the motto of the new president, and he quickly infused Washington with his desire for industriousness and efficiency. Foreign affairs were not exempt from this businesslike approach although they were not accorded any special priority. Hoover wanted either Hughes or Kellogg to be secretary of state and, when both refused, he turned to the little-known Henry Stimson.[1] Despite having once undertaken a special mission to Nicaragua, the new secretary of state showed minimal personal interest in Latin American affairs. However, continuity of Latin American policy was initially assisted by maintaining most of the serving ambassadors in their posts, including Edwin Morgan at Rio.

In fact, it was Herbert Hoover himself who was initially most active in attempting to improve relations with the southern republics. Prior to his inauguration he embarked upon a hemispheric tour lasting ten weeks and visiting ten countries. In a speech delivered in Honduras he stated his desire that inter-American relations should be those of "good neighbors."[2] The stop in Brazil was regarded as particularly successful. If only for a few days American newspapers were full of stories depicting the sights and charms of Rio. Cordial relations were also established between Hoover and Washington Luís. In June 1930 Hoover was especially gratified when his visit was returned by President-elect Júlio Prestes.

The Hoover administration sincerely aimed to pursue the policy of the good neighbor in Latin America, but diplomatic initiatives foundered upon events. The dream of eliminating poverty in the United States was exploded by the 1929 Wall Street crash, to be replaced by the somber realization that an era of "hard times" was at hand. Not only the United States, but the whole world was thrown into political and economic disorder. Even so, the outbreak of revolution in Brazil astounded officials in Washington and caught them unprepared. Moreover, confusion was heightened throughout the crisis by the poor communications between the State Department and the Rio embassy. Stimson insisted on a cautious and legalistic response that inevitably implied American support for the government in power. The victory of the rebels came as a shock and only served to underline the unpredictability and hazardous nature of diplomacy.

Outward progress and deceptive calm characterized the administration of Washington Luís from 1926 to 1930. The president continued the policy of Bernardes and extended executive control over the political system. Special emphasis was given to financial reform. Indeed, the achievement of a stable currency and rising exports prompted the *Washington Post* in May 1929 to claim that "Brazil has found the road to permanent prosperity and peace."[3] The American press also fully appreciated Brazil's friendship for the United States. "With Brazil our relations have always been most friendly," remarked the *New York Times*.[4] However, a mood of negativism continued to prevail at the Itamaraty. Not only did Brazil refuse to sign the Peace Pact, but it also resisted being directly associated with American efforts to mediate the Chaco dispute between Bolivia and Paraguay.[5]

As 1930 approached, Brazilian politics became almost totally absorbed with the question of presidential selection. Washington Luís sought a continuation of his own policies and exerted his patronage to the full to ensure the election of his fellow Paulista, Júlio Prestes. In September 1930 Edwin Morgan took his annual leave confident that order reigned in Brazil. A serious revolt occurred only a month later. It was not the first time that the ambassador was not present at his post during a crisis,[6] but the outbreak of revolution in October 1930 surprised and mystified Brazilians as much as foreigners. Diplomacy had no bearing on the outcome of what was purely a Brazilian matter. The political system was demoralized by twenty years of economic and political disorder.[7] When the army generals finally decided to turn against Washington Luís, their action spelled not only the defeat of executive aggrandizement of power but also the demise of the Old Republic.

A GOODWILL VISIT

It was scarcely surprising that the nomination of Herbert Hoover as Republican presidential candidate in June 1928 should cause "some apprehension" in Brazil.[8] Ever since his public broadside against Brazilian coffee policy only a few years earlier, Brazilians had remained wary of Hoover. While welcoming his conciliatory remarks communicated to the *Estado de São Paulo* in April 1926, Paulista officials were quick to dismiss rumors that he would be invited to visit their state.[9] Dispatches from the Brazilian embassy at Washington in 1927 still described the secretary of commerce as "arbitrary and dictatorial" and openly antagonistic toward Brazil.[10] During the 1928 election campaign the Brazilian press was inclined to view Al Smith sympathetically whereas Hoover was portrayed as "the exponent of dissolving materialism, of mechanical civilization, and of a cold blooded imperialism which characterizes the Yankees."[11]

On the other hand, coffee was no longer such a divisive issue between the two countries. In February 1928 Hoover used the occasion of a banquet held in New York for representatives of the Defense Institute to send a message praising the Institute's work in maintaining stable supplies of high-quality coffee.[12] The controversial issue was also carefully avoided during the presidential election campaign.[13] Silvino Gurgel do Amaral reported gratifyingly that the Republican candidate's speeches made no mention of foreign monopolies and did not reveal "his ancient hostility to Brazil concerning the coffee question."[14] Edwin Morgan confirmed that local attitudes had become more friendly. In his opinion, Brazilians believed that Hoover now held a much more understanding view of the policy of defense.[15] Any remaining anxieties were further allayed when Hoover's election to the presidency was quickly followed by the pleasing announcement that he would make a goodwill tour of Latin America prior to his inauguration.

The initiative revived memories of Elihu Root and gave a signal boost to Pan-Americanism.[16] The Brazilian ambassador at Washington was genuinely excited by what he saw as a reaffirmation of the traditional American-Brazilian friendship.[17] In welcoming news of the trip the *New York Times* particularly stressed the importance of visiting Brazil. "No country is more friendly to the United States than Brazil," remarked a typical editorial.[18] But the official itinerary accorded no special significance to the southern giant. Hoover evidently intended to visit as many Latin American countries as was feasible.[19] For once Brazil was last on the list simply as a result of Hoover's decision to depart from previous practice and set sail from San Francisco rather than the East. This meant that Rio would be his final port of call prior to returning to the United States. The stopover in the Brazilian capital was scheduled from Friday afternoon December 21 to Sunday evening December 23 and was allocated virtually the same amount of time as at Santiago and Buenos Aires.

Although Hoover sincerely wanted improved relations between the United States and all the nations of Latin America, he was careful to stress that his visit was not an official diplomatic mission. With the exception of Henry Fletcher, no diplomats were invited to join the touring party.[20] The desire to promote hemispheric goodwill was evident, but there were also other reasons for the trip. Indeed, Hoover's immediate aim was to escape, if only temporarily, from the political jungle of American spoils politics. "I agree with you," he informed Elihu Root, "that I should keep entirely out of Washington and also that I should keep in the background as much as possible."[21] The president-elect was also a great world traveler and wished to visit the one continent of the globe with which he was personally unfamiliar. Moreover, his pursuit of self-improvement made him view the tour as an admirable opportunity to expand his own knowledge. His personal baggage appropriately contained a formidable quantity of reading material on the countries to be visited.[22] Once the journey was under way, however, Hoover's speeches and press conferences frequently emphasized his desire to promote hemispheric peace and harmony. From this emerged what would later become known as the policy of the "good neighbor." Shortly after leaving California he told pressmen on board the *Maryland:*

> This is not a commercial trip but one intended to promote friendly relations, and if friendly relations are established, trade relations will follow automatically. . . . We must interpret these countries to our own people. We must show them they are entirely out of the state of savagery, although many of them are still in the early stages of development and we need to help them to greater stability. . . . We must feel our way along. I know we cannot accomplish this in one trip. If we do but part of that, we will have laid a foundation on which we must build for perhaps a century.[23]

After visiting the west coast of South America and the River Plate, Hoover arrived at Rio on December 21, 1928. A rapturous welcome awaited him. "Mr. Hoover's visit," remarked the *New York Times,* "is considered the most important event for some time." The American correspondent added: "Lima, Santiago, Buenos Aires and Montevideo all gave wonderful receptions to Mr. Hoover, but in point of numbers, enthusiasm, splendor of decorations and acclaim by the people, none has equaled the great welcome Brazil's metropolis staged today."[24] The Washington Luís administration organized lavish hospitality for the president-elect. It was characteristic of their American visitor to reveal little emotion, but there was no doubt that Hoover was personally impressed. This was indicated by his speech during the sumptuous banquet held at the Catete palace when he stated: "No one could fail to be moved by the hundreds of thousands of smiling men and women and joyous children who lined your streets in demonstration of the feeling they have toward my countrymen. No language can interpret the overwhelming waves of sentiment they have extended to us. It is itself proof of complete confidence in the serene and helpful friendship between our countries."[25]

The large American press contingent that accompanied Hoover was unanimously admiring in its praise for the host nation. "During the two and half days spent in Rio," noted Mark Sullivan of the *New York Herald Tribune,* "the cables of the United States carried an aggregate of more than 60,000 words, and every word was lyrical about Rio and Brazil."[26] The theme of the sleeping giant enjoyed special prominence. "The United States of Brazil," remarked the

Christian Science Monitor, "is a mighty realm of limitless potentialities, with vast interior regions still unmapped." The *New York Post* described Brazil as "a nation which staggers the imagination."²⁷ Special tributes were reserved for the capital. "It is literally the world's most beautiful city," wrote Sullivan. His colleague, Edwin McIntosh, was ecstatic over "a magnificent welcome from a magnificent city" and added: "Probably Mr. Hoover never will see a more beautiful and imposing scene than that afforded by Rio's harbor, with the city's red roof and yellow spires rimming the purple bay like a coral necklace and the rank green of the palm-clad mountains sheering skyward in the background."²⁸

Brazilians were delighted at the international attention paid to their country and its capital city. They were flattered to receive a visit from the next president of the United States and were determined to surpass Buenos Aires in their show of hospitality to their distinguished guest. The isolated references in the local press to Hoover as the representative of "a white country" and "the instrument of American imperialism"²⁹ were ignored as the Cariocas warmed to a man who dismissed the bodyguards assigned to his motorcade on the grounds that he needed no protection from Brazilians.³⁰ Political leaders were equally impressed and described the visit as an "epoch making event."³¹ The former minister of war, João Pandiá Calógeras, concluded that it "will enact wonders to create a better mutual understanding and an era of good-feeling among our peoples."³² Gratified by Hoover's parting message of thanks, the *Jornal do Brasil* summed up: "That man of few expressions, cold in appearance, experienced in life, economical in words, betrayed in a long radiogram his noble appreciation. His gratitude is sincere. And Brazil can hold it for certain that she has conquered a friend."³³

The president-elect was truly moved by his short stay in Brazil especially by the huge crowds that greeted his arrival and the spectacular display of fireworks that accompanied his departure. He let it be known that in all his world travels he had never quite experienced anything to compare with what nature had bestowed upon Rio.³⁴ Sightseeing was interesting, but work was not neglected. Between official functions it was noted that "Mr. Hoover has followed the custom established since the beginning of the trip and sat closeted with the native authorities discussing the life of the country." After meeting with President Washington Luís and other political and government leaders, Hoover declared that "Brazil's future was bright."³⁵

Despite the fine speeches and numerous gestures of friendship, little of substance resulted from Hoover's visit to Rio. On his way home, Hoover had little to say to the press about Brazil and preferred to talk in general terms about the whole of Latin America. He was at his most comfortable expounding upon the need for economic development. Above all, he prized financial stability and listed Brazil along with Venezuela, Paraguay, Colombia, Costa Rica, Uruguay, and Argentina as governments that had balanced their budgets.[36] No allusion was made to concrete diplomatic issues even though the Brazilian ambassador at Washington had originally warned that Hoover would try to persuade Brazil and Argentina to join the Kellogg-Briand Peace Pact.[37] There is, however, no evidence that this subject was raised by Hoover in his meetings with Brazilian officials.[38]

Despite all the ceremonial trappings, Hoover came to Latin America as a private citizen and not as a head of state with executive powers. Nevertheless, throughout the visit he was constantly in the public eye, requiring him to be circumspect in his public behavior and remarks. The danger of misinterpretation was ever present and occurred most notably at Buenos Aires where his comments on American intervention had been used by the local press to embarrass the Coolidge administration. Not surprisingly, Hoover became completely reticent on this particular subject during his stay in Brazil. The British ambassador at Rio cynically remarked that the president-elect "succeeded in refraining from saying anything of importance."[39] In fact, the visit merely emphasized the lame-duck condition of the Coolidge administration and thereby strengthened Brazil's determination to resist Kellogg's appeals to adhere to the Peace Pact. The Itamaraty later informed Silvino that Hoover's presence had given Brazil an opportunity not only to confirm its traditional friendly feeling for the United States but also to assert its independence of the American government.[40]

Nevertheless, the visit of a president-elect was an unprecedented event and helped to break down the barriers of indifference and misunderstanding that had become such a feature of United States–Brazilian relations during the 1920s. Personal contact had achieved wonders for Hoover's image in Brazil. He was no longer seen as a foe but a friend. At Hoover's inauguration in March 1929, Morgan reported Brazil's admiration for the new president and confidence that his term of office would see the achievement of many successes.[41] The emerging mood of good feeling between the two nations was expressed two months later by the *Washington Post* in an editorial praising "Brazil's Great Progress":

> Americans are well pleased with the remarkable progress of Brazil, as set forth by President Washington Luis in his annual message to the congress. . . . It furnishes proof that Brazil has found the road to permanent prosperity and peace. When the resources of that vast country are taken into account it becomes evident that within a few years Brazil will become one of the leading powers of the world. . . . The progress of Brazil benefits and encourages other nations, besides contributing to the assurance of peace in this hemisphere. The United States rejoices in the rise of this great republic in South America.[42]

Indeed, Brazil had much to be proud of. Under Washington Luís the federal government had achieved its first budget surplus since 1908. Symbolic of the country's economic advance was the building of impressive new highways linking Rio with Petrópolis and São Paulo. The latter city had become such a magnet for business and immigrants that it was known as the "Chicago" of South America. Americans were eager to invest and trade. Even though the United States still bought more than it sold, American exports to Brazil rose to a peak for the decade of $108 million in 1929. The adverse trade balance was offset, however, by the growing export of capital. After a lull in the mid-1920s a large number of American loans were floated in 1927 and 1928 so that by the end of the decade total American investment in Brazil had risen from $50 million to almost $500 million. In the process, the United States displaced Britain and became Brazil's leading supplier of new capital investment.[43]

Edwin Morgan was delighted by the advance of American economic influence, especially when it was at the expense of British business rivals. While acknowledging the achievements of the Washington Luís administration, he was not alone in warning that the country's prosperity depended "to an unwholesome extent" on earning foreign exchange from the export of coffee. The initial success of the policy of defense had encouraged new coffee planting so that bumper crops were expected from 1927 onward. The economic outlook was therefore decidedly uncertain. Moreover, although he welcomed the "eager desire" of American bankers to invest in Brazil, Morgan constantly advised "great caution" in the selection of borrowers.[44] In similar fashion, the perceptive American consul at São Paulo, Charles Cameron, referred disapprovingly to the "loan epidemic" of 1928. He was amazed to find American financiers willing to loan $3 million to Mato Grosso, a state whose resources he considered to be "very limited." In the consul's view: "Mato Grosso is a vast wilderness, an unknown quantity, and the development of its resources would seem to fall more properly to Brazilian than to foreign capital. The former would at least be spared the opposition of chauvinists, and the losses of Brazilian investors chargeable to any default of the Government or to bandits or revolutionists, would not create international animosities."[45]

Despite their advocacy of foreign loans, American officials were only too well aware of the risks involved. "Our trouble during this period," stated Grosvenor Jones of the Commerce Department in 1928, "was that so many banking houses of little experience in international finance stepped into the picture in an attempt to bring out loans."[46] Edwin Morgan worried that the availability of foreign capital was tempting the Brazilian federal and state governments "to indulge to an unwarranted extent in what should be considered a luxury and not adopted as an habitual practice." The ambassador was characteristically optimistic about Brazil's future, but he felt obliged to stress the warnings of the financial experts that "the limit of safe banking . . . has either been passed or is to be reached in the immediate future."[47]

The Wall Street crash intervened in October 1929 to render these strictures unnecessary if not obsolete. During the ensuing months the world was plunged into economic depression. No country was left unscathed by the severe contraction of international trade and investment. Indeed, Brazil's traditional dependence upon the world economy made it more vulnerable than most. The much-acclaimed deflationary policy pursued by the Washington Luís administration was jolted by the sudden collapse of export earnings. In just over a year coffee prices slumped by 45 percent. Initially American merchants took advantage of lower prices to stockpile, but in 1930 imports of coffee into the United States were drastically curtailed and fell to their lowest point since 1923. In terms of total trade with the United States, Brazilian exports fell by one-third from 1929 to 1930 while purchases from that country declined by almost one-half during the same period. The impact was devastating. No longer a beacon of prosperity, the state of São Paulo appealed to Washington Luís for federal assistance to stave off imminent bankruptcy. By the middle of 1930 Brazil's foreign debt had climbed to over $1 billion and could only be serviced with great difficulty.[48] Only a short time earlier Hoover had predicted a bright economic future for Brazil. It could hardly have been much consolation to Brazilians that he had said the same things even more fervently about the United States and had proved to be just as mistaken. In fact, the Brazilian political elite had little interest in Hoover or what was happening in the United States. Their attention was concentrated upon the 1930 presidential election. Undoubtedly Hoover's visit had promoted goodwill between Brazil and the United States. Other results were less easy to discern so that, in retrospect, Hoover's stay in Rio was no more than a pleasant interlude during a time when the Old Republic was fast sinking into political and economic crisis.

THE 1930 REVOLUTION

In the memorandum prepared for Hughes's visit to the 1922 Brazilian centennial, the Division of Latin American Affairs at the State Department described politics in Brazil as a struggle between those in power and those outside power. Personal rivalries predominated and became "most bitter during presidential elections."[49] This was true in 1922 but not in 1926 when Washington Luís enjoyed an unopposed election. However, a similar peaceful transfer of power appeared unlikely in 1930. According to the political tradition established by the "politics of the governors," the Paulista president should be followed by a Mineiro.[50] But Washington Luís insisted that he be succeeded by the governor of São Paulo, Júlio Prestes de Albuquerque. The states of Minas Gerais and Rio Grande do Sul predictably condemned what they regarded as a blatant maneuver to perpetuate the influence of São Paulo at their expense.

American opinion characteristically treated the machinations of Brazilian politics with supreme indifference. Among the very few individuals who gave any attention to this subject, there was an inclination to think favorably of Washington Luís. Before Hoover left for his tour of Latin America, he asked the financial expert, G. Butler Sherwell, to prepare background information on the countries to be visited. Sherwell singled out Brazil's friendliness and praised the "splendid administration record" of Washington Luís both as governor of São Paulo and president of the republic.[51] This impression was confirmed by firsthand experience and especially the little ways in which the Brazilian president craftily endeared himself to his American visitors. On receiving Hoover in Rio, Washington Luís responded to a question about his name by proudly acknowledging the link with George Washington and adding that his two brothers were called Benjamin Franklin and Lafayette. "The much-talked-of formality of South America," reported the *New York Times*, "was entirely lacking in the [Catete] palace."[52]

The public relations success of Washington Luís was confirmed in January 1929 by Assistant Secretary of State William Castle. Requested by Hoover to prepare a review of diplomatic postings in Latin America, Castle remarked: "Peru is at present, on the whole, the most friendly, except possibly Brazil, of the more important Latin American countries." In the case of Brazil, however, Castle believed that American diplomacy enjoyed the inestimable advantage of Edwin Morgan: "Morgan has had a very long diplomatic experience. He is admirably trained and has, according to all accounts, gained the complete confidence of the Brazilians. He is quite capable of doing practically all the work of the Embassy himself and likes to do it. I think it would be impossible to find another man who would fit so admirably into the picture as Morgan does and think that he, therefore, should without a doubt be kept."[53] Morgan had served so long at Rio that his name had become virtually synonymous with Brazil. Despite being only a year away from the retirement age of 65, he was considered irreplaceable and was asked to stay on as ambassador to Rio for a further five years.

The new secretary of state, Henry Stimson, was not so amenable. Unlike Castle and Morgan, he was not a member of the diplomatic "club." Determined to make his authority felt, Stimson's style of treating subordinate officials was frequently insensitive and abrasive.[54] In Morgan's case, this manifested itself in the following tersely worded stricture sent in May 1929:

> It is noted that very little information regarding political developments in Brazil has recently been received from the Embassy at Rio de Janeiro. Even though there are no events of outstanding importance to report it is very necessary that the Department should be kept informed regarding political matters, including the policies of the national government, the attitude and alignment of political parties and groups, and in general regarding all developments and trends of which

the Department should know in order to have at all times a clear picture of the existing situation. I should be very glad if you would furnish the Department with reports on these subjects at frequent intervals, dealing with the matter in as much detail as possible.[55]

Morgan responded with alacrity. In a two-page analysis of current Brazilian politics he observed that the selection of presidential candidates was "the principal political question which occupies public attention." Just as the infant United States had chosen its presidents from Virginia or Massachusetts, he noted that the majority of Brazil's leaders came from São Paulo, Minas Gerais, or Rio Grande do Sul. Various candidates had been proposed from these particular states although it was clear that Washington Luís favored the present governor of São Paulo, Júlio Prestes, "who is his creation and henchman." Morgan believed that the president's wishes would ultimately prevail "although much water will run under the bridge before his official nomination is gazetted."[56]

The receipt of this dispatch appears to have satisfied Stimson. No further personal requests were made for information about Brazil until the revolutionary crisis of October 1930. In the meantime the Latin American division resumed its responsibility for the supervision of Brazilian affairs while the secretary of state concentrated his attention on what he considered to be much more important matters such as Manchuria and the problem of world peace. It was just as well that Stimson did so for he would hardly have been amused by Morgan's report in June that the currently engrossing topic of both local and international significance in Rio was the visit of "Miss Brazil" to the United States as Brazil's representative in an international beauty pageant at Galveston.[57]

Having evidently contented his new master in Washington, Morgan was soon able to leave Brazil for his annual period of leave of absence. The embassy's third secretary, Rudolf Schoenfeld, assumed charge at Rio. From July through October he sent a regular flow of reports on political affairs to Washington. In August 1929 the chargé observed that politicians were obsessed with the issue of presidential selection "to the practical exclusion of other questions." During the following month he reported that Washington Luís was using all the patronage at his disposal, including the resources of the Bank of Brazil, to destroy the opposition.[58] In retaliation the states of Minas Gerais and Rio Grande do Sul formed the Liberal Alliance and chose as their presidential candidate the governor of Rio Grande do Sul, Getúlio Vargas. Perhaps because they did not originate from Morgan, Schoenfeld's dispatches attracted minimal attention at the State Department. In fact, officials were more impressed by the lengthy report prepared in September by the American military attaché at Rio, Major Lester Baker. What most interested them was not so much the attaché's admittedly "lucid exposition" of political affairs but his views on the prospects of coffee valorization. Baker's opinion that the threat of armed conflict loomed was simply passed over.[59]

After his return to Brazil in November 1929 Edwin Morgan still expressed confidence that Washington Luís would secure victory for Prestes. "The presidential power is the heir of the imperial power," he summed up. Nevertheless, Morgan regrettably noted that the president's "strong, obstinate personality" had directly contributed to the emergence of "exaggerated and uncontrolled political hatred" between the contending political factions.[60] Whoever was chosen, the ambassador predicted a year of political disturbance until the presidential inauguration scheduled for November 15, 1930. On the other hand, the Brazilian republic had enjoyed several decades marked by peaceful and orderly changes of government. While the breakdown of political consensus was alarming, Morgan wished to remind officials in Washington that "the Brazilian people, however, are peaceful by nature, and a similar propensity to disturb public order or to commit political crimes should not be attributed to them which characterizes other South American peoples."[61]

Indeed, the majority of state governors and political bosses duly conformed to the will of Washington Luís so that an impressive electoral victory was secured for Prestes in March 1930. Morgan was pleased to report that the expected disruption of order had not materialized, although he cautioned that "the political situation is still delicate." Nevertheless, his overall assessment was optimistic. "There is no reason to suppose," he believed, "that the peace of the country will be seriously disturbed or that the President of the Republic will lose control." This comforting news seemed to fit in well with the prevailing mood of officials in the Latin American division of the State Department. After all, the United States had experienced its own contentious national election only as recently as 1928. Once the people made their choice, the struggle was declared to be at an end. Consequently, William Manning minuted that Morgan's dispatch "is valuable, but it is such as is usually included in General Conditions Reports." He recommended that the Rio embassy continue to send reports on this subject, but that they did not merit a separate dispatch and should be relegated to inclusion in the appropriate section of the fortnightly surveys of "General Conditions."[62]

The Brazilian ambassador at Washington considered that American opinion was more than ever favorable to his country. He was delighted by another flattering editorial in the *Washington Post* that likened the Brazilian political system to that of the United States: "The election which has just been held in Brazil offers striking evidence of the success of the representative system of government in Latin America. This great South American republic has demonstrated its ability to maintain a government of the people, by the people and for the people." The editorial dismissed reports of "local disturbances" as "greatly magnified." In fact, the "lively" campaign was seen as convincing evidence that "Brazil has developed a strong two-party system which has proved effective in expressing the will of the people."[63]

The close relationship existing between the two republics was further exemplified by the decision of President-elect Júlio Prestes to visit the United States in June 1930. This was particularly gratifying to President Hoover who, according to Silvino, was visibly moved whenever Brazil was mentioned in conversation. In marked contrast to his earlier opinion, the Brazilian ambassador now regarded Hoover as "our biggest friend in the field of international politics."[64] This was illustrated in June 1929 by Hoover's personal invitation for Washington Luís to visit the White House. On that occasion, the Brazilian government had replied that the chief of state could not constitutionally leave the country. There was, however, no such barrier to prevent a president-elect from doing so.[65]

Only a year earlier Morgan had described Prestes as "the creation and henchman" of Washington Luís. He now portrayed the president-elect as "attractive, tall, vigorous, youthful and self-possessed" and predicted that "he will impress favorably the American public."[66] On the day of Prestes's arrival in the United States, John Barrett flatteringly described the Brazilian as the "Theodore Roosevelt of present-day Latin America." Barrett revealed that Theodore Roosevelt had met Prestes on his trip to Brazil in 1913–1914. The Roughrider was alleged to have told the young man that in time he would emulate his own career by becoming governor of his state and then president.[67] But Hoover needed little prompting to return some of the special attention that he had himself been shown at Rio only 18 months earlier. "Your presence," he told Prestes at a White House reception, "is but another evidence of that sincere and uninterrupted friendship which has always linked our countries together so that it can truly be described as traditional."[68]

The visit was doubly welcome in the United States because it came at a time of growing criticism in Latin America against proposals to increase the American tariff. As its own products were unlikely to be affected, Brazil could afford to be sympathetic. Moreover, even to think of Brazil helped lift some of the economic gloom that was fast descending upon the United States. "Brazil would appear to offer unlimited opportunities for the development of her marvelous resources," declared Max Winkler of the *New York Evening Post*. "Certainly, the resources of that enormous country," observed the *New York Times*, "are as yet but scratched."[69] Ambassador Silvino Gurgel do Amaral was happy to report that the American press treated the trip as "a memorable event." He was certain that it had further consolidated the friendship of the two peoples.[70] Prestes was also impressed by the "incredible and dizzying growth" of the United States.[71] After meeting with the president-elect on his return to São Paulo, Morgan recounted how Prestes had been "especially impressed" with the amount of time and attention given to him by President

Hoover. The ambassador optimistically concluded: "The President-elect impressed me as thoroughly American, with the intention of continuing the American orientation which has directed the foreign policy of Dr. Washington Luís."[72]

The British ambassador at Rio acknowledged the "highly flattering reception" given to Prestes in the United States. Seizing upon the fact that no announcement had been made of a major American loan, he concluded that "the visit would not appear to have produced much impression on either hosts or guests." The American consul at São Paulo, Charles Cameron, wrote, however, that the local press had followed the trip "with most intense interest" and that the lavish American hospitality had "undoubtedly created a warm reciprocal feeling on the part of the Brazilians."[73] Evidence of this had already been demonstrated in June when Morgan was informed that the Brazilian government wished to extend the naval contract due to expire in November. On September 1, Morgan had an audience with Washington Luís prior to taking his leave of absence in Europe. When the conversation turned to the matter of political unrest, the president sought to assure the ambassador that reports of disturbance in the South were unfounded and that "public order was complete." The next day Morgan telegraphed this information to Washington and shortly afterward sailed for France comfortable in the knowledge that recent events had marked a decided advance for United States–Brazilian relations.[74]

The rest of South America was not so calm. Worsening economic difficulties created a mood of pervasive political crisis. The Bolivian government had already fallen in March 1930. In late August the dictatorship of Leguía collapsed in Peru. On September 6 a military coup in Argentina compelled the resignation of President Irigoyen. Brazil's apparent immunity from revolutionary disorder was suddenly broken on October 3. Rebel forces mobilized in the North and the South and demanded the overthrow of Washington Luís and his replacement by Getúlio Vargas. With the backing of an estimated 30,000 troops in Rio Grande do Sul the *gaúcho* leader declared: "We are beginning a counter-revolution to obtain freedom and to restore the purity of the republican system."[75] The rebels quickly achieved their military objectives in the Northeast, but it was apparent that the decisive battle would take place when the army of Rio Grande do Sul attempted to enter the state of São Paulo.

Confusion reigned in Rio and no more so than at the American embassy where Morgan's absence exerted an unforeseen and detrimental effect upon American diplomacy. William Castle had admired Morgan's propensity to do all the diplomatic work of the embassy by himself. This same strength, however, became a distinct liability whenever the ambassador was away from his post. In September 1930 the inexperienced and ill-informed diplomatic secretary, S. Walter Washington, was left in charge of the embassy at Rio. Only

29 years old, the young chargé struggled to keep the State Department informed of events as the crisis unfolded.[76] Both his ability and resources were taxed to the limit. He explained his predicament to Stimson: "The gathering of information and the coding and decoding of telegrams to and from the Consulates in Brazil as well as to the Department, have occupied the full time of the American staff of this Embassy, which at present consists only of myself and two clerks."[77] During a press conference held at the State Department in late October a number of correspondents queried whether the embassy's dispatches were up-to-date. Secretary of State Stimson publicly insisted that he was "in constant communication" with his officials in Rio, but he later admitted privately that his knowledge of Brazilian affairs was "extremely meager."[78]

Ironically, only a few months earlier the Latin American division of the State Department had downgraded the importance of political reports from Brazil. Even as late as August the acting head of the division had stated that "a general movement against the federal authorities seems unlikely."[79] However, the sudden crisis shook officials out of their former complacency. The immediate priority was to ensure the safety of American citizens and property in the disturbed areas. How to achieve this posed a dilemma given the distance and lack of accurate information. Almost by default a reactive policy of watching and waiting was adopted. Such a response was sensible, but it also reflected the basic desire of American officials for the continuation of the political status quo. Consequently, American policy became identified with the preservation of the Washington Luís regime.

American diplomats had, however, no wish to interfere directly in the domestic affairs of Brazil. Like Thompson during the Naval Revolt, Walter Washington was primarily concerned about the protection of American citizens and their property. He was particularly apprehensive that serious fighting would break out in Pernambuco and suggested that a naval vessel visit the northeastern coast. "The Department," answered Stimson, "would be very loath to send any warships to Brazil." Conflicting information about events influenced this decision. In contrast to Argentina, Bolivia, and Peru during their times of revolution, Brazil did not appear to be experiencing mass demonstrations or widespread public disorder. There was also a concern that the image of the United States in Latin America would scarcely be improved by the sending of gunboats. Nonetheless, Stimson thought it wise to bring the matter before the U.S. Cabinet on October 10 and to secure agreement to place the cruiser *Pensacola* on standby in Brazilian waters. To Stimson's annoyance, this covert arrangement was made public knowledge only the next day by the Navy Department. The task of damage limitation was undertaken by Assistant Secretary of State Francis White, who spent the weekend explaining that the sending of the *Pensacola* was in no way intended to undermine the authority of the federal government of Brazil. It was described purely as a precautionary measure to assist the evacuation of foreigners should an emergency arise.[80]

While the government of Washington Luís was annoyed by the reported dispatch of an American gunboat to the Northeast, it was pleased to learn of the refusal of the Hoover administration to recognize the belligerent rights claimed by the rebels. During the Naval Revolt of 1893–1894, Secretary of State Gresham affirmed on a number of occasions that the provisional rebel government failed to meet the standards of recognition required by international law. In his opinion, to grant recognition "would be a gratuitous demonstration of moral support to the rebellion, and an unfriendly act towards Brazil."[81] In 1930 Stimson employed an identical argument in his evaluation of American diplomacy:

> The situation in Brazil arose out of internal politics and we looked upon such a state of affairs simply with the distress and regret that a country like ours, which believes in the ballot and peaceful methods for change of government, would look upon a change based upon violence. We saw nothing, therefore, to distinguish this revolution from an attempt to change a government by violence. Under those circumstances and under the principles of international law . . . it was the duty as well as the policy of this country to continue its good relations with the existing government, and we have done so.[82]

Whatever the rationale, the determination not to grant belligerent rights to the rebels implied American sympathy for Washington Luís. Furthermore, it appeared to influence the course of events in Brazil by allowing the federal government to purchase American military supplies. At issue was the completion of a contract for the sale of nine warplanes from the Curtis-Wright Company to the Brazilian government. "So long as a state of belligerency has not been recognized," declared the State Department's legal adviser on October 13, "a foreign government is free to supply or permit private individuals to supply arms to the government against which the revolt is in progress." While the memorandum added that this might incite retaliation from the insurgents, such a contingency was regarded as a political rather than a legal consideration. At a cabinet meeting on October 14, President Hoover raised just this question when he asked whether governmental participation in the proposed sale of American warplanes might incur "lasting enmity among the rebels in case they should finally be successful." But legal rather than political arguments carried the day. Stimson declared that the United States was under an obligation to honor existing contracts and he satisfactorily resolved the president's doubts by ensuring that the arms deal would be effected by private contractors and therefore not directly involve the United States government.[83]

Stimson's legalistic approach came to public attention on October 22, when it was announced that the United States was imposing an embargo on the export of weapons to Brazil. Trade under license was not affected, a qualification that permitted continued arms sales to the Brazilian government, although not to the rebels. The action was inevitably interpreted as conclusive evidence of American support for Washington Luís. One press article alleged that the embargo arose as a result of a personal request from the Brazilian president to Herbert Hoover. This was "the first time in American diplomatic history," remarked the *Washington Post* that "such a limitation has been placed on exportation of arms to a South American republic."[84] Stimson acted swiftly to dismiss charges of collusion between the two governments. On October 23 he stated that American policy was unchanged: "It is not a matter of choice on our part, but it is a practice of mankind known as international law. We have no personal bias and are doing nothing but attempting to carry out the law of mankind."[85] The pursuit of diplomatic rectitude was commendable, but the charge of bias was difficult to refute. Indeed, the Washington press corps could not have found Stimson's own attitude hard to discern. After a press conference on October 15 he wrote in his diary: "My object was to try to make a friendly impression towards Brazil, and to convey the idea that we were behind her." The effort succeeded only too well. On the following day the Washington correspondent of the *New York Times* reported that the United States government was pursuing "a policy of active friendship toward the Rio de Janeiro Government in its efforts to stamp out the Brazilian rebellion."[86]

It was hardly surprising that the Hoover administration should wish to see the continuance in power of a government with which it had established most friendly relations at the highest level. Moreover, ever since the outbreak of the revolt, telegrams from Walter Washington had confidently asserted that the federal troops had "the upperhand." Although the chargé did not deny that the "general situation" was "critical" and that it would require "a long time to subdue all the revolutionaries," he continued as late as October 21 to cite official statements that Washington Luís would retain power until his term of office ended in November.[87] A leading American journalist later disclosed that officials at the State Department had "almost no reports from Brazil," and that the cables received were "just as confused and not nearly so comprehensive as press dispatches."[88] One reason for this had been the strict enforcement of press censorship in Brazil so that the only information released expressed the government viewpoint. Consequently, Walter Washington found his access to information extremely restricted. If the chargé proved gullible, this was not entirely due to naïveté or lack of diplomatic experience; Edwin Morgan did not fundamentally disagree with the younger man's assessment of political events. During the first week of the crisis Morgan had been instructed by Stimson to cut short his leave in Europe and return to Brazil. His first telegram from Rio, dated October 23, acknowledged the evident lack of local enthusiasm for Washington Luís, but stated that the current military stalemate would only be broken if the president voluntarily consented to resign.[89]

Morgan added that the president's obstinate streak made him indifferent to the advice of sensible cabinet ministers such as Otávio Mangabeira.[90] Indeed, the Itamaraty had been deliberately relegated to an inactive role throughout the crisis. Nevertheless, Brazilian diplomacy did influence American attitudes as a result of the efforts of Ambassador Silvino Gurgel do Amaral who, in his conversations with State Department officials and American newsmen, faithfully communicated the official line that all was well. At his first meeting with Stimson after the revolt had broken out, Silvino ignored the crisis and concentrated instead on negotiations for the renewal of the naval contract. During the weeks that followed he constantly downplayed the seriousness of the fighting and, on one occasion, even inquired in his business-as-usual manner how the United States government intended to celebrate the inauguration of President-elect Júlio Prestes scheduled for November 15.[91] When a group of high-ranking army officers suddenly overthrew the federal government on October 24, the *Washington Post* observed that the astonishment of State Department officials "was nothing compared to the surprise experienced by Ambassador do Amaral."[92]

"Brazil Coup Stuns Washington Circles," read the headline of the *New York Times* on October 25.[93] Contrary to the expectation, if not the desire of the Hoover administration, the rebels had successfully seized power. The issue of the arms embargo only 48 hours earlier now appeared as a distinct embarrassment for State Department officials. Stimson, in particular, bore the brunt of criticism for backing the wrong side. The press corps facetiously called him "Wrong-Horse Harry." Journalists were so "excited" that Stimson felt compelled to alter his leisurely office schedule and submit to two press conferences on successive days. His diary recorded that he had to undergo "a rosy time."[94]

The question of the moment was whether the United States would approve the new government. Historically, American policy was averse to recognizing military coups. However, the moral guidelines associated with Woodrow Wilson had been relaxed in September when the Hoover administration had swiftly established diplomatic relations with the new military rulers of Argentina, Peru, and Bolivia.[95] But State Department officials were more circumspect about Brazil and reverted to the traditional policy of recognition. In the best diplomatic tradition, Stimson prevaricated. He argued that the unreliable nature of existing information from that country made it difficult to formulate an official response. It was known that a coup had definitely occurred in Rio, but the connection between the military junta and the rebel forces under Getúlio Vargas was unknown. Moreover, the State Department had made no effort to cultivate relations with the latter and knew very little about his background and personality.[96] Stimson's initial reaction was therefore to "go slow" and try to find out what exactly was taking place in Brazil. When the German ambassador visited the State Department on Monday, Oc-

tober 27, Stimson admitted that he still possessed "surprisingly little news."
The ambassador inquired whether the United States would recognize the new
regime, and the secretary of state replied: "I told him that the same scantiness
of news and difficulty of communication would probably prolong the time
which would be necessary to ascertain the basic facts upon which any recognition must be based. That we were anxious to help Brazil but it would probably take a considerable time to have the situation straightened out so that
a government would exist which would fulfill the necessary international
conditions."[97]

Stimson's plea for time to think was understandable, but it was also mixed
with the desire to delay recognition to America's best diplomatic advantage.
However, the strategy did not reckon with the pace of events in Brazil itself.
The question of recognition became a matter of some urgency as agreement
was quickly reached between the military junta and the rebels. Getúlio Vargas
arrived in Rio on October 31 and three days later announced the formation
of a provisional government. A number of distinguished figures were appointed
to cabinet office, including the experienced diplomat, Afrânio de Melo Franco,
as foreign minister; and a respected Paulista banker, José Maria Whitaker, as
minister of finance. The civil conflict was effectively over, and it was soon evident that several foreign powers, especially Britain, wished to recognize Getúlio. Morgan also reported that a number of Latin American countries were
on the point of establishing diplomatic relations with the new government.[98]
On Wednesday, November 5, Stimson sent a telegram asking for his ambassador's expert opinion: "My view of the situation at present is that owing to
the large extent and difficult character of the country, scantiness of communications, etc., we should go slow and we will not be hurried by the British in
determining what is the proper action for us to take, but in this matter I want
your full and frank views and recommendations."[99] But as Morgan considered
his reply, the British ambassador called at the State Department on Thursday
to advise that Britain intended to recognize the Brazilian government on Saturday, November 8. Francis White thanked the ambassador for this information
and stated that he was awaiting a dispatch from Morgan. Until this arrived,
White doubted "whether we would be in a position to make a decision in the
matter before the eighth."[100]

Morgan's answer was received early on Friday afternoon. Although favoring recognition as soon as possible, he was hesitant to recommend this action
until some form of popular election had been held to legitimize the status of
the revolutionary regime. The ambassador believed that this not only reflected
Stimson's instructions to proceed slowly but also that the consent of the governed was required before recognition could be granted.[101] However, with
British action only a few hours away, officials in Washington were perplexed
by their ambassador's constitutional reservations, which, if observed, would

"involve a very long delay." Morgan was informed that the United States had only very recently recognized Argentina, Bolivia, and Peru "upon the frank basis of control by a *de facto* government." Officials conveniently overlooked the fact that they had also expected those same regimes to hold elections as a condition of recognition. Instead of "full and frank views," Stimson now wanted an instant response to the question: "Are you willing to advise that the *de facto* control of the present Government of Brazil is sufficiently complete for similar prompt action?"[102]

The sudden emphasis on haste was surprising; earlier on Friday the Hoover cabinet had agreed that recognition need not be hurried. The likelihood of British recognition was mentioned, but its impact was discounted because Brazil was so economically dependent on trade with the United States.[103] According to Stimson, however, the mood of the meeting "was not very cheerful." In fact, "some rather nasty remarks" were made about the embargo. Stimson's pride must have been stung. The Brazilian business had brought him nothing but trouble, and perhaps he resolved to bring things to a conclusion. After receiving Morgan's telegram he decided to expedite matters by arranging a telegraph linkup between Washington and Rio for Saturday morning, November 8.[104]

"It is my opinion," telegraphed Morgan, "that the Provisional Government fully controls the country and is supported by the people." Conditions in Brazil were regarded as identical to those of Argentina in mid-September. When the ambassador therefore advised recognition, Stimson instructed him to do so immediately.[105] The telegraph linkup was made within 15 minutes. "A very quick and interesting performance," observed Stimson.[106] The same might be said for American diplomacy in this instance. In retrospect, the action appeared to express the realistic recognition policy emerging in response to a series of revolutionary upheavals in Latin America. But Brazil was treated differently than other governments. Stimson insisted that the United States would not be rushed into granting recognition even though other powers were on the point of doing so. American behavior in 1930 was more evocative of that which followed the fall of the empire. Like Dom Pedro in 1889, Washington Luís had clearly lost power. In each instance, however, there was a reluctance to admit the demise of a friendly ruler. There was also a disinclination to confer legitimacy upon a military coup. "A regime set up through revolution may not be representative of the people," warned the *Washington Post*.[107] Identical remarks had been made in 1889. When recognition was abruptly granted in November 1930, the action was not dissimilar to Blaine's impulsiveness in January 1890. The parallels are striking and show that a change of government in Brazil was a matter of some political concern in the United States. Of the other countries of Latin America, only Mexico and Cuba enjoyed a similar historical importance.[108]

Although the government of Getúlio Vargas was pleased, it attached no great significance to diplomatic recognition. The struggle to oust Washington Luís had been conducted without resort to appeals for assistance to any foreign powers. In fact, diplomacy had been an irrelevance. Once the revolt was under way the crucial task for the rebels was to persuade the military command in Rio to desert the president. The foreign powers had no meaningful role to play. The American embargo was a nuisance, but it came too late to have any bearing on events. Similarly, Stimson's delay in extending recognition was a matter of indifference to the victorious rebel leaders, who were absorbed with devising ways of implementing the "revolution." On November 11 they decreed the end of the Old Republic and established a virtual dictatorship.

On the other hand, the rebel movement had shown a concern to avoid damage to foreign citizens and their property. Some local hostility toward foreigners and especially Americans had surfaced in the Northeast, but this was believed to be due to working-class dissaffection. In the South, remarkable calm had prevailed. "American companies in Porto Alegre," reported the American consul at that city, "are very satisfied with the treatment given them in the protection of their property by the revolutionary government."[109] The appointment of a Paulista banker as minister of finance was also evidence of the desire of the new government to reassure both domestic and foreign opinion. Nevertheless, Stimson was disturbed to learn of extremist political activities, especially in São Paulo where the newly appointed interventor, João Alberto Lins de Barros, had allowed the Communist Party to organize. Morgan admitted that "communist agitators" had participated in the recent civil war, but he believed their influence had been greatly exaggerated:

> It is just as true now as formerly that the people of Brazil have no natural tendency to support communist theories. The necessities of life are in most parts of the country easy to obtain. Large and concentrated groups of mill hands and other laborers live only in São Paulo, Rio de Janeiro, Bahia and Pernambuco, most of whom are ignorant. When many are out of employment, rumors are easily circulated, and an opportunity is created for communist agitators to arouse disorders.

The ambassador added that the proud Paulistas were too accustomed to running their own affairs and resented being placed under the direction of a *tenente* from Pernambuco.[110]

In Morgan's opinion, Brazil was still an elitist society. Lacking education, the masses were politically inarticulate. More than a decade earlier he had observed that "public opinion, as representing the voice of the people, is not sufficiently developed in this country to overcome the opposition of the men in control."[111] The old political ways were so ingrained that they were likely to continue. Nevertheless, the central government had been overthrown by violence for the first time since 1889 and the ambassador sensed that significant changes were about to take place. "The revolution which has occurred in Brazil," he told Stimson, "is fundamental and will affect the future of the country profoundly."[112] In effect, Morgan was pronouncing an epitaph for the Old Republic and announcing the beginning of the era of Getúlio Vargas. More to the point, Morgan turned his back on the past by refusing to offer asylum to the now-discredited members of the deposed administration. Instead, he directed all his considerable influence and skill to rebuilding American prestige with the new political forces.[113]

The effort was necessary because some resentment did exist toward the United States because of its apparent support for the ousted Washington Luís. The arms embargo became a particular source of grievance. "This is not Nicaragua," asserted one of the new government ministers.[114] In the opinion of the British ambassador at Rio, "Americans are in the depths of gloom."[115] Indeed, one of the convenient means in which the new government asserted its independence and, at the same time, appeased nationalist supporters was to show its displeasure against the United States by requesting the termination of the naval mission. The French army mission was also to be withdrawn. No objection was raised in Washington. Any attempt to do so would only have provoked retaliation. The State Department was still dismayed by the turn of events and desired to be conciliatory. Moreover, officials acknowledged that the presence of foreign military advisers was an unnecessary luxury in a period of mounting economic depression.[116] Throughout 1930 Brazilian exports had continued to decline in value. Not only was the coffee industry in a state of paralysis but the nation's reserves of foreign exchange were also virtually exhausted. Indeed, one of the few positive actions taken by Washington Luís during the revolt had been to issue a moratorium on the payment of the foreign debt. This had been renewed by Getúlio Vargas. Like the rest of Latin America, Brazil appeared very likely to default on its international financial obligations. While State Department officials were sympathetic, they could hardly have been happy with the new regime's decision to spend large sums on buying up coffee stocks and to invite a British banker, Sir Otto Niemeyer, to visit Brazil to discuss the terms of a new funding loan.

On the surface, 1930 had been a bad year for American diplomacy in Brazil. The government preferred by the Hoover administration had collapsed and was replaced by a self-proclaimed "revolutionary" regime with pronounced nationalist tendencies. The British foreign office gloated over news of American embarrassments and took particular delight in describing the withdrawal of the naval mission as "a bitter pill for the Americans." However, the British ambassador at Rio judged the apparent setback as only "a temporary manifestation." This assessment was confirmed just over a year later when the Brazilian government requested the return of American naval instructors.[117]

The State Department's alleged partiality for Washington Luís aroused a certain amount of ill feeling, but it could hardly reverse a tradition of friendship between the United States and Brazil that stretched back beyond the establishment of the Brazilian republic.[118] The relationship was not merely sentimental, but reflected mutual interests. This became evident during the period of the Old Republic as diplomatic links were markedly strengthened. American goodwill and assistance proved invaluable to Brazilian statesmen in their successful efforts to resolve boundary disputes and play a more active role in hemispheric and world affairs. Moreover, the growing desire for increased commercial contact also brought the two countries closer together. "The United States," Rio Branco succinctly summed up in 1905, "are the principal market for our coffee and other products."[119] Although American merchants and politicians complained that the actual trade balance remained firmly in Brazil's favor, this was compensated by America's economic influence steadily growing in Brazil from the late-nineteenth century onward while that of European rivals correspondingly diminished.

Americans readily acknowledged and appreciated Brazil's friendliness. "Of all the countries in South America," observed Lloyd Griscom in 1906, "Brazil is most likely to respond quickly to our advances."[120] However, while American officials were delighted when Brazil became an ally in World War I or adopted a helpful role at Pan-American conferences, they resisted claims for special treatment and often displayed an attitude of indifference and disdain. In fact, the occasional talk of an alliance or partnership between the two "giants" was misleading. Such was the disparity of power between the two countries that the relationship could hardly be on equal terms. The Old Republic had to endure a number of slights, ranging from the unilateral abrogation of the reciprocity arrangement to the lack of consultation over the Peace Pact. Ambassador Frederic Stimson once remarked that the State Department believed that Brazil was "in its pocket."[121] The evident lack of mutual respect provoked Foreign Minister Mangabeira into protesting that Brazil wished to be the friend of the United States but not its servile follower.[122] The valorization disputes and the termination of the naval mission in 1930 served as instructive reminders of Brazilian sensitivity and capacity for retaliation.

The coincidence of the 1930 revolution and the onset of the Great Depression marked a historical watershed for both the United States and Brazil. Herbert Hoover's electoral defeat in 1932 underlined the collapse of the "Old Republican Order" and paved the way for the "New Deal" of Franklin D. Roosevelt.[123] One change desired by the new president was the termination of several diplomatic appointments, including that of Edwin Morgan, who duly resigned in April 1933. In Brazil itself, the Old Republic was replaced by the personal rule of Getúlio Vargas. Foreign policy became less elitist and more receptive to "nationalist" influences.[124] However, the adoption of a different form of political rhetoric could not disguise the reality that Brazil was still only a "sleeping" giant, whereas the gigantic power of the United States was undeniable. The idea of an equal relationship had been a pretense that had served the ambitions and vanities of the Old Republic's ruling elite. For a brief period under the skillful direction of Rio Branco and Joaquim Nabuco the concept had possessed some validity. Subsequently, however, the United States forged even further ahead in political prestige, economic wealth, and military power while Brazil sank into relative decline. Consequently, by 1930 the relationship was more unequal than ever. A certain amount of Brazilian resentment was inevitable. Nevertheless, despite the diplomatic embarrassment attending the fall of Washington Luís, the British ambassador at Rio considered that the United States stood "at a pinnacle" in Brazil and that this was a position that other foreign nations could not hope to rival.[125] So long as Brazil strove to fulfil its potential by looking outward in pursuit of overseas markets and diplomatic status, that country would continue to prize the friendship and assistance of the northern giant. Whenever the United States turned its attention to Latin American affairs it was similarly appreciative of the cooperative and cordial response that was generally forthcoming from Brazil. Prior to 1889 the two countries had been distant neighbors. By 1930 it was evident that they had established a tradition of diplomatic friendship that would endure into the future.

Notes

Bibliographical Essay

Index

NOTES

CHAPTER 1: *Sister Republics, 1889–1901*

1. December 20, 1889, *Congressional Record,* 51st Congress, 1st sess., 315.

2. This was part of a growing interest in Latin American affairs shown by American politicians, especially the controversial James G. Blaine. For a study of the diplomacy of this period see Joseph Smith, *Illusions of Conflict: Anglo-American Diplomacy Toward Latin America, 1865–1896* (Pittsburgh: University of Pittsburgh Press, 1979). On the link between economic motives and American foreign policy see William A. Williams, *The Roots of the Modern American Empire* (New York: Random House, 1969).

3. March 1, 1888, *Congressional Record,* 50th Congress, 1st sess., 1656.

4. Smith, *Illusions of Conflict,* 130–47.

5. During the period from 1890 to 1919 more than two million Europeans emigrated to Brazil. The corresponding number from the United States was a mere 6,691 or 0.25 percent of the total; see T. Lynn Smith, *Brazil: People and Institutions* (Baton Rouge: Louisiana State University Press, 1963), 137. With the exception of a few thousand Confederate exiles who settled in São Paulo immediately after the Civil War, organized emigration from the United States was unknown. Although the settlement established by the Confederate exiles quickly fragmented and lost its American identity, its existence did encourage the evangelical churches of the southern United States to establish several missions; see Blanche Weaver, "Confederate Immigrants and Evangelical Churches in Brazil," *Journal of Southern History* 17 (1952): 446–68. By the close of the nineteenth century a number of Protestant churches, hospitals, and schools had been successfully established including Mackenzie College in São Paulo. It was also estimated that there were one million Protestants in Brazil; see Erasmo Braga and Kenneth G. Grubb, *The Republic of Brazil: A Survey of the Religious Situation* (London: World Dominion Press, 1932), 59–61. The story of the Confederate exiles is recounted in William C. Griggs, *The Elusive Eden: Frank McMullan's Confederate Colony in Brazil* (Austin: University of Texas Press, 1987).

American travelers to Brazil also included explorers, geographers, and entrepreneurs attracted to the tropics by scientific curiosity and an appetite for exotic adventure. For the casual visitor Brazil was "the land of the cocoa and the palm" whose inhabitants were gentle, courteous and hospitable; see Thomas Ewbank, *Life in Brazil* (New York: Harper, 1856). American naval officers reminisced wistfully on the popularity of Rio for "the sprightliness of its amusements, the vivacity of its pleasure-loving people and their generous preference for Americans"; see Winfield S. Schley, *Forty-Five Years under the Flag* (New York: Appleton, 1904), 123. But there was also the constant dread of infectious diseases such as malaria, smallpox, typhus, cholera and especially yellow fever. The latter was transmitted from Africa in 1849 and epidemics became a regular occurrence. In Rio alone it was estimated that yellow fever had claimed more than 50,000 lives by the end of the century. Wealthy Brazilians and foreign diplomats escaped to the more agreeable climate of Petrópolis in the mountains beyond the capital, but the scourge of disease often made life uncomfortable. An American traveler reported that "the stranger almost takes his life in his hands" when walking through Rio; see Frank G. Carpenter, *South America* (Akron: Saalfield, 1903), 512. One distinctly unflattering impression of Rio was made by William E. Curtis who briefly visited the city in 1885 as the secretary of the Latin American Trade Commission: "Viewed from the deck of a ship in the harbor, the city of Rio looks like a fragment of fairy-land–a cluster of alabaster castles decorated with vines; but the illusion is instantly dispelled upon landing, for the streets are narrow, damp, dirty, reeking with repulsive odors, and filled with vermin-covered beggars and wolfish-looking dogs. The whole town seems to be in a continual perspiration, and the atmosphere is so enervating that the stranger feels an almost irresistible tendency to lie down;" *The Capitals of Spanish America* (New York: Praeger, 1969), 661.

6. Although the existence of the imperial court gave Brazil a higher standing than most Latin American countries, the American diplomatic establishment in Brazil was fairly typical of the majority of nineteenth-century posts in that it was invariably small and understaffed. From 1842 onward a resident minister headed the legation and was assisted by a diplomatic secretary who served as chargé d'affaires whenever the minister was absent. Communication with Washington was notoriously slow. Dispatches sent by sea mail usually took at least five weeks to reach their destination. Toward the end of the nineteenth century it became possible to use the telegraph service, although this was frowned upon for reasons of expense. In fact, American ministers in Brazil were rarely troubled with having to make urgent diplomatic decisions. Most business was of a consular and commercial nature and was administered by a consul-general at the American consulate in Rio. By 1900 additional consular representation was located in the state capitals of Pará, Maranhão, Pernambuco, Bahia, São Paulo and Rio Grande do Sul. Business was transacted entirely within the major cities and ports. Large areas of Brazil were unmapped and rudimentary transportation facilities made them virtually inaccessible. American officials therefore had little direct experience of the regional qualities and differences that interacted within Brazilian society. Invariably possessing a meager knowledge of Portuguese, they found it hard to relate to a society with a Latin culture. Consequently, a sense of confusion and helplessness often appeared in political dispatches. A common complaint alluded to "the excitable character of the people" that made diplomatic business so frustrating to conduct; see Adams to Blaine, no. 30, December 28, 1889, Washington, National Archives, Records of the Department of State, Record Group [hereafter cited as RG] 59, *Brazil*, Dispatches, 49.

7. Robert Adams of Pennsylvania took up his post as minister at Rio in July 1889 and remained until March 1890. Edwin Conger of Iowa served as minister from December 1890 until he was superseded by Thomas L. Thompson of California in

September 1893. Conger replaced Thompson in July 1897, but stayed in Rio for only six months. In January 1898 he was made minister to China. Colonel Charles Page Bryan of Illinois, who had refused the appointment to Peking, became minister to Brazil. The selection of consular officials was also dictated by political considerations; for an interesting example during the Harrison administration see J. Orton Kerbey, *An American Consul in Amazonia* (New York: Rudge, 1911). Although he did not know where Pará was, as "one of a thousand anxious seekers for a consulate," Kerbey was pleased to secure "one of the much coveted of a half dozen possible vacancies" (46).

8. Herman G. James offers a comprehensive study of the Brazilian constitution in *The Constitutional System of Brazil* (Washington: Carnegie Institution, 1923).

9. For example, only an estimated 2.7 percent of the population voted in the 1898 presidential election; see Joseph L. Love, "Political Participation in Brazil, 1881–1969," *Luso-Brazilian Review* 7 (1970): 7. The republic, which lasted from 1889 to 1930, was formerly known as the First Republic, but is more commonly referred to by historians as the Old Republic. For a perceptive analysis of its political, economic, and social structure see Edgard Carone, *A república velha: instituições e classes sociais* (São Paulo: Difel, 1970). A recent overview is Boris Fausto, "Brazil: The Social and Political Structure of the First Republic, 1889–1930," in *The Cambridge History of Latin America*, 5 vols., ed. Leslie Bethell (Cambridge: Cambridge University Press, 1986), 5:779–829. For a perceptive case study of the link between kinship and politics see Linda Lewin, *Politics and Parentela in Paraíba* (Princeton: Princeton University Press, 1987).

10. John D. Wirth, *Minas Gerais in the Brazilian Federation, 1889–1937* (Stanford: Stanford University Press, 1977), 177. The struggle for spoils also indicated that the federal government possessed considerable resources and consequent capacity for the exercise of governmental authority. On the role of the "state" see Steven Topik, "State Interventionism in a Liberal Regime: Brazil, 1889–1930," *Hispanic American Historical Review* 60 (1980): 593–616.

11. The Ministry of Foreign Relations was initially located in the Rua da Passeio and moved to the Rua da Glória during the 1850s. The Itamaraty palace had been constructed in 1851 as the Rio home of the Rocha Leão family, the counts of Itamaraty. It became the seat of the provisional government from 1889 to 1897. From 1897 to the creation of the new federal capital at Brasília in 1960, it was the headquarters of the foreign ministry. The staff employed by the foreign office fell from 38 in 1859 to 27 in 1902; see E. Bradford Burns, *The Unwritten Alliance: Rio-Branco and Brazilian-American Relations* (New York: Columbia University Press, 1966), 38. The decline was even more marked according to recent figures, which estimate the number of "funcionários" at 200 in 1889; see Alvaro Teixeira Soares, *História administrativa do Brasil: organização e administração do ministério dos estrangeiros* (Brasília: FUNCEP, 1984), 75.

12. Gilberto Freyre, *Order and Progress: Brazil from Monarchy to Republic*, trans. Rod W. Horton (New York: Knopf, 1970), 90. The founders of the Brazilian republic were more influenced by French positivism than American constitutional ideas. However, the desire for a federal system of government in which individual states enjoyed considerable powers of autonomy directed attention to the United States as a particularly relevant and appealing model. Although reservations were expressed about the excessive materialism and the practice of racial discrimination in the United States, Brazilians were impressed by that country's dynamic economic growth and technologi-

cal achievement. Americans were regarded as possessing an amazing capacity for work and inventiveness; see ibid., 94.

13. Thompson to Gresham, no. 348, April 15, 1895, and Thompson to Olney, no. 487, May 28, 1896, RG 59, *Brazil,* Dispatches, 59, 60.

14. The Jacobins were especially active in organizing antiforeign demonstrations. See June E. Hahner, *Poverty and Politics: The Urban Poor in Brazil, 1870–1920* (Albuquerque: University of New Mexico Press, 1986), 139–55, and Steven Topik, "Middle-Class Brazilian Nationalism, 1889–1930," *Social Science Quarterly* 59 (1978): 95–96. One of the most articulate critics of American imperialism was Eduardo Prado whose first edition of *A illusão americana* was confiscated by the police (a second edition was published in Paris two years later; see *A illusão americana* [Paris: A. Colin, 1895]). In common with the mass of educated Brazilians, Prado acknowledged a natural affinity with Portugal and European culture. England was admired for its urbane gentility. The influence of Italian opera was profound. France exercised a particular fascination and its civilization provided the inspiration and model for the Brazilian elite. Wealthy Brazilians such as Prado eagerly flocked to the Paris Exposition of 1889 to celebrate the centenary of the French Revolution. "Without a doubt the world is Paris," eulogized Prado. By contrast, American culture and manners were alien and repellent. "I can hardly wait," Prado wrote during a visit to the United States, "to free myself from this furnace of a country where it costs you a dollar to open your mouth and another dollar to close it"; quoted in Thomas E. Skidmore, "Eduardo Prado: A Conservative National Critic of the Early Brazilian Republic, 1889–1901," *Luso-Brazilian Review* 12 (1975): 149. For Prado's description of New York as "dirty and ugly" and Chicago as "the most brutal city in the world" see Darrell E. Levi, *The Prados of São Paulo, Brazil* (Athens: University of Georgia Press, 1987), 126.

15. Freyre, *Order and Progress,* 91–92; Thomas E. Skidmore, "Brazil's American Illusion: From Pedro II to the Coup of 1964," *Luso-Brazilian Review* 23 (1986): 73. A very readable account of Dom Pedro's visit is John H. Williams, "Brazil's Most Curious Monarch," *Americas* 36 (1984): 20–29. American visitors at the exhibition were also impressed by the Brazilian pavilion which displayed a wide variety of goods, including precious gems, stuffed parrots, and a Brazilian-made rifle. "Brazil was everywhere at the Centennial Exhibition, presenting a higher profile even than most European nations"; Williams, see ibid., 26.

16. William H. Ukers, *All About Coffee* (New York: Tea & Coffee Trade Journal Company, 1935), 451–52. Ukers relates the story that the "A" of Ariosa stood for Arbuckle, the "rio" for Rio and the "sa" for South America or Santos (452).

17. Compiled from Department of Commerce, Bureau of the Census, *Historical Statistics of the United States* (Washington: GPO, 1960), 903–07. Despite the relatively small figures, representing no more than 3 to 4 percent of total American trade, a profitable commercial relationship was established during the nineteenth century, ranking Brazil along with Cuba and Mexico as one of America's largest trading partners in Latin America. American merchants imported sugar, cocoa, and tobacco from northeastern Brazil, coffee from Rio and Santos and hides from the Plate region. Brazilians showed a preference for flour milled from the winter wheat of Maryland and Virginia and shipped via Baltimore. They also regularly purchased New England lard and dairy products.

18. Trail to Bayard, no. 72, January 21, 1886, RG 59, *Brazil*, Dispatches, 47. For an account of the ill-fated commission see Joseph Smith, "The Latin American Trade Commission of 1884–5," *Inter-American Economic Affairs* 24 (1971): 3–24.

19. See enclosure in MacDonell to Iddesleigh, no. 44, December 16, 1886, London, Public Record Office, Foreign Office Records [hereafter cited as FO], 13/621. The *Rio News* was an English-language weekly published by an American proprietor.

20. Frank R. Rutter, *South American Trade of Baltimore* (Baltimore: Johns Hopkins University Press, 1897), 31. Competition for the Brazilian trade also came from New Orleans and Newport News, but these ports were unable to provide adequate return cargoes and lacked the extensive railroad communications enjoyed by Baltimore and especially New York. From the Civil War to the 1880s New York controlled more than 60 percent of the import trade from Brazil. Baltimore's share was just over 20 percent; see ibid., 67.

21. Speech of James H. Blount of Georgia, *Congressional Record*, 45th Congress, 3d sess., 2131. John Roach was estimated to have lost one million dollars in his efforts to establish steamships to Brazil during the 1870s; see Leonard A. Swann, *John Roach, Maritime Entrepreneur* (Annapolis: U.S. Naval Academy, 1965), 102–24.

22. See Earl Richard Downes, "The Seeds of Influence: Brazil's 'Essentially Agricultural' Old Republic and the United States, 1910–1930" (Ph.D diss., University of Texas, 1986), 99. The USBMSC was formed by John Roach and Collis P. Huntington in 1882 and operated a line of steamers from New York and Newport News to Pará and Santos until going into bankruptcy in 1892.

23. See Carlos Süssekind de Mendonça, *Salvador de Mendonça: Democrata do Império e da República* (Rio: Instituto nacional do livro, 1960), 126–27.

24. The American consul-general at Rio told Brazilian officials that he had no knowledge of any discussions concerning a commercial treaty; see Jarvis to Bayard, no. 143, August 27, 1888, RG 59, *Brazil*, Dispatches, 48.

25. The Brazilian cabinet rejected the idea of a customs union. Minister of Finance Francisco Belisário warned that Brazil should not open its markets to "a new industrial nation, violently protectionist and brimming with expansion"; quoted in Humberto Bastos, *Rui Barbosa, ministro da independencia econômica do Brasil* (São Paulo: Martins editôra, 1951), 229–30. See also Francisco de Assis Barbosa, *Juscelino Kubitschek* (Rio: José Olympio, 1960), 104–05.

26. H. Clay Armstrong to Bayard, November 28, 1888, RG 59, *Brazil*, Dispatches, 48.

27. Blaine to Osborn, no. 9, December 1, 1881, RG 59, *Brazil*, Instructions, 17. Blaine's comment was written as part of the invitation for Brazil to attend his proposed Pan-American conference; Pereira da Costa to Rodrigo Augusto da Silva, April 12, 1889, and Pereira da Costa to Francisco Diana, August 8, 1889, Rio de Janeiro, Arquivo Histórico do Itamaraty, Missões Diplomáticas Brasileiras, Oficios [hereafter cited as AHI], 233/4/9.

28. Francisco Diana to Lafayette Pereira, June 18, 1889, AHI 273/3/5. See also Wyndham to Salisbury, no. 48, July 16, 1889, FO 13/661.

29. The American delegate, John B. Henderson, proposed "that this Conference welcome the United States of Brazil to the sisterhood of American Republics." The resolution was rejected on the grounds that the delegates lacked instructions and the

authority to recognize a change of government; see International American Conference, 1889–1890, *Minutes of the Conference* (Washington, D.C.: GPO, 1890), 28.

30. Adams to Blaine, no. 20, November 19, 1889, RG 59, *Brazil,* Dispatches, 48.

31. Blaine to Adams, November 30, 1889, ibid.

32. Salvador reported that Blaine was sympathetic to the turn of events; see José Afonso Mendonça Azevedo, *Vida e obra de Salvador de Mendonça* (Rio: Ministério das relações exteriores, 1971), 177.

33. Pedro I's heroic cry of "Independence or death" may have evoked memories of America's own struggle for freedom, but it could not alter the fact that he had been born and still remained a member of a European royal family. The Monroe administration hesitated to grant recognition. Its evident distaste for monarchy was eventually overcome in 1824 by the acceptance of political reality and desire for commercial advantage. "The form of government was not our concern," succinctly noted Secretary of State John Quincy Adams; quoted in Stanley E. Hilton, "The United States and Brazilian Independence," in *From Colony To Nation* ed. A. J. R. Russell-Wood (Baltimore: Johns Hopkins University Press, 1975), 128.

34. For a survey of American press opinion see J. Fred Rippy, "The United States and the Establishment of the Republic of Brazil," *Southwestern Political and Social Science Quarterly* 3 (1922): 39–53; Dom Pedro's abdication statement of November 16, 1889, is quoted in E. Bradford Burns, ed., *A Documentary History of Brazil* (New York: Knopf, 1966), 286.

35. For the debate of December 20, 1889, see *Congressional Record,* 51st Congress, 1st sess., 313–24.

36. See Salvador to Quintino Bocaiúva, no. 1, January 14, 1890, AHI 213/3/4.

37. *New York Sun,* December 20, 1889; *Nation,* January 2, 1890; *New York Times,* December 24, 1889.

38. The Chilean foreign minister later described Brazil's action as "a breach of faith"; see Kennedy to Salisbury, no. 36, April 27, 1890, FO 16/259. See also Robert N. Burr, *By Reason or Force: Chile and the Balancing of Power in South America, 1830–1905* (Berkeley and Los Angeles: University of California Press, 1965), 187–90.

39. Salvador to Quintino Bocaiúva, no. 3, January 14, 1890, AHI 273/3/4. In accordance with its republican tenets, the provisional government adopted a "collegiate system of decision-making" extending to all administrative matters including foreign policy; see Clodoaldo Bueno, "O cotidiano no processo de elaboração de decisões em política exterior e o início da república no Brasil," *História* 5–6 (1986–87): 11–17.

40. Burr, *Reason or Force,* 190. A competent account of Brazilian diplomacy during the early republic is Arthur Guimarães de Araujo Jorge, *Ensaios de história diplomática do Brasil no regímen repúblicano, 1889–1902* (Rio: Imprensa nacional, 1912), 53–84.

41. See Griggs, *Elusive Eden,* 41.

42. Salvador expected to be transferred to Switzerland in the spring of 1890. The confusion over rank between him and Amaral was ended in December 1890 when Salvador was confirmed as Brazilian minister to the United States. He held this post until May 1898. Two very useful collections of his correspondence are by Carlos Süssekind de Mendonça, and José Afonso Mendonça Azevedo, published in 1960 and 1971 respectively. See also the minister's own memoirs in Salvador de Mendonça, *A situação internacional do Brasil* (Paris: Garnier, 1913).

43. During the Pan-American conference Blaine was in the habit of calling Salvador by telephone in the morning so that the two men could meet and talk over business as they made their way to the conference hall; see Süssekind de Mendonça, *Salvador,* 145. In his memoirs, Charles Flint observed that Salvador was "a loyal friend of the United States and was treated by Secretary Blaine with great frankness"; see Charles R. Flint, *Memories of an Active Life* (New York: G. P. Putnam's Sons, 1923), 155.

44. Salvador was also involved in negotiating a commercial treaty with the United States. Later in the year he was instructed to explore the possibility of a political alliance; see Quintino Bocaiúva to Salvador, no. 11, September 2, 1890, AHI 273/3/5. It is interesting to note that a similar sense of vulnerability more than sixty years previously had motivated the Brazilian chargé at Washington to propose an alliance with the United States. The response of the Monroe administration in 1825 was decidedly cool; see Hilton, "United States and Brazilian Independence," 128–29.

45. Salvador noted that Charles Flint, Andrew Carnegie, and Thomas Jefferson Coolidge were especially active in helping to present his arguments personally to Blaine; see Süssekind de Mendonça, *Salvador,* 139–40 and Mendonça Azevedo, *Salvador,* 179–81.

46. The reasons for Blaine's decision are unknown. Contemporaries sometimes ascribed his erratic behavior to the fact that he was a hypochondriac. Salvador clearly believed that the arguments about European intervention were influential, but Blaine may also have been stung by Senator Turpie's criticism of the administration's recognition policy only a few days earlier. Turpie described Harrison as "lagging far behind the march of time and events" and, alluding to Blaine, he noted: "The whole Department of State have fallen under the spell of some slumbrous swoon of official inertia or under the guidance of the spirit of that old Saxon chieftain who was, from his dilatory habits on all occasions, named and called Athelstan the Unready"; see January 15, 1890, *Congressional Record,* 51st Congress, 1st sess., 584–85. The role of President Harrison in the question of the timing of recognition is also unclear. Although it was well known that the president was determined to be the final authority in foreign affairs, Salvador made no mention of any direct involvement by the White House. It would appear that this particular matter was left to Blaine's decision. On the personal rivalry between Harrison and Blaine see Harry J. Sievers, *Benjamin Harrison: Hoosier President* (Indianapolis: Bobbs-Merrill, 1968), 213–25. United States recognition of the Brazilian republic was officially granted on February 20, 1890. France followed suit in July 1890 and Britain in May 1891.

47. *Rio News,* February 10, 1890; Wyndham to Salisbury, no. 45, February 24 and no. 52, February 26, 1890, FO 13/666. Adams's resignation was accepted and he left his post on March 1, 1890. His successor, Edwin Conger, was not appointed until September. For examples of Adams's critical views on Deodoro see Adams to Blaine, no. 26, December 17 and no. 30, December 28, 1889, RG 59, *Brazil,* Dispatches, 49.

48. *New York Daily Tribune,* June 25, 1890; *New York Times,* June 24, 1890. The constitution came into effect in February 1891 and created a national government located in Rio and headed by an elected president. The powers of the executive were considerable, but were restricted by the legislature and judiciary. Significant constitutional powers were also reserved to the state governments. To American eyes, it ap-

peared that the new Brazilian form of government was virtually identical to their own.

49. Blaine did, however, attempt to restrict the offer of free sugar to Brazil alone; see Salvador to Quintino Bocaiúva, no. 7, May 9, and no. 9, June 8, 1890, AHI 273/3/4.

50. See David M. Pletcher, "Reciprocity and Latin America in the Early 1890s: A Foretaste of Dollar Diplomacy," *Pacific Historical Review* 47 (1978): 64–65.

51. The president was also empowered to impose retaliatory import duties on the goods of those countries he believed to be discriminating against American exports; see Smith, *Illusions of Conflict,* 143–47.

52. John W. Foster, *Diplomatic Memoirs,* 2 vols. (Boston: Houghton Mifflin, 1909), 2:7.

53. Mendonça Azevedo, *Salvador,* 158. On the importance of the American market for Brazilian sugar see Peter L. Eisenberg, *The Sugar Industry in Pernambuco* (Berkeley and Los Angeles: University of California Press, 1974), 22–25.

54. For an outline of the contents of the eventual agreement see Pletcher, "Reciprocity," 66.

55. See undated memorandum on "Loss of Revenue" by Foster, Library of Congress, John W. Foster Papers.

56. Conger to Blaine, no. 27, February 26; no. 30, March 6; and no. 40, April 2, 1891; RG 59, *Brazil,* Dispatches, 50.

57. *Rio News,* February 10, 1891.

58. The political background is presented in June E. Hahner, *Civilian-Military Relations in Brazil, 1889–1898* (Columbia: University of South Carolina Press, 1969), 34–46.

59. See the debate of February 11, 1891, in *Annães do congresso nacional,* 3:93–94.

60. Adam to Salisbury, no. 21, March 30, 1891, FO 13/681.

61. The Brazilian government was also placed under additional pressure from the British, French, and German ministers, who insisted that any tariff concessions granted to the Americans should be accorded to their own merchants. The British minister was instructed to inform the Itamaraty that the treaty had produced a "very bad effect" in England; see Adam to Salisbury, no. 17, March 21, 1891, ibid.

62. Adee to Conger, May 23, 1891, RG 59, *Brazil,* Instructions, 17.

63. Foster to Salvador, June 16, 1891 enclosed in Salvador to Justo Chermont, no. 8, June 19, 1891, AHI 233/4/10.

64. Conger to Blaine, no. 76, July 7, 1891, RG 59, *Brazil,* Dispatches, 51. The question whether Salvador had been deceived by Blaine attracted press comment in the United States, especially from the anti-Blaine *Nation;* see the *Nation,* October 8, November 19, December 3, 1891; April 7 and 14, 1892. For Salvador's response see his letter to the *New York Evening Post,* April 5, 1892.

65. Süssekind de Mendonça, *Salvador,* 153–62. A perceptive analysis of the reciprocity debate is Steven C. Topik, "Informal Empire? The U.S.–Brazilian Trade Treaty of 1891," (M.A. thesis, University of Texas, 1974), 46–67.

66. Conger to Blaine, no. 123, September 17, 1891, RG 59, *Brazil,* Dispatches, 51. For the allegation that bribery influenced the vote see Lawrence F. Hill, *Diplomatic Relations between the United States and Brazil* (Durham: Duke University Press, 1932), 271–72.

67. Conger to Blaine, no. 159, November 13, 1891, RG 59, *Brazil*, Dispatches, 52 and 53.

68. Conger to Blaine, no. 185, January 11, 1892, ibid., 53.

69. Wyndham to Salisbury, no. 88, May 6, 1892, FO 13/695.

70. *Rio News*, July 5, 1892; Gresham to Salvador, October 26, 1894, *Foreign Relations* [of the United States] (1894), 82. For an assessment of the effects of reciprocity see Lincoln Hutchinson, "Reciprocity with Brazil," *Political Science Quarterly* 18 (1903): 282–312. The evidence is ambiguous, but it seems that the treaty was "moderately beneficial" for American exports to Brazil; see Pletcher, "Reciprocity," 83–86.

71. Pauncefote to Salisbury, no. 154, July 10, 1891, FO 5/2120.

72. See James L. Laughlin and Henry P. Willis, *Reciprocity* (New York: Baker and Taylor, 1903), 218.

73. See Smith, *Illusions of Conflict*, 185–205.

74. For a general guide to the secondary literature on the Naval Revolt see Joseph Smith, "Britain and the Brazilian Naval Revolt of 1893–4," *Journal of Latin American Studies* 2 (1970): 175, n. 1.

75. A perceptive article on the enigmatic Floriano is June E. Hahner, "Floriano Peixoto, Brazil's 'Iron Marshal': A Re-Evaluation," *The Americas* 31 (1975): 252–71.

76. Matilda Gresham, *The Life of Walter Quintin Gresham, 1832–1895*, 2 vols. (Chicago: Rand, McNally, 1919), 2:777. For an example of Salvador's public relations activities see his articles "Republicanism in Brazil" and "Latest Aspects of the Brazilian Rebellion," *North American Review* 158 (1894): 8–15, 164–74. See also James F. Vivian, "United States Policy during the Brazilian Naval Revolt, 1893–94: The Case for American Neutrality," *American Neptune* 41 (1981): 253–56.

77. Floriano's attempt to acquire a fleet of fighting ships met with a very lukewarm response in the United States. The businessman, Charles Flint, claimed, however, that Americans reacted quickly and decisively; see Flint, *An Active Life*, 90–101. A fleet was eventually assembled, but it arrived too late to exert a direct military influence on events. One historian has described the ships as "a nondescript fleet" purchased "at an enormous price" and "manned by a motley crew"; see A. Curtis Wilgus, ed., *Argentina, Brazil and Chile Since Independence* (Washington, D.C., George Washington University Press, 1935), 232.

78. Thompson to Gresham, September 7, 1893, RG 59, *Brazil*, Dispatches, 54.

79. For an example of a contemporary view that the action of the foreign naval commanders was favorable to Floriano see Joaquim Nabuco, *A intervenção estrangeira durante a revolta de 1893* (São Paulo: Companhia editôra nacional, 1939), 48.

80. Gresham to Thompson, November 1, 1893, RG 59, *Brazil*, Instructions, 17.

81. *Rio News*, September 14, 1893.

82. The Department of the Navy judged that Stanton had violated Navy regulations by saluting the flag of a government not recognized by the United States. The action, however, was not considered to have been deliberate. Stanton suffered no loss of rank and was soon appointed to succeed Rear Admiral Benham as commander of the North Atlantic squadron. Benham was transferred to Rio to replace Picking.

83. Picking to Herbert, December 28, 1893, National Archives, Records of the Department of the Navy, RG 45, area 4, microfilm roll no. 26. Picking had attempted

to dissuade Stanton from firing a salute to Custódio, but he also found it difficult to resist the affinity and professional bonds that linked naval officers together. An awkward personal relationship developed with Thompson primarily because Picking accused the American minister of not treating Custódio like a gentleman; see Michael B. McCloskey, "The United States and the Brazilian Naval Revolt, 1893–1894," *The Americas* 2 (1946): 309, n. 41. Initially Picking believed that local sympathies were on the side of the rebels; see Picking to Herbert, November 4, 1893, RG 45, area 4, microfilm roll no. 26.

84. On the separatist movement in the south see Joseph L. Love, *Rio Grande do Sul and Brazilian Regionalism, 1882–1930* (Stanford: Stanford University Press, 1971), 57–72.

85. Thompson to Gresham, October 22 and 24, 1893, RG 59, *Brazil*, Dispatches, 55; Gresham to Thompson, October 25, 1893, ibid., Instructions, 18.

86. Thompson to Gresham, October 3 and December 13, 1893, ibid., Dispatches, 54 and 55.

87. Gresham to Thompson, January 9 and 30, 1894, ibid., Instructions, 18.

88. An informative account of Benham's naval action is William L. Clowes, *Four Modern Naval Campaigns* (London: Unit Library, 1902), 221–23.

89. Gresham to Thompson, January 30, 1894, RG 59, Brazil, Instructions, 18.

90. For example, Senator Anthony Higgins stated in 1895: "That Empire, becoming a republic, met with a rebellion, promoted and aided by European nations in the interest of their trade, which was advanced by the monarchical condition there, and was threatened with injury by American competition under the Republic"; see March 2, 1895, *Congressional Record*, 53d Congress, 3d sess., 3109. The importance of economic factors has also been stressed by historians, most notably Walter LaFeber, "United States Depression Diplomacy and the Brazilian Revolution, 1893–1894," *Hispanic American Historical Review* 40 (1960): 107–18. Gresham did insist on the continuance of American trade at Rio. What was at issue was not international commercial rivalry but observance of the principle that foreign merchants should be allowed to go about their business unhindered. The leading British journal on Latin American business affairs, the *South American Journal* (London), in its February 3, 1894 issue, expressed an identical view: "A group of discontented or ambitious military or naval officers commit an act of treason in seizing upon the ships of a nation, and immediately proceed to use them, in contravention of the expressed desire of the constituted authorities, to terrorise, injure, and obstruct foreign commerce. This is what has occurred in the Rio Bay, and we are of opinion that foreign commerce ought to be protected against such a state of affairs."

91. Gresham to Bayard, January 21, 1894, Library of Congress, Walter Q. Gresham Papers.

92. Picking to Herbert, October 14, 1893, RG 45, area 4, microfilm roll no. 26.

93. Report of the Secretary of the Navy, November 17, 1894, 53d Congress, 3d sess., House Doc. 1, 23. See also Charles W. Calhoun, "American Policy toward the Brazilian Naval Revolt of 1893–94: A Reexamination," *Diplomatic History* 4 (1980): 39–56.

94. Wyndham to Rosebery, no. 37, February 2, and no. 48, February 5, 1894, FO 13/724. Salvador was also acutely conscious of this local criticism; see Salvador de Mendonça, *Situação internacional*, 208–09.

95. The Floriano government actually attempted to stifle criticism of the United States by its confiscation of the first edition of Eduardo Prado's *A illusão americana*.

96. Custódio had similarly left Rio in December 1893. Without apparently much enthusiasm, he involved himself in various naval maneuvers in the south until April 1894 when he chose to seek political asylum in Argentina.

97. Thompson's dispatch of October 12, 1895, cited in 54th Congress, 1st sess., House Doc. 377, part 1, 92.

98. Gresham to Salvador, August 29, 1894, enclosed in Salvador to Carlos de Carvalho, no. 1, February 7, 1895, AHI 233/4/11.

99. *South American Journal* (London), September 29, 1894. The value of Brazilian coffee exports to the United States decreased during the late 1890s, but this was a consequence of falling world prices and depressed market conditions rather than changes in American tariff policy.

100. See Luiz Viana Filho, *A vida do barão do Rio Branco* (Rio: José Olympio, 1959), 210.

101. Moniz Bandeira, *Presença dos Estados Unidos no Brasil* (Rio de Janeiro: Civilização brasileira, 1973), 150. The friendly feeling toward Cleveland also resulted from the belief that he had assisted Brazil by persuading France to accept arbitration of the Amapá boundary dispute; see Joaquim Nabuco to Bacon, July 9, 1908, AHI 234/1/8. Argentine politicians tended to be critical of Cleveland's Venezuelan boundary policy and McKinley's intervention in Cuba; see Harold F. Peterson, *Argentina and the United States, 1810–1960* (Albany: State University of New York Press, 1964), 285.

102. Phipps to Salisbury, no. 37, May 21, 1899, FO 13/783. One writer describes Brazilian diplomacy as "perplexed and timid" during this period; see Francisco de Assis Barbosa, "A presidência Campos Sales," *Luso-Brazilian Review* 5 (1968): 19.

103. Phipps to Salisbury, no. 18, January 23, 1896, FO 13/757; Moore to Bryan, no. 61, July 30, 1898, RG 59, *Brazil, Instructions,* 18.

104. Chilean interest in Brazil is mentioned in José Zamudio Zamora, *Isidro Errázuriz, ministro en Brasil, 1897–98* (Santiago de Chile: Imprenta Universitaria, 1949); see also Burr, *Reason or Force,* 198–99, 254–55, and Miguel Angel Scenna, *Argentina-Brasil* (Buenos Aires: La Bastilla, 1975), 281–82.

105. The celebrated account of these events is Euclides da Cunha, *Os sertões,* translated by Samuel Putnam as *Rebellion in the Backlands* (Chicago: University of Chicago Press, 1944).

106. The inflationary period at the beginning of the republic was referred to as the *encilhamento.*

107. Thompson to Olney, no. 517, November 12, 1896, RG 59, *Brazil,* Dispatches, 60.

108. For requests for American warships see Thompson to Olney, no. 517, November 12, 1896 and Conger to Sherman, no. 58, November 10, 1897, RG 59, *Brazil,* Dispatches, 60 and 61. Street riots were a common occurrence in Rio and were especially frequent during the period from 1893 to 1897; see José Murilo de Carvalho, *Os bestializados* (São Paulo: Companhia das Letras, 1987), 70 and Hahner, *Poverty and Politics,* 147–50. For the *Wilmington* incident see Charles E. Stokes, "The Acre Revolutions, 1899–1903," (Ph.D. diss., Tulane University, 1974), 60–66.

109. The chances of successfully negotiating reciprocity arrangements with Latin

American countries were considerably reduced by the notable absence of sugar from the free list. One writer notes that the 1897 reciprocity provision was "complicated" and that its application was limited "to a series of mostly exotic and unimportant products"; see Pletcher, "Reciprocity," 88.

110. Rutter, *South American Trade Of Baltimore,* 56–57, 61. For an example of lobbying at the State Department by Baltimore merchants see Hay to Dawson, no. 266, November 16, 1901, RG 59, *Brazil,* Instructions, 18.

111. Conger to Sherman, no. 38, October 15, 1897, ibid., Dispatches, 61.

112. Hay to Bryan, no. 115, March 4, 1899, ibid., Instructions, 18.

113. Ibid.

114. Salvador to Dionísio Cerqueira, no. 5, April 3, and to William E. Curtis, April 6, 1897, AHI 234/4/12.

115. Nícia Vilela Luz, *A luta pela industrialização do Brasil: 1808 a 1930* (São Paulo: Difusão Européia do Livro, 1961), 111–23. For an example of how Campos Sales agreed to protectionist measures in return for political support from Minas Gerais see Wirth, *Minas Gerais,* 180.

116. Dawson to Sherman, no. 123, March 25, 1898, and to Hay, no. 383, January 3, 1902, RG 59, *Brazil,* Dispatches, 62 and 67. Joaquim Murtinho was actually critical of the policy of protection; see Carlos M. Peláez, "As consequências econômicas de ortodoxia monetária cambial e fiscal no Brasil entre 1889 e 1945," *Revista brasileira de economia* 25 (1971): 25–26.

117. Phipps to Salisbury, no. 40, August 13, 1899, FO 13/786.

118. Bryan to Hay, no. 309, February 12, 1901, RG 59, *Brazil,* Dispatches, 65. Argentina was also involved in protracted and ultimately unsuccessful reciprocity negotiations with the United States; see Harold F. Peterson, *Diplomat of the Americas: A Biography of William I. Buchanan* (Albany: State University of New York Press, 1971), 125–30.

119. Sherman to Conger, no. 73, November 16, 1897, RG 59, *Brazil,* Instructions, 18.

120. Dawson to Hay, no. 390, December 19, 1901, ibid., Dispatches, 67.

121. Assis Brasil to Olinto de Magalhães, no. 29, June 2, 1899, AHI 233/4/12.

122. Hay to Bryan, no. 213, October 2, 1900, RG 59, *Brazil,* Instructions, 18. Similar examples of Hay's forceful language are expressed in Hay to Bryan, telegram (hereafter abbreviated as tel.), July 11, and no. 266, November 16, 1901, ibid.

123. Bryan to Olinto de Magalhães, September 21, 1900, AHI 280/2/6.

124. Brazil's bumper coffee crop of 1901 contributed to the problem of overproduction that was depressing world coffee prices; see Celso Furtado, *The Economic Growth of Brazil,* trans. Ricardo W. de Aguiar and Eric C. Drysdale (Berkeley and Los Angeles: University of California Press, 1963), 194–95 and Carlos M. Peláez, "Análise econômica do programa brasileiro de sustentação do café, 1906–1945," *Revista brasileira de economia* 26 (1971): 31–44.

125. Despite his many talents, Assis Brasil was also typical of the Brazilian elite in that he lacked fluency in the English language; see Manoel de Oliveira Lima, *Memórias* (Rio: José Olympio, 1937), 168–72.

126. *Washington Post,* May 19, 1898; *New York Tribune,* March 21, 1898. Assis Brasil was also a rancher and had made a study of agricultural techniques and methods.

For his interest in American agriculture see Downes, "Seeds of Influence," 30–37. The appointment of Assis, however, owed more to the workings of spoils politics than commercial calculation. Assis had originally been selected as Brazilian minister to China, but did not proceed to that post. Throughout 1897 Foreign Minister Dionísio Cerqueira maneuvered to find a suitable alternative appointment. This was narrowed down to either Madrid or Washington and ultimately the latter was selected; see Süssekind de Mendonça, *Salvador,* 190–93.

127. This agreement was negotiated in Washington between Hay and Assis Brasil; see Hay to Bryan, no. 230, January 29, 1901, RG 59, *Brazil,* Instructions, 18.

128. Assis Brasil was described as "a great deal troubled and ashamed" that the arrangement had not been carried out; see Bryan to Hay, no. 342, July 17, 1901, ibid., Dispatches, 66. On the need for congressional sanction see Dawson to Olinto, November 13, 1901, and memorandum by Dawson, November 18, 1901, AHI 280/2/6.

129. Campos Sales had to be protected by police and soldiers en route from the presidential palace to the railroad station; see June E. Hahner, *Poverty and Politics,* 177–78.

130. Memorandum by Coleman to Root, January 3, 1906, RG 59, *Brazil,* Dispatches, 72. Chapman Coleman was an official in the Record Office of the State Department. Hay's desire to avoid difficulties with Brazil was in character with his generally indecisive approach to foreign affairs; see Richard H. Werking, *The Master Architects: Building the United States Foreign Service, 1890–1913* (Lexington: University Press of Kentucky, 1977), 90–91.

131. *Chicago Tribune,* December 14, 1901, quoted in A. Curtis Wilgus, "The Second International American Conference At Mexico City," *Hispanic American Historical Review* 11 (1931): 63, n.106.

132. See Tom E. Terrill, *The Tariff, Politics, and American Foreign Policy, 1874–1901* (Westport: Greenwood, 1973), 207–08.

CHAPTER 2: *Years of Approximation, 1902–1912*

1. Archibald C. Coolidge, *The United States as a World Power* (New York: Macmillan, 1908), 132.

2. Commerce Department, *Historical Statistics,* 903–07. See also Robert N. Seidel, "Progressive Pan Americanism: Development and United States Policy Toward South America, 1906–1931," (Ph.D. diss., Cornell University, 1973), 62–64. Despite the increasing volume of business with Latin America, most American trade and capital was exported primarily to Europe and Canada.

3. A good introductory survey is George E. Mowry, *The Era of Theodore Roosevelt and the Birth of Modern America, 1900–1912* (New York: Harper and Row, 1958). On progressivism and foreign policy see Seidel, "Pan Americanism." The Latin American division was "the most overworked in the department"; see Walter V. Scholes and Marie V. Scholes, *The Foreign Policies of the Taft Administration* (Columbia: University of Missouri Press, 1970), 19.

4. This anxiety was most eloquently expressed by Spanish-American writers such as Rubén Darío and José Enrique Rodó.

5. *Times* (London), August 9, 1906.

6. See Leo S. Rowe, "Our Trade Relations with South America," *North American Review* 184 (1907): 516, and Wilfred H. Schoff, "Investment of American Capital in Latin-American Countries," *Annals of the American Academy of Political and Social Science* 37 (1911): 67.

7. George A. Chamberlain, "A Letter From Brazil," *Atlantic Monthly* 90 (1902): 831. For statistics on the American share of Brazilian trade see Victor C. Valla, *A penetração norte-americano na economia brasileira, 1898–1928* (Rio: Livro Técnico, 1978), 13–18, and United States Tariff Commission, *Reciprocity and Commercial Treaties* (Washington, D.C.: GPO, 1919), 290.

8. Lloyd Griscom, *Diplomatically Speaking* (London: John Murray, 1941), 266–68, 277. Charles Page Bryan served as minister in Rio from April 1898 to December 1902. His replacement was David Thompson who presented his credentials in April 1903. Thompson was promoted to the rank of ambassador in January 1905 and stayed in Brazil until November 1905. Lloyd Griscom arrived at Rio in June 1906. He left in January 1907 and was replaced by Irving Dudley. The latter presented his credentials in April 1907 and remained as ambassador until September 1911. Edwin Morgan was notified of his transfer from Portugal to Brazil in January 1912. He arrived to take up his new post at Rio in June 1912.

9. Haggard to Grey, no. 23, April 7, 1907, FO 371/201.

10. See Scholes and Scholes, *Foreign Policies of Taft Administration,* 35.

11. *Times* (London), December 30, 1902.

12. The best biographies of Rio Branco are Luiz Viana Filho, *A vida do Barão do Rio Branco* (Rio: José Olympio, 1959), and Alvaro Lins, *Rio Branco: biografia pessoal e história política* (São Paulo: Companhia editôra nacional, 1965).

13. On Nabuco see Luiz Viana Filho, *A vida de Joaquim Nabuco* (São Paulo: Companhia editôra nacional, 1952), and Carolina Nabuco, *The Life of Joaquim Nabuco,* trans. Ronald Hilton (Stanford: Stanford University Press, 1950). The two immediate predecessors of Nabuco at Washington were Assis Brasil from May 1899 to April 1903 and Gomes Ferreira from October 1903 to May 1905. Nabuco served as Brazil's first ambassador until his death in January 1910. Domício da Gama was appointed as his successor in 1911.

14. The outstanding work on this subject is E. Bradford Burns, *The Unwritten Alliance: Rio Branco and Brazilian-American Relations* (New York: Columbia University Press, 1966). See also Frederic W. Ganzert, "The Baron do Rio Branco, Joaquim Nabuco and the Growth of Brazilian-American Friendship, 1900–1910," *Hispanic American Historical Review* 22 (1942): 432–51.

15. Quoted in Carolina Nabuco, *Nabuco,* 414.

16. Griscom to Root, July 16, 1906, RG 59, Numerical File (hereafter cited as NF) 1113/2.

17. Thompson to Hay, no. 143, May 4, 1904, RG 59, *Brazil,* Dispatches, 70. The period from 1903 to 1906 has been described as "the high tide of protectionism"; see Wirth, *Minas Gerais,* p. 44.

18. Griscom to Root, July 16, 1906, RG 59, NF 1113/2.

19. Clemenceau described his reception at Rio in 1910 as reflecting a "magnificent homage" to France; see Georges Clemenceau, *South America To-Day* (London:

Unwin, 1911), 235. The chapter on his visit was, however, much more of a travelogue than a political analysis. As such it was illustrative of contemporary European curiosity in Brazil and represented an example of the growing literature on the country that was appearing in French books and magazines. The Brazilian elite avidly devoured any praise emanating from Europe. For example, they were immensely flattered to learn that Portuguese had been adopted as one of the official languages at a scientific congress in Vienna and that a music festival held in the same city had performed compositions by the colonial musician, José Mauricio. With the exception of the personal attention bestowed on Joaquim Nabuco and Manoel de Oliveira Lima, American interest in Brazil was much less in evidence; see E. Bradford Burns, *A History of Brazil* (New York: Columbia University Press, 1980), 324. In fact, Brazilian art and literature were virtually unknown in the United States. Only a small handful of Brazilian literary works appeared in English-language versions during the nineteenth century and these were published in London. It was not until 1919–20 that the first English translations of Brazilian novels were published in the United States. They were José de Alencar, *The Jesuit* and Graça Aranha, *Canaan*. The barrier of language similarly frustrated the cultural curiosity of educated Brazilians who most often read American works not in their original English edition but in French translation. For example, the very popular *Uncle Tom's Cabin* was translated into French in 1853, but a Portuguese version was not published until 1881; see Samuel Putnam, *Marvelous Journey: A Survey of Four Centuries of Brazilian Writing* (New York: Knopf, 1948), 247, n. 19.

20. As a crude average about 250 Americans migrated annually to the Old Republic before the World War I. The majority were businessmen rather than settlers. For statistics see T. Smith, *Brazil*, 137; see also Rollie E. Poppino, *Brazil: The Land and the People* (New York: Oxford University Press, 1968), 195.

21. Rio Branco had requested the opportunity to be posted to Berlin. His admiration for France and Germany was always very evident and his "cultural preoccupations remained essentially European"; see Thomas E. Skidmore, *Black Into White: Race and Nationality in Brazilian Thought* (New York: Oxford University Press, 1974), 136.

22. Viana Filho, *Vida do Rio Branco*, 340–63. Rio Branco was also worried about possible clashes with the director-general, Cabo Frio. The baron initially suggested that Joaquim Nabuco was best suited for the post of foreign minister; see Burns, *Unwritten Alliance*, 34.

23. An informative study of the Acre dispute is Stokes, "Acre Revolutions." See also Frederic W. Ganzert, "The Boundary Controversy in the Upper Amazon between Brazil, Bolivia, and Peru, 1903–1909," *Hispanic American Historical Review* 14 (1934): 427–49, and Lewis A. Tambs, "Rubber, Rebels, and Rio Branco," ibid., 46 (1966): 254–73. The influx of settlers into Acre was part of a wider movement of population throughout the Amazon valley. Many migrants came from the Northeast, especially after a serious drought struck Ceará in 1879. By 1900 more than 60,000 Brazilians were estimated to be living in Acre; see Ganzert, "Boundary Controversy," 434.

24. The Argentine minister at La Paz was able to acquire a copy of the contract between the Bolivian government and the syndicate. This copy was given to the Brazilian minister at Buenos Aires; see Azevedo to Olinto, no. 6, April 27, 1902, AHI 206/1/12. The various foreign investors were officially described as the "Bolivian syndicate." Because it was headed by American entrepreneurs and its headquarters were

located in New York, the term "American syndicate" came into more popular use.

25. Chamberlain, "Letter from Brazil," 828.

26. Seeger to Hay, January 20, 1903, RG 59, *Brazil*, Dispatches, 68. Press reports confirmed "the bitter feeling now prevailing in Brazil against the United States"; see *New York Herald,* November 1, 1902.

27. Memorandum by Bryan, July 19, 1902, AHI 280/2/6.

28. Memorandum by Assis Brasil, June 19, 1902; Assis to Seabra, no. 7, November 18, 1902, ibid., 234/1/1. See also Moniz Bandeira, *Presença dos Estados Unidos,* 159–60. It had been initially reported that powerful individuals such as King Leopold of Belgium and the millionaire banker, J. Pierpont Morgan, had taken up shares in the syndicate; see Viana Filho, *Vida do Rio Branco,* 343. Moreover, anxiety was not only limited to Brazil. *La Nación* (Buenos Aires), April 13, 1902, described the syndicate as "a continental danger."

29. Seeger to Hay, January 20, 1903, RG 59, *Brazil,* Dispatches, 68. On Seeger's contention that the Amazon could not legally be closed, an official at the British foreign office minuted: "This is a remarkable declaration if authorized as it stands by the United States Government"; see Dering to Lansdowne, no. 1, January 20, 1903, FO 13/836. For the historic link between the United States and the Amazon see Percy A. Martin, "The Influence of the United States and the Opening of the Amazon to the World's Commerce," *Hispanic American Historical Review* 1 (1918): 146–62.

30. Hay to Bryan, no. 305, December 15, 1902, RG 59, *Brazil,* Instructions, 18. For an admiring obituary of the baron see John Bassett Moore, *The Collected Papers of John Bassett Moore,* 7 vols. (New Haven: Yale University Press, 1944), 3:438–40.

31. See Thompson to Hay, no. 147, May 12, 1904, and no. 252, January 15, 1905, *Brazil,* Dispatches, 70 and 71.

32. Enclosures in Assis Brasil to Rio Branco, no. 2, February 4 and no. 5, March 19, 1903, AHI 234/1/2. See also Moniz Bandeira, *Presença dos Estados Unidos,* 163.

33. See enclosures in Assis Brasil to Rio Branco, no. 3, February 19, 1903, AHI 234/1/2. The idea of buying out the syndicate originated while Olinto de Magalhães was foreign minister and had been proposed by Assis Brasil to representatives of the syndicate in October 1902.

34. Moore to Assis Brasil, January 25, 1903, ibid. For a fuller presentation of Moore's views see his article "Brazil and Peru Boundary Question" in Moore, *Collected Papers,* 3:120–42. The Brazilian legation retained Moore as their "regular counsel" for $2,000 per annum plus travel expenses. He was also paid an additional sum of $3,000 for consultation over the Acre dispute.

35. The first decade of the twentieth century was the high point of Brazil's rubber industry. World prices steadily increased so that in export value, rubber ranked second only to coffee. Although the bulk of rubber gathering and its profits were still located in Amazonas, the earnings from the Acre trade were more than sufficient to reimburse Brazil for its payments to the American syndicate and the Bolivian government. See Burns, *Unwritten Alliance,* 46. The Bolivians appeared to find the settlement highly satisfactory. One writer has noted: "The loss of the Acre District, however, despite its size, excited little interest among the majority of Bolivians"; see J. Valerie Fifer, *Bolivia: Land, Location, and Politics Since 1825* (Cambridge: Cambridge University Press, 1972), 130.

36. Dawson to Hay, no. 132, March 19, 1904, RG 59, *Brazil,* Dispatches, 69. On the recognition of Panama see Burns, *Unwritten Alliance,* 86–90.

37. Loomis to Thompson, tel., May 18, 1904; Hay to Thompson, tel., June 13, 1904, RG 59, *Brazil,* Instructions, 18. The British minister confirmed that Hay regarded Brazil's case as "absolutely unassailable"; see Dering to Lansdowne, no. 39, June 10, 1904, FO 13/843.

38. The agreement negotiated in 1904 was not formally ratified by the Brazilian and Peruvian governments until 1909. It confirmed Brazil's possession of more than 60,000 square miles of territory; Peru was awarded only 10,000 square miles.

39. Dawson to Hay, no. 383, January 3, 1902, RG 59, *Brazil,* Dispatches, 67.

40. *Times* (London), December 30, 1902.

41. Chamberlain, "Letter From Brazil," 831.

42. Bryan to Hay, no. 408, April 17, and no. 472, November 18, 1902, RG 59, *Brazil,* Dispatches, 67 and 68.

43. Thompson to Hay, no. 60, September 24, 1903, ibid.

44. The minister of finance, Leopoldo de Bulhões, was strongly in favor of tariff reform; see Afonso Arinos de Melo Franco, *Rodrigues Alves* (São Paulo: Universidade de São Paulo, 1973), 284, and Vilela Luz, *Luta pela industrialização,* 178–79.

45. One writer has observed that the annual budget law, although submitted in early May, was passed by Congress "in the greatest haste and amid the greatest confusion in the last days of December"; see James, *Constitutional System of Brazil,* 75. A similar pattern of events occurred very frequently in the United States Congress.

46. Thompson to Hay, no. 100, December 24, 1903, RG 59, *Brazil,* Dispatches, 69.

47. Dering to Lansdowne, no. 10, February 4, 1904, FO 13/843.

48. See Dering to Lansdowne, no. 24, April 18, 1904, ibid.

49. Dering to Lansdowne, no. 25, April 19, and no. 39, June 10, 1904, ibid.

50. Dawson to Hay, no. 122, February 15, 1904, RG 59, *Brazil,* Dispatches, 69; *A Notícia* (Rio), April 25, 1904, argued that "the North continues to remain forgotten."

51. Thompson to Hay, no. 142, April 27, and no. 188, June 24, 1904, RG 59, *Brazil,* Dispatches, 69 and 70. The reduction of duty on American flour aroused most criticism. A later American report concluded: "The flour-milling and wheat-importing interests of Brazil were powerful and influential, and did their utmost to bring the measure into popular disrepute"; see U.S. Tariff Commission, *Reciprocity,* 286.

52. See Sheppard (Manager of the Rio Flour Mills) to Dering, December 24, 1903; enclosed in Dering to Lansdowne, no. 56, December 30, 1903, FO 13/836.

53. Dering to Lansdowne, no. 24, April 18, 1904, FO 13/843.

54. U.S. Tariff Commission, *Reciprocity,* 300–01.

55. See Dering to Lansdowne, no. 27, April 30, 1904, FO 13/843.

56. Thompson to Hay, no. 142, April 27, 1904, RG 59, *Brazil,* Dispatches, 69.

57. See Hay to Thompson, tel., December 23, 1903, ibid., Instructions, 18; Thompson to Hay, tel., December 23 and no. 106, December 30, 1903, ibid., Dispatches, 69.

58. Rio Branco to Gomes Ferreira, tel., May 3, 1904, AHI 234/1/2. Thompson was later described as "a man of powerful personality" and also possessing a "sharp and

forthright tongue"; see Williams F. Sands, *Our Jungle Diplomacy* (Chapel Hill: University of North Carolina Press, 1944), 123. He also became involved in an unpleasant disagreement with Consul-General Seeger that resulted in a State Department inquiry and Thompson's transfer to Mexico City. See Lowther to Grey, no. 13, March 8, 1906, FO 368/8, and *Chicago Tribune*, December 22, 1905.

59. Rio Branco to Gomes Ferreira, no. 1, January 31, 1905, AHI 235/2/6.

60. Burns, *Unwritten Alliance*, 4–5. For the view that federal policy did not always directly benefit the export of coffee see Steven Topik, "The State's Contribution to the Development of Brazil's Internal Economy, 1850–1930," *Hispanic American Historical Review* 65 (1985): 209–10.

61. U.S. Tariff Commission, *Reciprocity*, 293.

62. Dering to Lansdowne, no. 71, October 29, 1904, FO 13/843.

63. Thompson to Domício da Gama, July 2, 1905, AHI 280/2/8; Thompson to Root, no. 76, August 21, 1905, RG 59, *Brazil*, Dispatches, 71.

64. Marie R. Wright, *The New Brazil* (Philadelphia: Barrie and Sons, 1907), 102; *Times* (London), September 13, 1909. See also Jeffrey D. Needell, *A Tropical "Belle Epoque"* (Cambridge: Cambridge University Press, 1987), 1–51.

65. Cabo Frio died in 1907. At the Itamaraty, Rio Branco enjoyed "praticamente carta branca"; see Melo Franco, *Rodrigues Alves*, 248. Nevertheless, Rio Branco regarded Cabo Frio as an old family friend and treated him tactfully; see Burns, *Unwritten Alliance*, 38.

66. Foreign diplomats were initially received in the "rose salon." Meetings and conferences took place in the "green and gold salon" while a large ballroom furnished in green and gold was used for major state functions. The most celebrated example of Rio Branco's high spending, however, was his provision of a luxurious bathroom at the Itamaraty. The minister of finance declared: "Never in my life have I heard of such an expensive bathroom"; see Burns, *Unwritten Alliance*, 39. During Rio Branco's tenure of office the number of diplomatic posts was raised from 54 to 73. Consular appointments were also increased from 22 in 1902 to 50 in 1915; see ibid., 50–51, and Carl M. Jenks, "The Structure of Diplomacy: An Analysis of Brazilian Foreign Relations in the Twentieth Century," (Ph.D. diss., Duke University, 1979), 162.

67. See Freyre, *Order and Progress*, 202–03. Rio Branco also looked for personal loyalty in the young men whom he appointed to diplomatic office. This was obviously a means of consolidating and ensuring his own ascendancy; see Alexandre de Barros, "The Formulation and Implementation of Brazilian Foreign Policy: Itamaraty and the New Actors," in *Latin American Nations In World Politics*, ed. Heraldo Muñoz and Joseph S. Tulchin (Boulder: Westview, 1984), 31.

68. João Pandiá Calógeras, *Rio Branco e a política exterior* (Rio: Imprensa nacional, 1916), 41. After the appearance of an alarmist editorial in the *Washington Post*, dated May 8, 1901, Hay expressed his anxiety over the German "plan" to colonize southern Brazil; see Assis to Olinto, May 11, 1900, AHI 234/1/1. A brief summary of contemporary thinking is Loretta Baum, "German Political Designs with Reference to Brazil," *Hispanic American Historical Review* 2 (1919): 586–99. State Department officials were always much more concerned about alleged German intrigues in the Caribbean rather than in South America; see Melvin Small, "The United States and the German 'Threat' to the Western Hemisphere, 1905–1914," *The Americas* 28 (1979): 252–70.

69. December 11, 1905, quoted in Burns, *Unwritten Alliance,* 148.

70. Ambassador Griscom once described José Carlos Rodrigues as "our permanent friend"; see Griscom to Root, July 16, 1906, RG 59, NF 1113/2.

71. As a further retort against the baron, Salvador de Mendonça remarked: "When Rio Branco sent Joaquim Nabuco to discover North America, it had already been discovered, measured, and delimited"; quoted in Richard Graham, *Britain and the Onset of Modernization in Brazil, 1850–1914* (Cambridge: Cambridge University Press, 1968), 313. It could also be argued that approximation was simply a continuation of the imperial diplomatic tradition, which sought an equilibrium among Brazil, the United States, and Spanish America. On this see Burns, *Unwritten Alliance,* chap. 7; José Honório Rodrigues, *Interêsse nacional e política externa* (Rio: Civilização braseira, 1966), 54–55; and Christopher J. R. Leuchars, "Brazilian Foreign Policy and the Great Powers, 1912–1930," (D.Phil thesis, University of Oxford, 1983), 16–18. An excellent brief analysis is Clodoaldo Bueno, "Política Exterior de Rio Branco," *Anais de História* 9 (1977): 101–25.

72. Assis Brasil to Rio Branco, no. 2, February 4, 1903, AHI 234/1/2. Despite the validity of Assis Brasil's point concerning diplomatic status, in fact, there was relatively little official diplomatic business to transact between Rio and Washington. The Brazilian legation in the nation's capital was tiny and its diplomatic staff only numbered a minister and a diplomatic secretary. Like Rio, the oppressive heat compelled an annual evacuation from the city for most of the summer. Of necessity the minister had to spend a good deal of time traveling between the various political "capitals" dotted along the eastern seaboard from Washington to Boston. Matters involving Brazil and the United States were usually confined to consular affairs and most of this routine business was concentrated in New York where a consul-general maintained his office. Additional Brazilian consulates were located in New Orleans, Baltimore, Chicago, Philadelphia, Norfolk, and Newport News.

73. Thompson to Hay, no. 247, January 3, 1905, RG 59, *Brazil,* Dispatches, 71. The Senate gave its consent to Thompson's promotion on January 20, 1905. Rio Branco reported this to the American minister. The latter received official confirmation by sea-mail during February; see Jenks, "Structure of Diplomacy," 231–32. Rio Branco fully appreciated the importance of titles of rank. Despite the legal abolition of such titles under the republic, he insisted on retaining his own courtesy title of baron. Consideration of rank also influenced his attitude toward foreign representatives. Consular officials bitterly complained of the baron's particular rudeness and attributed this to his spirit of revenge for the many years he served as consul at Liverpool; see Ernest Hambloch, *British Consul* (London: Harrap, 1938), 133–35.

74. Dering to Lansdowne, no. 16, March 18, 1905, FO 13/851. It was also believed that the extra cost of maintaining an embassy rather than a mission would deter other Latin American countries from following Brazil's example; see João Frank da Costa, *Joaquim Nabuco e a política exterior do Brasil,* (Rio: Gráfica record editôra, 1968), 58–59.

75. Thompson to Hay, no. 252, January 15, 1905, RG 59, *Brazil,* Dispatches, 71.

76. *Jornal do commercio* (Rio), March 16, 1905.

77. *O Paiz* (Rio), January 26, 1905.

78. Carolina Nabuco, *Nabuco,* 305–06. Nabuco had served as Brazilian consul at New York from 1876 to 1877. Despite his genuine belief in the desirability of ap-

proximation with the United States, he also considered himself an "Anglomaniac" and was reluctant to be transferred from London to Washington; see Joaquim Nabuco, *Minha Formação* (São Paulo: Companhia editôra nacional, 1934), 79–114, and Frank da Costa, *Nabuco,* 52.

79. *Jornal do Brasil* (Rio), January 14, 1905; Thompson to Hay, no. 263, February 1, and no. 9, March 18, 1905, RG 59, *Brazil,* Dispatches, 71.

80. Quoted in Peterson, *Diplomat of the Americas,* 196. The few specific references made by Roosevelt on Brazil also indicated his positive and friendly attitude. He had fond memories of Pedro II dating from the emperor's visit to New York in 1876. On one occasion Roosevelt remarked that he was perpetually mystified by two revolutions, the fall of Louis Philippe in France and the overthrow of Dom Pedro; see Oliveira Lima, *Memórias,* 19. Roosevelt's admiration for Brazil was evident in his account of his visit during 1913–1914. He noted: "The great progress of Brazil–and it has been an astonishing progress–has been made under the republic"; see Theodore Roosevelt, *Through the Brazilian Wilderness* (New York: Charles Scribner's Sons, 1914), 349.

81. See Tyler Dennett, *John Hay* (New York: Dodd, Mead, 1934), 264.

82. Root to Tillman, December 13, 1905, quoted in Philip C. Jessup, *Elihu Root,* 2 vols. (New York: Dodd, Mead, 1938), 1:469.

83. Gomes Pereira to Rio Branco, no. 1, January 7, 1904, AHI 234/1/2; Thompson to Hay, no. 32, June 6, 1903, RG 59, *Brazil,* Dispatches, 68.

84. Quoted in Frank da Costa, *Nabuco,* 224.

85. *Chicago Tribune,* November 15, 1905.

86. Nabuco to Rio Branco, tels., October 27 and November 14, 1905, AHI 235/2/14.

87. Richardson to Root, no. 113, December 1, 1905, RG 59, *Brazil,* Dispatches, 71.

88. Root to Nabuco, November 28, 1905, AHI 234/1/3.

89. Griscom, *Diplomatically Speaking,* 266–68. On social elitism in the foreign service at the time of Theodore Roosevelt see Thomas H. Etzold, *The Conduct of American Foreign Relations* (New York: Franklin Watts, 1977), 22–36 and Martin Weil, *A Pretty Good Club* (New York: Norton, 1978), 15–23.

90. *Washington Evening Star,* March 23, 1906.

91. Nabuco to Rio Branco, January 3, 1906, AHI 234/1/4.

92. On the *Panther* incident see Burns, *Unwritten Alliance,* 103–06 and Frank da Costa, *Nabuco,* 226–40.

93. For Griscom's initial impressions of Brazil see Griscom to Root, July 16, 1906, RG 59, NF 1113/2.

94. See William N. Nelson, "Status and Prestige as a Factor in Brazilian Foreign Policy, 1905–1908," (Ph.D. diss., Louisiana State University, 1981), 24–26. Nabuco's friendship with Pena dated from 1866 when they were fellow students at the São Paulo Law School. Rodrigues Alves was also a member of the same class.

95. Alvaro Lins, *Rio-Branco,* 350. No extensive lobbying had been undertaken to select the site of the Pan-American conference and, in fact, Rio was a surprise choice; see Melo Franco, *Rodrigues Alves,* 293. Rio Branco attempted to reassure Latin American opinion by giving a long interview to an Argentine correspondent on July 25; see *La Nación* (Buenos Aires), July 26, 1906.

96. *New York Evening Post,* November 27, 1905. Root's biographer has described

his decision to visit South America as a "spontaneous initiative"; see Jessup, *Root,* 1:474.

97. See Elihu Root, *Latin America and the United States* (Cambridge: Harvard University Press, 1917), 45–52. Root's choice of clothes at Bahia was described as "characteristic and comfortable American fashion"; see Clayton Sedgwick Cooper, *The Brazilians and Their Country* (New York: Frederick A. Stokes, 1917), 5. Even in tropical temperatures, it was customary for middle-class Brazilian men to follow European fashion and wear black coats and tophats in public. To dress in a lightweight white suit was considered a scandal in Brazilian society; see Needell, *Tropical "Belle Epoque,"* 169–71.

98. Griscom to Root, July 16, 1906, RG 59, NF 1113/2.

99. "Europe will pay much more attention to the doings of the Congress with Mr. Root there, than it would were he not to go to it," commented the *Times* (London), June 25, 1906.

100. Griscom, *Diplomatically Speaking,* p. 274; Jessup, *Elihu Root,* 1:478–79; the Senate building had originally been the Brazilian pavilion at the St. Louis Fair in 1904. With his usual flair for publicity, Rio Branco named the building after Monroe immediately after Root made his celebrated speech on July 31.

101. Quoted in Burns, *Unwritten Alliance,* 110.

102. A general description of the conference is A. Curtis Wilgus, "The Third International American Conference at Rio de Janeiro, 1906," *Hispanic American Historical Review* 12 (1932): 420–56. For a contemporary Brazilian impression see Luís Gurgel do Amaral, *O meu velho Itamarati* (Rio: Imprensa nacional, 1947), 123–31.

103. Paul S. Reinsch, quoted in Wilgus, "Third American Conference," 451.

104. See Jessup, *Elihu Root,* 1:479–80.

105. Quoted in Root, *Latin America and the United States,* 10. Rui Barbosa commented: "These words reverberated through the length and breadth of our continent, as the American evangel of peace and of justice"; quoted in ibid., 3.

106. *Times* (London), August 9, 1906.

107. Nabuco could hardly accept the post of foreign minister so long as Rio Branco clearly wished to stay on; see Carolina Nabuco, *Nabuco,* 329–30 and Nelson, "Status and Prestige in Brazilian Foreign Policy," 26. Only after Nabuco had left Brazil for Washington in October, did the British minister consider it "almost certain" that Rio Branco would remain as head of the Itamaraty; see Barclay to Grey, no. 58, October 22, 1906, FO 371/12.

108. Quoted in Jessup, *Elihu Root,* 1:483.

109. The proposal of a similar arrangement involving the United States and Mexico also "evaporated;" see Robert F. Smith, "Latin America, the United States and the European Powers, 1830–1930," in *Cambridge History of Latin America,* ed. Leslie Bethell, 4:103. Brazil's diplomatic usefulness, however, was evident in 1908 when the State Department temporarily entrusted the care of American interests in Venezuela to the Brazilian legation at Caracas. This example of close diplomatic cooperation was flattering to Brazil, but was not the equivalent of an alliance. Further research is needed to clarify when the idea of an alliance was discarded, but a lecture delivered by Taft in 1913 on the Monroe Doctrine throws light on the thinking of the State Department. While he approved in principle the idea of seeking the assistance of the powerful countries of South America, Taft feared "that these Powers would be loath to assume responsibility or burden in the matter of the welfare of a government like one of the

Central American republics, or Haiti or Santo Domingo so remote from them and so near to us." He concluded: "If action in respect of any republic of South America were necessary under the Monroe Doctrine, the joining of the ABC powers with the United States might involve suspicion and jealousy on the part of other South American republics not quite so prosperous or so stable as the ABC powers. Thus, instead of helping the situation, the participation of part of the South American governments might only complicate it"; see William H. Taft, *The United States and Peace* (New York: Charles Scribner's Sons, 1914), 20–21.

110. Haggard to Grey, no. 23, April 7, 1907, FO 371/201.

111. Of the nations of Latin America, only Mexico and Brazil had been invited to the 1899 conference. The proposal to hold the second conference in 1906 also clashed with a meeting to revise the Red Cross convention at Geneva. On the diplomatic background see Calvin D. Davis, *The United States and the Second Hague Peace Conference* (Durham: Duke University Press, 1975).

112. Ibid., 133; Root, *Latin America and the United States,* 10.

113. The choice was between Rui and Joaquim Nabuco. For the controversy over the appointment see Nelson, "Status and Prestige in Brazilian Foreign Policy," 39–66, and Luiz Viana Filho, *A vida de Rui Barbosa* (São Paulo: Companhia editôra nacional, 1960), 33.

114. Nabuco to Root, May 25, 1907, quoted in Nelson, "Status and Prestige in Brazilian Foreign Policy," 74. Root later wrote to Choate on May 31, 1907, that "the United States does not care . . . about the so-called honors," but that American assistance to the Latin Americans "will be repaid ten times over by their appreciation provided they do not think we are discriminating in favor of one against another"; quoted in ibid., 88.

115. Root openly discussed with Nabuco the policy that the United States would pursue at the conference; see ibid., 72–80.

116. Davis, *Second Hague Peace Conference,* 126–27.

117. Rio Branco succinctly summed up: "We pay our debts, and, furthermore, we are creditors to Uruguay and Paraguay"; quoted in Hildebrando Accioly, "O Barão do Rio Branco e a Segunda Conferência da Haia," *Revista do Instituto Histórico e Geográfico Brasileiro* 187 (1945): 73.

118. *La Nación* (Buenos Aires), July 26, 1906.

119. Davis, *Second Hague Peace Conference,* 170–71, 257–58.

120. Ibid., 257. Brazil had also earlier supported the proposal by the American delegation that private property should be immune from capture at sea.

121. Quoted in Nelson, "Status and Prestige in Brazilian Foreign Policy," 145. Rui paid Stead £800 to write an "advertisement" in the *Review of Reviews*. This took the form of a lengthy article entitled "Brazil at The Hague"; ibid., 137.

122. Silvino Gurgel do Amaral to Rio Branco, no. 3, September 3, 1907, AHI 234/1/7; Root's comment is quoted in Jessup, *Elihu Root,* 2:78. See also Nelson, "Status and Prestige in Brazilian Foreign Policy," 92–99, 104–12.

123. Rio Branco later told Nabuco that he held Choate personally responsible for the difficulties at The Hague and criticized the American delegate for being "unfaithful to the Pan-American policy followed since Blaine"; quoted in Nelson, "Status and Prestige in Brazilian Foreign Policy," 186.

124. Quoted in Davis, *Second Hague Peace Conference*, 272. Although some commentators described Rui as "muy verbosa," it was agreed that his efforts had led to Brazil being "discovered" at The Hague; see ibid. To what extent Rui was simply following Rio Branco's instructions or acting independently is unknown. Certainly, there was regular telegraphic communication between the two men. State Department officials were also puzzled. "We had supposed that Ruy Barbosa's egotism and chauvinism were responsible for his course," noted Alvey A. Adee in January 1908, "but it now seems he merely obeyed orders"; quoted in Nelson, "Status and Prestige in Brazilian Foreign Policy," 193.

125. Haggard to Grey, no. 65, September 7, 1907, FO 371/200.

126. Haggard to Grey, no. 83, October 21, 1907, ibid.; Nabuco's comment is quoted in Nelson, "Status and Prestige in Brazilian Foreign Policy," 188.

127. Thompson to Hay, no. 252, January 15, 1905, RG 59, *Brazil*, Dispatches, 71.

128. Thompson to Hay, no. 9, March 18, 1905, ibid. The population of Brazil in 1906 was just over 14 million compared to Argentina's population of 5 million. Griscom noted the diplomatic strains resulting from the publication in Buenos Aires of population statistics stating that 8 million Brazilians were "of negro race"; see Griscom to Root, no. 37, September 20, 1906, RG 59, NF 1070/3 and Burns, *Unwritten Alliance*, 182.

129. Moniz Bandeira, *Presença dos Estados Unidos*, 170–71. Brazilian warships were dispatched to Paraguay in 1904; see Rio Branco to Gomes Ferreira, tel., no. 31, November 24, 1904, AHI 234/1/2. For a perceptive analysis of Argentine-Brazilian relations in the twentieth century see Stanley E. Hilton, "The Argentine Factor in Twentieth-Century Brazilian Foreign Policy Strategy," *Political Science Quarterly* 100 (1985): 27–51.

130. For reports of Argentine resentment see Von Hoonholtz to Rio Branco, no. 22, July 13, 1906, and Assis Brasil to Rio Branco, no. 12, November 15, 1906, AHI 206/2/1. Rio Branco once expressed the view that the reduction of duty in favor of American flour had almost brought war with Argentina in 1906; see Haggard to Grey, no. 1, January 5, 1907, FO 368/91.

131. Beaupré to Root, no. 592, August 19, 1907, RG 59, NF 6047/2.

132. Quoted in Clodoaldo Bueno, "O Rearmamento Naval Brasileiro e a Rivalidade Brasil-Argentina em 1906–1908," *História* 1 (1982): 29.

133. See Stanley E. Hilton, "The Armed Forces and Industrialists in Modern Brazil: The Drive for Military Autonomy (1889–1954)," *Hispanic American Historical Review* 62 (1982): 629–73.

134. Beaupré to Root, no. 592, August 19, 1907, RG 59, NF 6047/2.

135. Nabuco to Rio Branco, no. 1, January 3, 1907, AHI 234/1/6.

136. Griscom to Root, no. 37, September 20, 1906, RG 59, NF 1070/3.

137. Haggard to Grey, no. 1, January 5, 1907, FO 368/91.

138. Lorillard to Root, no. 121, March 26, 1907, RG 59, NF 6047/1. A procession of hundreds of yachts and small boats filled the bay to re-create a Venetian regatta in honor of the man who was judged to be Brazil's best friend in Argentina.

139. Haggard to Grey, no. 22, April 4, 1907, FO 371/200. The lukewarm reception for Dudley may have represented an element of retaliation for the "humiliating" experience suffered by Joaquim Nabuco when returning to the United States in No-

vember 1906. Punctilious immigration authorities apparently submitted the ambassador to embarrassing personal questions such as asking if he possessed a criminal record or how had he raised the money to pay for his passage. Root personally visited Nabuco the next day to present his government's apology. Griscom predicted, however, the possibility of retaliation and confirmed that the incident had "produced a most disagreeable impression in Brazil and seriously offended the national susceptibilities"; see Griscom to Root, no. 63, November 28, 1906, RG 59 NF 2372/4–8, and Nelson, "Status and Prestige in Brazilian Foreign Policy," 33–35. Mischievous as ever, Alvey Adee suggested a New Year's telegram from Roosevelt to President Pena to "preen the ruffled plumage of Brazil a little." He added: "As a Spaniard once said to me 'We Latins pay great attention to ticket!' [meaning *etiquette*]"; memorandum from Adee to Root, n.d., RG 59, NF 2372/4–8.

140. Dudley to Root, no. 176, May 6, and no. 182, May 21, 1908, RG 59, NF 6047/9 and 11.

141. See minute dated October 22, 1908, on Eddy to Root, no. 18, September 16, 1908, RG 59, NF 15865/1; Adee to Eddy, tel., December 19, 1908, ibid., NF 1070/25.

142. Rio Branco to Nabuco, December 8, 1908, AHI 234/1/8. See also Clodoaldo Bueno, "Política Exterior de Rio Branco," 109. It is interesting to note that Rio Branco showed no inclination to return Root's visit. Much to the dissatisfaction of Joaquim Nabuco, Rio Branco discouraged such suggestions by pleading ill health; see Maurício Nabuco, *Reminiscências sérias e frívolas* (Rio: Pongetti, 1969), 32.

143. Haggard to Grey, no. 83, October 21, 1907, FO 371/200.

144. Rio Branco to Nabuco, no. 73, November 22, 1909, AHI 234/1/9. This question was referred to as the Alsop Claims. For a discussion see Burns, *Unwritten Alliance*, 135–39.

145. See enclosures in Nabuco to Rio Branco, no. 8, December 1, and no. 9, December 15, 1909, AHI 234/1/9. Knox later proved amenable to persuasion and Nabuco attributed this to the personal intervention of Elihu Root.

146. The personal antipathy between the two foreign ministers had exploded into public recrimination in 1908 when Zeballos published the contents of a coded telegram sent via the Buenos Aires telegraph by Rio Branco to the Brazilian minister at Santiago. Zeballos alleged that Rio Branco was planning war against Argentina. Rio Branco was, however, able to show that the charge was false and malicious. An embarrassed Zeballos was forced to resign.

147. Dudley to Knox, no. 582, August 27, 1910, RG 59, Decimal File [hereafter cited as DF] 1910–29, 732.35/20.

148. Undated memorandum by Domício da Gama, Coleção Domício da Gama, Instituto Histórico e Geográfico Brasileiro, Rio de Janeiro.

149. Fletcher to Knox, no. 7, September 24, 1910, and memorandum by Adee, October 31, 1910, RG 59, DF 1910–29, 725.3211/23 and 24. The State Department considered that the ABC alliance was "inspired by anti-American feeling"; see memorandum by Henry L. Janes of the Latin American Division, February 1, 1912, ibid., 725.3211/33. See also Scenna, *Argentina-Brasil*, 296–98.

150. William H. Becker, *The Dynamics of Business-Government Relations: Industry and Exports, 1893–1921* (Chicago: University of Chicago Press, 1982) 91–112; Emily S.

Rosenberg, *Spreading the American Dream: American Economic and Cultural Expansion, 1890–1945* (New York: Hill and Wang, 1982), 56–57.

151. See Patrick D. DeFroscia, "The Diplomacy of Elihu Root, 1905–1909" (Ph.D. diss., Temple University, 1976), 104–05.

152. Speech at Santos, August 7, 1906, quoted in Root, *Latin America and the United States*, 42.

153. The executive was given authority by Congress to introduce preferential rates for one year. The list of goods was the same as 1904 with the addition of refrigerators, pianos, scales, and windmills.

154. See U.S. Tariff Commission, *Reciprocity*, 293–300; Cheetham to Grey, no. 41, July 9, 1908, FO 368/173.

155. *New York Times*, October 15, 1906.

156. 59th Congress 2d sess., Senate Doc. 365, 26.

157. November 23, 1906, quoted in Jessup, *Elihu Root*, 1:489–91.

158. Brazil showed more initiative and enterprise in 1906 when the Lloyd Brasileiro Company established a line of steamships from Rio to New York. The company quickly acquired a reputation for inefficiency and poor service and required heavy subsidies from the Brazilian government; see D. C. M. Platt, ed., *Business Imperialism, 1840–1930* (Oxford: Oxford University Press, 1977), 143–44.

159. Chamberlain, "Letter From Brazil," 821.

160. Root, *Latin America and the United States*, 43.

161. Frederic Emory, "Causes of Our Failure to Develop South-American Trade," *Annals of the American Academy of Political and Social Science* 22 (1903): 155.

162. Griscom to Root, July 16, 1906, RG 59, NF 1113/2; Griscom, *Diplomatically Speaking*, 270.

163. Although Rio Branco's movements were much more unpredictable and abrupt, the practice of switching between Rio and Petrópolis did not begin with him. It had started during the last decades of Dom Pedro's rule when the emperor and his family showed an increasing preference to reside for most of the year in the cooler and healthier climate of Petrópolis almost 30 miles away from Rio. Emerging from its humble beginnings as an agricultural community, the small city became known as the "Versailles" of Brazil. Consequently, diplomatic missions, including the American legation, were located there while more temporary accommodations were rented in Rio. Telegraphic communication was established with Rio as early as 1857, but diplomats were compelled to shuttle frequently between the two places by a combination of boat, funicular, and railroad.

164. Haggard to Grey, no. 97, November 16, 1907, FO 371/200. The same dispatch also presented a most unflattering picture of the great Brazilian statesman: "His slovenliness and untidiness are appalling. His table is covered literally a foot high with documents in their turn covered with dust. This is probably the dust-heap into which disappear many of our carefully prepared private letters and memoranda on pressing matters and possibly even our Notes, of which we never hear anything again. His memory is worse than bad, which causes him to make the most egregious 'gaffes,' so what chance has one? One speaks to him and he forgets all about this also, and so on 'ad infinitum.'"

165. The royal visit in May 1908 was intended to be the high point of a celebration to mark the centenary of the opening of the ports of Brazil to foreign trade. The British minister noted that Rio Branco eagerly awaited the event. "The visit of a European monarch," he reported, "would set the seal on the claim of Brazil to be the first among South American nations and to rank among the powers of the world"; see Cheetham to Grey, no. 12, February 9, 1908, FO 371/402. Unfortunately, the assassination of King Carlos prevented the state visit from taking place.

166. See Barclay to Grey, no. 50, September 7, 1906, FO 368/8; Haggard to Grey, no. 1, January 5, 1907, ibid., 368/91.

167. Dudley to Rio Branco, December 31, 1909, AHI 280/2/9. There was a slight increase in the volume of exports from the United States to Brazil after 1906, but the American share of the market remained relatively unchanged. Even though articles receiving preference made up less than 12 percent of total American exports, discontent focused primarily on the failure to expand sales of wheat and flour. The commercial reality was that Argentine flour was less expensive and enjoyed cheaper freight rates. Most Brazilian flour mills were also located in the South and preferred to import from Argentina. Consequently, the preferential tariff was of little advantage to American flour exporters. Nonetheless, there were some gains. Notably, the value of exports of india rubber manufactures tripled from 1906 to 1911. Items such as American typewriters, pianos, and windmills had been virtually unknown and gained a foothold in the Brazilian market as a result of preference. In 1910 when the reduction was extended to cement, American exports of cement to Brazil climbed from $7,116 to $276,624 within two years and to $766,915 in 1913; see U.S. Tariff Commission, *Reciprocity*, 285–313.

168. See Barclay to Grey, no. 45, August 8, 1906, FO 371/13. Griscom acknowledged that there was "considerable doubt" whether Pena would continue approximation, but he was relieved to report the friendly nature of Pena's inaugural presidential address; see Griscom to Root, no. 63, November 28, 1906, RG 59, NF 2372/4–8.

169. Haggard to Grey, no. 14, March 8, 1907, FO 368/91. The British minister likened the United States to a "cuckoo" which aimed "to turn us out of the nest to get all the worms for itself"; see Haggard to Grey, no. 1, January 5, 1907, ibid.

170. Quoted in Werking, *Master Architects*, 162.

171. Francis Huntington-Wilson, *Memoirs of an Ex-Diplomat* (Boston: B. Humphries, 1945), 166, 170–71.

172. See Scholes and Scholes, *Foreign Policies of Taft Administration*, 27–31 and Huntington-Wilson, *Memoirs*, 140.

173. Nabuco to Rio Branco, no. 16, May 5, and no. 22, August 5, 1909, AHI 234/1/9.

174. See Haggard to Grey, no. 29, March 29, 1910, FO 371/832.

175. Throughout the nineteenth century American diplomats frequently assumed a superior and condescending attitude in their dealings with Brazilian officials. The pompous tone was reflected in such statements as that of the American chargé, Condy Raguet, who described the arrest of seamen from an American ship in 1826 as "the greatest outrage upon civilization, that had ever been practiced in modern days"; quoted in Hill, *Diplomatic Relations*, 44.

176. Rives to Rio Branco, November 7, 1911, AHI 280/2/9.

177. Huntington-Wilson to Bath Iron Works, July 20, 1910, RG 59, DF 1910–

29, 832.34/21A. American promotional efforts were, however, directed more to Argentina than Brazil. The director of the Pan-American Union, John Barrett, expressed a typical comment when he observed: "Argentina buys more from us than any other Latin American Republic, with the exception of Mexico and Cuba, and offers a larger undeveloped field for our exports than any other southern nation"; see Barrett to Carr, August 14, 1909, RG 59, NF 1302/76. See also Harold F. Peterson, *Argentina and the United States, 1810–1960* (Albany: State University of New York Press, 1964), 293–97, and Seward W. Livermore, "Battleship Diplomacy in South America: 1905–1925," *Journal of Modern History* 16 (1944): 31–48.

178. Huntington-Wilson to Dudley, tel., March 23, 1910, RG 59, NF 23178/1.

179. Knox to Dudley, tel., December 6, 1910, RG 59, DF 1910–29, 832.3421/12.

180. Knox to Rives, no. 326, October 18, 1911, ibid., 832.34/73.

181. Rio Branco to Rives, no. 8, December 28, 1911, enclosed in Rives to Knox, no. 788, January 7, 1912, ibid.

182. See undated memorandum by Janes, ibid. The submarine order was eventually won by an Italian company.

183. See Scholes and Scholes, *Foreign Policies of Taft Administration*, 16–17.

184. Huntington-Wilson to Domício, January 20, 1912, RG 59, DF 1910–29, 832.3421/26A.

185. Domício to Huntington-Wilson, January 29, 1912, ibid., 832.3421/27.

186. Domício to Rio Branco, no. 1, January 31, 1912, AHI 234/1/13. This dispatch was sent by sea-mail and arrived at the Itamaraty after Rio Branco's death in February 1912. The proposed marine arsenal at Rio had been under discussion since the beginning of the republic. Actual work was commenced by a French company in 1910, but this soon ran into severe financial difficulties. Huntington-Wilson hoped to secure the transfer of the contract to an American company, but his timing proved misguided. The project was riddled with so many problems that it had fallen into abeyance; see Hilton, "Armed Forces and Industrialists," 640.

187. Haggard to Grey, no. 8, January 30, 1912, FO 371/1302.

188. Rio Branco to Rives, no. 8, December 28, 1911, enclosed in Rives to Knox, no. 788, January 7, 1912, RG 59, DF 1910–29, 832.34/73; Rio Branco to Domício, December 31, 1911, quoted in Rodrigues, *Interêsse nacional*, 31.

189. Haggard to Grey, no. 14, February 14, 1912, FO 371/1302. The British diplomat added: "The only time that I ever heard him say anything showing irritation against the United States was on the last occasion but one on which I saw him."

190. Dudley to Knox, no. 626, December 16, 1910, and no. 694, April 11, 1911, RG 59, DF 1910–29, 832.00 and 832.34/52. Dudley concluded: "The spirit of the Brazilian people has become less militant and their ambition for naval preeminence in South America is at this writing reduced to a comparatively low ebb." The pride of the Brazilian elite was also stung by the international publicity given to the fact that the vast majority of the mutineers were blacks and mulattoes. The mutiny was led by a black sailor, João Candido.

191. James R. Scobie, *Argentina: A City and A Nation* (New York: Oxford University Press, 1971), 164.

192. Peterson, *Argentina and the United States*, 293–99. Brazilian diplomatic prestige suffered a further galling reverse at the Pan-American meeting when the Brazilian

delegation was compelled to withdraw its motion seeking Latin American affirmation of the Monroe Doctrine. For the Buenos Aires conference see Thomas F. McGann, *Argentina, the United States, and the Inter-American System, 1880–1914* (Cambridge: Harvard University Press, 1957), 275–86. In a private conversation, the American minister at Buenos Aires revealed an Argentine version of "approximation" when he reported to Knox that Argentine Foreign Minister Victoriano de la Plaza "was determined that Argentina should act in accord with you and follow your lead in all matters touching South American affairs"; Sherrill to Knox, no. 301, March 28, 1910, RG 59, DF 1910–29, 711.235.

193. Minute on Griscom to Root, no. 37, September 20, 1906, RG 59, NF 1070/3.

194. Sherrill to Knox, no. 38, July 29, 1909, ibid., 1070/75.

195. Sherrill to Knox, no. 122, October 14, 1909, ibid., 1302/73.

196. Despite his sincere admiration for the hustle and bustle of American society, Nabuco had once mused whether "humanity would lose anything essential" should this way of life suddenly disappear; see Nabuco, *Minha Formação*, 157.

197. Domício to Hermes da Fonseca, December 29, 1911, Coleção da Gama, Instituto Histórico e Geográfico Brasileiro, Rio de Janeiro. Domício arrived at Washington in June 1911 to take up the post of Brazilian ambassador. He remained in this capacity for more than seven years until November 1918 when he was appointed foreign minister.

CHAPTER 3: *Conflict and Conformity, 1912–1920*

1. See speech quoted in *New York Times,* March 12, 1913.

2. For an overview of the growth of American trade with Latin America see João F. Normano, *The Struggle For South America* (London: Allen and Unwin, 1931), 21–47.

3. On the growth of the federal government see Rosenberg, *Spreading the American Dream,* 63–86, and Seidel, "Progressive Pan Americanism," 67–135.

4. Roosevelt, *Brazilian Wilderness,* 349. Another common American perception was reflected by an American traveler who visited Bahia and commented: "The population is about one hundred and fifty thousand, and most of the people are black, very black. These colored people, combined with the heat, made me long again for São Paulo and southern Brazil"; see Roger Babson, *The Future of South America* (Boston: Little, Brown, 1918), 313.

5. Lilian E. Elliott, *Brazil* (New York: Macmillan, 1917), 102.

6. On the economic and social crisis see Carlos S. Bakota, "Crisis and the Middle Classes: The Ascendancy of Brazilian Nationalism: 1914–1922" (Ph.D. diss., University of California, Los Angeles, 1973), 26–39.

7. Morgan to Lansing, no. 1149, February 21, and no. 1210, April 12, 1918, RG 59, DF 1910–29, 763.72/9378 and 832.00/181.

8. A perceptive survey of this debate is Skidmore, *Black Into White,* 145–72. For the emergence of a similar concern over the nation's military vulnerability see

Frank D. McCann, "The Formative Period of Twentieth-Century Brazilian Army Thought, 1900–1922," *Hispanic American Historical Review* 64 (1984): 737–65.

9. Domício to Rio Branco, no. 1, January 31, 1912, AHI 234/1/13.

10. Quoted in Lewis House, "Edwin V. Morgan and Brazilian-American Diplomatic Relations 1912–1933" (Ph.D. diss., New York University, 1969), 19. The racial barrier toward Brazilian-American understanding also received prominent mention in a British report on the navies of South America: "The feeling in the United States on the colour question is so acute that no one with coloured blood can be associated as an equal, and this feeling is not disguised. Under these circumstances it is impossible for any real friendship between the United States of America and any South American States. In Brazil nearly every one is coloured, some very distinctly, and in the other states a great deal of Indian blood is seen"; see Captain Horace Hood to Grey, November 3, 1908, FO 371/403.

11. Haggard to Grey, no. 8, January 30, 1912, FO 371/1302. Domício's appearance was also a topic of conversation in Brazil where he was described as "mulatinho rosado"; see Heitor Lyra, *Minha vida diplomática,* 2 vols. (Brasília: Editôra Universidade de Brasília, 1981), 1:79.

12. For a brief biographical sketch see Rodrigo Octávio Filho, "Lauro Müller," *Revista do Instituto Histórico e Geográfico Brasileiro* 265 (1964): 172–88. Müller's political astuteness was summed up in his nickname of "the fox with the girded sword."

13. Rives to Knox, tel., February 15, and no. 305, February 17, 1912, RG 59, DF 1910–29, 832.002/7 and 10.

14. Müller to Domício, February 23, 1912 and Domício to Müller, February 24, 1912, AHI 234/1/13. See also Rodrigues, *Interésse Nacional,* 30, and Lyra, *Vida Diplomática,* 1:97–98. Müller's enquiry was ill-timed because Knox was absent from Washington on a tour of Central America and Taft was absorbed with his own reelection campaign. Domício observed that the president gave little attention to "matters of remote interest"; see Domício to Müller, tel., no. 15, February 24, 1912, AHI 235/4/2. For public criticism of Hermes da Fonseca see Rives to Knox, no. 838, May 7, 1912, RG 59 DF 1910–29, 832.032/3; the American chargé considered that Hermes "has shown little or no aptitude for the high position he holds, and his moral prestige with the thinking public has become practically nil."

15. *La Razón* (Buenos Aires), April 11, 1912; *La Nación* (Buenos Aires), March 7, 1912.

16. The two presidents had previously exchanged visits in 1899–1900. The repetition of this event marked a symbolic reaffirmation of friendship between the two nations.

17. Brazilian displeasure over valorization was underlined by the fact that Morgan was received on his arrival by the Brazilian minister to Ecuador and not by Müller who pleaded pressure of business. Haggard to Grey, no. 33, May 28, and no. 54, July 7, 1912, FO 368/656 and 371/1303.

18. Grevstad to Knox, no. 108, February 13, 1912, RG 59, DF 1910–29, 732.33/15.

19. Haggard to Grey, no. 25, March 26, no. 30, May 20, no. 33, May 28, and no. 42, July 16, 1912, FO 368/656.

20. See Leon F. Sensabaugh, "The Coffee-Trust Question in United States–Brazilian Relations: 1912–1913," *Hispanic American Historical Review* 26 (1946): 480.

21. A valorization scheme was briefly attempted by the imperial government in 1870, but was abandoned after heavy losses; see Ukers, *All About Coffee*, 462. On the history of valorization see Thomas H. Holloway, *The Brazilian Coffee Valorization of 1906* (Madison: University of Wisconsin Press, 1975).

22. Sielcken was also involved in the financing of São Paulo's 1906 valorization scheme. For a brief portrait of the man who arrived in the United States as a poor German immigrant and became "many times a millionaire" see Ukers, *All About Coffee*, 448–51. Contrary to the view held by officials in Washington, Sielcken was no servile tool of the Brazilians. To secure Sielcken's acquiescence in 1906 the government of São Paulo had to send its commissioner to plead with him at his estate in Baden-Baden, Germany. As Ukers notes: "It was Sielcken's hour of triumph. For years he had been soliciting Brazil. Now the tables were turned, and Brazil was asking favors of Sielcken" (459).

23. Valla, "Os Estados Unidos na economia brasileira," 149.

24. Lima e Silva to Rio Branco, no. 9, April 29, 1911, AHI 234/1/12; *Washington Post*, February 24, 1911. See also memorandum by Huntington-Wilson, March 10, 1911, DF 1910–29, 832.60/72.

25. Holloway, *Brazilian Coffee Valorization*, 56–83.

26. The "Chantland Report" was reprinted in *Foreign Relations* (1913), 39–52.

27. Domício to Müller, no. 2, April 18, 1912, AHI 234/1/13. On the valorization operations in the United States see Holloway, *Brazilian Coffee Valorization*, 69–75. The New York court granted a temporary restraining order to prevent disposal of the coffee.

28. In a curt note Knox informed Wickersham of Domício's protest and stated that "we have no information except that seen in the newspapers"; see Knox to Wickersham, May 21, 1912, RG 59, DF 1910–29, 832.6133/91A.

29. *Washington Post*, May 24, 1912. Domício did, however, pay at least one private visit to Wickersham; see *New York Times*, May 23, 1912.

30. The response of President Taft to the visits by Domício and Root is unknown. After a cabinet meeting on May 22, Taft had "a long conference" with Wickersham; see *New York Times*, May 23, 1912. The president's legal background and training was likely to have persuaded him not to intervene in a matter that was sub judice.

31. Sielcken also retained Kennedy as his legal counsel.

32. Kennedy's analysis is enclosed in Domício to Müller, no. 4, May 30, 1912, AHI 234/1/3.

33. Haggard to Grey, no. 54, June 19, 1913, FO 371/1581.

34. *New York Herald*, May 28, 1912.

35. Huntington-Wilson to Janes, September 24, 1912, RG 59, DF 1910–29, 832.6133/103. For press comment that Knox and Wickersham were "at odds over coffee" see *Washington Post*, May 29, 1912.

36. Knox to Morgan, tel., May 31, 1912, RG 59, DF 1910–29, 832.6133/88A. Lauro Müller was critical of Domício's action, which departed from his instructions not to include mention of the coffee dispute in the speech. Domício stated, however, that on his return to Long Island he had found various telegrams from Enéas Martins,

one of which stressed that he should attend the banquet and make reference to the valorization question. Domício also argued that his speech had been well received by Americans and that Elihu Root considered his remarks to be "fully justified." Moreover, it was also evident that the ambassador's spirited speech did not lack supporters in Brazil. Despite rumors that he was to be recalled, Domício remained at his post in Washington; see Domício to Müller, no. 38, tel., May 24, 1912, and no. 43, tel., May 30, 1912, AHI 234/1/13.

37. House, "Morgan," 2–4.

38. The British minister considered that Morgan "overdoes" his work. He also regarded the ambassador as "urbane and affable" though "somewhat oppressively so." Another irritant was the fact that Morgan was "very rich and throws his money about" and that this, "of course, appeals to Brazilian love of show"; see Haggard to Grey, no. 6, January 13, 1913, FO 371/1580.

39. Morgan possessed a fine collection of Oriental art and his private patronage extended to providing funds for Brazilian artists to visit Europe; see House, "Morgan," 5. Despite serving as minister to Portugal, Morgan was unable to converse fluently in Portuguese. His private secretary at Lisbon described him as "a poor linguist," but added that "he had the faculty of winning the respect and liking of people to whom he couldn't talk"; see Hugh Wilson, *The Education of a Diplomat* (New York: Longman, Green, 1938), 27. Certainly, Morgan's gregarious personality and generous hospitality was in marked contrast to his predecessor, Irving Dudley, who rarely entertained. While the British minister considered Dudley as "a sensible and hard-working man, perhaps of a rather better stamp than the usual run of United States' representatives in South American republics," he noted that Mrs Dudley had attracted adverse social comment and was "quite an impossible woman, who is apparently accustomed to no society, and who is, moreover, subject to 'attacks of nerves' on the slightest provocation"; see Haggard to Grey, no. 36, April 5, 1908, FO 371/403. A foreign official minuted: "The account of the U.S. embassy is the reverse of impressive."

40. House, "Morgan," 4. Morgan's personal regard for Brazilians earned him many compliments. As a lowly clerk at the Itamaraty, Luís Gurgel do Amaral was flattered and highly impressed that Morgan would talk to him. He had personal experience of dealing with all the American ambassadors since Griscom and considered Morgan "unforgettable"; see Luís Gurgel do Amaral, *Meu Velho Itamarati*, 193. Morgan's longstanding personal friend, Maurício Nabuco, paid him the simple but sincere tribute that he was "very popular"; see Nabuco, *Reminiscências*, 18. On the other hand, Morgan did not enjoy such good relations with his fellow Americans. The feeling was that he preferred Brazilian society; see House, "Morgan," 35. From time to time there were also allusions to his effeminate character. "He lacks the necessary strong, manly character to assume the leadership of his compatriots," noted a British ambassador; see Alston to Chamberlain, no. 16, January 25, 1927, FO 371/11966.

41. For the quotation from the *Jornal do commercio* see Haggard to Grey, no. 54, June 19, 1913, FO 371/1581. The American embassy was relocated in Rio at 30 Rua de Carvalho; see House, "Morgan," 8. During the 1920s an impressive new building was constructed along what became known as the Avenida Presidente Wilson in the center of the city. Morgan never lost sight of the importance of Rio although he did spend increasingly more time in São Paulo as the latter city became the hub not only

of Brazil's business activity but also of its intellectual and artistic life. Morgan also maintained a residence in Petrópolis and chose to retire there on his departure from the foreign service in 1933. Consequently, his first few months and his last months in Brazil were spent in the old imperial city.

42. For example, see the views of Rodrigues Alves in Melo Franco, *Rodrigues Alves,* 670–71, 675. In their demands for retaliation against the United States, the Paulistas gained the support of rubber interests from Amazonas. As the Far East became a major supplier of rubber, they lost their monopoly virtually overnight. After reaching a peak in 1910, prices fell by almost 70 percent within three years. The United States was Brazil's biggest market for rubber, and there was a suspicion that American speculators were manipulating prices to their own advantage. Rubber valorization schemes were mooted, but proved unsuccessful. In contrast to coffee, there were alternative sources of supply and no Herman Sielcken existed in the rubber business; see E. Bradford Burns, *A History of Brazil,* 338–39.

43. Müller to Domício, tel., March 7, 1913, AHI 235/4/2.

44. A State Department official who had recently returned from Brazil reported surprise that the United States had not requested Domício's recall. He was also told by "a friend of Lauro Müller" that the Itamaraty "planned to replace Da Gama within a few months because of the 'gaffe' they felt he had perpetrated"; see minute on Huntington-Wilson to Janes, September 24, 1912, RG 59, DF 1910–29, 832.6133/103.

45. Haggard to Grey, no. 61, September 22, 1912, FO 368/656, and no. 6, January 13, 1913, FO 371/1580. The British minister added that Müller "is himself a past master in the arts of dissimulation." Müller was also highly cultured and was an elected member of the prestigious Brazilian Academy of Letters; see Freyre, *Order and Progress,* xvii.

46. When Morgan fell ill at the close of 1912 and was briefly out of communication with Washington, Müller worried that Washington would misinterpret Brazilian policy. The foreign minister described Morgan as a "peacemaker"; see Müller to Domício, tels., January 3 and March 7, 1913, AHI 235/4/2.

47. Morgan to Knox, no. 40, August 29, 1912, RG 59, DF 1910–29, 732.62/3. Huntington-Wilson approved the idea in principle and saw it as a return for Root's visit in 1906. But no special significance was attached to the visit of a Brazilian foreign minister. Indeed, the assistant secretary of state stressed to Morgan that the initiative must be seen to come from Brazil. Otherwise the countries of South America might think that the United States was "voluntarily extending to Brazil marked courtesies which were not being shown to each of them"; see Huntington-Wilson to Morgan, no. 31, October 22, 1912, ibid.

48. Domício predicted in June that the controversy would soon be resolved; see Domício to Müller, no. 5, June 19, 1912, AHI 234/1/13.

49. April 26, 1911, *Congressional Record,* 62d Congress, 1st sess., 642.

50. See Sensabaugh, "Coffee-Trust Question," 486–89.

51. Rodrigues Alves to Müller, December 17, 1912; quoted in Melo Franco, *Rodrigues Alves,* 675.

52. Wickersham to Knox, December 4; Knox to Morgan, tel., December 5; Huntington-Wilson to Morgan, tel., December 14, 1912, RG 59, DF 1910–29, 832.6133/114 and 117/A. By pressing for a demurrer in the New York court, Sielcken

implied that the Justice Department lacked sufficient evidence to press the original suit. Sielcken was persuaded to withdraw his motion, although it is not clear at whose instigation. Huntington-Wilson was surprised at Domício's apparent lack of knowledge of current developments in the dispute. Domício's inattentiveness to diplomatic business may partly be explained by absences from Washington arising from his marriage in November to a Texan widow, Mrs Arthur Hearn. In addition, the Brazilian ambassador was virtually ignored by Müller in the transaction of official business between the Itamaraty and the State Department; see Knox to Wickersham, December 5, 1912, ibid., 832.6133/115, and Melo Franco, *Rodrigues Alves,* 667–68.

53. Morgan to Müller, no. 55, December 23, 1912, AHI 280/2/11.

54. Morgan to Knox, tel., January 5, 1913, RG 59, DF 1910–29, 832.6133/125.

55. Knox to Wickersham, January 6 and Wickersham to Knox, January 10, 1913, ibid., 832.6133/125 and 129. Knox told Morgan that the State Department "regrets that the Department of Justice is not willing magnanimously to accede to the request"; see Knox to Morgan, tel., January 14, 1913, ibid., 832.6133/129.

56. Knox to Morgan, tel., January 18 and Wickersham to Knox, January 21, 1913, ibid., 832.6133/130 and 133.

57. Haggard to Grey, no. 6, January 13, 1913, FO 371/1580.

58. Domício to Müller, tel., no. 74, November 5, 1912, AHI 234/1/13. A few weeks later Domício sent a clipping entitled "Wilson May Change Our Foreign Policy" from the *New York Sun,* dated November 19, 1912. Most of the article was underlined with red lines indicating the Itamaraty's considerable interest; see Domício to Müller, no. 31, November 22, 1912, AHI 234/1/13.

59. Morgan to Knox, tel., January 24; Knox to Morgan, tel., January 29; and Huntington-Wilson to Knox, January 29, 1913, RG 59, DF 1910–29, 832.6133/134 and 144. In his revealing memorandum to Knox, Huntington-Wilson also regarded the Norris bill as "startlingly broad" and, citing the example of cotton, he queried whether it might prevent the United States from introducing its own valorization scheme. He was also concerned about the bill's possible application to the German government's potash monopoly. "If, for example," he remarked, "it were found that under this law we should have to put the German potash monopoly's agent in jail it might give rise to quite an incident." Complications with Brazil were clearly of a much lesser order.

60. Haggard to Grey, no. 10, February 3, 1913, FO 368/796; Morgan to Knox, tel., February 14, 1913, RG 59, DF 1910–29, 832.6133/142.

61. See memoranda by Huntington-Wilson and Pepper, the Foreign Trade Adviser, February 18; enclosed with Knox to Morgan., tel., February 18, 1913, RG 59, DF 1910–29, 832.6133/142. The assistant chief of the Latin American Division, Seth Low Pierrepont, advised against issuing a threat to tax coffee "because it is felt that the Brazilians are confident, perhaps not without reason, that it would be impossible to place a duty upon coffee in this country"; see Pierrepont to Huntington-Wilson, February 18, 1913, ibid.

62. Müller to Domício, March 6, and Domício to Müller, April 3, 1913, AHI 234/2/1.

63. Officials were distressed by Long's appointment; see Werking, *Master Architects,* 246.

64. Memorandum by Pierrepont, March 8, 1913, RG 59, DF 1910–29, 832.6133/

154. Pierrepont's frustration was fully shared by European diplomats. Not only those of the United States, but most foreign companies were discouraged from establishing offices in Brazil by the many local difficulties involved in transacting business. American businessmen proved the most reluctant so that by 1910 only 40 American companies were registered in Brazil. The number almost doubled during the next three years, but several experienced difficulties necessitating State Department involvement. A particularly awkward case concerned the Amazon Wireless Company. During the valorization controversy, officials attempted to assist the company in its claims against the state government of Amazonas, but were eventually compelled to acquiesce in its expropriation by the Brazilian government. For registration of American companies see Downes, "Seeds of Influence," 90. On Amazon Wireless see James J. Schwoch, "The United States and the Global Growth of Radio, 1900–1930" (Ph.D. diss., Northwestern University, 1985), 50–51.

65. *New York Herald,* April 3, 1913.

66. Domício to Müller, tel., no. 74, November 5, 1912, AHI 234/1/13; Domício to Bryan, March 31, RG 59, DF 1910–29, 832.6133/153. Although the American stocks were liquidated, almost two million bags of coffee were still stored in various European ports.

67. Morgan to Bryan, tel., March 5, 1913, RG 59, DF 1910–29, 832.6133/148.

68. Norris to Bryan, April 11, 1913, ibid., 832.6133/156.

69. Bryan to McReynolds, April 3, and McReynolds to Bryan, April 17, 1913, ibid., 832.6133/153A and 157; Bryan to Domício, April 12, and Domício to Bryan, April 24, 1913, ibid., 832.6133/159A and 160.

70. In his careful evaluation of valorization, one writer has concluded: "It thus seems probable that the consumer eventually paid most of the cost of the scheme." It is also debatable whether the individual Brazilian producer gained from the scheme; see Holloway, *Brazilian Coffee Valorization,* 76–84, quotation is from p. 83.

71. *La Prensa* (Buenos Aires), August 9, 1912; *La Nación* (Buenos Aires), September 17, 1912. Approximation was described in Spanish as "la política de acercamiento."

72. *La Nación* (Buenos Aires), June 15, 1912; *Jornal do commercio* (Rio), August 7, 1912.

73. Haggard to Grey, no. 37, June 30, and no. 42, July 16, 1912, FO 368/656.

74. Haggard to Grey, no. 30, May 20, and no. 37, June 30, 1912, ibid. The American chargé described Enéas Martins as "thoroughly familiar with the political plans and ambitions of the late Rio Branco"; see Rives to Knox, no. 305, February 17, 1912, RG 59, DF 1910–29, 832.002/10.

75. Rives observed that the new post was part of a restructuring of the Itamaraty copied from the reorganization of the State Department; Rives to Knox, no. 305, February 17, 1912, RG 59, DF 1910–29, 832.002/10.

76. Haggard to Grey, no. 54, June 19, 1913, FO 371/1581. In what seemed a mood of despair the British minister noted that "the difficulties of doing business with the Brazilian Government, already great and unusual during the life of Baron de Rio Branco, have increased rather than diminished under his successor"; see Haggard to Grey, no. 11, February 2, 1913, FO 371/1580.

77. *La Argentina* (Buenos Aires), February 14, 1913.

78. Haggard to Grey, no. 47, May 17, 1913, FO 371/1580.

79. Morgan first mentioned the idea of Müller's visit in August 1912 when he noted that the latter had received a large signed portrait of the German Kaiser in memory of his recent trip to Germany. The ambassador also revealed that the foreign minister's son intended to study engineering in the United States. In his reply to Morgan, Huntington-Wilson disclosed that Charles Sutter of the Business Men's League of St. Louis had indicated that he could raise $50,000 toward Müller's travel expenses within the United States; see Morgan to Knox, no. 40, August 29, and Huntington-Wilson to Morgan, no. 31, October 22, 1912, RG 59, DF 1910–29, 732.62/3.

80. Originally, Morgan asked permission to accompany Müller on his visit. The State Department refused on the ostensible grounds that the ambassador would be absent from his post for too long. The British minister regarded Morgan's request to form part of Müller's "suite" as an example of his characteristic "obsequiousness" and reported disparagingly: "His Government has apparently however taken a higher view of the dignity of an Ambassador of a Great Power than His Excellency is apt to assert for himself"; see Haggard to Grey, no. 44, May 12, 1913, FO 371/1580. When Morgan left the official party at Bahia, he decided to make a short tour of the Northeast. On a visit to a sugar plantation, he slipped and fell into a vat of sugar. "This episode brought the ambassador almost as much publicity in Brazil as the goodwill visit of Dr. Müller and his entourage"; see House, "Morgan," 31.

81. Haggard considered that Müller was "dazzled" by his reception in the United States; see Haggard to Grey, no. 110, October 4, 1913, FO 368/796. For an account of the visit see Harry O. Sandberg, "Mission of Dr. Lauro S. Müller to the United States," *Bulletin of the Pan-American Union* 37 (1913): 1–13, and House, "Morgan," 30–36.

82. *New York Times,* June 19, 1913.

83. Ibid., July 20, 1913.

84. Ibid., March 12, 1913, and Arthur S. Link, *Wilson: The New Freedom* (Princeton: Princeton University Press, 1956), 320.

85. Seward W. Livermore, "'Deserving Democrats': The Foreign Service under Woodrow Wilson," *South Atlantic Quarterly* 69 (1970): 144–60. On the administration's Latin American appointments, one critic wrote: "A clearer case of partisan political debauchery cannot be imagined"; see George Harvey, "The Diplomats of Democracy," *North American Review* 199 (1914): 172. The anxieties of Fletcher and House are mentioned in Mark T. Gilderhus, *Pan American Visions: Woodrow Wilson in the Western Hemisphere, 1913–1921* (Tucson: University of Arizona Press, 1986), 13–14.

86. The resignation of John B. Moore from the State Department in March 1914 prompted one newspaper to condemn "the deplorable disorganization" of the department since Bryan had taken charge; see the *Sun* (New York), March 5, 1914.

87. Speech by Wilson, October 25, 1913, cited in Arthur S. Link, ed., *The Papers of Woodrow Wilson* (Princeton: Princeton University Press, 1966–), 28:441.

88. Domício to Müller, tel., no. 74, November 5, 1912, AHI 234/1/13; Domício to Bryan, March 31, 1913, RG 59, DF 1910–29, 832.6133/153.

89. Francisco Vinhosa, "A diplomacia brasileira e a revolução mexicana, 1913–1915," *Revista do Instituto Histórico e Geográfico Brasileiro* 327 (1980): 33.

90. See telegrams enclosed in Domício to Müller, no. 9, May 12, 1914, AHI 234/2/2. Lauro Müller possessed a "conciliatory nature"; see Lyra, *Vida Diplomática,* 1:31.

91. On Wilson and Mexico in general see Kendrick A. Clements, "Woodrow Wilson's Mexican Policy, 1913–15," *Diplomatic History* 4 (1980): 113–36. See also Vinhosa, "A diplomacia brasileira," 19–81 and Cristián Guerrero Yoacham, *Las Conferencias del Niagara Falls* (Santiago de Chile: Andres Bello, 1966).

92. Bolivia, Uruguay, and Guatemala were referred to as the BUG nations. A note of arrogance was apparent in Wilson's comment: "Our idea was . . . to include in the cooperative conference also, the three ranking ministers next after them in the Latin American group; but it would be well to sound out the beginning of the alphabet first"; Wilson to Lansing, June 22, 1915; quoted in Link, *Wilson Papers,* 33:437.

93. Domício to Müller, tel., no. 16, September 29, 1915, AHI 234/2/4.

94. Domício to Lansing, September 27, 1915, ibid; Arthur S. Link, *Wilson: The Struggle for Neutrality* (Princeton: Princeton University Press, 1960), 638; Lansing to Wilson, September 18, 1915; quoted in Link, *Wilson Papers,* 34:487–88.

95. See John Coogan, *The End of Neutrality: The United States, Britain, and Maritime Rights 1899–1915* (Ithaca: Cornell University Press, 1981).

96. House Diary, November 25, 1914; quoted in Link, *Wilson Papers,* 31:355. On a later occasion House told Wilson and Lansing that "there were no objections whatever to the Germans going to South America in great numbers and getting peaceful control of the governments." In the colonel's opinion this "would probably be of benefit to the Americas rather than a detriment, for the German population would be in every way preferable to the population now in the majority of South American countries"; see House Diary, October 15, 1915, quoted in ibid., 35:71.

97. House Diary, December 16, 1914, quoted in ibid., 31:469. Annual Message to Congress, December 7, 1915; quoted in ibid., 35:296.

98. House Diary, December 16, 1914; quoted in ibid., 31:469. Bryan to Wilson, May 19, 1915; quoted in State Department, *Lansing Papers,* 2:485. In 1916 Wilson and House considered that Britain might even become a signatory of the treaty; see House Diary, May 3, 1916; quoted in Link, *Wilson Papers,* 36:601–02. The tortuous course of negotiations is examined in Mark T. Gilderhus, "Pan-American Initiatives: The Wilson Presidency and 'Regional Integration,' 1916–17," *Diplomatic History* 4 (1980): 409–23.

99. House Diary, December 16, 1914; quoted in Link, *Wilson Papers,* 31:470. Gilderhus, *Pan American Visions,* 53. Presumably Edwin Morgan suffered the same embarrassment as Fletcher. Since Chile was the major obstacle to the conclusion of the treaty, Fletcher assumed an active role in the negotiating process and was even called back to Washington to lend his expertise. Morgan appears to have played little part in the discussions.

100. House Diary, June 24, 1915; quoted in Link, *Wilson Papers,* 33:449. House dismissed Bryan as "essentially a talker."

101. Lansing to House, October 6, 1915; quoted in ibid., 35:34. The pressure persisted. Some months later Wilson told House that "he was continually prodding Lansing"; see House Diary, March 29, 1916; quoted in ibid., 36:380.

102. House Diary, December 19, 1914; quoted in ibid., 31:497. House to Lansing, October 12, 1915; quoted in ibid., 35:54.

103. House Diary, December 19, 1914; quoted in ibid., 31:497. Bryan to Wilson, May 19, 1915; quoted in State Department, *Lansing Papers*, 2:484–85.

104. Fletcher to Bryan, tel., January 2, 1915, RG 59, DF 1910–29, 725.3211/39. Bryan had already secured the assent of a number of governments, including that of Brazil in July 1914, to draft treaties in which it was agreed to submit disputes to arbitration after allowing a one-year "cooling-off" period.

105. Peel to Balfour, no. 40, May 27, 1918, FO 371/3168; *New York Times*, May 25, 1915.

106. Bryan to Schoenfeld, tel., April 27, 1915, RG 59, DF 1910–29, 725.3211/44.

107. Wilson to Bryan, April 26, 1915, ibid., 725.3211/46.

108. Morgan to Lansing, no. 689, October 18, 1915, ibid., 725.3211/76.

109. Bryan to Wilson, December 17, 1914, ibid., 763.72119/35; State Department memorandum, November 17, 1914; quoted in Emily S. Rosenberg, *World War I and the Growth of United States Predominance in Latin America* (New York: Garland, 1987): 9–10.

110. William G. McAdoo, *Crowded Years* (Boston: Houghton Mifflin, 1931), 351. See also John J. Broesamle, *William Gibbs McAdoo* (Port Washington: Kennikat, 1973), 201–11.

111. See Seidel, "Progressive Pan Americanism," 70–86, and Burton I. Kaufman, "United States Trade with Latin America: The War Years," *Journal of American History* 57 (1971): 354–59.

112. Morgan to Bryan, tel., August 3, 1914, RG 59, DF 1910–29, 832.51/71; Robertson to Grey, no. 19, April 23, 1915, FO 371/2294. The establishment in 1915 of an office in Rio of the American Chamber of Commerce provided further evidence of the American economic drive.

113. Downes, "Seeds of Influence," 178.

114. Although American exports to Brazil fell in absolute value, so sharp was the decline in total Brazilian imports that the American share of the import trade actually increased from 15 percent in 1913 to over 30 percent in 1915; see Edward E. Pratt, "Trade Conditions in Latin America as Affected by the European War," *Annals of the American Academy of Political and Social Science* 60 (1915): 80–81. Downes, in "Seeds of Influence," estimates that the American share rose from 23 percent to 43 percent (211). The question whether World War I stimulated or retarded Brazilian economic development has attracted considerable scholarly debate but no firm conclusion. A useful survey is Carlos M. Peláez, "World War I and the Economy of Brazil," *Journal of Interdisciplinary History* 7 (1977): 683–89.

115. The complaint was stressed by McAdoo on his brief visit to Rio in March 1916; see Downes, "Seeds of Influence," 208.

116. The dearth of American merchant shipping remained a major obstacle to the increase in inter-American trade. For McAdoo's views see Broesamle, *McAdoo*, 210–11. An American traveler observed: "The most conspicuous laggard in the Brazilian shipping world is the United States"; see Elliott, *Brazil*, 164. Another lamented that "the ships of Uncle Sam . . . are conspicuously absent"; see Cooper, *Brazilians and their Country*, 236.

117. *Times* (London), March 18, 1914; Morgan to Bryan, no. 346, April 1, 1914, RG 59, DF 1910–29, 832.00/122, and no. 497, November 27, 1914, ibid., 832.002/18.

118. O'Sullivan-Beare to Grey, no. 6, February 5, 1915, FO 368/1233. For trade statistics see Victor Valla, "Os Estados Unidos e a influência estrangeira na economia brasileira: um período de transição (1904–1928)," *Revista de História* 45 (1972): 146–64.

119. Morgan to Bryan, personal communication, August 19, 1914, RG 59, DF 1910–29, 832.51/79; Morgan to Lansing, tel., September 14, 1916, ibid., 832.51/122; Polk to Morgan, tel., October 21, 1916, ibid., 832.51/125; Harry N. Scheiber, "World War I as Entrepreneurial Opportunity: Willard Straight and the American International Corporation," *Political Science Quarterly* 84 (1969): 501. Straight was vice president of the American International Corporation. The AIC's interest in Europe resulted from Straight's visit there in the spring of 1916. One State Department official referred to Straight's "pessimism regarding Latin-America in general"; see Wright to Morgan, personal communication, November 22, 1916, RG 59, DF 1910–29, 832.51/143. In 1917 American bankers showed more interest in a larger scheme involving the reorganization of Brazil's finances; see memorandum by the chief of the Latin American Division, Jordan Herbert Stabler, March 15, 1917, ibid., 832.51/148.

120. Elliott, *Brazil,* 286.

121. Morgan to J. Butler Wright, personal communication, September 12, 1916, RG 59, DF 1910–29, 832.51/129. Joshua Butler Wright's long diplomatic career included several posts in Washington and overseas. He retained a long-standing interest in Latin American affairs and ultimately served as ambassador to Uruguay and Cuba.

122. *Proceedings of the First Pan American Financial Conference* (Washington: GPO, 1915), 341–46.

123. See minute by Gottschalk on Maddin Summers (Consul at São Paulo) to secretary of state, no. 16, July 2, 1915, RG 59, DF 1910–29, 832.51/101.

124. Robert Mayer, "The Origins of the American Banking Empire in Latin America," *Journal of Inter-American Studies* 15 (1973): 60–76.

125. Bryan to Wilson, March 11, 1915, quoted in Link, *Wilson Papers,* 32:364.

126. See Peterson, *Argentina and United States,* 340–42.

127. For examples of Müller's proposals see Morgan to Bryan, August 19, 1914, RG 59, DF 1910–29, 832.50/79 and Morgan to Lansing, tel., March 31, 1916, ibid., 763.72/2546.

128. On leave in the United States during 1916, the American ambassador to Argentina was depressed that Wilson didn't wish to know about Argentine affairs. "Coming from a country where, though more remote from the war than we were, the people thought of nothing else, the indifference of our own people was amazing to me," observed the ambassador; see Frederic J. Stimson, *My United States* (New York: Charles Scribner's Sons, 1931), 352–53.

129. Ernest Hambloch, *British Consul* (London: Harrap, 1938), 246.

130. Morgan to Lansing, no. 1037, November 5, 1917, RG 59, DF 1910–29, 832.20/15.

131. Morgan to Bryan, private, August 19, 1914, ibid., 832.51/79. The navy remained demoralized by the 1910 mutiny. Financial stringency also compelled the sale to Turkey in 1913 of what had been intended to be Brazil's third major battleship, the *Rio de Janeiro.*

132. Morgan to Bryan, no. 231, August 13, 1913, RG 59, DF 1910–29, 832.00/113.

133. Dudley to Knox, no. 560, July 17, 1910, ibid., 832.20; Rives to Knox, tel., October 12, 1911, ibid., 832.20/1, and tel., February 15, 1912, ibid., 832.002/7. Hermes da Fonseca had paid an earlier visit to Germany in 1908; see McCann, "Twentieth-Century Brazilian Army Thought," 746.

134. Peel to Balfour, no. 23, March 25, 1918, FO 371/3167. The subject has recently been examined by Frederick C. Luebke, *Germans in Brazil* (Baton Rouge: Louisiana State University Press, 1987).

135. See Leuchars, "Brazilian Foreign Policy," 83–86. The German government realized that any payment made to Brazil would be quickly transferred to Britain or France.

136. See memorandum on "Internal Conditions" by British War Trade Intelligence Department, November 13, 1916, FO 371/2900. Brazilians protested that a German name did not necessarily signify German nationality. The insistence on the right of search and the black list also evoked memories of traditional British high-handedness toward Brazil.

137. See João Dunshee de Abranches, *A illusão brasileira* (Rio: Imprensa nacional, 1917). The author's views earned him the nickname of "Deutsch" from Rui Barbosa.

138. Peel to Balfour, no. 23, March 25, 1918, FO 371/3167. For an analysis of pro-German opinion see Luebke, *Germans in Brazil,* 83–118 and Skidmore, *Black Into White,* 150–52.

139. Memorandum by British War Trade Intelligence Department, November 30, 1916, FO 371/2900.

140. Rui's celebrated address was delivered at Buenos Aires on July 14, 1916, and is quoted in Percy A. Martin, *Latin America and the War* (Baltimore: Johns Hopkins University Press, 1925), 50. The Brazilian press also strongly favored the Allies; see Nelson Werneck Sodré, *História da imprensa no Brasil* (Rio: Civilização brasileira, 1966), 392. See also Francisco Vinhosa, "O Brasil e a primeira guerra mundial" (doctoral thesis, Universidade de São Paulo, 1984), 13–27. The League For The Allies was known as the *Liga pelos Aliados.*

141. Peel to foreign secretary, no. 33, December 28, 1915, FO 368/1494. For the views of Brazilian nationalists see Bakota, "Crisis and the Middle Classes" and Barbosa Lima Sobrinho, *Presença de Alberto Tôrres* (Rio: Editôra civilização, 1968).

142. Morgan to Lansing, tel., March 31, 1916, and Lansing to Morgan, tel., April 6, 1916, RG 59, DF 1910–29, 763.72/2546.

143. Colloquy, August 30, 1916; quoted in Link, *Wilson Papers,* 38:116.

144. Fletcher to House, April 12, 1916; quoted in ibid., 36:479. Lansing to Wilson, February 19, 1916; quoted in ibid., 36:197.

145. Morgan reported that "as far as Rio is concerned, the German propaganda is fruitless"; see Morgan to Lansing, no. 636, August 9, 1915, RG 59, DF 1910–29, 763.72/2087; no. 497, November 27, 1914, ibid., 832.002/18; no. 804, July 31, and no. 820, September 25, 1916, ibid., 763.7211/3949 and 4133.

146. Peel to Balfour, no. 40, May 27, 1918, FO 371/3168.

147. Morgan to Lansing, no. 804, July 31, 1916, RG 59, DF 1910–29, 763.7211/3949.

148. Morgan to Lansing, no. 796, June 5, 1916, ibid., 832.021/10; see minute on Gottschalk to secretary of state, no. 485, June 9, 1916, ibid., 832.021/14. Müller

had frequent periods of ill health and wished to rest because of a liver complaint. A trip to a European spa was ruled out by the war.

149. Fletcher to Lansing, June 16, 1916; quoted in Link, *Wilson Papers,* 37:242. Wilson was highly pleased and wrote: "Fletcher seems to have pressed this matter very wisely and successfully"; see Wilson to Lansing, June 21, 1916; quoted in ibid., 37:271.

150. Domício to Ministério das Relações Exteriores, tel., July 3, 1916, AHI 235/3/6.

151. Memorandum by Fletcher to Lansing, August 9, 1916; quoted in Link, *Wilson Papers,* 38:18. Müller had two meetings with Butler Wright in New York. However, the coup de grace to American hopes had been delivered even before Müller arrived, when Naón refused to sign the treaty because of the tense state of relations currently existing between the United States and Mexico.

152. Sousa Dantas was transferred from Buenos Aires to take up the post of under secretary of state for foreign affairs. For most of 1916 he acted as virtual foreign minister. Müller's decline in authority was also indicated by the increasingly active role exerted by President Venceslau Brás in the formulation of diplomacy.

153. Peel to Grey, tel., no. 493, November 25 and December 7, 1916, FO 371/2900; Peel to Balfour, no. 23, March 25, 1918, FO 371/3167. Anxiety about future retaliatory policies was conditioned by the period of neutrality in which Brazil suffered from the imposition of Allied maritime restrictions and frequent threats to limit and even prohibit the import of coffee. For example, the British decision to embargo coffee imports in February 1917 was regarded in Brazil as a deliberate act designed to force Brazil into joining the war.

154. House Diary, January 12, 1917; quoted in Link, *Wilson Papers,* 40:463.

155. Quoted in Downes, "Seeds of Influence," 217.

156. Domício to Müller, no. 6, February 24, 1917, AHI 234/2/7; Benson to Lansing, tel., January 8, 1917, RG 59, DF 1910–29, 763.72119/236.

157. Domício to Lansing, February 14, 1917, AHI 234/2/7.

158. *New York Tribune,* February 4, 1917. The *New York Times* regularly printed brief notices of Brazil's attitude toward the war.

159. Benson to Lansing, tel., February 5, 1917, RG 59, DF 1910–29, 763.72/3216.

160. Frederic Stimson to Lansing, tel., March 3, 1917, ibid., 763.72119/486; Müller regarded the proposal as "too protracted and vain"; see Domício to Lansing, February 14, 1917, AHI 234/2/7; Rosenberg, "Continental Solidarity," 318–20.

161. Benson to Lansing, tel., February 5, 1917, RG 59, DF 1910–29, 763.72/3216.

162. Martin, *Latin America and the War,* 53; *Washington Post,* February 12, 1917.

163. The most serious riots occurred in Porto Alegre on April 15–16. See Luebke, *Germans in Brazil,* 119–46.

164. Domício to Lansing, April 10, 1917, RG 59, DF 1910–29, 832.635/4.

165. Polk to Lansing, April 7, and Lansing to Wilson, April 8, 1917; quoted in Link, *Wilson Papers,* 42:14–15.

166. Peel to Balfour, no. 23, March 25, 1918, FO 371/3167.

167. Polk to Lansing, April 7, 1917; quoted in Link, *Wilson Papers,* 42:15.

168. See *New York Times,* April 9, 1917. The State Department was particularly

concerned about ensuring supplies of manganese ore for the American steel industry. The temporary closure of traditional suppliers such as Russia and India enhanced the importance of imports from Brazil; Lansing to Benson, April 3, 1917, RG 59, DF 1910–29, 832.635/1.

169. Wilson to Lansing, April 12 and 13, 1917; quoted in Link, *Wilson Papers,* 42:44, 54.

170. Lansing to Wilson, April 8, and Wilson to Lansing, April 13, 1917; quoted in Link, *Wilson Papers,* 42:14, 54.

171. Wilson to Lansing, April 20, 1917; quoted in Gilderhus, *Pan American Visions,* 94.

172. *New York Times,* April 9, 1917.

173. For example, see *Washington Post,* April 9, 1917.

174. One scholar has recently presented the interesting argument that the measure was deliberately designed to frustrate and delay retaliatory action against Germany; see Luebke, *Germans in Brazil,* 149.

175. Benson to Lansing, tel., no. 911, April 30, May 3 and 4, 1917, RG 59, DF 1910–29, 763.72/4773, 5090 and 4376; Gottschalk to Lansing, April 10, 1917, ibid., 763.62/4. The American press also contained alarming reports of the extent of German influence in Brazil and even predicted the imminence of civil war; for an example, see *New York Tribune,* April 13, 1917. Domício acted quickly to deny these reports; see Domício to Müller, no. 2, March 3, 1917, AHI 234/2/7, and no. 87, April 24, 1917, AHI 234/2/8.

176. Lauro's resignation was softened by the proposal that he be the next president of the Military Club; see Leuchars, "Brazilian Foreign Policy," 119–20. Venceslau Brás may have offered Lauro an alternative cabinet post although it was generally held that he "did not have the courage to defend his foreign minister"; see Lyra, *Vida Diplomática,* 1:31 and Luebke, *Germans in Brazil,* 150–51. Despite the termination of his presidential ambitions and his formal departure from office, Lauro remained influential. Morgan later described him as "the principal adviser" of Bernardes on foreign affairs; Morgan to Kellogg, no. 2620, August 4, 1926, RG 59, DF 1910–29, 832.00/587.

177. Benson to Lansing, tel., May 5, 1917, RG 59, DF 1910–29, 832.002/23. A typical headline was "Brazilian Foreign Minister In Favor Of Joining Allies"; see *New York Herald,* May 6, 1917.

178. Lansing to Wilson, May 17, 1917, RG 59, DF 1910–29, 763.72/13420.

179. Domício to Nilo Peçanha, no. 108, May 18, 1917, AHI 234/2/8.

180. On Caperton's mission see David Healy, "Admiral William B. Caperton and United States Naval Diplomacy in South America, 1917–1919," *Journal of Latin American Studies* 8 (1976): 297–323. The admiral's original instructions were to patrol the South Atlantic. His decision to visit Rio was prompted by Morgan's urgent request for an American naval presence; see Downes, "Seeds of Influence," 228.

181. *New York Tribune,* June 5, 1917.

182. Benson to Lansing, no. 920, May 11, 1917, RG 59, DF 1910–29, 763.72/5042.

183. *New York Evening Post,* April 11, 1917.

184. Foreign Office to Peel, tel., July 27, 1917, FO 371/2901.

185. The British minister reported that the revocation of neutrality was a direct

result of the refusal of the American government to grant a loan to Brazil; Peel to Foreign Office, tel., no. 341, June 30, 1917, FO 371/1706.

186. Foreign Office to Spring Rice, tel., June 21, 1917, ibid. France claimed to have sufficient supplies to last for at least two years.

187. Morgan to Lansing, tel., May 19, 1917, RG 59, DF 1910–29, 763.76/4856.

188. Morgan to Lansing, tel., August 22, 1917, ibid., 832.85/12. The matter was not strictly diplomatic business as formal negotiations were conducted by the Ministry of Finance rather than the Itamaraty. Secret discussions were also pursued by private intermediaries who were paid large commissions for their efforts. "It is unfortunate," lamented Morgan, "that the moral standards of the Brazilian Government are still so undeveloped that it cannot conduct large operations in which graft and its accompanying evils do not play a leading part"; Morgan to Lansing, tel., January 22, 1918, ibid., 832.85/70. See also Morgan to Lansing, no. 1080, December 8, 1917 and no. 1100, January 8, 1918, ibid., 832.85/59 and 65.

189. Morgan to Lansing, tel., October 29, 1917, ibid., 832.85/51.

190. Lansing to Morgan, tel., November 1, and Morgan to Lansing, tel., November 29, 1917, ibid., 832.85/53A and 54. A formal arrangement was signed in December by which Brazil leased 30 ships for one year. In return, France paid a cash sum of 110 million francs and agreed to purchase a substantial quantity of Brazilian primary products including two million bags of coffee.

191. *New York Evening Post,* April 11, 1917.

192. Quoted in Luebke, *Germans in Brazil,* 159. For the official Brazilian version of events, see the correspondence printed in Brazilian Ministry for Foreign Affairs, *The Brazilian Green Book* (London: Allen and Unwin, 1918). The Venceslau administration also used the declaration of war to impose states of siege and to repress domestic social unrest.

193. Peel to Balfour, no. 23, March 25, 1918, FO 371/3167.

194. Robert Lansing, *War Memoirs of Robert Lansing* (Indianapolis: Bobbs-Merrill, 1935), 316.

195. Count Luxburg was the German minister at Buenos Aires. His letters to Berlin were intercepted by British intelligence and passed on to the United States government. Lansing decided to reveal extracts critical of the Argentine government in order to expose German duplicity; see Peterson, *Argentina and the United States,* 310–14.

196. See Spring-Rice to Foreign Office, tel., August 7, 1917, and minute by Sperling, August 8, 1917, FO 371/2901.

197. Nilo Peçanha to Domício, no. 211, November 14, 1917, AHI 234/2/9; Morgan to Lansing, no. 1058, November 14, 1917, RG 59, DF 1910–29, 763.72/7974; *New York Herald,* October 29, 1917; and *Washington Post,* November 1, 1917.

198. Daniels to Lansing, November 16, 1917, RG 59, DF 1910–29, 732.35/29.

199. *Jornal do commercio* (Rio), May 23, 1917, quoted in Martin, *Latin America and the War,* 64.

200. Peel to Curzon, no. 89, May 20, 1919, FO 371/3654.

201. Nilo Peçanha has been described as "a mulatto of very humble origin"; see Gilberto Freyre, *New World in the Tropics* (New York: Knopf, 1959), 191. This was evidently a cause of difficulty in his dealings with American officials. A State Department memorandum later summed up that Nilo Peçanha "was not friendly to Ameri-

can interests because of our color prejudices"; memorandum by Division of Latin American Affairs, August 22, 1922, RG 59, DF 1910–29, 832.00/255.

202. Morgan to Lansing, no. 1210, April 12, 1918, RG 59, DF 1910–29, 832.00/181. Brazil's military participation in the war was slight and consisted of a small army mission and pilots sent to France and naval patrols in the South Atlantic. The contribution that gained most public attention was the work of Brazilian doctors and nurses on the western front.

203. Quoted in Rosenberg, *United States Predominance,* 85.

204. Peel to Balfour, no. 40, May 27, 1918, FO 371/3168.

205. It must have been of even less consolation to Morgan when Lansing remarked that the arrangement with France was "most unsatisfactory." Lansing to Page, tel., December 5, 1917, RG 59, DF 1910–29, 832.85/56A.

206. Morgan to Lansing, no. 1037, November 5, 1917, ibid., 832.20/15. The strong links between Brazilian army officers and Germany had, of course, been sundered by the war. Nonetheless, despite the prewar admiration for German methods and equipment, the government of São Paulo had contracted a French military mission in 1906 to reorganize the state's militia forces. The mission was considered a notable success. French propaganda also claimed to have been instrumental in transforming American farm boys into soldiers on the western front in Europe; see Frank D. McCann, "The Brazilian Army and the Pursuit of Arms Independence, 1899–1979," in *War, Business and World Military-Industrial Complexes,* ed. Benjamin F. Cooling (Port Washington: Kennikat, 1981), 176–77.

207. Morgan to Lansing, no. 828, October 18, 1916, RG 59, DF 1910–29, 832.30/13.

208. Morgan to Lansing, no. 1037, November 5, and no. 1052, November 13, 1917, ibid., 832.20/15 and 16.

209. Daniels to Lansing, November 16, 1917, and Morgan to Lansing, no. 1094, January 4, 1918, ibid., 832.30/19 and 37. Morgan was also concerned that the attitude of the Navy Department would prevent the Electric Boat Company of Connecticut from winning a valuable order for a submarine for the Brazilian navy; see Morgan to Lansing, no. 1078, December 8, 1917, ibid., 832.34/118.

210. Daniels to Lansing, January 16, 1918, ibid., 832.30/25; Lansing to Morgan, tel., February 7, and no. 396, February 21, 1918, ibid., 832.30/27. The Navy Department saw little military advantage to be gained from naval missions to South America; see Joseph S. Tulchin, *The Aftermath of War: World War I and U.S. Policy Toward Latin America* (New York: New York University Press, 1971), 35, and Joseph Smith, "American Diplomacy and the Naval Mission to Brazil, 1917–30," *Inter-American Economic Affairs* 35 (1981): 73–91.

211. Morgan to Lansing, tel., December 1, 1917, and Lansing to Morgan, tel., February 7, 1918, RG 59, DF 1910–29, 832.30/22 and 27.

212. Morgan to Lansing, no. 941, June 20, 1917, ibid., 763.72/5871; see Healy, "Caperton and U.S. Naval Diplomacy," 309–11 and David F. Trask, *Captains and Cabinets: Anglo-American Naval Relations, 1917–1918* (Columbia: University of Missouri Press, 1972), 89–90.

213. Morgan to Lansing, tel., December 2, 1917, and no. 1143, February 6, 1918, RG 59, DF 1910–29, 763.72/7945 and 9019; Daniels to Lansing, January 26,

1918, ibid., 763.72/8654; Morgan to Lansing, no. 1452, February 5, 1919, ibid., 832.30/140. For a description of the squadron's tour of duty see Arthur Saldanha da Gama, *A marinha do Brasil na primeira guerra mundial* (Rio: Caperni editôra, 1982).

214. See William H. Becker, *The Dynamics of Business-Government Relations: Industry and Exports, 1893–1921* (Chicago: University of Chicago Press, 1982), 113–30, Burton I. Kaufman, *Efficiency and Expansion: Foreign Trade Organization in the Wilson Administration, 1913–21* (Westport: Greenwood, 1974), 76–80.

215. Isaac F. Marcosson, *Caravans of Commerce* (New York: Harper and Bros., 1926), 48–49.

216. Redfield to Polk, January 27, 1917, RG 59, DF 1910–29, 832.51/141.

217. Seidel, "Progressive Pan Americanism," 103–20; McAdoo to Wilson, January 3, 1917, quoted in ibid., 102.

218. Lansing to McAdoo, March 14, 1918, RG 59, DF 1910–29, 832.51/173; memoranda by Stabler, May 1, 4, and 23, 1918, ibid., 832.51/177, 178 and 179. Treasury officials also included Brazil in an ambitious scheme by which the Latin American governments would deposit their gold reserves with the United States Federal Reserve System. The proposal met with studied silence from the Brazilian government; see Rosenberg, *United States Predominance*, 93–94.

219. See Downes, "Seeds of Influence," 240–44.

220. Morgan to Lansing, no. 1133, January 26, 1918, RG 59, DF 1910–29, 832.635/53.

221. Peel to Balfour, no. 40, May 27, 1918, FO 371/3168.

222. Morgan to Lansing, tel., June 4, 1918, *Foreign Relations* (supp. 1, part 1, 1918), 700–01.

223. Stimson, *My United States*, 294. When asked to survey press opinion, Morgan reported that Brazilian newspapers "are curiously reticent in commenting upon war news." The ambassador stressed the provincial nature of news coverage and added: "The local press devotes itself to local news of the town in which it is located and does not even cover the other cities and states of Brazil"; Morgan to Lansing, no. 1149, February 21, 1918, RG 59, DF 1910–29, 763.72/9378.

224. Lansing to Morgan, tels., September 20 and October 8, 1918, RG 59, DF 1910–29, 720–21, 734–35.

225. Lansing to Laughlin, tel., May 29, 1918, ibid., 698. See also Emily S. Rosenberg, "Anglo-American Economic Rivalry in Brazil during World War I," *Diplomatic History* 2 (1978): 138–40.

226. Morgan to Lansing, no. 1324, July 22, 1918, RG 59, DF 1910–29, 832.3421/42. See also the remarks of the State Department official, Gordon Auchincloss, quoted in Rosenberg, "Anglo-American Rivalry," 138. On the de Bunsen mission see FO 371/3484. The Latin American Division of the State Department prepared plans to send an equivalent American mission, but these were not acted upon. Only a year earlier the *New York Times* had predicted that Wilson was about to send a special mission to Brazil. The failure of these missions to materialize confirms the insularity of officials in Washington and gives a hollow ring to their criticism of the commercial efforts of their more enterprising European rivals; see Rosenberg, *United States Predominance*, 95, and *New York Times*, July 1, 1917.

227. Morgan to Lansing, no. 1078, December 8, 1917, RG 59, DF 1910–29, 832.34/118.

228. See Valla, "Estados Unidos na economia brasileira," 150, 162.

229. Peel to Curzon, no. 89, May 20, 1919, FO 371/3654; Hambloch to Department of Overseas Trade, March 24, 1919, FO 368/2073. Although Brazilians admired American business efficiency, they also complained about the "trickery of the Yankee" in commercial dealings; see Cooper, *Brazilians and their Country*, p. 369.

230. Morgan to Lansing, no. 1210, April 12, 1918, RG 59, DF 1910–29, 832.00/181. On American economic gains in Brazil see Rosenberg, "Anglo-American Economic Rivalry," 149–52.

231. Morgan to Lansing, n. 1473, March 20, 1919, RG 59, DF 1910–29, 763.72119/4509.

232. Peel to Curzon, no. 46, February 28, no. 76, April 2, and no. 95, May 31, 1919, FO 371/3653.

233. Peel to Curzon, no. 95, May 31, 1919, FO 371/3653; Morgan to Lansing, no. 1508, June 3, 1919, RG 59, DF 1910–29, 763.72119/5421. The statement of Alberto Tôrres is from *A Noite* (Rio), December 29, 1915; quoted in Barbosa Lima Sobrinho, *Presença de Alberto Tôrres*, 438.

234. Quoted in Peel to Balfour, no. 134, December 14, 1918, FO 371/3653.

235. Gilderhus, *Pan American Visions*, 138–39.

236. Minute by Sperling on Peel to Curzon, no. 66, April 9, 1919, FO 371/3653; Hambloch to Department of Overseas Trade, March 24, 1919, FO 368/2073.

237. Morgan to Lansing, no. 1310, July 6, 1918, RG 59, DF 1910–29, 832.00/155. In a private meeting with Morgan in June, the president-elect stated that his foreign policy would be "based on the approximation of Brazil with the United States and on continental solidarity"; see Morgan to Lansing, tel., June 18, 1918, ibid., 832.00/152.

238. Morgan privately let it be known that his government objected to Rui's appointment; see Peel to Balfour, no. 133, December 7, 1918, FO 371/3653 and Moniz Bandeira, *Presença dos Estados Unidos*, 203. The matter was further complicated by the illness of Rodrigues Alves and the meddling of Vice President Delfim Moreira; see Lyra, *Vida Diplomática*, 1:87–91.

239. Department of State, *Papers Relating to the Foreign Relations of the United States: the Paris Peace Conference, 1919*, 13 vols. (Washington: GPO, 1942–47), 1:386.

240. Domício to Ipanema Moreira, no. 5, January 9, and no. 11, January 18, 1919, AHI 234/2/11; Morgan to Lansing, tel., January 8, and Polk to Lansing, tel., January 10, 1919, RG 59, DF 1910–29, 763.72119/3325.

241. Domício had personally requested Lansing to present his views to Wilson; see Lyra, *Vida Diplomática*, 1:94.

242. Meeting of the Council of Ten, January 13, 1919; quoted in Link, *Wilson Papers*, 54:45–6; Arthur Walworth, *Wilson and His Peacemakers* (New York: Norton, 1986), 16–19. Domício stated that Wilson had once described Brazil to him as "a nation as disinterested as the U.S.A." The precise context is unknown and it may well have been an example of typical diplomatic flattery. However, if taken at face value, the remark gives an insight into why Wilson pleaded so strongly for Brazil's extra repre-

sentation; see Domício to Lansing, April 18, 1919, RG 59, DF 1910–29, 711.32/23.

243. Morgan to Lansing, no. 1342, August 10, 1918, RG 59, DF 1910–29, 832.00/154. Brazil and Uruguay were each assigned one full committee place and were the only Latin American nations so honored.

244. In 1919 the mark had declined to 10 percent of its 1914 value.

245. On Brazil and the peace conference see Leuchars, "Brazilian Foreign Policy," 142–73, and Martin, *Latin America and the War*, 98–106. See also Epitácio Pessoa, *Pela verdade* (Rio: Francisco Alves, 1925).

246. Leuchars, "Brazilian Foreign Policy," 155. The coffee money was transferred to Brazil in the early 1920s, but it appears that it was still paid in depreciated marks. The state of São Paulo probably made a loss of 90 percent on the transaction; see Steven Topik, *The Political Economy of the Brazilian State, 1889–1930* (Austin: University of Texas Press, 1987), 87. The struggle over the coffee money foreshadowed a later debate over world terms of trade. While Europeans were critical of Brazil's selfishness, Brazilians complained that their nation's increased volume of exports during the past decade had not resulted in larger export revenues; see Elias T. Saliba, ed., *Idéias econômicas de Cincinato Braga* (Brasília: Senado federal, 1983), 181–230.

247. Quoted in Link, *Wilson Papers*, 58:37.

248. See Pessoa, *Pela verdade*, 26–42, and Epitácio's presidential message of May 3, 1920; quoted in Morgan to Colby, no. 1652, June 16, 1920, RG 59, DF 1910–29, 832.032/22.

249. A summary of the American legal opinion is contained in memorandum from the Office of the Solicitor, October 14, 1920, RG 59, DF 1910–29, 832.85/123.

250. Morgan to Colby, tel., December 1, 1920, RG 59, DF 1910–29, 832.85/124.

251. Wilson's favorable image in Brazil was, however, tarnished by his refusal to allow Italy to annex the city of Fiume. The British minister reported the strength of ethnic loyalties to the Old World. In his opinion, "sympathy is all on the side of Italy" and Wilson "is considered here as having adopted an unaccommodating as well as dictatorial attitude in seeking to impose his views on the allied nations"; Peel to Curzon, no. 76, April 28, 1919, FO 371/3653.

252. Domício to Lansing, April 18, 1919, RG 59, DF 1910–29, 711.32/23. Morgan commented that he and Domício had "worked 'hand in hand' to complete the chain between the Department and the Brazilian and American Delegations in Paris"; see Morgan to Lansing, no. 1526, July 31, 1919, ibid., 832.001P43/7. Domício's diplomatic contribution, however, is given scanty mention in Laurita Pessoa Gabaglia, *Epitácio Pessoa* (Rio: José Olympio, 1951). One Brazilian diplomat calls this "a falsification of history"; see Lyra, *Vida Diplomática*, 1:87.

253. Adee to Morgan, tel., July 18, 1919, RG 59, DF 1910–29, 711.32/23A.

254. Morgan considered Epitácio "a safe although not a brilliant choice." He singled out "vanity and arrogance" as Epitácio's principal weaknesses; Morgan to Lansing, no. 1461, February 26, 1919, ibid., 832.00/171.

255. Adee to Morgan, tel., July 18, 1919, ibid., 711.32/23A. For a representative example of Epitácio's speeches see the *New York Times*, June 25, 1919. Epitácio's election also affected diplomatic relations by forcing the resignation of Domício in July 1919 and his later transfer to the London embassy. Morgan described the foreign minister's departure as arousing "general regret," but he seemed to be more interested

and impressed by the emergence of a new president who "shows every intention of ruling"; Morgan to Lansing, no. 1526, July 31, 1919, RG 59, DF 1910–29, 832. 001P43/7. If Domício's fall from grace was a blow to United States–Brazilian relations, so was the resignation of Lansing only six months later. Domestic political factors had effectively sundered the "chain" that had worked so closely during the peace conference.

256. Hambloch to Department of Overseas Trade, December 6, 1920, FO 371/5535.

257. For trade statistics see Valla, "Estados Unidos na economia brasileira," 162.

258. Adee to Morgan, no. 609, August 14, 1920, RG 59, DF 1910–29, 832.51/ 207A.

259. Chilton to Curzon, no. 227, December 27, 1920, FO 371/5536. On his visit to Rio, it was notable that Secretary of State Colby made a point of explaining to the local chapter of the American Chamber of Commerce that American financial policy was not responsible for the fluctuations in exchange rates; see *New York Times,* December 24, 1920.

260. One scholar describes the State Department in 1919 as "a messenger service for the Peace Commission" and concludes that the function of the Latin American Division was "reduced to gathering information"; see Tulchin, *Aftermath of War,* 52–58. Another example of the prevailing diplomatic confusion was the failure to utilize the large amount of information prepared on Latin American issues; see Lawrence Gelfand, *The Inquiry: American Preparations for Peace, 1917–1919* (New Haven: Yale University Press, 1963).

261. Daniel M. Smith, *Aftermath of War: Bainbridge Colby and Wilsonian Diplomacy, 1920–1921* (Philadelphia: American Philosophical Society, 1970), 141–52, and Daniel M. Smith, "Bainbridge Colby and the Good Neighbor Policy, 1920–21," *Mississippi Valley Historical Review* 50 (1963): 56–78. The Wilson administration originally intended General Pershing to tour South America, but the general's interventions in the Mexican Revolution made him a singularly inappropriate choice.

262. State Department to Stimson; quoted in Smith, *Aftermath of War,* 145. The Argentine government was reluctant to receive Colby and delayed announcing a formal invitation until the secretary of state had actually left the United States and was en route to Brazil.

263. For Colby's speech see *New York Times,* December 25, 1920.

264. Morgan to State Department, January 8, 1921, RG 59, DF 1910–29, 832.00/ 203; Chilton to Curzon, no. 29, February 16, 1921, FO 371/5539. Colby's sympathy for Latin America was regarded as sincere and did leave a lasting impression; see Silvino Gurgel do Amaral to Mangabeira, tel., no. 146, September 19, 1928, AHI 235/3/11.

265. Chilton to Curzon, no. 227, December 27, 1920, FO 371/5536.

CHAPTER 4: *Misunderstandings and Bruised Feelings, 1921–1928*

1. See Melvyn P. Leffler, "1921–1932: Expansionist Impulses and Domestic Constraints," in *Economics and World Power,* ed. William H. Becker and Samuel F. Wells

(New York: Columbia University Press, 1984), 225–75, and John Braeman, "Power and Diplomacy: The 1920's Reappraised," *Review of Politics* 44 (1982): 360.

2. See Kenneth J. Grieb, *The Latin American Policy of Warren G. Harding* (Fort Worth: Texas Christian University Press, 1976), 1–15, and L. Ethan Ellis, *Frank B. Kellogg and American Foreign Relations, 1925–1929* (New Brunswick: Rutgers University Press, 1961), 1–13.

3. Seidel, "Progressive Pan Americanism," 145–47, and Rosenberg, *Spreading the American Dream,* 138–60.

4. The American consul at São Paulo did complain, however, of lack of sufficient staff to keep pace with the increase of commercial work; see Charles Cameron to White, January 29, 1928, RG 59, DF 1910–29, 711.32/37.

5. Alston to Chamberlain, no. 16, January 25, 1927, FO 371/11966. A visiting American diplomat reported in 1922 that Morgan's "fetes are of an oriental magnificence." He added: "From every side in Rio I heard how popular Mr. Morgan was, particularly among the Brazilians, and from all hearsay we seem to have the right man in the right place"; Blair to Castle, June 8, 1922, William R. Castle Papers, Hoover Presidential Library. Percy Blair stopped at Rio en route to taking up his post of secretary of the American legation at Buenos Aires.

6. Morgan's advisory role was typical of professional diplomats during the 1920s; see Robert D. Schulzinger, *The Making of the Diplomatic Mind* (Middletown: Wesleyan University Press, 1975), 139–40. In terms of background and professionalism, Morgan remained a member of the elitist "club" of foreign service officers. Replying to a private letter on the 1924 São Paulo revolt Francis White warmly thanked Morgan: "It is very helpful to have your views on the situation and I am most grateful to you for writing to me in such detail. I trust Brazil will soon find a way out of her difficulties. If there is any one who can help her to do so you are certainly the one"; White to Morgan, September 18, 1924, RG 59, DF 1910–29, 832.00/584.

7. The service was operated by the Munson Shipping Line; see Herman G. James, *Brazil After a Century of Independence* (New York: Macmillan, 1925), 544.

8. *Wall Street Journal,* September 10, 1924. While Morgan was a keen advocate of increased American investment, he also advised caution in advancing loans to "backwater states." In his opinion, these invariably risked an "unhappy fate"; see Morgan to Kellogg, no. 2418, August 18, 1925, RG 59, DF 1910–29, 832.51C32/35.

9. Valla, *Penetração Norte-Americana,* 125–26.

10. Memorandum by Division of Latin American Affairs, August 22, 1922, RG 59, DF 1910–29, 832.00/255; Morgan to Hughes, no. 2023, February 22, 1923, ibid., 832.00/268, and Morgan to Kellogg, no. 2970, March 12, 1928, ibid. 832.00/Political Reports/4.

11. Silvino to Mangabeira, no. 202, May 31, 1928, AHI 235/1/1.

12. Roy Nash, *The Conquest of Brazil* (London: Jonathan Cape, 1926), 345. The statement had been originally made by a Brazilian doctor in 1916.

13. Isaac F. Marcosson, *Caravans of Commerce,* 285.

14. James, *Brazil After Independence,* vii. Students of literature were better served by the publication in 1922 of Isaac Goldberg's study. Despite his sympathetic approach to the subject, Goldberg concluded: "Brazilian literature, as is highly evident, is not one of the major divisions of world letters. It lacks continuity, it is too largely deriva-

tive, too poor in masterpieces"; *Brazilian Literature* (New York: Core Collection Books, 1978), 125.

15. Gilberto Amado, *Presença na política* (Rio: José Olympio, 1960), 213.

16. Fletcher to Kellogg, August 16, 1927, RG 59, Havana Conference, Entry 144, Box 425.

17. *Washington Post,* August 30, 1922, and *New York Herald Tribune,* December 23, 1926.

18. Morgan to Hughes, no. 2300, January 7, 1925, RG 59, DF 1910–29, 832.002/43.

19. On monetary policy see Winston Fritsch, *External Constraints on Economic Policy in Brazil, 1889–1930* (Pittsburgh: University of Pittsburgh Press, 1988), 53–117, and Topik, "State's Contribution to Brazil's Internal Economy," 205–12.

20. Topik, "Middle-Class Brazilian Nationalism," 97–101, and Skidmore, *Black Into White,* 173–79. The links between modernism and politics are examined in Ilan Rachum, "Nationalism and Revolution in Brazil, 1922–1930" (Ph.D diss., Columbia University, 1970). Nationalism also strongly influenced military officers and contributed to the rise of "tenentismo"; see McCann, "Formative Period of Brazilian Army Thought," 737–65. Another manifestation of national sensitivity surfaced in criticism of Japanese immigration. "I do not believe," stated Morgan in 1924, "that Japanese immigration will ever become popular or successful in Brazil." Nevertheless, State Department officials were obviously concerned by the threat of the "yellow peril" and stamped this dispatch "Strictly Confidential." In 1926 Morgan ominously reported that 5,000 Japanese immigrants were arriving annually and that Japan "is giving more attention, therefore, to commercial expansion and investment of capital"; Morgan to Hughes, November 11, 1924, and Morgan to Kellogg, no. 2720, December 22, 1926, RG 59, DF 1910–29, 832.00/465 and 608. For an interesting account of the confluence of Brazilian and American official attitudes toward restricting black migration see Teresa Meade and Gregory A. Pirio, "In Search of the Afro-American 'Eldorado': Attempts by North American Blacks to Enter Brazil in the 1920s," *Luso-Brazilian Review* 25 (1988): 85–110.

21. *Saturday Evening Post* (Philadelphia), November 7, 1925. Not only South Americans, but America's own "lost generation" was drawn to Paris during the 1920s.

22. See Cameron to White, January 29, 1928, RG 59, DF 1910–29, 711.32/37. When Arthur Hayes Sulzberger visited Rio in August 1928 he announced the intention of the *New York Times* to appoint a local correspondent to remedy the dearth of news from South America. The correspondent, however, was hardly assigned an easy task since he would be responsible not only for Brazil but also Uruguay, Argentina, and Chile.

23. Isaac Marcosson observed that "Yankee motors and movies have done more to put us on the South American map than years of academic propaganda, congressional trips, sentimental talk about Pan-Americanism and sporadic worship of the Monroe Doctrine"; see *Saturday Evening Post* (Philadelphia), July 11, 1925.

24. Sebastião Sampaio, "The New Understanding between the United States and Latin America," *Current History* 29 (1927): 906.

25. The private protest of the Brazilian ambassador at Washington drew an "apology" from Will Hays; see Hays to Rowe, October 25, 1927, AHI 234/4/11. "The Girl

From Rio" was distributed in 1927 and presented the standard Hollywood plot of passion, jealousy, murder, false arrest, and the ultimate triumph of true love. What made it different from a hundred similar movies was its title and the introduction of local color in the shape of dancers, coffee planters, American consuls, and frequent reference to the fact that events were supposedly taking place in Rio. Unfortunately, the Brazilian characters were given Spanish rather than Portuguese names.

26. Morgan to Kellogg, no. 2811, May 27, 1927, RG 59, DF 1920–29, 832.00/626.

27. Paget to Curzon, no. 48, April 5, 1920, FO 371/4435.

28. Alston to Chamberlain, no. 17, January 30, 1929, FO 371/13468.

29. For the view that Harding's interest in disarmament diminished after his election see Thomas H. Buckley, *The United States and the Washington Conference, 1921–1922* (Knoxville: University of Tennessee Press, 1974), 10–11.

30. Azevedo Marques to Cochrane de Alencar, tel., no. 62, October 10, 1921, AHI 235/4/5; Cochrane de Alencar to Azevedo Marques, tels., no. 64, September 26 and no. 80, December 30, 1921, AHI 235/3/8b.

31. Quoted in Stanley E. Hilton, "Brazil and the Post-Versailles World: Elite Images and Foreign Policy Strategy, 1919–1929," *Journal of Latin American Studies* 12 (1980): 343.

32. Afonso Arinos de Melo Franco, *Um estadista da república: Afrânio de Melo Franco e seu tempo* (Rio: José Olympio, 1955), 1117.

33. On the sheer difficulty of effecting military reorganization see João Pandiá Calógeras, *Problemas de administração* (São Paulo: Companhia editôra nacional, 1938). Pandiá Calógeras served as minister of war during the administration of Epitácio Pessoa. Foreign missions were expensive because their personnel insisted on financial privileges and payment of salaries in their own national currency.

34. Crosby to Hughes, no. 1959, July 25, 1922, RG 59, DF 1910–29, 832.20/30. Sheldon Crosby assumed charge of embassy affairs during the periods when Morgan took leave of absence in mid-1922 and mid-1924.

35. The British minister reported that Morgan had unsuccessfully sought a transfer to Rome in 1920; see Chilton to Curzon, no. 1, January 1, 1921, FO 371/5537. During 1921 Morgan resided for most of the year in São Paulo and was rumored to have suffered a nervous breakdown; see Tilley to Curzon, no. 28, January 20, 1922, FO 371/7190.

36. Morgan to Hughes, tel., no. 21, March 4, 1922, RG 59, DF 1910–29, 832. 30/47. See also the similar arguments presented by the American Chamber of Commerce at Rio contained in Schurz to Hoover, tel., March 21, 1922, Herbert Hoover Presidential Library, Hoover Papers, Commerce, Box 59. William L. Schurz served as commercial attaché at the Rio embassy.

37. Schurz reported that "the older officers . . . are almost uniformly in favor of a British mission, while the majority of the younger officers are pro-American"; Schurz to Klein, April 17, 1922, Herbert Hoover Presidential Library, Hoover Papers, Commerce, Box 152.

38. Morgan to Hughes, tel., no. 21, March 4, 1922, RG 59, DF 1910–29, 832. 30/47. Epitácio Pessoa acted despotically and sought to exercise a veto power over all matters pertaining to the Itamaraty; see Lyra, *Vida diplomática,* 1:104.

39. The Navy Department was traditionally reluctant to allow its personnel to

undertake duties on behalf of foreign governments. Largely at the instigation of the State Department, Congress had passed a law to legalize this practice in 1920; see Tulchin, *The Aftermath of War,* 35. The continuing problem of interdepartmental communications bordered on farce when the Navy Department announced that Vogelgesang could not be released for service in the Brazilian "Naval Museum"; see Michael L. Krenn, "Lions in the Woods: the United States Confronts Economic Nationalism, 1917–29" (Ph.D diss., Rutgers University, 1985), 286–87.

40. Morgan to Hughes, tel., no. 36, March 29, 1922, RG 59, DF 1910–29, 832.30/50.

41. Sparrow to McNamee, June 8, 1922, ibid., 832.30/69. Luke McNamee served in the Office of Naval Intelligence, Department of the Navy.

42. Crosby to Hughes, tel., no. 49, May 19, 1922, ibid, 832.415/23.

43. Hughes to Lodge, August 16 and Lodge to Hughes, August 17, 1921, ibid., 832.607B/6A and 7; Hughes to Crosby, tel., no. 59, May 20, 1922, ibid., 832.415/ 23. See also Seidel, "Progressive Pan Americanism," 269–70.

44. Hughes to Crosby, tel., no. 43, April 17 and no. 57, May 12, 1922, RG 59, DF 1910–29, 832.30/53; Hughes to Harding, May 1922, ibid., 832.415; Tilley to Curzon, no. 162, June 6, 1922, FO 371/7184.

45. *Times* (London), September 20, 1922; Tilley to Curzon, tel., no. 105, July 25, 1922, FO 371/7186.

46. *New York Tribune,* August 20, 1922.

47. Downes, "Seeds of Influence," 371–73, and Schwoch, "United States and Global Growth of Radio," 150.

48. Tilley to Curzon, no. 62, February 22, 1923, FO 371/8431. One example of the ill fortune attending the best of motives was the sorry saga of the attempt of local American merchants to erect a Brazilian "Statue of Liberty." The statue was commissioned in the United States, but arrived too late for the centennial. It was eventually placed close to the American embassy at Rio in 1942; see Downes, "Seeds of Influence," 372.

49. Brazilian dismay was expressed at some of the appointments made to the American commission, especially that of Mrs Henrietta Livermore of New York. The American commercial attaché noted that "women have no place in public affairs in Brazil and the people are very conservative about having foreign innovations of this kind thrust upon them"; Schurz to Klein, January 18, 1922, Hoover Papers, Commerce, Box 152. Schurz's admonition had no effect.

50. Tilley to Curzon, no. 257, September 21, 1922, FO 371/7184 and no. 261, September 24, 1922, FO 371/7193. The impression made by President José de Almeida of Portugal was quite profound; see Amado, *Presença na política,* 103–05.

51. Hughes to Denby, October 20, 1922, RG 59, DF 1910–29, 832.30/74. At full strength the naval mission consisted of 16 officers and 19 petty officers. As head of the mission, Vogelgesang assumed the rank of admiral.

52. Morgan to Hughes, no. 2102, October 30, 1923, ibid., 832.20/34.

53. Morgan regarded the admiral's appointment as "the most unfortunate one which the President has made"; see Morgan to Hughes, no. 1987, November 15 and no. 1996, November 28, 1922, ibid., 832.00/262 and 832.30/87.

54. Zeballos's comment appeared in *La Prensa* (Buenos Aires), May 19, 1922,

and was enclosed in Riddle to Hughes, no. 52, May 24, 1922, RG 59, DF 1910–29, 832.20/29. During this same period the American minister at Asuncion reported that disturbances in Paraguay were creating diplomatic tension between Argentina and Brazil; see O'Toole to Hughes, no. 1168, September 23, 1922, ibid., 732.34/2.

55. Morgan to Hughes, no. 2102, October 30, 1923, RG 59, DF 1910–29, 832.20/34. On American efforts to reassure Argentina see Riddle to Hughes, tel., no. 75, December 20, 1922, Hughes to Riddle, tel., no. 60, December 21, 1922 and January 17, 1923, ibid., 832.30/89 and 97. The terms of the contract were kept secret at the request of the Brazilian government.

56. Morgan to Hughes, no. 2021, February 20, 1923, ibid., 832.30/97. The American ambassador did not wish to see either Brazil or Argentina become more powerful than the other. In an unusually frank dispatch he suggested that the secession of the states south of Rio would have beneficial results: "The senseless rivalry and jealousy between Argentine and Brasil would be diminished should such a State come into existence, and the peace of the Continent would be more certainly assured"; Morgan to Hughes, no. 2287, November 29, 1924, ibid., 832.00/476.

57. Cochrane de Alencar to Azevedo Marques, no. 98, September 11, 1922, AHI 234/3/3; Morgan to Hughes, September 16, 1922, RG 59, DF 1910–29, 832.00/256.

58. Pacheco had been editor of the *Jornal do commercio*. His appointment as foreign minister came as a surprise; see Lyra, *Vida Diplomática*, 2:23. The British ambassador reported that Morgan "takes a gloomy view of Dr. Pacheco's appointment" and considers him "a politician and journalist with probable ambitions towards the Presidency"; Tilley to Curzon, no. 315, November 9, 1922, FO 371/7193.

59. Tilley to Curzon, no. 341, November 28, 1922, FO 371/7193.

60. Pacheco to Cochrane de Alencar, tel., no. 89, November 24, 1922, AHI 235/4/5; Cochrane de Alencar to Pacecho, tel., no. 138, November 30, 1922, AHI 235/3/8B; Pacheco to Cochrane de Alencar, tel., no. 94, December 2, 1922, AHI 235/4/5.

61. Melo Franco, *Estadista da República*, 1119–20.

62. Bateman to Curzon, December 20, 1922, FO 371/8456.

63. Pacheco to Brazilian embassy at Washington, tels., nos. 11 and 14, February 12, 1923, AHI 235/4/6.

64. *O Jornal* (Rio), January 6, 1923.

65. Geddes to Foreign Office, no. 47, February 1, 1923, FO 371/8456.

66. Cochrane de Alencar to Pacheco, tel., no. 138, November 30, 1922, AHI 235/3/8B; Hughes to Harding, November 28, 1922; quoted in Grieb, *Harding's Latin American Policy*, 180.

67. Stewart to Curzon, no. 132, May 7, 1923, FO 371/8457.

68. See Melo Franco, *Estadista da República*, 1113–48.

69. The words of General Tasso Fragoso are quoted in ibid., 1122. The principal Brazilian representatives at Santiago were the head of the delegation, Afrânio de Melo Franco, and the Brazilian ambassador to Chile, Silvino Gurgel do Amaral.

70. Undated memorandum "Instructions to Delegates of the U.S.A. to the 5th International Conference of American States, Santiago, Chile" and memorandum by General B. H. Wells, War Department, January 27, 1923, RG 59, Santiago Conference, Entry 126, Box 358.

71. Morgan to Hughes, no. 2019, February 8, 1923, ibid.

72. Melo Franco to Pacheco, tel., no. 60, April 26, 1923, AHI 273/3/16.

73. Stewart to Curzon, no. 132, May 7, 1923, FO 371/8457.

74. Cochrane de Alencar was instructed by Pacheco to find out the views of Harding and Hughes. The Brazilian ambassador reported that Harding was cautious and that Hughes was unduly sensitive to the fact that Fletcher had taken an initiative on his own; see Melo Franco, *Estadista da República*, 1143–44.

75. Memorandum by J. Butler Wright, April 28, 1923, and "Department of State Press Release," June 4, 1923, RG 59, Santiago Conference, Entry 126, Box 358.

76. Morgan to Hughes, no. 2138, January 24, 1924, RG 59, DF 1910–29, 725.3211/87.

77. Tilley to Curzon, no. 312, December 24, 1923, FO 371/9513. One Brazilian diplomat reminisced how Vogelgesang once told him "with tears in his eyes" how Bernardes had resolutely refused the navy small amounts of fuel while allowing the expenditure of more than 30,000 contos a year for official cars; see Maurício Nabuco, *Reminiscências*, 68–69.

78. Crosby to Hughes, no. 2203, May 26, 1924, RG 59, DF 1910–29, 832.30/111.

79. Tilley to Chamberlain, no. 153, April 24, 1925, FO 371/10609. Foreign Office officials regarded Bernardes as "anti-American"; see Tilley to Curzon, no. 62, February 22, 1923, FO 371/8431.

80. Crosby to Hughes, tel., no. 24, June 6, and Hughes to Crosby, tel., no. 18, June 11, 1924, RG 59, DF 1910–29, 832.34/182.

81. Crosby to Hughes, tel., June 15, 1924, ibid., 832.34/185, and no. 2220, June 18, 1924, ibid., 832.20/38; Hughes to Crosby, tel., no. 27, June 26, 1924, ibid., 832.34/185.

82. Division of Latin American Affairs to Hughes, May 29, 1924, ibid., 832.20/36.

83. Hughes to Riddle, tel., no. 60, December 21, 1922, ibid., 832.30/89.

84. Memorandum by Division of Latin American Affairs, December 4, 1923, ibid., 832.30/103.

85. Morgan to Hughes, no. 2243, August 19, 1924, ibid., 832.00/419. Since the rising of the "tenentes" at Copacabana in July 1922, the Old Republic was plagued by fears of military revolt; see John D. Wirth, "Tenentismo in the Brazilian Revolution of 1930," *Hispanic American Historical Review* 44 (1964): 161–79.

86. Hughes to Morgan, tel., no. 77, December 9 and Morgan to Hughes, tel., no. 103, December 10, 1924, RG 59, DF 1910–29, 832.34/188A and 189. Despite its ambitious plans, the Bernardes administration actually placed only one major naval order. This was for a submarine from the Ansaldo Company of Italy, which came into service in 1927. In the original bidding for the contract, Ansaldo tendered a bid of 13,680 milréis. Its two American competitors, Electric Boat Company and Bethlehem Steel Company offered the highest bids of 23,655 and 32,775 milréis respectively. Morgan acknowledged the superior quality of the American submarine, but he also reported: "In view, however, of the determination of the President to reduce expenditures in all departments, the decision will probably be based on prices and on the familiarity of the officers and men of the Brasilian Navy with the Italian, rather than the American type"; see Morgan to Hughes, no. 2375, May 30, 1925, ibid., 832.34/193.

87. Morgan to Hughes, no. 2308, January 20, 1925, ibid., 832.30/120; Ramsay to Chamberlain, no. 360, October 14, 1925, FO 371/10609; Morgan to Kellogg, no. 23, March 30, 1926, RG 59, DF 1910-29, 832.30/136.

88. See minute on Morgan to Kellogg, no. 23, March 30, 1926 and also Kellogg to Morgan, tel., no. 10, April 6, 1926, RG 59, DF 1910-29, 832.30/136 and 131.

89. Morgan to Kellogg, no. 2559, May 16, 1926, ibid., 832.30/137.

90. J. Butler Wright to H. W. Atkinson, December 27, 1926, ibid., 832.20/45. Atkinson, a citizen of Baltimore, had requested information about the State Department's Latin American policy. His query was prompted by public disquiet that the United States was supporting the build up of armaments in South America; see Kenneth F. Woods, "'Imperialistic America': A Landmark in the Development of U.S. Policy toward Latin America," *Inter-American Economic Affairs* 21 (1967): 55-72.

91. See Captain A. T. Beauregard. "The U.S. Naval Mission to Brazil: A Review of Naval Mission Problems," (November 1939); enclosed in Burdett to Hull, no. 2235, December 18, 1939, RG 59, DF 1930-39, 832.30/339.

92. For trade statistics see Commerce Department, *Historical Statistics,* 903-07, and Valla, "Estados Unidos na Economia Brasileira," 158-63. Coffee prices are cited in Peláez, "Programa de Sustentação do Café," 68.

93. See Carlos M. Peláez, "As consequências econômicas da ortodoxia monetária cambial e fiscal no Brasil entre 1889 e 1945," *Revista brasileira de economia* 25 (1971): 58, and Topik, "States' Contribution to Brazil's Internal Economy," 211.

94. On Farquhar's difficulties with the Bernardes administration see Charles A. Gauld, *The Last Titan: Percival Farquhar* (Stanford: Institute of Hispanic American and Luso-Brazilian Studies, 1964), 285-86. Farquhar frequently appeared in Washington to lobby support for his Brazilian ventures. Officials were impressed by the potential of the Itabira scheme, but they also realized the political controversy surrounding Farquhar and only gave him qualified support. Farquhar received even less assistance from American officials in Brazil. In 1924 he complained to the State Department that Morgan "had actively opposed him and his associates." The ambassador sent back a devastating reply in which he alluded to Farquhar's several business failures and record of poor judgment. "That gentleman's exaggerated optimism," summed up Morgan, "often leads him to assume and subsequently to represent that a condition exists which is founded upon opinion rather than fact"; see Leland Harrison to Morgan, April 16, and Morgan to Hughes, no. 2267, October 15, 1924, RG 59, DF 1910-29, 832.6351Itl/16 and 18.

95. Alston to Chamberlain, no. 214, December 1, 1927, FO 371/11964, and Crosby to Kellogg, no. 2226, July 8, 1924, RG 59, DF 1910-29, 832.635 It/11. Bernardes was especially concerned about alleged American imperialist designs upon the Amazon region; see Love, *Rio Grande do Sul and Brazilian Regionalism,* 125.

96. See statistical tables in Commerce Department, *Historical Statistics,* 903-07; Valla, "Estados Unidos na Economia Brasileira," 158-63; Rosenberg, "Anglo-American Economic Rivalry," 149-50; Bill Albert, *South America and the First World War* (Cambridge: Cambridge University Press, 1988), 94. For a contemporary view of the rapid American economic advance see Normano, *Struggle for South America,* 21-72.

97. *Jornal do commercio* (Rio), February 17, 1928. "It is obvious," confirmed the British ambassador, "that as long as the United States remains by far the largest pur-

chaser of Brazilian coffee, which during the year was responsible for £70 million worth of Brazil's total export trade of £90 million odd, she must continue to play an important role in Brazil"; Tilley to Chamberlain, no. 153, April 24, 1925, FO 371/10609. For trade figures see Commerce Department, *Historical Statistics*, 903–07; Valla, *Penetração Norte-Americana*, 123–30; Downes, "Seeds of Influence," 459.

98. From 1915 to 1930 it has been estimated that Brazil borrowed £54.3 million from London and £86.5 million from New York; see Marcelo de Paiva Abreu, "Anglo-Brazilian Economic Relations and the Consolidation of American Pre-Eminence in Brazil, 1930–1945," in *Latin America, Economic Imperialism and the State*, ed. Christopher Abel and Colin M. Lewis (London: Athlone, 1985), 381. Despite the evident surge of Wall Street's interest in Brazil during the 1920s, that country remained second to Argentina as the most popular area of American investment in South America; see Max Winkler, *Investments of United States Capital in Latin America* (Boston: World Peace Foundation, 1929), 274–85.

99. The stress on long-term corporate investment was in contrast to the interest shown during the last half of the previous decade in setting up branch banks and mounting a challenge to the financial services offered by Britain; see Carl P. Parrini, *Heir to Empire: United States Economic Diplomacy, 1916–1923* (Pittsburgh: University of Pittsburgh Press, 1969), 131. The number of American branch banks in Latin America declined from 75 in 1921 to 46 in 1922; ibid., p. 117.

100. The observation of Isaac F. Marcosson, *Saturday Evening Post*, October 24, 1925.

101. For the term "outpost of Yankee enterprise" see ibid. On Ford Motor Company in Brazil see Downes, "Seeds of Influence," 423–54, and Allan Nevins and Frank E. Hill, *Ford: Expansion and Challenge, 1915–1933* (New York: Charles Scribner's Sons, 1957), 230–38, 375. In typical American progressive fashion the city of Fordlandia was meant not just to involve the construction of industrial plant and transportation facilities but also the provision of services for employees such as housing, schools, and medical care. A recent study states that Ford was "cozened" into paying $125,000 for land that he might well have received at no cost from the state government of Pará; see Warren Dean, *Brazil and the Struggle for Rubber* (Cambridge: Cambridge University Press, 1987), 72.

102. See Joan Hoff Wilson, *American Business & Foreign Policy 1920–1933* (Boston: Beacon, 1973), 65–100, and Rosenberg, *Spreading the American Dream*, 138–43.

103. Hughes to Morgan, tel., January 6, 1923, *Foreign Relations* (1923), 454.

104. Topik, *Political Economy of Brazilian State*, 153.

105. Hughes to Morgan, tel., January 6, 1923, Foreign Relations (1923), 454.

106. Stewart to Curzon, no. 173, June 26, 1923, FO 371/8426. Although the commercial agreement with Belgium only allowed a limited preferential duty to certain Belgian goods, its extension to other countries was complicated by Brazil's desire not to do anything that might upset the visit of King Albert of Belgium to Brazil in 1922.

107. Morgan to Hughes, January 15 and April 26, 1923, *Foreign Relations* (1923), 455–56. The inclusion of a retaliatory provision in the 1922 tariff prompted some speculation in Brazil that the Harding administration might impose a tax on coffee should a commercial treaty not be forthcoming. British reports suggested that Bernardes believed stocks of coffee were currently so low in the United States that American retalia-

tion was unlikely; see Stewart to Curzon, no. 173, June 26, 1923, FO 371/8426. It was also very likely that the abrasive tone of Hughes's initial correspondence was communicated to the Itamaraty in a more tactful manner by Morgan; see Leuchars, "Brazilian Foreign Policy," 250–51.

108. American negotiators were easily outmaneuvered. What had originally been a straightforward request to negotiate a most-favored-nation treaty was deliberately complicated by Brazilian attempts to secure reductions in American import duty on manganese, mica, nuts, and sugar. When American officials queried Brazil's stated unwillingness to conclude commercial treaties by referring to the Belgian agreement of 1920, Brazilian negotiators pointed out that the United States similarly reserved its own sovereign right to maintain a special commercial agreement with Cuba; see *Foreign Relations* (1923), 455–59.

109. Britain also failed in its attempt to secure a commercial treaty with Brazil. The setback to American policy in Brazil was not untypical. Only eight agreements were signed by 1929; see Wilson, *American Business and Foreign Policy,* 92.

110. Memorandum by Stabler, March 15, 1917, and McAdoo to Lansing, October 19, 1918, RG 59, DF 1910–29, 832.51/148 and 185. McAdoo also proposed that the Treasury purchase and control the former German banks in Brazil; see Parrini, *Heir to Empire,* 132.

111. American diplomacy was particularly active in helping to break the cable monopolies held in Brazil by the British Western Telegraph Company and thereby enabling American companies to establish a cable network covering the whole of Latin America; see Tulchin, *Aftermath of War,* 206–33, and Rosenberg, "Anglo-American Economic Rivalry," 143–48.

112. In 1920 the Commerce Department was almost deprived of funds for its network of commercial attachés; see Becker, *Business-Government Relations,* 166.

113. Hoover's policies are expertly analyzed in Joseph Brandes, *Herbert Hoover and Economic Diplomacy* (Pittsburgh: University of Pittsburgh Press, 1962); Craig Lloyd, *Aggressive Introvert* (Columbus: Ohio State University Press, 1972); and Ellis W. Hawley, "Herbert Hoover, the Commerce Secretariat, and the Vision of an 'Associative State,' 1921–1928," *Journal of American History* 41 (1974): 116–39.

114. Hoover to Harding, November 30, 1921, Hoover Papers, Commerce, Box 480. See also Joan Hoff Wilson, *Herbert Hoover* (Boston: Little, Brown, 1975), 180.

115. See Tulchin, *Aftermath of War,* 155–85; Rosenberg, *Spreading the American Dream,* 138–60; Seidel, "Progressive Pan Americanism," 503–11.

116. White to Dillon, Read and Company, September 26, 1927, RG 59, DF 1910–29, 832.51/501.

117. Adee to Morgan, no. 609, August 14, 1920, ibid., 832.51/207A.

118. Grew to Walker and Roberts, Inc., October 18, 1924, ibid., 832.51SA6.

119. Grew to Hoover, March 4, 1926, ibid., 832.51SA6/71.

120. The chief of the foodstuffs division at the Commerce Department believed that the Brazilians "are undoubtedly afraid that we may take some action"; see Montgomery to Emmet, August 9, 1922, Hoover Papers, Commerce, Box 59.

121. The financial intervention of the Epitácio Pessoa administration is known as the "third" valorization. The "second" valorization had occurred in 1918 when the Venceslau Brás administration had sought to counter the effects of an overabundant

supply of coffee resulting from the 1917–18 crop. For an outline of valorization policy see Peláez, "Programa de Sustentação do Café," 64–81.

122. Topik, *Political Economy of Brazilian State*, 88–89. The general financial instability prevailing in Brazil made British bankers cautious to advance any further credits until the 1922 loan was liquidated; see Fritsch, *External Constraints on Brazil*, 81.

123. Jones to Hoover, April 5, 1922, Hoover Papers, Commerce, Box 59. Grosvenor Jones worked in the Finance Division of the Commerce Department.

124. Manning to White, August 1, 1922, RG 59, DF 1910–29, 832.6133/189. William R. Manning served in the Latin American Division of the State Department.

125. On the competition for the American coffee market see Valla, *Penetração Norte-Americano*, 141–42.

126. The National Coffee Roasters Association was actually more concerned about securing adequate supplies of coffee than rising prices. It suspected that the Paulista authorities were making secret sales to its main American rivals organized in the Green Coffee Importers Association. By enlisting the support of Hoover, the Roasters Association hoped to increase its own bargaining leverage with the Coffee Institute. It was proved correct.

127. Morgan to Hughes, no. 2002, December 14, 1922, RG 59, DF 1910–29, 832.6133/197.

128. Klein to Hoover, July 13, 1923, and March 15, 1924, Hoover Papers, Commerce, Box 117.

129. See Seidel, "Progressive Pan Americanism," 434–39, and Brandes, *Hoover and Economic Diplomacy*, 130–38.

130. Silvino Gurgel do Amaral to Pacheco, no. 167, November 19, 1925, AHI 234/4/5.

131. Hoover to Couzens, September 15, 1925, Hoover Papers, Commerce, Box 231. James Couzens was U.S. senator for Michigan.

132. Seidel, "Progressive Pan Americanism," 451–52, and Brandes, *Hoover and Economic Diplomacy*, 131–33.

133. This strict attitude had already been put into effect during 1924; see memorandum by the Office of Economic Adviser, October 15, 1924, RG 59, DF 1910–29, 832.51SA6.

134. Memorandum by Harrison, March 18, 1925, ibid., 832.51SA6/8; memorandum by Stokes, March 24, 1925, Hoover Papers, Commerce, Box 231; Grosvenor Jones to Stokes, April 30, 1925, ibid., Box 222. Harold Phelps Stokes served as Hoover's personal assistant.

135. Manning to White, June 15, 1925, RG 59, DF 1910–29, 832.51SA6/12.

136. See *New York Times*, January 2, 1925, and Seidel, "Progressive Pan Americanism," 439–40. The Paulista authorities regularly spent large sums to promote coffee sales in the United States and were estimated to have allocated $1 million for this purpose in 1919; see Seidel, "Progressive Pan Americanism," 432, n. 20. In 1926 Klein remarked that the Coffee Institute had $500,000 to spend "for propaganda purposes in this country." He had no doubt that the money was "being squandered in the usual Latin American manner"; Klein to Hoover, May 5, 1926, Hoover Papers, Commerce, Box 117.

137. Seidel, "Progressive Pan Americanism," 438–49.

138. Memorandum by Hoover, August 25, 1925, Hoover Papers, Commerce, Box 231. See also Seidel, "Progressive Pan Americanism," 449–65.

139. Silvino Gurgel do Amaral to Pacheco, no. 2, October 24, and no. 92, November 5, 1925, AHI 234/4/5. Silvino had taken charge of the Brazilian embassy in June. His purpose in rushing to see Hoover in late October was not to discuss the coffee question but to forestall publication by the Commerce Department of a highly critical report on Brazil's rubber supplies. Hoover reassured Silvino that the contents of the report were not so unfavorable as had been rumored. Although Hoover's speech before the Erie chamber of commerce did not mention this particular subject, the Brazilian ambassador was convinced that Hoover was personally opposed to the cultivation of rubber on a large scale in the Amazon region. However, while acknowledging the difficulties of transportation and cultivation, Commerce Department officials were keen to advocate American investment in Brazilian rubber; see the statement made by Klein to the *New York World,* January 12, 1926.

140. Silvino Gurgel do Amaral to Pacheco, no. 97, November 19, 1925, AHI 234/4/5. The British ambassador similarly suspected that Hoover's campaign against the rubber cartel was motivated by presidential ambition. I am indebted to George H. Nash for this information.

141. See Press Clippings, November 1925, Hoover Papers. Press interest still focused on Hoover's attack on the British rubber cartel rather than the coffee question.

142. Kellogg to Hoover, October 31 and Hoover to Kellogg, November 4, 1925, Hoover Papers, Commerce, Box 231.

143. Speyer to Harrison, November 10 and November 25, 1925, RG 59, DF 1910–29, 832.51SA6/47. See also Joseph Brandes, "Product Diplomacy: Herbert Hoover's Anti-Monopoly Campaign at Home and Abroad," in *Herbert Hoover as Secretary of Commerce,* ed. Ellis W. Hawley, (Iowa City: University of Iowa Press, 1981), 193.

144. Harrison to Speyer, November 21, 1925, RG 59, DF 1910–29, 832.51SA6/47. Before this reply was drafted Hoover had already upstaged the State Department by announcing at a press conference on November 12 that "the Administration does not believe the New York banking houses will wish to provide loans which might be diverted to support the coffee speculation which has been in progress for the past year at the hands of the coffee combination in Sao Paulo, Brazil"; see "Statement by Hoover at Press Conference," November 12, 1925, Hoover Papers, Commerce, Box 231.

145. Morgan to Kellogg, tel., no. 74, December 1, 1925, RG 59, DF 1910–29, 832.51SA6/46.

146. Hoover to Kellogg, November 28, 1925, Hoover Papers, Commerce, Box 231.

147. Hoover to McCreery (Hard and Rand, Inc., New York), January 5, 1926, ibid.

148. E. H. Marsters (President of Capitol Lunch Stores, Boston) to Hoover, January 14, and Mrs Ada Orsinger to Hoover, January 6, 1926, ibid.

149. Hoover to Marster, February 25, 1926, ibid., Box 208.

150. Coste to Hoover, November 25, 1925, ibid., Box 117; Speyer to Hoover, December 9, 1925, ibid., Box 231.

151. Morgan to Kellogg, tel., no. 74, December 1, 1925, RG 59, DF 1910–29, 832.51SA6/46, and no. 2470G, December 12, 1925, ibid., 832.00/545.

152. Klein to Schurz, November 24, 1925; quoted in Seidel, "Progressive Pan Americanism," 468.

153. Memorandum by Hoover, December 24, 1925, Hoover Papers, Commerce, Box 208.

154. Schurz to Klein, January 13, 1926, ibid., Box 231.

155. Morgan to Kellogg, no. 2482, January 12, 1926, RG 59, DF 1910–29, 832.51SA6/68. At the same time, Morgan reported that *O Jornal* of Rio had published on January 8 the most anti-American article to have appeared in the press for a "considerable period"; see Woods, "'Imperialist America,'" 67.

156. *O Jornal* (Rio), January 7, 1926.

157. The Commerce Department had also sought to develop alternative sources of supply by encouraging coffee cultivation in Central America and the Caribbean islands. The immediate results were discouraging and merely confirmed Brazil's preeminence in this commodity.

158. *New York Times,* January 8, 1926. Hoover was giving evidence on monopolies before the House committee on interstate and foreign commerce. For the moderate tone ultimately adopted in the committee's report see *New York Journal of Commerce,* March 16, 1926, and *New York Times,* March 21, 1926.

159. Memorandum of interview between Hoover and Rangel de Nestor Pestana, April 10, 1926, Hoover Papers, Commerce, Box 231. The interview was published in the *Estado de São Paulo* on April 13, 1926. For Schurz's views see Klein to Hoover, May 15, 1926, Hoover Papers, Commerce, Box 231. Hoover's change of tactics has never been satisfactorily explained. When confronted by setbacks Hoover could retreat into introversion and suffer from depression; see the essay by Gerald D. Nash in *Herbert Hoover and the Crisis of American Capitalism,* ed. J. Joseph Huthmacher and Warren I. Susman (Cambridge: Schenkman, 1973), 103. On the other hand, Hoover was modifying rather than reversing his coffee policy. The publicity attached to his opposition to valorization obscured the fact that Hoover's goodwill toward the Paulista coffee industry was sincere. "I hold to the fact," he told Felix Coste, "that the sound basis for building up a coffee planting industry for protecting the coffee planter and the American consumer lies in the path of an abandonment of all restraint of every character." He wanted the Defense Institute not to buy up surpluses and fix prices at artificial levels but to seek ways of improving and increasing coffee cultivation. His pet idea was the use of American loans to set up agricultural banks to provide credit for the small coffee planter; see Hoover to Coste, December 4, 1925, Hoover Papers, Commerce, Box 231, and Seidel, "Progressive Pan Americanism," 473–83. The problem for Hoover was how to persuade Brazilians to accept economic plans dictated from Washington.

160. Memorandum by Silvino Gurgel do Amaral, February 1, 1926, RG 59, DF 1910–29, 832.6133/233. Silvino had earlier described Klein as Hoover's "eminence grise"; Silvino to Pacheco, no. 2, October 24, 1925, AHI 234/4/5.

161. Memorandum by Kellogg, February 18 and Kellogg to Gurgel, March 13, 1926, RG 59, DF 1910–29, 832.6133/233 and 234.

162. Ramsey to Chamberlain, no. 7, January 8, 1926, FO 371/11115.

163. Brazil's pretensions to hemispheric leadership were also assisted by Argentina's decision to abstain from active involvement in the League's affairs; see Percy A. Martin, "Latin America and the League of Nations," *American Political Science Review*

20 (1926): 14–30. A brief survey of Brazil's policy toward the League is Warren H. Kelchner, *Latin American Relations with the League of Nations* (Boston: World Peace Foundation, 1929), 54–74.

164. Hélio Lobo to Ministério das Relações Exteriores (hereafter cited as MRE), April 8, 1923; cited in Hilton, "Brazil and Post-Versailles World," 352. Hélio Lobo was the Brazilian consul-general at New York.

165. Lyra, *Vida Diplomática*, 2:109.

166. Increases in Brazilian diplomatic resources were directed mainly to Europe; see Jenks, "Structure of Diplomacy," 176–78.

167. Another honor was the Assembly's election in 1923 of Epitácio Pessoa to the International Court of Justice at The Hague. One newspaper described this as a "brilliant and well deserved success" for Brazilian diplomacy. "Members of the great world assembly," it proudly observed, "gave fresh proofs of their recognition of the culture, loyalty and prestige of our people and our international policy"; *Jornal do commercio* (Rio), September 14, 1923.

168. Brazil's record of participation in the League's affairs was hardly distinguished. One critic summed up that Brazil's "negligence has beaten all records"; see José Carlos de Macedo Soares, *Brazil and the League of Nations* (Paris: A. Pedone, 1928), 165.

169. Morgan to Kellogg, no. 2398G, July 12, 1925, RG 59, DF 1910–29, 832.00/522. The diplomatic effort to secure a permanent seat had commenced in 1923; see Melo Franco, *Estadista da República*, 1166–76.

170. The remark of the British ambassador at Berlin was directed at Poland; see David Carlton, "Great Britain and the League Council Crisis of 1926," *Historical Journal* 11 (1968): 355.

171. Pacheco to Melo Franco, September 23, 1923; cited in Melo Franco, *Estadista da República*, 1174. The French government implied a measure of support for Brazil, but it was evident that France's real aim was to secure the election of Poland to the Council. A devious diplomatic game resulted in which Brazil was "simply used as a catspaw"; see Macedo Soares, *Brazil and the League of Nations*, 134.

172. *O Jornal* (Rio), September 25, 1925. See also Macedo Soares, *Brazil and the League of Nations*, 97–102, and Leuchars, "Brazilian Foreign Policy," 174–99, 264–306.

173. Tilley to Chamberlain, no. 78, March 5, 1925, FO 371/10607.

174. In much less controversial circumstances in 1921 Brazil had used its power of veto to defeat Spain's application for a permanent seat on the Council.

175. Bernardes to Melo Franco, tel., March 12, 1926; quoted in Melo Franco, *Estadista da República*, 1244.

176. In somewhat overdramatic fashion one Brazilian diplomat described the meeting of the Council as "the most solemn and important in its history"; Lyra, *Vida Diplomática*, 2:133.

177. For reasons of his own personal safety Bernardes rarely ventured from Petrópolis or the Catete palace and ruled virtually by means of a permanent state of siege.

178. Quoted in Alston to Chamberlain, no. 85, April 26, 1927, FO 371/11967. See also Macedo Soares, *Brazil and the League of Nations*, 111–34.

179. MRE to Brazilian embassy at Washington, tel., no. 6, February 23, 1926, AHI 235/4/6; Silvino to MRE, tels., no. 40, February 25, no. 42, February 25, and no. 54, March 4, 1926, AHI 235/3/10. The Itamaraty believed that Brazil was not

totally devoid of support beyond Latin America. Sweden and Canada were regarded as supporters of Brazil's case, and a residual feeling persisted that France and Italy were basically sympathetic.

180. Memorandum by Melo Franco, December 3, 1925; quoted in Melo Franco, *Estadista da República,* 1236. In similar vein Heitor Lyra observed that "when Brazil found itself in difficulty, then they all joined against us"; Lyra, *Vida Diplomática,* 2:98.

181. Alston to Chamberlain, no. 85, April 26, 1927, FO 371/11967.

182. Alston to Chamberlain, tel., June 4, 1926, FO 371/11117. In an attempt to influence Bernardes's attitude toward the League, the Foreign Office informed British bankers that a loan to Brazil would not be looked on with favor. A cool response was forthcoming from the financiers. At a meeting in April 1926 one banker told the foreign secretary: "We have financed Brazil since her independence and to allow her to go to America would mean a great loss to this country." The foreign secretary was unmoved and indicated that the government placed the future of the League of Nations above considerations of Anglo-American economic rivalry in Brazil; see Fritsch, *External Constraints on Brazil,* 117.

183. Tilley to Foreign Office, July 6, 1925; cited in Hilton, "Brazil and the Post-Versailles World," 352.

184. Two years' notice of withdrawal was required so that Brazil did not technically leave the League until 1928.

185. See minutes on Alston to Tyrell, tel., no. 42, September 15, 1927, FO 371/11965. On Morgan's visit to Bernardes see Macedo Soares, *Brazil and League of Nations,* 142.

186. *New York World,* June 18, 1926.

187. *New York Times,* June 17, 1926.

188. *New York World,* June 15, 1926; *Philadelphia Public Ledger,* June 15, 1926.

189. Morgan to Kellogg, no. 2594, June 23, 1926, RG 59, DF 1910–29, 832.00/583; Alston to Chamberlain, no. 153, July 12, 1926, FO 371/11117.

190. Harrison to Morgan, August 21, 1926, RG 59, DF 1910–29, 711.322/2A; Daniels to Kellogg, tel., no. 71, September 27 and Kellogg to Daniels, no. 1178, October 18, 1926, ibid., 711.322/3. While Morgan was on his annual leave of absence, Thomas L. Daniels assumed charge of the American embassy at Rio from August through November 1926.

191. Daniels to Kellogg, no. 2683, October 23, 1926, ibid., 711.322/6. The economic attaché, William L. Schurz, warned, however, that Washington Luís "has been strongly anti-American"; see Klein to Hoover, Hoover Papers, Commerce, Box 208.

192. See Francisca Isabel Schurig Vieira, "O Pensamento Político-Administrativo e a Política Financeira de Washington Luís," *Revista de História* 20 (1960): 105–46.

193. Daniels to Kellogg, tel., no. 78, October 14, 1926, RG 59, DF 1910–29, 832.002/46.

194. Daniels to Kellogg, no. 2686G, October 26, 1926, ibid., 832.00/599; "Political Notes" by the American vice consul at Bahia, Allan Dawson, November 9, 1926, ibid., 832.00/603; Lyra, *Vida Diplomática,* 2:227.

195. *O Jornal* (Rio), February 20, 1927. See also the comment that Washington Luís intended to dominate his cabinet in Daniels to Kellogg, no. 2648, September 10,

1926, RG 59, DF 1910–29, 832.01/5 and Gilberto Amado, *Depois da política* (Rio: José Olympio, 1960), 6–7.

196. A commercial treaty between Brazil and the United States was eventually concluded in 1935.

197. Morgan to Kellogg, no. 2860G, August 17, 1927, RG 59, DF 1910–29, 832.00/635. By way of explanation the ambassador added that "local affairs interest the public more than those which are associated with a greater distance."

198. *O Jornal* (Rio), December 31, 1926; *Jornal do commercio* (Rio), March 11, 1927; *Gazeta de notícias* (Rio), February 1, 1927. However, the antigovernment *Correio da manhã* was scathing toward American intervention; see *Correio da manhã* (Rio), December 8, 1927. "This editorial is an isolated one," observed the American chargé, "and finds no echo in the main body of Brazilian public opinion; Schoenfeld to Kellogg, no. 2913G, December 10, 1927, RG 59, DF 1910–29, 832.00/641. Rudolf Schoenfeld acted as chargé d'affaires at the Rio embassy from 1927 until late 1929.

199. Kellogg to Fletcher, July 26, 1927, RG 59, Havana Conference, Entry 144, Box 425.

200. Fletcher to Kellogg, August 16; Kellogg to Hughes, October 1; and Kellogg to Coolidge, October 10, 1927, ibid.

201. Morgan to Kellogg, no. 2874, September 28, and no. 2903, November 15, 1927, ibid. For the official instructions given to the Brazilian delegation see MRE to Silvino, tel., no. 89, October 5, 1927, AHI 235/3/11.

202. For a brief outline of Mangabeira's conduct of foreign affairs see Yves de Oliveira, *Otávio Mangabeira* (Rio: Editôra Saga, 1971), 83–111.

203. Schoenfeld to Kellogg, no. 2906G, November 24, 1927, RG 59, DF 1910–29, 832.00/640. Financial bonuses and increased leave were introduced in 1928 "to overcome among Brazilian diplomatic officers an aversion to serve at South American posts." More attention was also given to maintaining diplomatic relations with the Central American and Caribbean republics; see Morgan to Kellogg, no. 2804G, May 14, 1927, and no. 2952G, February 1, 1928, ibid., 832.00/623 and 832.00/Political Reports/2.

204. Rodrigues Alves to MRE, tel., no. 6, January 9, 1928, AHI 208/2/6.

205. Silvino to MRE, tel., no. 204, November 3 and December 26, 1927, AHI 235/3/11.

206. Rodrigues Alves to MRE, no. 39, February 13, 1928, AHI 208/2/6. The Argentine foreign minister described Pueyrredón as "an engine out of control."

207. Rodrigues Alves to MRE, tel., no. 21, February 12, 1928, ibid., and Silvino to MRE, tel., no. 13, January 27, 1928, AHI 235/3/11. Brazil also assisted the United States by questioning the meaning of "intervention." Citing the example of health programs organized by the Rockefeller Foundation in Latin America, the Brazilian delegation argued that "intervention" in the affairs of other states could be beneficial. This was instrumental in preventing the blanket condemnation of intervention desired by some of the critics of the United States; see Morgan to Kellogg, no. 2966G, February 18, 1928, RG 59, DF 1910–29, 832.00/Political Reports/3.

208. Silvino to MRE, no. 51, February 20, and no. 70, February 23, 1928, AHI 234/4/12.

209. Alston to Chamberlain, no. 17, January 30, 1929, FO 371/13468.

210. The aim of Brazilian policy was "consolidating our friendship with the United States without annoying Argentina"; see MRE to Silvino, tel., no. 18, February 24, 1928, AHI 235/3/11.

211. See Morgan to Kellogg, no. 2975G, March 15, 1928, RG 59, DF 1910–29, 832.00/Political Reports/4. Brazil was also very complimentary toward American diplomatic efforts to resolve the Tacna-Arica dispute at this time. One newspaper remarked that the United States government "is always ready to serve as a mediator for attaining continental peace"; see *Jornal do Brasil* (Rio), July 15, 1928.

212. For the general diplomatic background to the pact see Robert H. Ferrell, *Peace In Their Time: The Origins of the Kellogg-Briand Pact* (New Haven: Yale University Press, 1952).

213. Morgan to Kellogg, no. 3028, July 6, 1928, RG 59, DF 1910–29, 711.3212/AntiWar/5.

214. Kellogg to Morgan, tel., June 29, 1928, ibid., 711.3212/AntiWar/3.

215. *Jornal do Brasil* (Rio), August 30, 1928.

216. Morgan to Kellogg, no. 3049, August 22, 1928, RG 59, DF 1910–29, 711.3212/AntiWar/11.

217. Silvino to MRE, tel., no. 138, September 1, 1928, AHI 235/3/11.

218. Morgan to Kellogg, tel., September 1, and no. 3058, September 6, 1928, RG 59, DF 1910–29, 711.3212/AntiWar/10 and 14.

219. In addition, the wish to exclude Spain from the signing ceremony also influenced the decision to leave out the Latin American nations; see Ellis, *Kellogg and American Foreign Relations*, 209.

220. Silvino to MRE, tel., no. 142, September 13; MRE to Silvino, tel., no. 73, September 15; Silvino to MRE, tel., no. 146, September 19, 1928, AHI 235/3/11. Even the sympathetic Morgan believed, however, that Brazil was being influenced by Argentina; see Morgan to Kellogg, no. 3058, September 6, 1928, RG 59, DF 1910–29, 711.3212/AntiWar/14.

221. Castle to McClure, September 14, 1928, RG 59, DF 1910–29, 711.3212/AntiWar/no document file number. William Castle was an assistant secretary of state. Wallace McClure served in the Treaty Division of the State Department.

222. Kellogg to Morgan, tel., September 14, 1928, ibid., 711.3212/AntiWar/13.

223. Morgan to Kellogg, no. 3071, September 26, ibid., 711.3212/AntiWar/16.

224. Kellogg to Morgan, tel., October 9, 1928, ibid., 711.3212/AntiWar/15.

225. Silvino to MRE, no. 328, September 17, 1928, AHI 235/1/2 and tel., no. 162, October 12, 1928, AHI 235/3/11; memorandum by White, October 13 and White to Silvino, October 13, 1928, RG 59, DF 1910–29, 711.3212/AntiWar/17 and 18.

226. Morgan to Kellogg, no. 3075, October 13, 1928, RG 59, DF 1910–29, 711.3212/AntiWar/20.

227. Memorandum by Kellogg, January 31, 1929, ibid., 711.3212/AntiWar/24. Kellogg remarked that Silvino was in favor of Brazil's adherence although the Brazilian ambassador's own report of the same interview mentions that he gave a guarded reply simply restating his government's position; see Silvino to MRE, tel., no. 45, January 31, 1929, AHI 235/3/12.

228. Kellogg to Morgan, tel., January 31, 1929, RG 59, DF 1910–29, 711.3212/AntiWar/23.

229. Morgan to Kellogg, tel., February 10, 1929, ibid., 711.3212/AntiWar/25. Brazil eventually gave its adherence to the Peace Pact in May 1934.

230. MRE to Silvino, tel., no. 36, February 15, 1929, AHI 235/3/12; Alston to Chamberlain, no. 69, April 23, 1929, FO 371/13469. In January 1929 Brazil gave a further demonstration of its capacity for diplomatic awkwardness by refusing to join the Pan-American arbitration commission proposed by the Washington Conference on Conciliation and Arbitration. This was particularly dismaying to the State Department because Brazil's membership had already been reported in the American press.

231. For example, see the Itamaraty's desire for a "major understanding" with Argentina expressed in MRE to Rodrigues Alves, tel., October 2, 1928, AHI 208/2/6. One diplomat considered that the basic aim of Mangabeira's continental strategy was an "entente" with Argentina; see Lyra, *Vida Diplomática,* 2:229.

232. Silvino to MRE, tel., no. 146, September 19, 1928, AHI 235/3/11.

CHAPTER 5: *Demise of an Era, 1928–1930*

1. Richard N. Current, *Secretary Stimson* (New Brunswick: Rutgers University Press, 1954), 43–44, and Robert Ferrell, *American Diplomacy in the Great Depression: Hoover–Stimson Foreign Policy, 1929–33* (New Haven: Yale University Press, 1957), 34–54.

2. Alexander DeConde, *Herbert Hoover's Latin-American Policy* (New York: Octagon Books, 1970), 17–18.

3. *Washington Post,* May 6, 1929.

4. *New York Times,* June 11, 1930.

5. Despite concern over the rise of Argentine influence in the region, the Itamaraty hesitated to side with either Paraguay or Bolivia over the Chaco question. Another example of the prevailing negative mood of Brazilian diplomacy was the decision not to rejoin the League of Nations. On the Chaco controversy see Leslie R. Rout, *Politics of the Chaco Peace Conference, 1935–1939* (Austin: University of Texas Press, 1970).

6. Morgan was absent during the São Paulo revolt of July 1924 as he was again to be during the 1932 revolt in that city. In 1906, when serving as ambassador to Cuba, Morgan was reprimanded by Theodore Roosevelt for being away in Europe at a time of grave political crisis on the island. Perhaps Morgan was unfortunate in that these crises coincided with his periods of leave. However, the writer cannot help thinking of the admonition in Oscar Wilde's *The Importance of Being Earnest* that one lost opportunity may be regarded as a misfortune but that more than two looks like carelessness.

7. See Boris Fausto, *A revolução de 1930* (São Paulo: Editôra brasiliense, 1970).

8. Morgan to Kellogg, no. 3024, July 2, 1928, RG 59, DF 1910–29, 832. 6133/293.

9. *O Jornal* (Rio), July 11, 1926.

10. Silvino to MRE, no. 7, May 16 and no. 24, June 22, 1927, AHI 234/4/10.

11. See article by Daniel de Carvalho in *O Paiz* (Rio), December 21, 1928.

12. Seidel, "Progressive Pan Americanism," 488–89. At about the same time the Commerce Department was instrumental in persuading American bankers not to give a loan to the Defense Institute; ibid., 483.

13. The American embassy at Rio instructed its officials to abstain from "official

intervention" in the coffee question; see Brandes, *Hoover and Economic Diplomacy,* 134.

14. Silvino to MRE, no. 287, August 18, 1928, AHI 235/1/2.

15. Morgan to Kellogg, no. 3024, July 2, 1928, RG 59, DF 1910–29, 832.6133/293.

16. In fact, only days after the presidential election Root had personally urged Hoover to make the trip to Latin America; see Root to Hoover, November 10, 1928, Hoover Papers, Campaign-Transition, Box 59.

17. The Brazilian ambassador considered that Hoover's visit "signifies a new point of departure in our relations"; see Silvino to MRE, tel., no. 177, November 9, and tel., no. 184, November 10, 1928, AHI 235/3/11.

18. *New York Times,* November 12, 1928.

19. The countries not visited were Mexico, Panama, Bolivia, Paraguay, Colombia, Venezuela, and the Caribbean republics.

20. The Hoover Papers contain an undated memorandum from Fletcher that obviously was intended to brief Hoover on his visit. Fletcher stated: "Good will is the mission of the tour . . . the visit is so important in these countries that those who may have had unfavorable impressions of North Americans are prepared to date a new attitude from this time. Do you give them a chance?" Hoover Papers, Campaign-Transition, Box 170.

21. Hoover to Root, November 16, 1928; ibid., Box 59.

22. See Klein to Ash, November 12, 1928; ibid., Box 44.

23. Press Meeting, November 20, 1928; ibid., Box 170.

24. *New York Times,* December 23, 1928. For a contrasting British view that the occasion attracted only "mildly curious spectators" see Alston to Chamberlain, no. 17, January 30, 1929, FO 371/13468.

25. See *New York Herald Tribune,* December 23, 1928.

26. *Review of Reviews* (New York), 79 (1929), 53–57.

27. *Christian Science Monitor,* December 22, 1928; *New York Post,* December 21, 1928.

28. *New York Herald Tribune,* December 22 and 23, 1928.

29. *A Crítica* (Rio), December 21, 1928. Politeness required that no direct reference was made to the fact that Hoover was known to be unsympathetic to blacks and that he personally favored restrictions on immigration into the United States. In 1924 he had stated his regret that Puerto Ricans were admitted as immigrants while "Nordics" were being excluded; see Alexander DeConde, "Herbert Hoover's Foreign Policy: A Retrospective Assessment," in *Herbert Hoover Reassessed,* 96th Congress, 2d sess., Senate Doc. 96–63 (Washington D.C.: GPO, 1981), 316.

30. *New York Herald Tribune,* December 23, 1928.

31. *Wileman's Brazilian Review* (Rio), December 27, 1928.

32. *O Jornal* (Rio), December 22, 1928.

33. *Jornal do Brasil* (Rio), December 26, 1928.

34. *New York Evening Post,* December 22, 1928.

35. *New York Star,* December 24, 1928.

36. Press Meeting, December 31, 1928, Hoover Papers, Campaign-Transition, Box 170.

37. Silvino to MRE, tel., no. 184, November 10, 1928, AHI 235/3/11.

38. Hoover did mention the coffee question in his talks with Washington Luís; see Seidel, "Progressive Pan Americanism," 493.

39. Alston to Chamberlain, no. 17, January 30, 1929, FO 371/13468. For the controversy surrounding Hoover's statements made in Argentina see DeConde, *Hoover's Latin-American Policy,* 21–22.

40. MRE to Silvino, tel., no. 36, February 15, 1929, AHI 235/3/12.

41. Morgan to Stimson, no. 3128G, March 13, 1929, RG 59, DF 1910–29, 832.00/General Conditions/17. Hoover still remained ambivalent in his attitude toward valorization. In May 1929 the State Department stated that the president wished American bankers not to participate in a coffee loan to São Paulo. However, despite objections from Commerce Department officials, Hoover reversed this policy in April 1930; See Fritsch, *External Constraints On Brazil,* 147 and Seidel, "Progressive Pan Americanism," 498.

42. *Washington Post,* May 6, 1929.

43. For economic statistics see Valla, "Estados Unidos na economia brasileira," 162–63, Winkler, *Investments of U.S. Capital,* 274–85, and Normano, *Struggle For South America,* 34–47. A contemporary estimate was that 80 percent of new capital in 1928 was derived from the United States; see Seidel, "Progressive Pan Americanism," 558.

44. Morgan to Kellogg, no. 2753G, February 16, and no. 2822G, June 11, 1927, RG 59, DF 1910–29, 832.00/615 and 630.

45. See reports by Cameron, no. 72, "Mato Grosso and Its Finances," December 24, 1927, ibid., 832.51M43/2, and no. 232, "Parana State Loan," April 22, 1929, ibid., 832.51P21/9.

46. Quoted in Seidel, "Progressive Pan Americanism," 557. The publication from 1925 to 1929 of numerous "Special Circulars" on investment prospects in Brazil indicated that the Commerce Department was actively interested in promoting American loans to that country; see ibid., 551–58.

47. Morgan to Kellogg, no. 2884, October 12, 1927, RG 59, DF 1910–29, 832.52/505.

48. For a descriptive survey of the economic crisis see Jordan M. Young, *The Brazilian Revolution of 1930 and Its Aftermath* (New Brunswick: Rutgers University Press, 1967), 70–80 and Fritsch, *External Constraints on Brazil,* 138–59.

49. Memorandum on "Brazil" by Division of Latin American Affairs, August 22, 1922, RG 59, DF 1910–29, 832.00/255.

50. The same tradition was also referred to as "café com leite."

51. Undated memorandum by Sherwell, Hoover Papers, Campaign-Transition, Box 167.

52. *Correio da manhã* (Rio), December 22, 1928; *New York Times,* December 24, 1928.

53. Castle to Hoover, January 21, 1929, Hoover Papers, Presidential, Box 67.

54. Ferrell, *American Diplomacy in the Great Depression,* 38–39.

55. Stimson to Morgan, no. 1449, May 23, 1929, RG 59, DF 1910–29, 832.00/644A.

56. Morgan to Stimson, no. 3175, June 14, 1929, ibid., 832.00/646.

57. Morgan to Stimson, no. 3171G, June 5, 1929, ibid., 832.00/General Conditions/20. Brazil's representative, Miss Olga Bergamini de Sá, did not win the pageant.

The American chargé reported that the result "has given rise to no untoward reaction locally, despite the notable interest and optimism with which her trip was accompanied"; Schoenfeld to Stimson, no. 3185G, July 1, 1929; ibid., 832.00/General Conditions/21.

58. Schoenfeld to Stimson, no. 3213G, August 21, 1929, ibid., 832.00/General Conditions/23, and no. 3227, September 7, 1929, ibid., 832.00/Presidential Campaigns/6.

59. Report no. 888 by Major Lester Baker on "Current Political Situation in Brazil," September 10, 1929, ibid., 832.00 (no separate file number). In keeping with the negative mood of the period, State Department officials were pleased to learn that Brazilian newspapers were "practically silent" on the controversial subject of American military intervention in Haiti. Morgan to Stimson, tel., no. 59, December 23, 1929, ibid., 838.00/2655.

60. Morgan to Stimson, no. 3271, December 18, 1929, ibid., 832.00/Presidential Campaigns/10. The ambassador was particularly appalled by the occurrence of political assassination. After the murder of Sousa Filho in the lobby of the congressional building he noted: "So long as the majority of Brazilians are accustomed to carry revolvers or knives as a part of their daily equipment, in moments of anger arising from whatever cause, murders . . . are not unlikely to occur in moments of passion"; Morgan to Stimson, no. 3274, December 30, 1929, ibid., 832.00/652.

61. Morgan to Stimson, no. 3290, February 11, and no. 3321, April 8, 1930, RG 59, DF 1930–39, 832.00/654 and 656.

62. See minute by Manning on Morgan to Stimson, no. 3321, April 8, 1930, ibid., 832.00/656.

63. Silvino to MRE, no. 115, March 15, 1930, AHI 235/1/10; *Washington Post*, March 7, 1930. The American editors overlooked the fact that no more than 5 percent of Brazil's population had cast their votes in the presidential election.

64. Silvino to MRE, no. 448, September 5, 1929, AHI 235/1/8.

65. Silvino to MRE, tel., no. 159, June 22, 1929, and MRE to Silvino, tel., no. 102, July 1, 1929, AHI 235/3/12. Prestes's trip also included a visit to Europe as well as the United States.

66. Morgan to Stimson, no. 3346, May 14, 1930, RG 59, DF 1930–39, 832.001/Julio Prestes/47.

67. Barrett to Richey, June 9, 1930, Hoover Papers, Presidential, Box 981. Lawrence Richey was Hoover's private secretary.

68. *Public Papers of the Presidents of the United States, Herbert Hoover, 1930* (Washington, D.C.: GPO, 1976), 226.

69. *New York Times,* June 11, 1930; *New York Evening Post,* June 14, 1930.

70. Silvino to MRE, no. 248, June 30, 1930, AHI 235/1/11. The arrival of Prestes at New York was actually described on shortwave radio by the National Broadcasting Company. However, the topic of the moment on the East coast was not Prestes but the forthcoming boxing contest between Jack Sharkey of the United States and the German champion, Max Schmeling; see *New York Evening Post,* June 9, 1930.

71. Speech by Prestes, June 14, 1930, Hoover Papers, Presidential, Box 981.

72. Morgan to Stimson, no. 3397, August 13, 1930, RG 59, DF 1930–39, 832.001/Julio Prestes/169.

73. Seeds to Henderson, no. 42, February 23, 1931, FO 371/15067; Cameron to Morgan, August 1, 1930, RG 59, DF 1930–39, 832.00/664.

74. Morgan to Stimson, tel., no. 53, September 2, 1930, ibid., 832.00/666.

75. Quoted in Love, *Rio Grande do Sul and Brazilian Regionalism,* 241.

76. The British ambassador remarked that Morgan would tolerate only one diplomatic secretary serving under him. He was so jealous that he had deliberately kept Walter Washington "in utter darkness, or at the best a dim twilight"; see Seeds to Henderson, no. 2, January 3, 1931, FO 371/15065. This view of Morgan as difficult and aloof contrasts with an earlier and much more sympathetic recollection by Hugh Wilson who served as his private secretary at Lisbon in 1911: "I took leave of Mr. Morgan with real regret. He had taken endless trouble to train me in detail, and the example of his technique with foreign officials has often been useful. . . . He knew his job and did his best to teach it to me. I had no claim on him and was grateful for his kindness"; *Education of a Diplomat,* 27.

77. Washington to Stimson, no. 3435, October 15, 1930, RG 59, DF 1930–39, 832.00/Revolutions/172.

78. Memorandum of Press Conference, October 24, 1930 and Stimson to Morgan, tel., no. 78, November 5, 1930, ibid., 832.00/Revolutions/169 and 199.

79. Memorandum by Thurston to Schoenfeld, August 1, 1930, ibid., 832.00/661.

80. Washington to Stimson, tel., no. 78, October 9; Stimson to Washington, tel., no. 57, October 8, and tel., no. 60, October 11, 1930, ibid., 832.00/Revolutions/29, 37 and 44; photocopy of Henry L. Stimson Diary [hereafter cited as Stimson Diary], Herbert Hoover Presidential Library, October 10, 1930. "As usual the Navy leaked," commented Stimson. The *Pensacola* did not actually reach Bahia until October 25 by which time the civil war was over.

81. Gresham to Thompson, October 25, 1893, RG 59, *Brazil,* Instructions, 18.

82. Memorandum of Press Conference, October 24, 1930, RG 59, DF 1930–39, 832.00/Revolutions/169. The revolt in Brazil was regarded as possessing the characteristics not of a typical Latin American coup but of the American Civil War. "The struggle," stated one newspaper editorial, "takes the form of a war between States"; see *New York Times,* October 8, 1930. The same analogy was also present in the minds of American diplomats. Reviewing the issue a few years later in 1933, an official concluded: "With reference to the revolutionists . . . they had not formed a real Government, similar to that of the Confederacy in our Civil War, which held complete control over a considerable expanse of territory. The situation appeared to the Department to be merely a case of the attempt of a disappointed faction to overthrow the constituted authorities. Consequently, the question of recognizing the belligerency of the insurgents was not viewed with favor"; see "Review of Questions of Major Interest in the Relations of the United States with Latin American Countries, 1929–1933," 1:10–11, Hoover Papers, Presidential, Cabinet Offices, Box 49.

83. Memorandum by Hackworth, October 13, 1930, RG 59, DF 1930–39, 832.01/23; memorandum by Stimson, October 14, 1930, ibid., 832.248/10. Green H. Hackworth acted as Solicitor to the State Department.

84. *Washington Post,* October 23, 1930. The embargo actually originated from within the State Department. The confusion arose because Stimson sought to conceal this by asking Silvino to make a formal request prior to its issue. See Stimson Diary,

October 22, 1930. To Stimson's embarrassment it was revealed that his subterfuge was unnecessary owing to the existence of a convention dating from the 1928 Havana Conference that called upon signatories to export arms only to legally constituted authorities during periods of civil disorder. The United States had ratified this convention only as recently as June 1930.

85. "Press Release," October 23, 1930; cited in *Foreign Relations* (1930), 1:443.

86. Stimson Diary, October 15, 1930; *New York Times,* October 16, 1930.

87. Washington to Stimson, no. 3435, October 15, and tel., October 21, 1930, RG 59, DF 1930–39, 832.00/Revolutions/172 and 123. Information was so scarce that as late as October 17 one daily was reporting that "the rebels now face a desperate situation, in which every day of delay and disappointment works for the demoralization of their forces and a public reaction against them"; *Washington Post,* October 17, 1930.

88. See the comments of Drew Pearson in *Baltimore Sun,* November 9, 1930. The fact that the Commerce Department had all along predicted a victory for the rebels also perplexed journalists and made them question the accuracy of the State Department's sources of information; see British Chancery at Washington to the Foreign Office, November 14, 1930, FO 371/14202.

89. Morgan to Stimson, tel., no. 121, October 23, 1930, RG 59, DF 1930–39, 832.00/Revolutions/140. A British report noted later: "Mr. Morgan may be putting all the blame now on Mr. Washington but he must have been equally blind himself, for we know as a fact that on his first day back (when things were working up for a crisis) he spent hours paying social calls on ladies etc., apparently satisfied that all was for the best. The extreme depression in which Sir William Seeds found him immediately after the revolution of October 24th showed what a blow it had been to him"; see British Chancery at Washington to Foreign Office, December 29, 1930, FO 371/15059.

90. Morgan to Stimson, tel., no. 121, October 23, 1930, RG 59, DF 1930–39, 832.00/Revolutions/140.

91. Memorandum by White, October 16, 1930, ibid., 832.00/Revolutions/112.

92. *Washington Post,* October 25, 1930.

93. *New York Times,* October 25, 1930.

94. Stimson Diary, October 24–25, 1930. On Stimson's attempts to justify his policy see Current, *Stimson,* 52–55.

95. The State Department circular dated September 17, 1930 is cited in *Foreign Relations* (1930) 1:387–89.

96. State Department dispatches contain few references to Getúlio Vargas before his rise to power in 1930. He had served as minister of finance from 1926 to 1927 and was reputed to be competent and honest. The image of a regional politico rather than a national leader was underlined by Morgan's description of him in 1927 as "a conciliatory and conservative politician of considerable authority with the Rio Grande 'bancada'"; Morgan to Kellogg, no. 2847, August 2, 1927, RG 59, DF 1910–29, 832.00/634.

97. Memorandum by Stimson, October 27, 1930, RG 59, DF 1930–39, 832.00/Revolutions/168.

98. Morgan to Stimson, tel., no. 137, November 3, 1930, ibid., 832.01.1.

99. Stimson to Morgan, tel., no. 78, November 5, 1930, ibid., 832.00/Revolutions/199.

100. Memorandum by White, November 6, 1930, ibid., 832.01/13.

101. Morgan to Stimson, tel., no. 144, November 7, 1930, ibid., 832.00/Revolutions/200. The British ambassador at Rio considered that Morgan "was hampered from the outset" by his government's insistence on "the necessity for a revolutionary Government to legalise their status by some form of popular election"; Seeds to Henderson, no. 190, November 10, 1930, FO 371/14203.

102. Stimson to Morgan, tels., November 7 and 8, Morgan to Stimson, tel., November 8, 1930, RG 59, DF 1930–39, 832.01/3, 6B, 21A and 22. On learning that the United States government could not make a decision before November 8, the Foreign Office actually proposed to delay its own action until November 10. When the British ambassador informed the State Department of this, White had to reply that his own government had already decided to recognize. For this and similar embarrassment concerning France see Joseph Smith, "United States Diplomacy Toward Political Revolt in Brazil, 1889–1930," *Inter-American Economic Affairs* 37 (1983): 19–20.

103. Stimson Diary, November 7, 1930. The Washington correspondent of the *New York Times* faithfully reported: "There is confidence here that, regardless of immediate political and diplomatic developments, trade between the United States and Brazil will not be adversely affected. Economic currents are such, it is contended, that business is certain to be maintained in strong volume between the two countries and particularly because of advantages to Brazil"; *New York Times,* October 26, 1930.

104. Stimson Diary, November 7, 1930.

105. The statement is printed in Morgan to Stimson, tel., November 8, 1930, *Foreign Relations* (1930), 1:451. By November 8 the new Brazilian government had established diplomatic relations with Argentina, Britain, Chile, France, Portugal, United States, Uruguay, and the Vatican.

106. Stimson Diary, November 8, 1930.

107. *Washington Post,* November 4, 1930.

108. The recognition of Mexico and Brazil in 1822–1823 had also caused particular problems for American diplomacy.

109. Nasmith to Stimson, tel., October 17, 1930, *Foreign Relations* (1930), 1: 438–39. The anti-American demonstrations in the Northeast were motivated by nationalist sensitivity against the sheer size of American business interests and the suspicion that Americans were responsible for the prevailing economic distress. The British consul at Pernambuco reported the local fear "that American interests in Brazil are becoming so far-reaching as to be likely to affect ultimately the independence and integrity of the Republic"; Mackness to Henderson, no. 34, November 12, 1930, FO 371/14203.

110. Morgan to Stimson, no. 3494, December 27, 1930, RG 59, DF 1930–39, 832.00B/21, and no. 3470, December 5, 1930, ibid., 832.00/693. In an earlier dispatch Morgan had sought to reassure the State Department that the display of red flags commemorating the rebel victory "indicate revolution and not communism"; Morgan to Stimson, tel., no. 124, October 24, 1930, ibid., 832.00/Revolutions/146. In fact, Morgan had never given much credence to the threat of communism in Brazil. His longest dispatch on this subject was in 1926 and ended with the conclusion: "There are probably few countries where the Communist or Socialist Parties find less terrain in which to operate successfully than in Brasil, which for many years to come will re-

main agricultural, on account of the uncultivated and productive conditions of her soil and the scarcity of population in comparison to acreage. Industries and manufactures occupy the attention of only a small portion of the population and will continue to do so until the vast unoccupied areas are filled"; Morgan to Kellogg, no. 2623, August 6, 1926, ibid., 832.00B.

111. Morgan to Lansing, no. 1052, November 13, 1917, RG 59, DF 1910–29, 832.20/16.

112. Morgan to Stimson, November 12, 1930, RG 59, DF 1930–39, 832.00/ Revolutions/227.

113. The British ambassador at Rio was critical of "the indecent way in which Morgan ran down his former friends in order to ingratiate himself with the new administration"; see British Chancery at Washington to Foreign Office, December 29, 1930, FO 371/15059. A different slant was given by Maurício Nabuco who recalled Morgan saying to him that the doors of the embassy would be closed to those seeking asylum but that he could enter by the kitchen door; see Nabuco, *Reminiscências*, 78.

114. Lindolfo Collor, quoted in Moniz Bandeira, *Presença dos Estados Unidos*, 227.

115. Seeds to Henderson, no. 190, November 10, 1930, and no. 42, February 23, FO 371/14203 and 15067.

116. Memorandum by White, October 31, 1930, RG 59, DF 1930–39, 832.30/ 216. Agreement to renew the naval contract had been reached during October, but Stimson resisted Silvino's suggestion that this be formally communicated to the provisional government; see Stimson Diary, October 31, 1930.

117. Seeds to Foreign Office, no. 145, December 1, 1930, FO 371/14203. On the return of American naval instructors see memorandum by Stimson, March 10, 1932, RG 59, DF 1930–39, 832.30/237.

118. The friendly tone of relations was established in May 1808. President Thomas Jefferson symbolically sent a message of welcome to the Portuguese royal family when he learned of their safe crossing from Lisbon to Brazil.

119. Rio Branco to Gomes Ferreira, no. 1, January 31, 1905, AHI 235/2/6.

120. Griscom to Root, July 16, 1906, RG 59, NF 1113/2.

121. Stimson, *My United States*, 294.

122. MRE to Silvino, tel., no. 36, February 15, 1929, AHI 235/3/12.

123. The concept of the collapse of the "old order" is taken from Arthur M. Schlesinger, Jr., *The Crisis of the Old Order: 1919–1933* (Boston: Houghton Mifflin, 1957).

124. On Brazilian foreign policy after 1930 see Stanley E. Hilton, *Brazil and the Great Powers, 1930–1939* (Austin: University of Texas Press, 1975), and John D. Wirth, *The Politics of Brazilian Development, 1930–1954* (Stanford: Stanford University Press, 1969).

125. Seeds to Henderson, no. 42, February 23, 1931, FO 371/15067.

BIBLIOGRAPHICAL ESSAY

The notes are intended to provide a supplement to the text and to serve as a reference and guide to further reading material. The following essay lists the bibliographical aids, documentary sources, and a selection of the main secondary works that have been used for this study.

BIBLIOGRAPHIES

There is no single bibliography on diplomatic relations between the United States and Brazil. The essential reference source for books and articles on Latin America is the annual *Handbook of Latin American Studies* (Cambridge: Harvard University Press, 1936–1951; Gainesville: University of Florida Press, 1961–). For works on American diplomacy selective use should be made of Richard D. Burns, ed., *Guide to American Foreign Relations since 1700* (Santa Barbara, Calif.: ABC-Clio, 1983) and David F. Trask, Michael C. Meyer, and Roger R. Trask, eds., *A Bibliography of United States–Latin American Relations since 1910* (Lincoln: University of Nebraska Press, 1968). Other useful references for American history and Latin American studies are Frank Freidel, ed., *Harvard Guide to American History,* 2 vols. (Cambridge: Harvard University Press, 1974), and Charles C. Griffin and J. Benedict Warren, eds., *Latin America: A Guide to the Historical Literature* (Austin: University of Texas Press, 1971). The standard but dated bibliography on Brazilian works in general is Rubens Borba de Moraes and William Berrien, eds., *Manual bibliográfico de estudos brasileiros* (Rio: Souza, 1949). Excellent guides to more recent studies on Brazilian history are Robert M. Levine, *Brazil, 1822–1930: An Annotated Bibliography for Social Historians* (New York: Garland, 1983), and Thomas E. Skidmore, "The Historiography of Brazil, 1889–1964," *Hispanic American Historical Review* 55 (1975): 716–48, and 56 (1976): 81–109.

DOCUMENTARY SOURCES

The fundamental manuscript sources consulted were the unpublished records of the Department of State and the Brazilian Ministry of Foreign Relations. American diplomatic correspondence relating to Brazil can be examined at the National Archives in Washington, D.C. Brazilian records up to 1930 were made available to me at the Arquivo Histórico do Itamaraty in Rio. I also made extensive use of the Foreign Office volumes on relations between Britain and Brazil located in the Public Record Office, London. The papers of other government departments and a few private papers were also consulted, but their value for this particular study proved limited. Useful supplementary information was found in newspapers such as the *New York Times* and the *Times* (London). Moreover, a large number of diplomatic dispatches, especially those from the Brazilian embassy at Washington, regularly contained clippings and thereby provided an invaluable summary of press opinion. The study of American foreign relations is also greatly facilitated by the fact that most American diplomatic records for the period up to 1929 can be purchased in microfilm form. A small amount of correspondence is printed in the State Department's annual *Papers Relating to the Foreign Relations of the United States* and the Itamaraty's annual *Relatório do ministério das relações exteriores.*

GENERAL WORKS

The historical literature on United States–Brazilian relations has been dominated by American historians and they have accorded relatively little attention to the period of the Old Republic. The notable exceptions are Victor C. Valla, *A penetração norte-americano na economia brasileira, 1898–1928* (Rio: Livro Técnico, 1978), and Earl Richard Downes, "The Seeds of Influence: Brazil's 'Essentially Agricultural' Old Republic and the United States, 1910–1930" (Ph.D diss., University of Texas, 1986), which both highlight economic factors. Of the older studies, traditional diplomatic history is well represented by Lawrence F. Hill, *Diplomatic Relations between the United States and Brazil* (Durham: Duke University Press, 1932); Lawrence F. Hill, "The United States," in *Brazil,* ed. Lawrence F. Hill (Berkeley and Los Angeles: University of California Press, 1947), 344–66; and the sections on relations with Brazil in Graham H. Stuart, *Latin America and the United States* (New York: Appleton-Century-Crofts, 1955), 413–47, and J. Lloyd Mecham, *A Survey of United States–Latin American Relations* (New York: Houghton Mifflin, 1965), 432–58. The most recent American studies by Roger W. Fontaine, *Brazil and the United States* (Washington, D.C.: American Enterprise Institute for Public Policy Research, 1974), and Robert G. Wesson, *The United States and Brazil: Limits of Influence* (New York: Praeger, 1981), adopt a more analytical approach, but are preoccupied with contemporary issues and only briefly mention the historical background. A brief and perceptive essay is Thomas E. Skidmore, "Brazil's American Illusion: From Dom Pedro II to the Coup of 1964," *Luso-Brazilian Review* 23 (1986): 71–84. The virtual American monopoly of the historical interpretation on this subject has, however, been vigorously challenged by Moniz Bandeira, *Presença dos Estados Unidos no Brasil* (Rio: Civilização brasileira, 1973) although only a small portion of this ambitious study is concerned with the Old Republic.

For the history of the Brazilian republic the best guide for English readers is José Maria Bello, *A History of Modern Brazil, 1889–1964,* trans. James L. Taylor (Stanford: Stanford University Press, 1966). Joseph L. Love, *Rio Grande do Sul and Brazilian Regionalism, 1882–1930* (Stanford: Stanford University Press, 1971) is also informative on political matters. The relevant sections of E. Bradford Burns, *A History of Brazil* (New York: Columbia University Press, 1970) are also recommended. Gilberto Freyre, *Order and Progress: Brazil from Monarchy to Republic,* trans. Rod W. Horton (New York: Knopf, 1970), expresses the ideas of the period, while the social structure is analyzed by Edgard Carone, *A república velha: instituições e classes sociais* (São Paulo: Difel, 1970), and Boris Fausto, "Brazil: The Social and Political Structure of the First Republic, 1889–1930," in *The Cambridge History of Latin America,* 5 vols. to date, ed. Leslie Bethell (Cambridge: Cambridge University Press, 1986–), 5:779–829.

Of the many works on Brazilian economic history see Celso Furtado, *The Economic Growth of Brazil,* trans. Ricardo W. de Aguiar and Eric C. Drysdale (Berkeley and Los Angeles: University of California Press, 1963), and Annibal V. Villela and Wilson Suzigan, *Política do governo e crescimento da economia brasileira, 1889–1945* (Rio: INPES, 1973). For statistics on Brazilian trade and investment see Victor Valla, "Os Estados Unidos e a influencia estrangeira na economia brasileira: um período de transição (1904– 1928)," *Revista de História* 44 (1972): 143–64, and Max Winkler, *Investments of United States Capital in Latin America* (Boston: World Peace Foundation, 1929). The study of the economy of the Old Republic has now been enormously aided by the appearance of Steven Topik, *The Political Economy of the Brazilian State, 1889–1930* (Austin: University of Texas Press, 1987), and Winston Fritsch, *External Constraints on Economic Policy in Brazil, 1889–1930* (Pittsburgh: University of Pittsburgh Press, 1988).

An excellent analysis of Brazilian diplomacy is José Honório Rodrigues, *Interésse nacional e política externa* (Rio: Civilização brasileira, 1966). This interpretation is also conveniently summarized in the same author's "The Foundations of Brazil's Foreign Policy," *International Affairs* 38 (1962): 324–38. Among the standard works on Brazilian foreign policy the following are useful: Delgado de Carvalho, *História diplomática do Brasil* (São Paulo: Companhia editôra nacional, 1959); Pedro Calmon, *Brasil e América* (Rio: José Olympio, 1943); and the recent short survey by Amado Luiz Cervo and Clodoaldo Bueno, *A política externa brasileira, 1822–1985* (São Paulo: Editôra Atica, 1986). Extremely valuable for the whole period of the Old Republic are the insights and diplomatic documents contained in Heitor Lyra, *Minha vida diplomática,* 2 vols. (Brasília: Universidade de Brasília, 1981), and Afonso Arinos de Melo Franco, *Um estadista da República: Afrânio de Melo franca e seu tempo,* 3 vols. (Rio: José Olympio, 1955). For the views of American scholars see Lawrence F. Hill, "Europe and the South American Neighbors," in *Brazil,* ed. Lawrence F. Hill, 325–43, and the perceptive analysis of Bradford E. Burns, "Tradition and Variation in Brazilian Foreign Policy," *Journal of Inter-American Studies* 9 (1967): 195–212. The pervasive influence of Argentina on Brazilian diplomacy can be studied in Miguel Angel Scenna, *Argentina-Brasil: Cuatro siglos de rivalidad* (Buenos Aires, Argentina: Las Bastilla, 1975) and Harold F. Peterson, *Argentina and the United States, 1810–1960* (Albany: State University of New York Press, 1964).

SISTER REPUBLICS, 1889–1901

The rise of the United States to the status of a world power is discussed in Charles S. Campbell, *The Transformation of American Foreign Relations, 1865–1900* (New York: Harper and Row, 1976), and Robert L. Beisner, *From the Old Diplomacy to the New,*

1865–1900 (New York: Crowell, 1975). On the growing American interest in Latin America see Joseph Smith, *Illusions of Conflict: Anglo-American Diplomacy toward Latin America, 1865–1896* (Pittsburgh: University of Pittsburgh Press, 1979). The influence of economic factors on American policy is presented in Walter LaFeber, *The New Empire: An Interpretation of American Expansion, 1860–1898* (Ithaca: Cornell University Press, 1963). The best guide to the complex question of reciprocity is David M. Pletcher, "Reciprocity and Latin America in the Early 1890s: A Foretaste of Dollar Diplomacy," *Pacific Historical Review* 47 (1978): 53–89. A survey of American press opinion on the fall of the republic is contained in J. Fred Rippy, "The United States and the Establishment of the Republic of Brazil," *Southwestern Political and Social Science Quarterly* 3 (1922): 39–53.

The literature on Brazilian affairs is much less abundant. For a guide to political events see the general works of Bello and Love. Also useful are Eduardo Kugelmas, "A primeira república no período de 1891 a 1909," in *Pequenos estudos de ciência política*, ed. Paula Beiguelman (São Paulo: Pioneira editôra, 1973), 189–225, and June E. Hahner, *Civilian-Military Relations in Brazil, 1889–1898* (Columbia: University of South Carolina Press, 1969). On the diplomatic events of this period see Arthur Guimarães de Araujo Jorge, *Ensaios de história diplomática do Brasil no regímen republicano, 1889–1902* (Rio: Imprensa nacional, 1912). An excellent introduction to the wider diplomatic perspective is Robert N. Burr, *By Reason Or Force: Chile and the Balancing of Power in South America, 1830–1905* (Berkeley and Los Angeles: University of California Press, 1965). An indispensable work for the study of diplomacy is Salvador de Mendonça, *A situação internacional do Brasil* (Paris: Garnier, 1913). Two invaluable collections of Salvador's correspondence are Carlos Süssekind de Mendonça, *Salvador de Mendonça: Democrata do império e de república* (Rio: Instituto nacional do livro, 1960), and José Afonso Mendonça Azevedo, *Vida e obra de Salvador de Mendonça* (Rio: Ministério das relações exteriores, 1971).

The Naval Revolt has attracted increasing attention from historians. Still informative are Sergio Corrêa da Costa, *A diplomacia do marechal: Intervenção estrangeira na revolta da armada* (Rio: Tempo brasileiro, 1979), and Michael B. McCloskey, "The United States and the Brazilian Naval Revolt, 1893–1894," *The Americas* 2 (1946): 296–321. Economic factors are stressed in Walter LaFeber, "United States Depression Diplomacy and the Brazilian Revolution, 1893–1894," *Hispanic American Historical Review* 40 (1960): 107–18. British attitudes are examined by Joseph Smith, "Britain and the Brazilian Naval Revolt of 1893–4," *Journal of Latin American Studies* 2 (1970): 175–98. The historical debate has been further enlivened by the following articles: Charles W. Calhoun, "American Policy toward the Brazilian Naval Revolt of 1893–94: A Reexamination," *Diplomatic History* 4 (1980): 39–56; James F. Vivian, "United States Policy during the Brazilian Naval Revolt, 1893–94: The Case for American Neutrality," *American Neptune* 41 (1981): 245–61; and Clodoaldo Bueno, "A diplomacia da 'Consolidação': a intervenção estrangeira na revolta da armada (1893/94)," *História* 3 (1984): 33–52.

YEARS OF APPROXIMATION, 1902–1912

The period from 1902 to 1912 is admirably interpreted in E. Bradford Burns, *The Unwritten Alliance: Rio Branco and Brazilian-American Relations* (New York: Columbia University Press, 1966). Frederic W. Ganzert, "The Baron do Rio Branco, Joaquim Nabuco and the Growth of Brazilian-American Friendship, 1900–1910," *Hispanic American Historical Review* 22 (1942): 432–51, is now very dated. More useful are William N. Nelson, "Status and Prestige as a Factor in Brazilian Foreign Policy, 1905–1908" (Ph.D diss., Louisiana State University, 1981), and Carl M. Jenks, "The Structure of Diplomacy: An Analysis of Brazilian Foreign Relations in the Twentieth Century" (Ph.D diss., Duke University, 1979), which provides excellent insights on the nature of Brazilian diplomacy.

The best biographies of Rio Branco are Alvaro Lins, *Rio Branco: biografia pessoal e história política* (São Paulo: Companhia editôra nacional, 1965), and Luiz Viana Filho, *A vida do barão do Rio Branco* (Rio: José Olympio, 1959). A perceptive modern analysis is Clodoaldo Bueno, "Política Exterior de Rio Branco," *Anais de História* 9 (1977): 101–25. On Nabuco see Luiz Viana Filho, *A vida de Joaquim Nabuco* (São Paulo: Companhia editôra nacional, 1952), and Carolina Nabuco, *The Life of Joaquim Nabuco*, trans. Ronald Hilton (Stanford: Stanford University Press, 1950). An excellent study of Nabuco's diplomacy is João Frank da Costa, *Joaquim Nabuco e a política exterior do Brasil* (Rio: Gráfica record editôra, 1968). For his personal views, especially on the United States, consult Joaquim Nabuco, *Minha formação* (São Paulo: Companhia editôra nacional, 1934).

The outstanding overview of the relationship between progressivism and American foreign policy toward Latin America is Robert N. Seidel, "Progressive Pan Americanism: Development and United States Policy toward South America, 1906–1931" (Ph.D diss., Cornell University, 1973). A succinct analysis of American diplomacy during the era of Theodore Roosevelt is Raymond E. Esthus, "Isolationism and World Power," *Diplomatic History* 2 (1978): 117–29. The standard biography of Root is Philip C. Jessup, *Elihu Root*, 2 vols. (New York: Dodd, Mead, 1938). For a less comprehensive but more modern treatment see Patrick D. DeFroscia, "The Diplomacy of Elihu Root, 1905–1909" (Ph.D diss., Temple University, 1976). Walter V. and Marie V. Scholes, *The Foreign Policies of the Taft Administration* (Columbia: University of Missouri Press, 1970), says little about Brazil, but provides the basic study of the Latin American policy of the Taft presidency. For the views of contemporary American diplomats see Francis M. Huntington-Wilson, *Memoirs of an Ex-Diplomat* (Boston: B. Humphries, 1945), and Lloyd Griscom, *Diplomatically Speaking* (London: John Murray, 1941).

A fine study of the Acre dispute is Charles E. Stokes, "The Acre Revolutions, 1899–1903: A Study in Brazilian Expansionism" (Ph.D diss., Tulane University, 1974). Useful information on this question can be found in Lewis A. Tambs, "Rubber, Rebels, and Rio Branco," *Hispanic American Historical Review* 66 (1966): 254–73; Frederic W. Ganzert, "The Boundary Controversy in the Upper Amazon between Brazil, Bolivia, and Peru, 1903–1909," *Hispanic American Historical Review* 14 (1934): 427–49; and Warren Dean, *Brazil and the Struggle for Rubber: A Study in Environmental History* (Cambridge: Cambridge University Press, 1987). John Bassett Moore, "Brazil and Peru Boundary Question" in *The Collected Papers of John Bassett Moore*, 7 vols. (New Haven: Yale University Press, 1944), 3:120–42, provides a valuable insight into contemporary opinions on the matter.

The Pan-American conference system has received authoritative examination by Samuel G. Inman, *Inter-American Conferences, 1826–1954: History and Problems* (Washington, D.C.: University Press of Washington D.C.: 1965). For descriptive accounts of the Rio conference see Thomas F. McGann, *Argentina, the United States, and the Inter-American System, 1880–1914* (Cambridge: Harvard University Press, 1957), and A. Curtis Wilgus, "The Third International American Conference at Rio de Janeiro, 1906," *Hispanic American Historical Review* 12 (1932): 420–56. The leading work on the Hague peace conference is Calvin D. Davis, *The United States and the Second Hague Peace Conference* (Durham: Duke University Press, 1975).

CONFLICT AND CONFORMITY, 1912–1920

Two excellent works on this period are Seidel, "Progressive Pan Americanism," 67–135, and Christopher J. R. Leuchars, "Brazilian Foreign Policy and the Great Powers, 1912–1930" (D.Phil. thesis, University of Oxford, 1983). The history of valorization is considered by Thomas H. Holloway, *The Brazilian Coffee Valorization of 1906* (Madison: University of Wisconsin Press, 1975), and Carlos M. Peláez, "Análise econômico do programa brasileiro de sustentação do café, 1906–1945," *Revista brasileira de economia* 25 (1971): 5–211. The diplomatic controversy is described in Leon F. Sensabaugh, "The Coffee-Trust Question in United States-Brazilian Relations: 1912–1913," *Hispanic American Historical Review* 26 (1946): 480–96. Some useful information can also be found in William H. Ukers, *All About Coffee* (New York: Tea & Coffee Trade Journal Company, 1935), and Afonso Arinos de Melo Franco, *Rodrigues Alves: apogeu e declínio de presidencialismo,* 2 vols. (São Paulo: Universidade de São Paulo, 1973).

The life and times of Woodrow Wilson are considered in Arthur S. Link, *Wilson,* 5 vols. (Princeton: Princeton University Press, 1947–   ), and Arthur S. Link, ed., *The Papers of Woodrow Wilson,* 62 vols to date (Princeton: Princeton University Press, 1966–   ). An informative analysis of the diplomacy of the Mexican crisis is Francisco Vinhosa, "A diplomacia brasileira e a revolução mexicana, 1913–1915," *Revista Instituto Histórico e Geográfico Brasileiro* 327 (1980): 19–81. The story of the Pan-American treaty is explained by Mark T. Gilderhus, "Pan-American Initiatives: the Wilson Presidency and 'Regional Integration,' 1914–17," *Diplomatic History* 4 (1980): 409–23, and his more extended study, *Pan American Visions: Woodrow Wilson in the Western Hemisphere, 1913–1921* (Tucson: University of Arizona Press). The standard work on hemispheric diplomacy and World War I remains Percy A. Martin, *Latin America and the War* (Baltimore: Johns Hopkins University Press, 1925). Important new information is contained in Emily S. Rosenberg, "World War I and 'Continental Solidarity,'" *The Americas* 31 (1975): 313–34. Still useful is the official account of Brazilian policy in Brazilian Ministry for Foreign Affairs, *The Brazilian Green Book* (London: Allen and Unwin, 1918).

Wartime developments in Brazil have received relatively little attention from political and diplomatic historians. Thomas E. Skidmore, *Black Into White: Race and Nationality in Brazilian Thought* (New York: Oxford University Press, 1974), and Carlos S. Bakota, "Crisis and the Middle Classes: The Ascendancy of Brazilian Nationalism: 1914–1922" (Ph.D diss., University of California, Los Angeles, 1973), are good introductions to Brazilian ideas of the period. Also useful are Francisco de Assis Barbosa, *Juscelino Kubitschek: uma revisão na política brasileira* (Rio: José Olympio, 1960), Barbosa Lima Sobrinho, *Presença de Alberto Tôrres* (Rio: Editôra civilização, 1968), and João Dunshee de Abranches, *A illusão brasileira* (Rio: Imprensa nacional, 1917).

An important scholarly work on the question of the economic influence of the war is Bill Albert, *South America and the First World War: The Impact of the War on Brazil, Argentina, Peru and Chile* (Cambridge: Cambridge University Press, 1988). American aspects are given more emphasis in Carl P. Parrini, *Heir To Empire: United States Economic Diplomacy, 1916–1923* (Pittsburgh: University of Pittsburgh Press, 1969). Economic relations between the United States and Latin America are examined in Burton I. Kaufman, "United States Trade with Latin America: the War Years," *Journal of American History* 57 (1971): 342–63, and Robert Mayer, "The Origins of the American Banking Empire in Latin America," *Journal of Inter-American Studies* 15 (1973): 60–76. Emily S. Rosenberg, in "Anglo-American Economic Rivalry in Brazil during World War I," *Diplomatic History* 2 (1978): 131–52, explores the battle for the Brazilian market. On American diplomatic initiatives affecting Brazil see David Healy, "Admiral William B. Caperton and United States Naval Diplomacy in South America, 1917–1919," *Journal of Latin American Studies* 8 (1976): 297–323, and Daniel M. Smith, *Aftermath of War: Bainbridge Colby and Wilsonian Diplomacy, 1920–1921* (Philadelphia: American Philosophical Society, 1970). A disappointingly descriptive outline of the diplomatic career of Edwin Morgan is presented in Lewis House, "Edwin V. Morgan and Brazilian-American Diplomatic Relations, 1912–1933" (Ph.D diss., New York University, 1969).

MISUNDERSTANDINGS AND BRUISED FEELINGS, 1921–1928

A competent survey of American diplomacy is L. Ethan Ellis, *Republican Foreign Policy, 1921–1933* (New Brunswick: Rutgers University Press, 1968). Also informative is L. Ethan Ellis, *Frank B. Kellogg and American Foreign Relations, 1925–1929* (New Brunswick: Rutgers University Press, 1961). Economic factors are given more prominence in Joan Hoff Wilson, *American Business & Foreign Policy 1920–1933* (Boston: Beacon, 1973). Indispensable studies on American policy toward Latin America are Joseph S. Tulchin, *The Aftermath of War: World War I and U.S. Policy toward Latin America* (New York: New York University Press, 1971), and Kenneth J. Grieb, *The Latin American Policy of Warren G. Harding* (Fort Worth: Texas Christian University Press, 1976). On the reemergence of the coffee dispute see Seidel, "Progressive Pan Americanism," 418–99, and Joseph Brandes, *Herbert Hoover and Economic Diplomacy: Department of Commerce Policy, 1921–1928* (Pittsburgh: University of Pittsburgh Press, 1962). João F. Normano, *The Struggle For South America: Economy and Ideology* (London: Allen and Unwin, 1931), describes the economic inroads made by the United States throughout Latin America.

Historical writing on Brazilian political affairs during the 1920s is relatively meager and the subject is best approached through the broader surveys mentioned in the section on "General Works." Brazilian diplomacy, however, receives more attention from Seidel and Leuchars and is expertly examined in Stanley E. Hilton, "Brazil and the Post-Versailles World: Elite Images and Foreign Policy Strategy, 1919-1929," *Journal of Latin American Studies* 12 (1980): 341–64. The naval mission is considered by Joseph Smith, "American Diplomacy and the Naval Mission to Brazil, 1917–30," *Inter-American*

Economic Affairs 35 (1981): 73–91. The literature on the League of Nations issue is virtually restricted to the contemporary studies of Warren H. Kelchner, *Latin American Relations with the League of Nations* (Boston: World Peace Foundation, 1929), and José Carlos de Macedo Soares, *Brazil and the League of Nations* (Paris: A. Pedone, 1928). Much more useful are the memoirs of Heitor Lyra and the biography of Afrânio de Melo Franco mentioned above. Though it scarcely mentions Brazil, the essential work on the Peace Pact is Robert H. Ferrell, *Peace In Their Time: The Origins of the Kellogg-Briand Pact* (New Haven: Yale University Press, 1952).

DEMISE OF AN ERA, 1928–1930

Two readable guides to American policy are Robert Ferrell, *American Diplomacy in the Great Depression: Hoover–Stimson Foreign Policy, 1929–33* (New Haven: Yale University Press, 1957), and Richard N. Current, *Secretary Stimson: A Study in Statecraft* (New Brunswick: Rutgers University Press, 1954). Hoover's attitudes toward his southern neighbors are described in Alexander DeConde, *Herbert Hoover's Latin-American Policy* (New York: Octagon Books, 1970). Diplomatic relations between the United States and Brazil are mentioned in Joseph Smith, "United States Diplomacy Toward Political Revolt in Brazil, 1889–1930," *Inter-American Economic Affairs* 37 (1983): 3–21, and Donald W. Giffin, "The Normal Years: Brazilian-American Relations, 1930–1939" (Ph.D diss., Vanderbilt University, 1962).

The events of the 1930 Revolution are competently considered by Jordan M. Young, *The Brazilian Revolution of 1930 and Its Aftermath* (New Brunswick: Rutgers University Press, 1967). Useful insights are also found in John D. Wirth, "Tenentismo in the Brazilian Revolution of 1930," *Hispanic American Historical Review* 44 (1964): 161–79, and Thomas E. Skidmore, *Politics in Brazil* (New York: Oxford University Press, 1967). Two excellent examples of Brazilian scholarship are Edgard Carone, *Revoluções do Brasil contemporâneo, 1922–1938* (São Paulo: Difel, 1968), and Boris Fausto, *A revolução de 1930: historiografia e história* (São Paulo: Editôra brasiliense, 1970). The story of United States relations after 1930 can be approached through John D. Wirth, *The Politics of Brazilian Development* (Stanford: Stanford University Press, 1969), and Stanley E. Hilton, *Brazil and the Great Powers, 1930–1939: The Politics of Trade Rivalry* (Austin: University of Texas Press, 1975).

INDEX

Pitt Latin American Series
Cole Blasier, Editor

USSR POLICIES

Discreet Partners: Argentina and the USSR Since 1917
Aldo César Vacs

The Giant's Rival: The USSR and Latin America
Cole Blasier

Mexico Through Russian Eyes, 1806–1940
William Harrison Richardson

OTHER NATIONAL STUDIES

Black Labor on a White Canal: Panama, 1904–1981
Michael L. Conniff

The Catholic Church and Politics in Nicaragua and Costa Rica
Philip J. Williams

The Origins of the Peruvian Labor Movement, 1883–1919
Peter Blanchard

The Overthrow of Allende and the Politics of Chile, 1964–1976
Paul E. Sigmund

Peru and the International Monetary Fund
Thomas Scheetz

Primary Medical Care in Chile: Accessibility Under Military Rule
Joseph L. Scarpaci

Rebirth of the Paraguayan Republic: The First Colorado Era, 1878–1904
Harris G. Warren

Restructuring Domination: Industrialists and the State in Ecuador
Catherine M. Conaghan

A Revolution Aborted: The Lessons of Grenada
Jorge Heine, Editor

SOCIAL SECURITY

Ascent to Bankruptcy: Financing Social Security in Latin America
Carmelo Mesa-Lago

The Politics of Social Security in Brazil
James M. Malloy

Social Security in Latin America: Pressure Groups, Stratification, and Inequality
Carmelo Mesa-Lago

OTHER STUDIES

Authoritarians and Democrats: Regime Transition in Latin America
James M. Malloy and Mitchell A. Seligson, Editors

The Catholic Church and Politics in Nicaragua and Costa Rica
Philip J. Williams

Female and Male in Latin America: Essays
Ann Pescatello, Editor